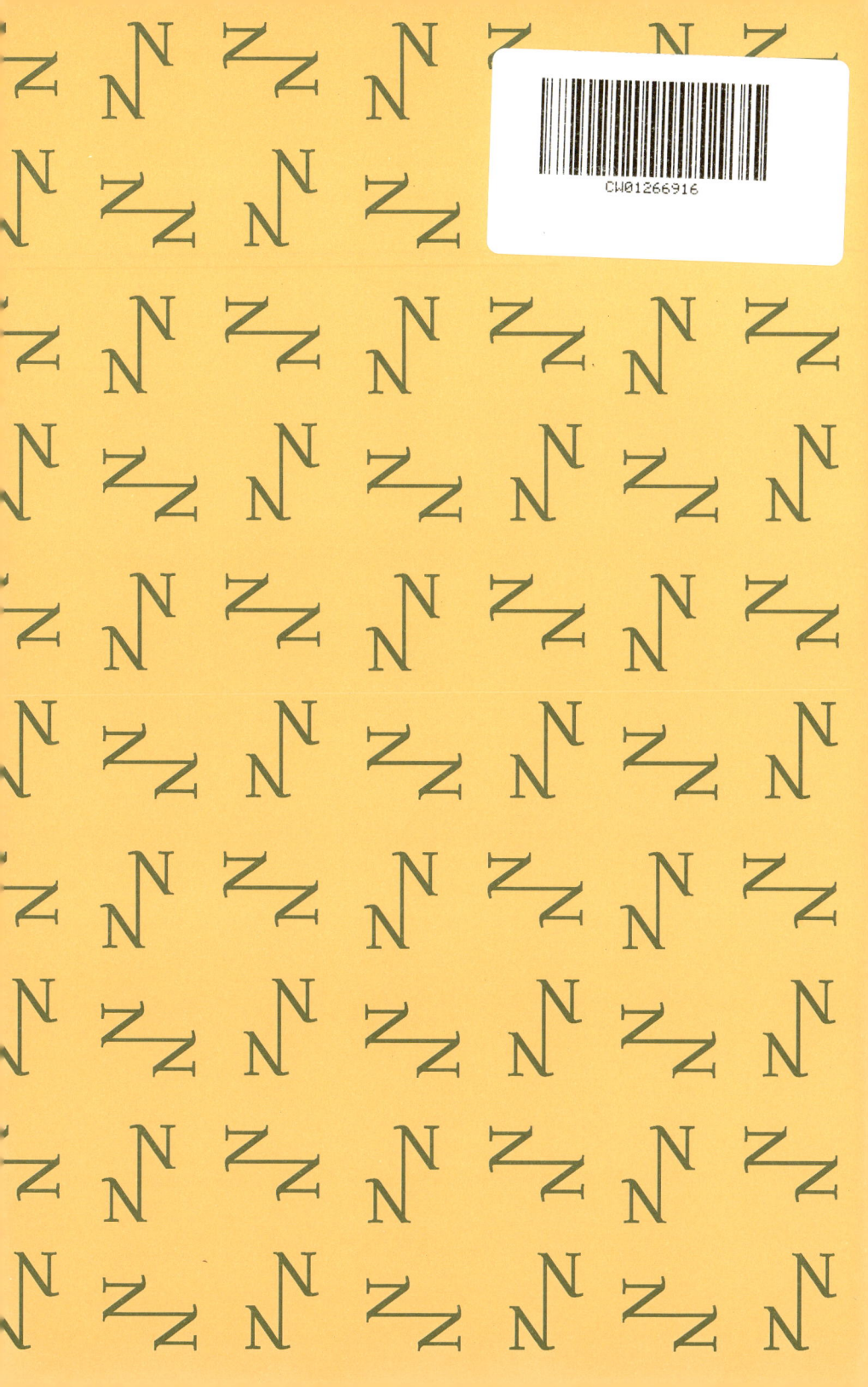

THE NEW NATURALIST LIBRARY

A SURVEY OF BRITISH NATURAL HISTORY

BRECON BEACONS

EDITORS
SARAH A. CORBET, ScD
DAVID STREETER, MBE, FIBıol
JIM FLEGG, OBE, FIHort
Prof. JONATHAN SILVERTOWN

*

The aim of this series is to interest the general
reader in the wildlife of Britain by recapturing
the enquiring spirit of the old naturalists.
The editors believe that the natural pride of
the British public in the native flora and fauna,
to which must be added concern for their
conservation, is best fostered by maintaining
a high standard of accuracy combined with
clarity of exposition in presenting the results
of modern scientific research.

THE NEW NATURALIST LIBRARY

BRECON BEACONS

JONATHAN MULLARD

This edition published in 2014 by William Collins,
an imprint of HarperCollins Publishers

HarperCollins Publishers
77–85 Fulham Palace Road
London W6 8JB

williamcollinsbooks.com

First published 2014

© Jonathan Mullard, 2014

All rights reserved. No part of this publication may be reproduced, stored in a retrieval system or transmitted in any form or by any means, electronic, mechanical, photocopying, recording or otherwise, without the prior written permission of the copyright owner.

A CIP catalogue record for this book is available from the British Library.

Set in FF Nexus

Edited and designed by
D & N Publishing
Baydon, Wiltshire

Printed in Hong Kong by Printing Express

Hardback
ISBN 978-0-00-736770-2

Paperback
ISBN 978-0-00-736769-6

All reasonable efforts have been made by the authors to trace the copyright owners of the material quoted in this book and of any images reproduced in this book. In the event that the authors or publishers are notified of any mistakes or omissions by copyright owners after publication of this book, the authors and the publisher will endeavour to rectify the position accordingly for any subsequent printing.

In memory of Alfred Russel Wallace, who developed his skills as a naturalist in the Brecon Beacons.

There are many facts in this volume – but already I have forgotten most of them. I couldn't pass an examination on them. That doesn't worry me; it is merely a question of memory – which can be refreshed at any minute. The point is I have grasped the facts (and of course I do remember the chief ones). Having grasped them, then thought followed, and emotion followed, and I drew nearer to the mystery.

John Stewart Collis, *Down to Earth*

Contents

Editors' Preface ix
Author's Foreword and Acknowledgements xi

1. An Upland Landscape 1
2. Geology and Scenery 19
3. Creation and Loss 57
4. Mountains and Moorlands 91
5. The Ffridd 143
6. Rivers and Waterfalls 153
7. Cave Systems 197
8. Wetlands 221
9. Woodlands 261
10. Ancient and Special Trees 289
11. Churches and Chapels 311
12. Farmland 329

13 Landscape Futures 351

Appendix 1 Designated Sites and Nature Reserves 363

Appendix 2 Organisations and Contacts 371

References and Further Reading 374
Species Index 385
General Index 408

Editors' Preface

RECENT YEARS HAVE SEEN A number of regional volumes added to The New Naturalist Library, not the least of which is Jonathan Mullard's *Gower*, published in 2006. With *Brecon Beacons* we reach another landmark, as it is ten years since we last published a wholly new account of a national park, that being Angus Lunn's *Northumberland*, which appeared in 2004, although Dartmoor has since been revisited. In 1957, the Brecon Beacons became the last of the clutch of ten English and Welsh national parks to be set up following the passing of the National Parks and Access to the Countryside Act, 1949, and the third and last of the three Welsh parks. This famous mountainous landscape of South Wales forms an important biogeographical link between Dartmoor and Exmoor to the south and the main mass of the Welsh mountains and Snowdonia to the north. At 886 m, Pen y Fan is the highest point in southern Britain.

On first acquaintance the Brecon Beacons can give the impression of a rather uniform area of upland moorland, but these initial perceptions are misleading since a more intimate familiarity will reveal a countryside of remarkable variety and diversity, full of unexpected revelations. For ten years Jonathan Mullard was a senior countryside officer in South Wales, during which time he developed a deep understanding of and empathy for this unique landscape to which he returns as often as his current responsibilities allow.

The regional volumes pose a particular challenge to the author, as at one level there is a need for a broad overarching approach that unravels the character of the landscape whilst at the same time the text must provide a balanced story of its detailed natural history. In *Brecon Beacons* Jonathan Mullard achieves a seamless marriage between these two approaches. The major habitats are set in the context of climate, geology and scenery whilst his remarkable facility as an all-round naturalist is revealed in accounts like that of Britain's rarest woodlouse lurking under stones on the slopes of Tarren yr Esgob and the story of the moss new to Britain that had been completely overlooked until its discovery in 2006.

The *ffridd*, that uniquely Welsh interface between upland and lowland, gets its own special treatment, and there is a fascinating account of the invertebrate fauna of the famous caves. The importance of churchyards as wildlife habitats is increasingly being recognised but few can match the story of the blind ghost slug discovered new to science in the churchyard of Brecon Cathedral!

As one might expect from a professional planner and countryside manager, the final chapter is a particularly authoritative look into the future, although we are told at the outset where the Beacons' true destiny lies: '[King] Arthur now lies asleep with his knights in a cave under Dinas Rock, near Pontneddfechan, waiting for a call to defend Britain'.

Author's Foreword and Acknowledgements

THIS IS THE FIRST COMPREHENSIVE BOOK to be published about the wildlife of the Brecon Beacons. I have written it because although a large number of people visit the area comparatively few are aware of the flora and fauna that exist in this seemingly wild and inhospitable mountain landscape and its immediate surroundings. I have also taken the opportunity to describe the area because I believe the Beacons, more so than many other landscapes, represent a possibility – the possibility for change and the creation of a new countryside. Given the right circumstances, the landscape could be richer in wildlife than it is at present, while still retaining the essence of the mountains. To achieve this successfully there needs to be a wider appreciation of the present and potential distribution of species in the area, and of their interactions with people.

That said, throughout most of the book I have consciously avoided a detailed discussion of the activities of the landowners and conservation bodies, including the National Park Authority, that play a part in the management of the area. (It is heavily managed, although apparently natural in the eyes of the general visitor.) I have instead concentrated on the wildlife, and people's experience of it. My approach is similar to that of Leslie Harvey, joint author of the first New Naturalist volume on Dartmoor, who wrote 'I am not reconciled to the view of man as the centre about which the affairs of the world revolve. The account I present of Dartmoor is therefore as objective as I have been able to make it, relating directly to the plants and animals which live there, and to the ways in which human arbitrariness may affect them' (Harvey & St Ledger Gordon 1953).

'Human arbitrariness' is indeed starting to affect the plants and animals found in the Brecon Beacons on a previously unimagined scale, and the warming climate makes the consequences of these actions ever more unpredictable. The need to think about new ways in which the landscape and wildlife of the area might develop over the coming decades is therefore becoming more urgent. Over the past 40 years the mean temperature of Wales has increased by about 1 °C overall, leading to a longer and warmer growing season. This does not necessarily mean that it is going to be sunnier, as the very wet and cloudy summer of 2012 showed, warm air holds more moisture than cold air. Whether the second wettest year on record is an indication of future weather conditions remains to be seen, but all these effects will have far-reaching consequences for the landscape of the Brecon Beacons, whether we act or not. Taking positive action, however, may help to mitigate the worst effects of our changing climate and provide space for wildlife to adapt.

I first visited the Brecon Beacons in the late 1970s, when climate change was hardly considered, following in the footsteps of Alfred Watkins, seeking out ancient alignments across the landscape. This brought me inevitably to the Vale of Ewyas and Llanthony Priory, where Watkins had recorded 'straight tracks' across the hillsides. I was struck at once by the almost otherworldly nature of the area. At that time no vapour trails from budget airlines scarred the skies above and the whole area seemed forgotten. The appearance of a red kite above the priory, then an extremely rare sight, added to the feeling of a very different landscape and left me with an impression which subsequent visits and an increased knowledge of the area have failed to erase. That visit was the first of many. Later, while living in Swansea, I explored the upper Swansea Valley and the western end of the Beacons; a very different landscape from lowland and coastal Gower, where I was working at the time. It is, however, countryside that takes time to explore, and few naturalists have a detailed knowledge of the whole area.

Although this is a book written in English about an area of Wales, I have resisted the irritating habit of translating Welsh place names into their English equivalent, except in one or two cases where knowing the meaning of a topographical name adds to an understanding of the subject under discussion. *Ban*, one of a number of words for 'mountain' or 'summit' is, for instance, the first element of *Bannau Brycheiniog* (Brecon Beacons) and also occurs in mutated form in *Pen y Fan*, the highest point of the Beacons.

The large-scale Ordnance Survey maps covering the Brecon Beacons are a useful companion to this book and show many of the sites that I have described. The book is not, however, intended as a field guide and, although a considerable area of the National Park and its surroundings is accessible to the public, the description or mention of any site does not necessarily imply that there is access to it, or that a right of way exists. An account of an area or site, or its appearance on a photograph or map, should not therefore be taken as an invitation to visit.

Finally, writing a book such as this often exposes the personal thoughts of the author, intentionally or unintentionally. It should be noted that the views expressed in these pages are his alone and do not necessarily represent the position of past or current employers.

ACKNOWLEDGEMENTS

While this book was being written and prepared for publication there was a great deal of organisational change in the public sector in Wales, with the Countryside Council for Wales, Environment Agency Wales and Forestry Commission Wales being combined into a 'single environmental body' called Natural Resources Wales. British Waterways also ceased to exist and its functions were taken over by the Canal and River Trust. For simplicity I have, however, elected to refer to the separate organisations as they existed while I was developing the text.

If there is one person I must thank above all for his support of this project it is Graham Motley, Senior Conservation Officer for the Countryside Council for Wales (CCW), who from the beginning saw the value of a book on the area, kindly supplied information, read the draft text, and shared a number of days in the field. Other CCW staff have also been immensely helpful, including Sam Bosanquet, John Wohlgemuth, James Latham, Adrian Fowles and Mike Howe. Gareth Owen, formerly of CCW, suggested how I might approach the geological material, while another previous CCW employee, Ian Morgan, provided a valuable perspective on the wildlife at the eastern end of the Beacons.

Another enthusiastic supporter has been Tim Rich of the National Museum of Wales, who has also walked the mountains with me and ensured that I did not forget the whitebeams and hawkweeds, amongst many other plants. His colleagues Graham Oliver, Ben Rowson and Chris Cleal supplied information on molluscs and fossil plants.

A number of National Park Authority staff have also been extremely helpful, including Alan Bowring, who read the chapter on geology and scenery, Paul Sinnadurai and Gareth Ellis. Steve Smith provided essential information on the management of the Blorenge and his personal project on whinchats and other associated birds.

Joe Daggett of the National Trust kindly briefed me on the Trust's acquisition policy in the Beacons and wildlife sightings on Trust land. James Tinney and Paul Dann of Forestry Commission Wales explained the organisation's approach to the area. Mark Robinson of British Waterways sent me details of the Monmouthshire and Brecon Canal records from the 2010 British Waterways wildlife survey.

A number of other people have also contributed advice about their specialist areas. Phil and Diane Morgan of the Just Mammals Consultancy provided data on mammals. Russell Hobson and Judy Burroughs of Butterfly Conservation Wales helped with butterflies and moths, while Dave Grundy and Norman Lowe recounted the details of the various expeditions in search of the Silurian moth. Graham Proudlove of Manchester University gave me access to information on cave invertebrates, as did Andrew Lewington. Steve Oram, Orchard Project Coordinator for the People's Trust for Endangered Species, kindly provided information on their ongoing orchard survey. Oliver Brown, Environment Agency, explained current conservation measures for white-clawed crayfish. Sian Laws, Wildlife Management Adviser to the Welsh Government, supplied information on sightings of possible big cats. Jerry Lewis of the Llangorse Ringing Group discussed the Group's activities, as well as sharing the results of his own long-running dipper study. Andrew King clarified the position on bird sightings and provided a number of ornithological contacts. Richard Pryce explained the distribution of rare plants in the Llandeilo area. Tim Hills of the Ancient Yew Group accessed the group's database on yew trees. Fiona Cooper contributed thoughts on black poplars. David Hill and Janet Simkin of the British Lichen Society collated survey information. Ray Woods let me have further details on lichens and mosses. Steve Wilce described his experiences of barn owls. Richard Hartnup helped me with the section on soils. Fellow New Naturalist author Peter Marren and Adam Cormack, Communications Manager with the Wildlife Trusts, provided the background to the Rothschild archive. Owen McKnight, Librarian at Jesus College Oxford, clarified the history of the *Red Book of Hergest*. Barry Attoe, Search Room Manager at the British Postal Museum and Archive, explained the role of the Post Office Surveyors Department. The staff of the Science Reading Room in the British Library have also helped to locate a number of obscure references.

Many of the above have also supplied a number of excellent photographs, as did Harold Grenfell, who helped so much with *Gower*, my first book in the series. Other photographers I must acknowledge are Peter Birch, Roy Blewitt, Nigel Davies, Jeremy Early, Mark Fisher, Nick Greatorex-Davies, Melvin Grey, Philip Halling, Christopher Hatch, Roger Key, René and Peter van der Krogt, John Light, Brendan Marris, Allan Nutt, Alan Parfit, George Peterken, Alan Richards, Paul Richards, David Robinson, Gilles San Martin, Jonathan Saville, Duncan Schlee and John Windust.

I also wish to thank Myles Archibald and Julia Koppitz of HarperCollins, and the New Naturalist Editorial Board, especially David Streeter, for their continued support. Having collected the New Naturalists for many years I was delighted to be offered the opportunity to write my previous book, and then to produce this volume.

In conclusion, I must express gratitude to my wife Melanie and my daughters Caitlin and Bethan for agreeing to take all their holidays over the last few years in the Brecon Beacons, forsaking sunnier climes for the joys of damp Welsh mountains and the chance to explore the hidden wonders of the area. I hope they agree that the end result was worth it.

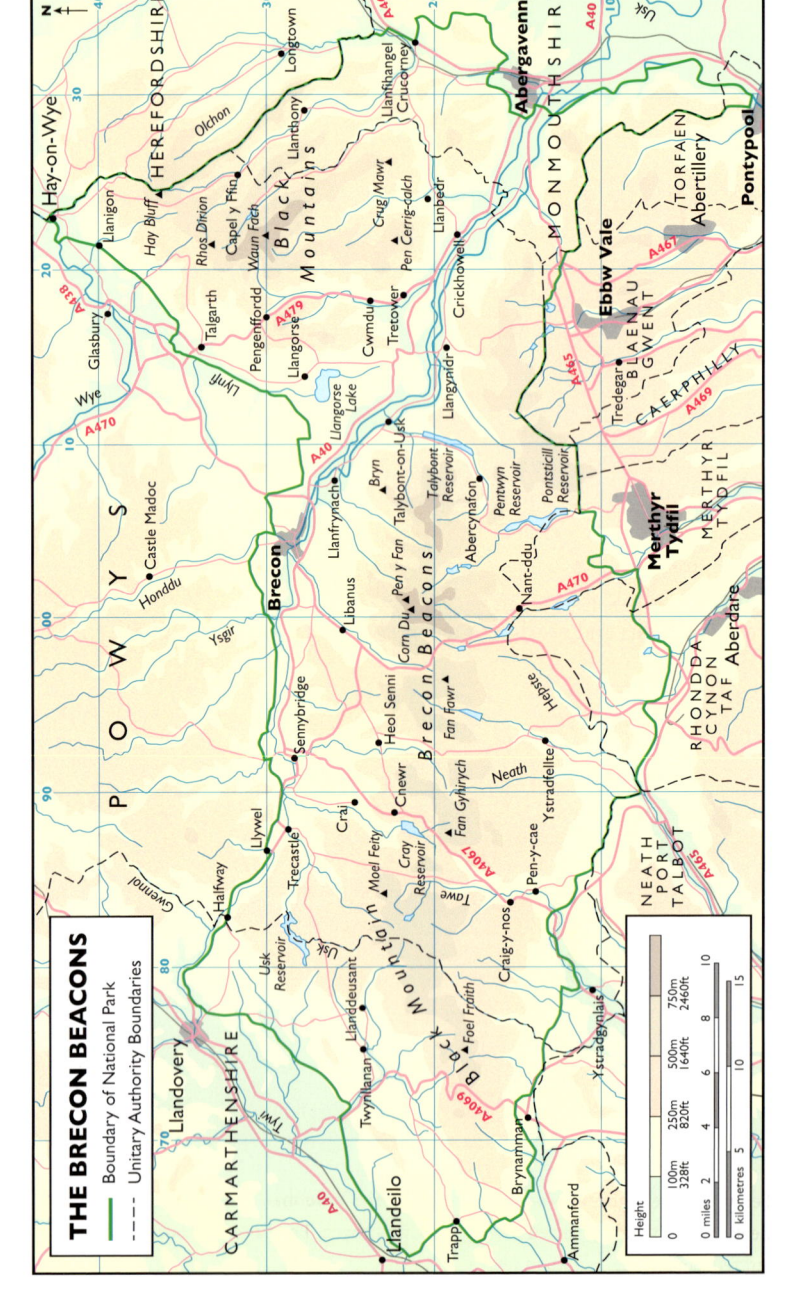

Chapter 1

An Upland Landscape

THE BRECON BEACONS ARE ONE of the most impressive upland areas in Wales. Although mountains, hills and moorlands dominate the country and 40 per cent of the Welsh land mass lies above the 250 m contour, such areas are scarce in southern Britain. The Brecon Beacons thus form an important link between Dartmoor and Exmoor and the more extensive uplands of Snowdonia and northern England (Fig. 1). In his New Naturalist

FIG 1. Pen y Fan, the highest point in Britain south of Snowdonia, and Corn Du, the second highest peak in South Wales, viewed from Craig Cwm Llwch. The path has worn down to the underlying red sandstone. (Jonathan Mullard)

volume *Nature Conservation in Britain*, Dudley Stamp, one of the best-known British geographers of the twentieth century, wrote that 'On the Old Red Sandstone, largely in Brecon, are large expanses of uninhabited, forbidding moorland, large parts of which lie in the Brecon Beacons National Park' (Stamp 1969). First impressions of an endless expanse of 'forbidding moorland' and rough pasture though are misleading. The Beacons are a multi-layered landscape, and with a little searching an astonishing variety of habitats can be found in the area, ranging from extensive cave systems to limestone crags and rich meadows. This variety supports thousands of species, some of which are found nowhere else on Earth.

The landscape in which these plants and animals occur is also a landscape rich in myths and legends, including a number involving King Arthur. One of Arthur's tasks, for example, was to rid the Brecon Beacons of a pack of enchanted wild boars that were terrorising the local people. He chased them, and on Mynydd Du, in the west of the area, picked up a large stone and hurled it at the pack, killing the leader on the edge of the valley near Craig y Fran Gorge. Its body rolled down the valley and into the river now known as the Afon Twrch, 'river of the boar'. The stone Arthur used, Carreg Fryn Fras, is still to be found on the mountain, but geologists have a different explanation for its origins, as it is a glacial erratic. Perhaps worn out by his exertions, Arthur now lies asleep with his knights in a cave under Dinas Rock, near Pontneddfechan, waiting for a call to defend Britain. Other legends also involve elements of natural history, as in the tale of the Physicians of Myddfai who practised herbal medicine in this remote village on the northern slopes of the Beacons for over 500 years, collecting their materials from the mountains.

NAMES

Covering over 1,300 km^2, the mountains dominate the skyline south of Brecon and their summit, Pen y Fan, at 886 m, is the highest point in southern Britain. Together with Corn Du, Cribyn and Fan y Big, Pen y Fan is part of a long ridge which forms a horseshoe around the head of the Taf Fechan river to the southeast, with long parallel spurs extending to the northeast. Strictly the name 'Brecon Beacons' refers only to the peaks south of Brecon, which form the central section of the area covered by this book, but in practice today the term is used to cover the full width of the range that divides South Wales from Mid Wales, and throughout this book the term 'Brecon Beacons', or simply 'the Beacons', will be used to refer to the mountains and their immediate surroundings. There are four distinct blocks of hills cut through by major river valleys, and from west to east these are Mynydd Du (Black Mountain), Fforest Fawr (Great Forest), the Brecon Beacons themselves, and the Black Mountains. The interconnected ridgelines of the Black Mountains are separated from the summits of the Brecon Beacons by the valley of the River Usk. The Usk is the principal river of the Beacons, rising on Mynydd Du in the west, flowing east through Sennybridge and Brecon and then south through Crickhowell, eventually entering the Severn Estuary at Newport. It has been suggested (Owen *et al.* 2007) that its Welsh name, Afon Wysg, is derived from 'pysg' (fish) but there are other theories.

Today most people take the name Brecon Beacons for granted, but it dates back to the time when a complex warning system consisting of a chain of intervisible hill beacons was established. There are many Beacon Hills marked on maps, and most of them take the name from their use as sites for beacons as part of Britain's early warning system in Elizabethan times, when they were lit to warn of the coming of the Spanish Armada. In many cases their origin can be traced back even earlier, to the start of the troubles with France in the fourteenth century, when cross-Channel raids constantly highlighted the threat of invasion. News of the approaching enemy was conveyed along the coast and inland by fire signals. Such a chain would include a high point which would be visible from a wide area, and Pen y Fan is ideal for this purpose (Fig. 2). The view from the summit, on all sides, is extensive – it is said that on a clear day

FIG 2. Pen y Fan and Corn Du from Cwm Llwch to the north. The valley is a popular area with visitors. (Jonathan Mullard)

twelve or thirteen counties can be seen, as well as the Bristol Channel from Swansea to Chepstow. A bonfire was lit on the summit in 1887 to celebrate Queen Victoria's Golden Jubilee, and ten years later, in 1897, to celebrate her Diamond Jubilee. This practice has continued up until the present day. On 31 December 1992 a beacon was lit on the summit to mark the beginning of the European Market, presumably in celebration rather than as a warning and, more recently, to celebrate the turn of the millennium. Appropriately enough, the logo of the Brecon Beacons National Park Authority is a flaming beacon.

The mountain range is sometimes also known as 'the Vans', a term used much more frequently in the Victorian period when the Reverend Augustin Ley, a keen botanist based in Herefordshire, recorded, for instance, that:

> The whole range of hills has been well named, when spoken of collectively as 'the Vans': the Welsh term 'Y Fan' (one of the many words meaning 'a top' or 'a ridge') being applied more frequently to the undulating 'ridges' or 'tops' which they present, than to those of any other group of mountains in the principality.

In the sixteenth century it seems that the whole area was known as the Black Mountain; which is probably why, even today, the western end of the massif is known as the Black Mountain and the eastern end as the Black Mountains. The Black Mountains are frequently confused by visitors with the Black Mountain, and to complicate matters further there is a peak in the Black Mountains called the Black Hill – the latter probably being the source for the title of Bruce Chatwin's novel *On the Black Hill*. To avoid uncertainty, in this book the Black Mountain will be referred to by its Welsh name, Mynydd Du. The earliest source for the name Black Mountain appears to be the antiquarian John Leland, who, 'in or about the years 1536–1539', referred to a mountain range extending between Carmarthen and Monmouth as follows (Toulmin Smith 1906):

> Among the montaynes of that shire Blak Montayne is most famose, for he strecchith, as I have lerned, his rootes on one side within a iiii. or V. myles of Monemuth, and on the other side as nere to Cairmerdin.

'Black' in this instance seems to have referred to 'dark, gloomy or daunting', since before the late eighteenth century the mountainous areas of Wales were viewed as wasteland when compared with the rich and productive lowlands. Similarly Daniel Defoe, in his description of the area related later in this chapter, refers to 'these horrid mountains'. Samuel Lewis, author of *A Topographical Dictionary of Wales* (1833), in describing the Beacons recorded that 'the most elevated western

FIG 3. Gospel Pass in the Black Mountains, at 549 m, is the highest road pass in Wales. The name is derived from the Third Crusade in the twelfth century, which passed through the area preaching to raise funds for the expedition. (Harold Grenfell)

summits ... are called the Black Mountains, probably from the dark and frowning aspect which they assume when their covering of heath is out of bloom.' The mountains are indeed elevated, the Gospel Pass in the Black Mountains being the highest road pass in Wales, exceeding even those in Snowdonia (Fig. 3).

There is a suggestion too that the names Hatterall Hill and Mynydd y Gader may also once have been used to apply to the entire range of the Black Mountains, though the former is now used only to refer to the easternmost ridge, and the latter, in the form Pen y Gadair Fawr, is the name now given to the second-highest summit. Part of the Black Mountains extends into England, and the eastern side of the Hatterall Ridge, along which the Offa's Dyke National Trail passes, and the Olchon Valley, both indisputably part of the range, are in Herefordshire.

Leland also noted that 'Though this be al one montayne, yet many partes of him have sundry names', and in his historical novel *People of the Black Mountains* Raymond Williams (1989) described some of these 'sundry names' as follows:

The ridges of your five fingers and the plateau of the back of your hand are now called the Black Mountains. Your thumb is Crib y Gath or the Cats Back. Your first finger is Hatterall Hill. Your second finger is Ffawyddog with Bal Mawr at the knuckle. Your third finger is Gader with Gader Fawr at the knuckle. Your little finger is Allt Mawr and its nail is Crug Hywel giving its name to Crickhowell below it. On the back of your hand are Twyn y Llech and Twmpa and Rhos Dirion and Waun Fach. Mynwy and Olchon flow from Twyn y Llech. Honddu flows from Twyn y Llech and Twmpa. Grwyne Fawr flows from Rhos Dirion. Grwyne Fechan and Rhiangoll flow from Waun Fach. You hold the shapes in the names in your hand.

The Black Hill is known locally as 'The Cat's Back', since when it is viewed from Herefordshire it looks like a crouching cat about to pounce.

Unfortunately there are few local names of plants and animals recorded from the Brecon Beacons, and most of these are English. The first comprehensive Welsh county avifauna, The Birds of Breconshire, was published in 1882 by Edward Cambridge Phillips, and in this he noted that the redstart *Phoenicurus phoenicurus* 'is invariably called here "firebrand tail", and is very common in the gardens around Brecon and in the woods of the county. The Welsh is "Llost-rhuddyn", red tail.' Phillips goes on to say:

It is, however, much to be regretted that many of the Welsh names applied to various species of birds at the present day are generic and not specific. The deep Welsh known to cultured Welshmen is rarely used in every-day life, and scarcely ever written, hence many of the old Welsh names of birds have died out, and in their stead names of general application have come into vogue such as are in common use in South Wales at the present day.

DESIGNATIONS

Much of the area covered by this book was designated as a National Park in 1957, the Brecon Beacons being the last of the ten National Parks created in the 1950s and the third of the three Welsh National Parks, after Snowdonia in 1951 and Pembrokeshire Coast in 1952. The Brecon Beacons and Black Mountains had been suggested as being suitable for National Park status as early as 1931, but the Second World War intervened and it was not until 1947, in a report of the newly formed National Parks Committee, that a proposal was made for a 'Brecon Beacons and Black Mountains National Park'. The Committee considered that the magnificent mountain scenery (Fig. 4), with almost unlimited access for walkers, clearly formed an area of 'high recreational value', being close to the

FIG 4. The road from Llanddeusant to Blaenau, with Bannau Sir Gaer, Picws Du and Fan Brycheiniog in the distance. (Jonathan Mullard)

populated areas of South Wales. In the description of the proposed National Park it highlighted the wealth of archaeological and historical interest within the area, including religious sites such as Llanthony Priory. Progress on the designation was slow, however, until questions were raised in the House of Commons. Formal consultations then took place with local authorities and, after a great deal of debate about the proposed boundary, the National Park was designated on 17 April 1957 (Woolmore 2011).

The final boundary of the National Park excluded the Olchon Valley and the Herefordshire Black Mountains, because of possible administrative problems, not because the area lacked 'scenic merit' (Fig. 5). This part of England was subsequently considered for inclusion in various reviews of National Park boundaries, but the issue remains 'unfinished business'. It is a border landscape with a transition from the wide, fertile Golden Valley in the east to the edge of the Black Mountains in the west.

The Brecon Beacons also include a large part of the Blaenavon Industrial Landscape World Heritage Site, one of the most significant examples of development in the early years of the Industrial Revolution in Wales. Although the focus of the designation is the head of the Afon Lwyd, which includes

FIG 5. The Olchon Valley and Herefordshire Black Mountains viewed from Longtown Castle: indisputably part of the mountain range but outside the boundary of the current National Park. (Jonathan Mullard)

FIG 6. Sugar Loaf common, the first property to be acquired by the National Trust in the Brecon Beacons, viewed from Llangattock on the other side of the Usk Valley. (Graham Motley)

Blaenavon Ironworks and the oldest areas of iron and coal extraction between Blaenavon and Pwll Du, more than 40 per cent of the World Heritage Site falls within the National Park boundary. During the Industrial Revolution the hillsides around Blaenavon were heavily worked, but as the industries declined the landscape recovered. The area is now the focus of the Forgotten Landscapes Project, which aims to conserve the wildlife and historic features in the landscape.

Because of the importance of the area the National Trust owns over 5,000 hectares of the Brecon Beacons, including large areas of common land. The first property to be acquired by the Trust was part of the Sugar Loaf common, which was donated in 1936 (Fig. 6). This was followed three years later by the open hill land of Skirrid Fawr. The major acquisition, however, was the central massif of the Beacons, covering 3,328 hectares, which was a gift from the Eagle Star insurance company in 1964. The property was accepted because the area was seen as important for its landscape value – the potential of the uplands for access, wildlife conservation and archaeology not being recognised at the time. Public access was not an issue either, since there were relatively few people at the time interested in hill-walking, and as a result the property came to the Trust un-endowed – that is, without any funds for its maintenance. Since then the number of walkers has increased greatly and the footpaths have been substantially eroded. This has increased the cost of managing the area: the main routes have had to be hardened, and in some places stone-pitched footpaths have been constructed.

Other land was accumulated piecemeal as opportunities presented themselves. For example, land at Coelbren was acquired by the National Trust over a 39-year period between 1947 and 1986.

EARLY VISITORS

Probably the first person to publish an account of the Brecon Beacons was the twelfth-century chronicler Gerald of Wales (Giraldus Cambrensis). As Archdeacon of Brecknock he toured his homeland and wrote the *Itinerarium Cambriae* ('Journey through Wales') and *Cambriae Descriptio* ('Description of Wales'), which included a number of references to sites in the area, including important descriptions of Llangorse Lake (Thorpe 1978).

Another much later visitor was Daniel Defoe, best known as the author of *Robinson Crusoe*. His three-volume travel book, *A Tour Thro' the Whole Island of Great Britain*, was published between 1724 and 1727, and was innovative partly because Defoe had actually visited the places he described. In 1724 Defoe entered Brecknockshire, which he found 'mountainous to an extremity, except on the side of Radnor, where it is something more low and level. It is well watered by the Wye, and the Uske, two rivers mentioned before; upon the latter stands the town of Brecknock the capital of the county.' He then goes on to list some of the features in the area: 'Kyrton-Beacon, Tumberlow, Blorench, Penvail, and Skirridan, are some of the names of these horrid mountains.'

> We began with Brecknock, being willing to see the highest of the mountains, which are said to be hereabouts; and indeed, except I had still an idea of the height of the Alps, and of those mighty mountains of America, the Andes, which we see very often in the South-Seas, 20 leagues from the shore: I say except that I had still an idea of those countries on my mind, I should have been surprized at the sight of these hills; nay, (as it was) the Andes and the Alps, tho' immensely high, yet they stand together, and they are as mountains, pil'd upon mountains, and hills upon hills; whereas sometimes we see these mountains rising up at once, from the lowest valleys, to the highest summits which makes the height look horrid and frightful, even worse than those mountains abroad; which tho' much higher, rise as it were, one behind another: So that the ascent seems gradual, and consequently less surprising.

From the late eighteenth century onwards, however, it was for its wild, rugged, mountainous scenery that Wales became famous and subsequently much visited. On an October day in 1854, George Borrow recorded his trip from Llandovery across Mynydd Du in Wild Wales. Braving occasional showers of rain and hail he only caught 'a glimpse of some very lofty hills which I supposed to be the Black Mountains. It was a mere glimpse, for scarcely had I descried them when mist settled down and totally obscured them from my view.' The day improved, however, and he noted that:

> In two or three hours I came to a glen, the sides of which were beautifully wooded. On my left was a river, which came roaring down from a range of lofty mountains right before me to the south-east. The river, as I was told by a lad, was the Sawdde or Southey, the lofty range the Black Mountains. Passed a pretty village on my right standing something in the shape of a semicircle, and in about half-an-hour came to a bridge over a river which I supposed to be the Sawdde which I had already seen, but which I subsequently learned was an altogether different stream. It was running from the south, a wild, fierce flood, amidst rocks and stones, the waves all roaring and foaming.

FIG 7. The Afon Sawdde in the 'beautifully wooded glen' seen by George Borrow on his journey through 'Wild Wales'. (Graham Motley)

This was Borrow's only sight of the Brecon Beacons as he journeyed though Wales (Fig. 7), but his writings, together with those of other contemporary travellers, started the Victorian interest in Wales, its scenery and people.

WEATHER

Wet weather is always a possibility when visiting the Brecon Beacons. The British Bryological Society, for instance, which exists to promote the study of mosses and liverworts, held its Annual Meeting and Excursion at Brecon from 12 to 19 August 1927. Their journal records that:

> The weather conditions were somewhat adverse; owing to the heavy rainfall the Usk and the mountain streams were so swollen that the riparian bryophytes were submerged and the waterfalls so overbrimming that the rocks were unapproachable in places. In spite of this, some good work was done, and several records were

added to the County Flora. The Brecon Beacons were visited twice; there was some excellent ground on the fine cliffs and crags of Craig Cerig Gleisiad, where ravens and buzzards circled round the cliff-tops. Heavy rain unfortunately curtailed the visit to Sennybridge and the Usk valley. A fine drive across high moorland led the way into the delightful wooded cwm of the Hepste, but the excess of water in the streams and falls made the visit somewhat tantalizing.

The high rainfall has created a number of habitats that are dependent on a constant supply of fresh water, and the uplands of the Brecon Beacons play an important role in the distribution of fresh water in South Wales, with the Usk, Monnow, Nedd and Tawe all originating in the uplands. The main river is the Usk, rising on the northern side of the Brecon Beacons and flowing eastwards to cut across the mountain chain, while the northeast is drained by the Wye and the west by the Tywi. To the south, the moorland slopes down to a region of porous limestone pavements and a rocky terrain of rivers, waterfalls and vast underground cave systems such as the Dan yr Ogof showcaves, the largest system of subterranean caverns in western Europe.

Nearly 350 years earlier William Camden, in his great work *Britannia*, a topographical and historical survey of all of Great Britain and Ireland, first published in 1586, summarised the situation well (Camden 1607):

Now the raine, which mountaines breed, falleth here verie often, the windes blow strong, and all winter time almost it is continuallie cloudy and misty weather. And yet notwithstanding (such is the healthfull temperature of the ayre, which, the grosser it is, the gentler and milder it is), and verie seldome there are any diseases heere.

The area's rainy weather is also captured in a huge mural cut deep into the plaster of the walls of St Mary's church at Llanfair Kilgeddin, located in a bend of the Usk to the southeast of the Beacons (Fig. 8). This was created by Heywood Sumner, a well-known 'Arts and Crafts' artist, in 1888. Sgraffito, the technique by which individual layers of coloured plaster are applied to a wall and then scraped back at varying depths to create a picture, was used to depict 'blustering cumulus clouds casting slanting rain over the familiar outlines of neighbouring hills, Skirrid and Sugarloaf, and Blorenge rising underneath a rainbow' (Hughes 2006). No longer in use, the church is cared for by the Friends of Friendless Churches, an organisation which campaigns for and rescues redundant historic churches threatened by demolition and decay. It is probably their most popular church, attracting hundreds of visitors each year.

FIG 8. Rain over Skirrid, Sugar Loaf and Blorenge, pictured in sgraffito on the wall of St Mary's church, Llanfair Kilgeddin, by Heywood Sumner in 1888. (Jonathan Mullard)

DARK SKIES

As well as being an area with high rainfall, the Brecon Beacons, especially the northern and western parts, are one of the few dark areas still remaining in the British Isles. In 2013, after campaigning by the National Park Authority and the National Park Society, the area became an international dark sky reserve – only the fifth place in the world to gain the award from the International Dark Sky Association. The Beacons has been designated at the 'Silver Tier' level, meaning that while the skies above the area are affected to some extent by light pollution they are still remarkably dark, making it an excellent place to see the Milky Way and other night sky objects. The aim is to combat increasing light pollution and mitigate the worst effects of this on both people and wildlife. Increased levels of artificial lighting prevent people seeing the night sky, disrupt ecosystems, affect human rhythms, and waste energy. Owl numbers in Britain, for instance, are decreasing, and studies have shown that light pollution reduces the suitable area of feeding habitat for them. Night-flying moths are also adversely affected by artificial lights, as are riverflies. The term riverflies covers mayflies, caddisflies and stoneflies, and it has been shown that artificial light can cause the adult insects to become disorientated and attract them away from the water. The action being taken to reduce light pollution therefore has the potential to improve conditions for a wide variety of wildlife.

NATURALISTS IN THE BEACONS

Light pollution was not an issue for the early naturalists and residents of the Brecon Beacons. People such as Henry Vaughan (1621–1695), one of the best-known of the British 'metaphysical poets', who spent most of his life in Llansantffraed in the Usk Valley, would have had a very different appreciation of the night sky. In his poem *The World*, for instance, he states:

> *I saw Eternity the other night*
> *Like a great Ring of pure and endless light,*
> *All calm as it was bright;*
> *And round beneath it,*
> *Time, in hours, days, years,*
> *Driven by the spheres,*
> *Like a vast shadow moved, in which the world*
> *And all her train were hurled.*

Vaughan chose the name Silurist to describe his work, the name deriving from his reverence of the Silures, the tribe of pre-Roman South Wales which resisted the Romans. It also reflects the deep affection Vaughan felt towards the mountains and the valley of the Usk, where he spent most of his life. His love

FIG 9. The grave of Henry Vaughan under an ancient yew in the churchyard at Llansantffraed. (Jonathan Mullard)

FIG 10. The statute of Edward Lhuyd (1660–1709), famous Welsh naturalist, outside Aberystwyth hospital. (René and Peter van der Krogt)

of nature and mysticism influenced the work of poets such as Wordsworth, Tennyson and Siegfried Sassoon. Though Vaughan apparently left no specific records of wildlife, he could reasonably be counted as one of the area's early naturalists. His poem 'Man', for example, includes the following verse:

> Weighing the steadfastnesse and state
> Of some mean things which here below reside
> Where birds like watchful Clocks the noiseless date
> And Intercourse of times divide,
> Where Bees at night get home and hive, and flowrs
> Early, as well as late
> Rise with the Sun, and set in the same bowrs.

Henry Vaughan was little celebrated during his lifetime, but after his death his reputation developed rapidly. He is buried under an ancient yew in the churchyard of St Bridget's, Llansantffraed (Fig. 9).

Given the perceptions of the Brecon Beacons, however, until the nineteenth century there were few naturalists prepared to explore the area. One of the exceptions was Edward Lhuyd (Fig. 10), the famous Welsh naturalist (though he was

FIG 11. Alfred Russel Wallace (1823–1913), who developed his skills as a naturalist in the Brecon Beacons and surrounding areas. (Hulton-Deutsch Collection/Corbis)

actually born in Loppington, Shropshire). In 1684, Lhuyd was appointed as assistant to Robert Plot, the Keeper of the Ashmolean Museum in Oxford, and he replaced him as Keeper in 1690. Later, he worked on revised descriptions of all the Welsh counties for Edmund Gibson's new English edition of Camden's *Britannia*, and this inspired him to plan an ambitious natural and human history of Wales, *Archaeologia Britannica*. Lhuyd was a polymath who made important contributions to the emerging disciplines of botany, geology, antiquities and philology. He was part of the new order of experimental science, scorning the earlier naturalists – 'who, til this last century contented themselves with bare reading and scribbling paper.' The project led to an extended research tour with his trained helpers William Jones, Robert Wynne and David Parry, from 1697 to 1701, during which he spent a considerable amount of time in Wales (Mullard 2006). One of his early visits was to the Beacons and, as explained later in this book, he was a careful observer of the fossils and wildlife to be found in the area.

Another well-known naturalist associated with the area is Alfred Russel Wallace, who independently came up with the theory of evolution (Fig. 11). His letter to Darwin subsequently provoked the latter to publish *On the Origin of Species* in 1859. Wallace has been described by the American biologist E. O. Wilson as 'one of the most important figures of nineteenth-century biology and in character among its most admirable.' He spent around two years in the area, living in Neath and working with his brother on a number of projects, including designing and building the Mechanics' Institute where he gave a number of lectures. His leisure time he spent 'wandering about this beautiful district, on my part in search of insects, while my brother always had his eyes open for any uncommon bird or reptile.' It was during this time that Wallace's interest in natural history emerged and developed, and the Beacons played a crucial role in developing his field skills. He climbed to the summit of Pen y Fan, visited prehistoric sites, collected rare insects and once spent an uncomfortable night in the entrance to Porth yr Ogof cave in order to 'try sleeping out-of-doors, with no shelter or bed but what nature provided' as he and his brother were 'at this time determined, if possible, to go abroad into more or less wild countries.' Wallace subsequently achieved his aim, becoming the pre-eminent collector and tropical field biologist of his generation. In fact, by the time of his death in 1913 Wallace was probably the world's most famous scientist – although since then he has been almost completely overshadowed by Darwin.

Other Victorian naturalists included the Reverend Augustin Ley, mentioned earlier, a Herefordshire vicar who spent much of his spare time riding around Wales on horseback, indulging his passionate interest in natural history. After the early death of his wife in 1878, Ley immersed himself in his clerical duties and botany. For the next thirty years he searched Herefordshire and neighbouring counties on the Welsh border for plants, recording, collecting and discovering many uncommon species. His pioneering explorations of the Brecon Beacons and the Wye Valley, from the early 1870s onwards, resulted in many exciting discoveries, including rare species of whitebeam (Lawley undated).

Ley may have been exceptionally enthusiastic, even by the standards of his age, but he was not alone in his interest in the flora of the area. W. Bowles Barrett, a botanist based in Weymouth who published extensively on the botany of Dorset, also produced a series of papers in the *Journal of Botany* for 1885, which he considered a contribution towards a Flora of Breconshire. Ley considered that 'These papers contain an accurate and exhaustive summary of the Flora of the county. They afford far the fullest list of the flowering plants of Breconshire known to exist and but little has been added, and that chiefly in the critical genera of *Rubus* and *Hieracium*, to the flora of the county since the date of their publication.' A short note on the 'Flora of Breconshire' was also published by Reginald W. Phillips, head of the Department of Botany at University College, Bangor (Phillips 1892). Phillips was born in the Beacons at Talgarth on October 15, 1854, the same month and year that George Borrow crossed Mynydd Du. Another Phillips, Edward Cambridge Phillips, has already been mentioned for his pioneering work on the birdlife of the area.

Work on the 'critical genera' of *Rubus* (blackberries and dewberries) and *Hieracium* (the hawkweeds) has continued to this day, though there is as yet no up-to-date flora for the area. Riddelsdell's hawkweed *Hieracium riddelsdellii*, for example, is a rare Welsh endemic plant, all the known sites of which are in the Brecon Beacons, with the main population occurring on the Craig y Nos Ridge on the west side of the Tawe Valley. It is not just these plants, however, that are receiving attention. There are probably more naturalists active at present, working across a wider range of subjects, than at any other time in the area's history, but the information is fragmented and sometimes hard to find. It is thanks to many of these people that it has been possible to bring the material together in this book.

RECREATION

Recreational use of the area has changed dramatically since Wallace wrote that 'As Brecknockshire is comparatively little known, and few English tourists make the ascent of the Beacons, a short account of then will be both interesting and instructive' (Wallace 1905). Of all the mountain areas in Britain, the Brecon Beacons are probably the most accessible. The main road from Brecon to Merthyr Tydfil passes near to the summit of Pen y Fan, rendering it a relatively short walk from a highway. During the summer, hundreds of people every day take advantage of this and go to the highest point to take in the view. The Beacons are now a major recreational resource for a very wide range of people, and are used by numerous outdoor activity centres (Fig. 12). According to the findings of a survey conducted in 1994, the estimated number of visitor days to the National Park was 3.6 million (Pratt-Heaton 1999). It is impossible to calculate exactly how many visitors the area receives, but this figure is probably still roughly correct today. Recreation plays a large part in the rural economy, supporting around 2,000 jobs in the area. There are downsides though, in the form of eroded footpaths and, very occasionally, congested roads. Not surprisingly in a National Park, the 1994 survey highlighted that over 60 per cent of visitors come for the scenery, while around 45 per cent are also interested in wildlife.

The scenery that attracts these visitors is, of course, dependent on the underlying geology, and this is the subject of the next chapter.

FIG 12. Pony trekkers in a lane near Llangorse village. (Jonathan Mullard)

Chapter 2

Geology and Scenery

THE RELATIONSHIP BETWEEN GEOLOGY AND SCENERY is rarely as clear as it is in the Brecon Beacons. Consisting entirely of sedimentary rocks, which derive from material laid down by ancient rivers and seas, their subsequent movement and erosion have created a distinctive landscape, with steep scarp slopes alternating with gentler dip slopes.

Most of the rocks are Old Red Sandstone from the Devonian period, around 417 to 355 million years ago, when the amalgamation of continental plates resulted in a new continent, known as the Old Red Continent or Euramerica. During the Carboniferous period, a time of active mountain formation, this became a part of a major supercontinent, Pangaea. Around 200 million years ago, however, the Pangaean supercontinent broke up and the component parts moved away from each other. They are still moving today, and it has been suggested that they will eventually join up again in a new 'Pangaea Ultima'. All these movements created huge changes in flora and fauna and they are still going on today, though over such a long timescale that we are unable to perceive them. From this perspective the current flora and fauna of the Beacons represent only a passing moment in the geological calendar.

In the south a narrow band of limestone, derived from rises and falls in sea level during the Carboniferous period, stretches from the Blorenge in the east to Carreg Cennen in the west. Over 70 km in length and up to 3 km in width, this band contains some of the most spectacular landscapes in Britain. Located between the Old Red Sandstone to the north and the Millstone Grit to the south, it is an area of countryside characterised by natural cliffs, quarry faces, rocky outcrops, limestone pavements and calcareous grassland. At lower elevations there is a distinctive landscape of wooded gorges, caves, swallow holes, and

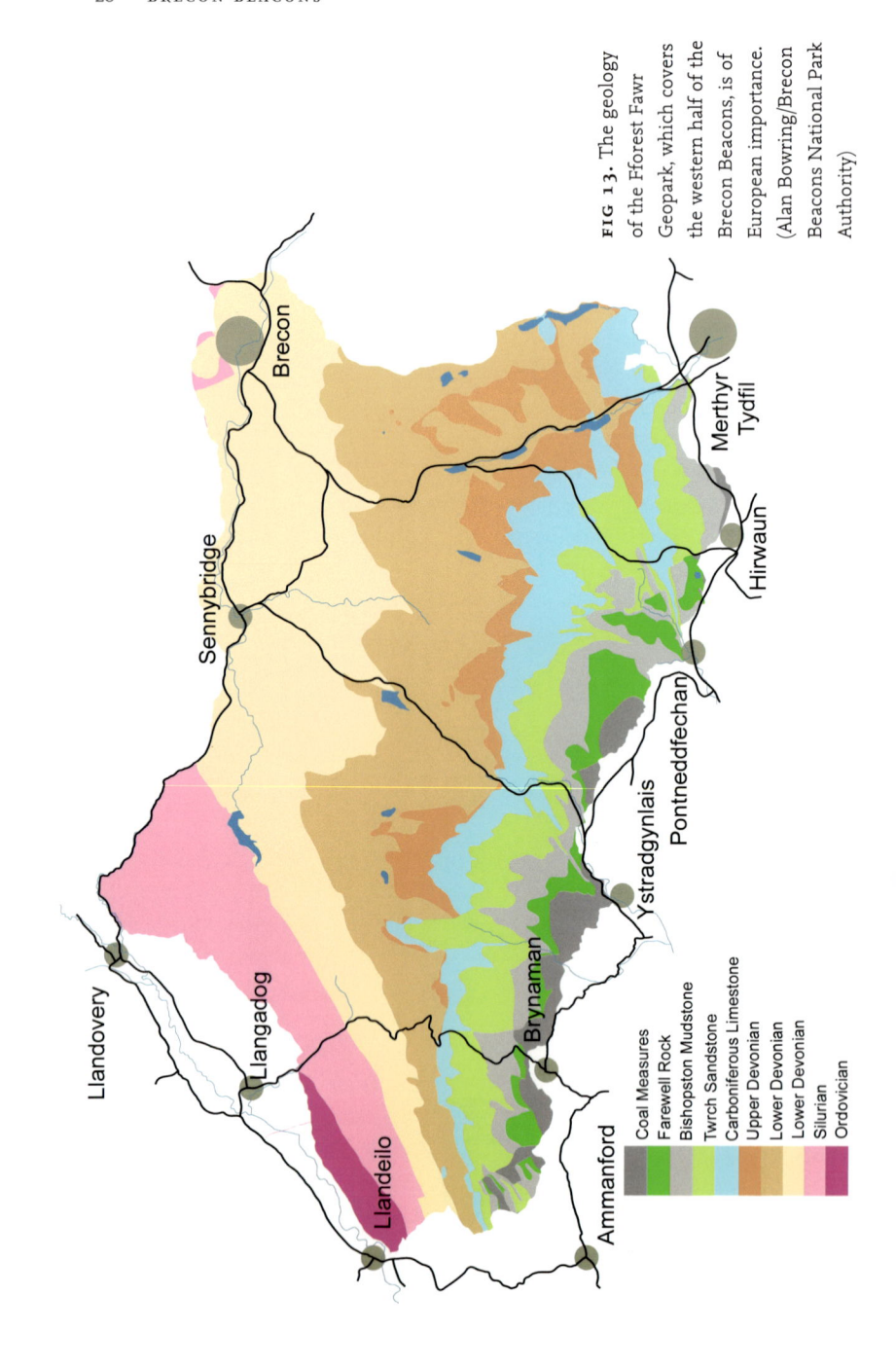

FIG 13. The geology of the Fforest Fawr Geopark, which covers the western half of the Brecon Beacons, is of European importance. (Alan Bowring/Brecon Beacons National Park Authority)

waterfalls, epitomised by the area around Coed y Rhaeadr. Some of the largest cave systems in Britain occur in the limestone, and these are described, together with the waterfalls, in later chapters. Further south again are areas of Millstone Grit and Coal Measures, which were heavily exploited, during the nineteenth and twentieth centuries, in the Industrial Revolution.

In the recent geological past the Beacons were one of the most southerly areas in Britain to be subjected to glaciation during the last glacial period, which lasted from 110,000 to 10,000 years ago, and the evidence for this can be seen across both the sandstone and limestone, with bare striated rock marked by the passage of glaciers and erratic boulders and moraines: material transported by a glacier and then deposited.

Today the importance of the geological heritage has been recognised by the designation of the western half of the Beacons as the Fforest Fawr Geopark (Fig. 13). A partnership between the National Park Authority, the British Geological Survey and Cardiff University, the Geopark, which is part of a European network, aims to conserve, protect and explain the geological heritage of the area.

PIONEER GEOLOGISTS

The rocks found in the Brecon Beacons, both sandstone and limestone, are critically important in the study of the Earth's history, containing evidence for the changes in sea level mentioned above, the emergence of life from the oceans onto land and the influence of major mountain-building events. The area has therefore been the subject of significant research and mapping ever since the mid-nineteenth century, when, at the suggestion of William Buckland, the pioneering English geologist Roderick Murchison (Fig. 14) and Adam Sedgewick studied the Old Red Sandstone and the underlying rocks.

Murchison, later to become President of the Geological Society, first came to the Beacons in 1831 to attempt to discover whether the greywacke rocks, which lie

FIG 14. Sir Roderick Impey Murchison (1792–1871) was a Scottish geologist who, following a visit to the Brecon Beacons, first described and investigated the Silurian system. Hulton-Deutsch Collection/Corbis)

beneath the sandstone, could be grouped into a definite order of succession. Greywacke is a variety of hard dark-coloured sandstone containing angular grains of quartz feldspar and small rock fragments set in fine clay. The result of Murchison's explorations in the Beacons was the establishment of the 'Silurian system', in which he grouped, for the first time, a remarkable series of formations, each with distinctive organic remains very different from those of other rocks. These researches, together with descriptions of the economically important coalfields and overlying formations in South Wales and the English border counties, were described in his book *The Silurian System*, published in 1839.

ORDOVICIAN AND SILURIAN

The Silurian rocks and the preceding Ordovician strata represent the oldest rocks in the Beacons. They were formed towards the end of a long period during which mud and sand accumulated on the floor of the sea and were consolidated as the waters retreated. Both periods were named after Welsh tribes – the Ordovices, who inhabited much of central and North Wales, and the Silures, who occupied most of South Wales before the Roman invasion. The rocks only occur in the west of the Beacons, in a narrow band between Llandeilo and Llandovery, and they represent the remains of the Towy anticline, a convex geological fold with the oldest strata at its core. The Ordovician rocks comprise a complex mix of mudstones, limestones and sandstones and indicate a worldwide fall in sea level as a major ice age set in. At the beginning of the Silurian, the land that would eventually become Wales and England lay far to the south of the Equator, separated by an ocean from a large continent to its north. Scotland was a part of this more northerly continent, along with Greenland and much of North America. Like the earlier rocks, those from the Silurian are mostly mudstones, siltstones and sandstones, some of which were deposited in deep water on a continental shelf.

The boundary between the Ordovician and the Silurian periods marks the second-largest extinction event in the history of the Earth, after the Permian extinction 252 million years ago. About 450 to 440 million years ago two bursts of extinction, separated by a million years, occurred. At this time life was confined to the seas and oceans, and more than 60 per cent of marine invertebrates died. The immediate cause of extinction appears to have been the movement of a supercontinent known as Gondwana into the region of the South Pole, which led to global cooling, another glaciation and a fall in sea levels that disrupted, or eliminated, habitats along the continental shelves.

SILURIAN/DEVONIAN BOUNDARY

The boundary between the Silurian and the following Devonian period is exemplified by Cwar Glas Quarry and the Sawdde Gorge. Designated as a Site of Special Scientific Interest (SSSI) and a Geological Conservation Review Site, it is considered to be one of the best localities in Britain for the study of this important sequence of rocks. Lying beneath shallow tropical seas for most of the Silurian, this area became terrestrial in the Devonian, and this change can clearly be seen in the rocks of the gorge, which change from blue-grey mudstones and siltstones to yellow-green siltstones and sandstones. The Brecon Beacons is renowned for its early fossil fishes, and slabs of sandstone have been found here which show zigzag trails made by a primitive fish on the bed of an ancient lake. Ripple marks left by the sea can also still be seen in the sandstone on the summit of Pen y Fan. The fresh, or brackish, water in which the rock was laid down was not rich in vertebrate life, however, and, unlike the situation in the limestone, actual fossil fish are uncommon; most of the fossils found at the site represent a rich fauna of marine invertebrates.

One of the significant evolutionary milestones during the Silurian was the appearance of jawed and bony fish, but to date little evidence of these has been found in the Beacons. The abandoned quarry at Cwar Glas, however, contains the remains of a jawless fish *Archaegonaspis ludensis*, the earliest known species of British heterostracan, a group of armoured, jawless, bottom-dwelling fishes (Fig. 15). The discovery of this fossil fish in the nineteenth century was important because it showed that 'true fishes' existed in beds underlying the Ludlow Bone Bed (418–416 million years old), which was previously thought to contain the oldest fish remains. The only surviving jawless fishes today are the hagfishes, and the lampreys described in Chapter 6.

DEVONIAN

The Old Red Sandstone records the environmental change from marine to terrestrial conditions as the shallow seas, which were home to the early fossil fishes described above, silted up. The sandstone covers three-quarters of the Beacons and forms the north- and northeast-facing escarpments of the principal mountain blocks, as well as the plateaux to the north and south of these scarps. It represents an extraordinary period of the Earth's history, when vertebrates developed in the seas and rivers and emerged onto the land, the first vascular plants spread across the continents, and terrestrial arthropods became well

FIG 15. Cwar Glas Quarry, a key site for the fossil remains of the jawless fish *Archaegonaspis ludensis*. The ripple marks from an ancient seabed are preserved on the vertical face of the rock. (Alan Bowring)

established. The red colour of the rocks arises from the presence of iron oxide, but not all the Old Red Sandstone is red, or indeed sandstone. The sequence also includes conglomerates, mudstones, siltstones and thin limestones, and their colours range from grey and green, through red, to purple. The Old Red Sandstone has been widely used as a building stone across those regions where it outcrops, a notable example being Brecon Cathedral.

FIG 16. Llandyfan Church with its roof of Tilestones was built in 1864–65 on the site of a small chapel adjacent to Ffynnon Gwyddfaen, which is the source of the River Gwyddfân. The effect of runoff from the lead flashing on the mosses covering the roof is clear. (Harold Grenfell)

There are six divisions of the Old Red Sandstone. The oldest rocks, representing the transition between the Silurian and Devonian, are the Tilestones and the Red Marls, both of which are found in valleys and the lower hills. The Tilestones are so named because they are easy to split into thin slabs. The impressive remains of workings along the outcrop can be traced for miles across the countryside at places such as Mynydd Myddfai, and the stone has been used for the roofs of many buildings in the west of the Brecon Beacons, including Llandyfan Church (Fig. 16).

Above the Marls are the Senni Beds, which are exposed along the Senni and other rivers flowing northwards into the Usk from the uplands (Fig. 17). These sandstones, dull red or green in colour, offer varying resistance to the running water; in some locations they are solid and unbroken, while in other situations they are broken and flaky.

The mountains are formed from two of the most resistant Devonian rocks, the Brownstones and the Plateau Beds. Brownstones predominate, consisting of inter-bedded red marls, brown sandstones and conglomerates. One of the best exposures is the steep northern face of Pen y Fan, which consists of a regular

FIG 17. The Senni Valley gives its name to the Senni Beds, which are exposed along the watercourses in the area. (Harold Grenfell)

horizontal pattern of Brownstones, with the harder bands standing out as steps and shelves. These steps and shelves, for the most part inaccessible to grazing sheep, as described in Chapter 4, hold the most interesting of the current vegetation communities. The summit of Pen y Fan, however, consists of an outlier of the overlying Plateau Beds, the conglomerates and sandstones which give the mountains their distinctive flat profile.

The youngest Devonian rocks, the Grey Grits, are formed from a mixture of quartz grits and sandstones. These outcrop in the south next to the rocks of the following Cretaceous period. The lonely Bryniau Gleision uplands, the Blue-Grey Hills, between the Taf Fawr and Talybont reservoirs, are formed from Grey Grits, as are some of the areas between Taf Fawr and the village of Penderyn.

FOSSIL PLANTS

Some of the earliest vascular land plants have been found in the Brecon Beacons, appearing as dark smudges in the rocks. The fossils are around 417 million years old and date to the early Devonian. Among the moss forests and bacterial and algal mats that had developed during the Silurian, primitive rooted plants such as *Gosslingia breconensis* and *Tarella trowenii* appeared, helping to create the first stable soils and sheltering arthropods such as mites and scorpions, along with the first insects. (*Gosslingia breconensis* is one of a small number of species named after the area, the others including a modern dandelion, Brecon dandelion *Taraxacum breconense*, and a microspecies of bramble, *Rubus breconensis*.) These early Devonian plants, ancestors of the clubmosses that dominated much of the land vegetation later in the Carboniferous coal swamps, were no more than a few centimetres tall and probably spread largely by vegetative growth. Clubmosses found in the Beacons today, thought to be similar to these earliest plants, include stag's horn clubmoss *Lycopodium clavatum*, which is abundant in several locations amongst the heather on the Blorenge, with small, scale-like leaves, spores borne in sporangia at the bases of the leaves, branching stems and generally a simple form (Fig. 18).

Gosslingia breconensis was first discovered in Craig y Fro Quarry in the early 1920s by Mr F. N. Gossling of the Post Office Surveyors Department, who informed Professor A. H. Cox at Cardiff University of the discovery. At that time the Post Office had a very large Surveyors Department, the staff being responsible for inspecting sub post offices, suggesting improvements to the postal system and drawing up contracts. It was quite a varied role, but the work consisted largely of inspection tours, and in this role Gossling must have passed Craig y Fro and the

FIG 18. Stag's horn clubmoss, thought to be similar to the earliest vascular plants, amongst the heather on the Blorenge. (Jonathan Mullard)

other quarries along the main Brecon to Merthyr road many times in the course of his duties. Craig y Fro, sometimes known as 'Brecon Beacons Quarry', and the other nearby quarries were probably the source of stone for the enclosure walls built in the neighbourhood, and consequently they date from the wall-building phase of the nineteenth century (Fig. 19). They have remained fresh because of their use as lay-bys.

Professor Cox and Albert Heard subsequently examined the locality, the latter writing a paper which was published in the *Quarterly Journal of the Geological Society* in 1927 in which he noted, 'In naming the plant *Gosslingia breconensis* I have pleasure in associating with the first described Old Red Sandstone plant from Wales the name of Mr F. N. Gossling, who was the first observer of the fossil locality.' Albert Heard subsequently spent over a year trying to 'obtain internal structures from the plant remains' and was finally rewarded in his efforts to etch the polished surface when concentrated nitric acid was used as a reagent. In the meantime, as Heard described it, 'While the work on these plants has been in progress, other investigators have observed the new plant locality.' These other investigators included Mr W. Wickham King FGS and Miss Daisy Williams of Swansea, who in 1925 'kindly withdrew from

FIG 19. Craig y Fro Quarry, the 'type locality' for *Gosslingia breconensis*, a primitive rooted plant of the Silurian period and one of a few species named after the area. *Gosslingia* was discovered by Mr. F. N. Gossling of the Post Office Surveyors Department in the 1920s. (Jonathan Mullard)

FIG 20. Close up of a fertile branch of *Gosslingia breconensis*, showing the sporangia attached laterally along the length of the stem. Scale bar = 10 mm. (National Museum of Wales)

the *Geological Magazine* a paper on the Brecon plant locality.' Heard was obviously keen not to be usurped in his naming and description.

Since the 1920s further scientific papers have been written on the fossil floras found here, and Craig y Fro is now recognised as having some of the best preserved and most completely known Devonian plant fossils in Britain, second only in quality to those found in the internationally renowned Rhynie Chert locality in Scotland. As a consequence, in the 1980s the quarry and its immediate surroundings were notified as a Geological Conservation Review Site in recognition of their national and international significance. The sediments now exposed by quarrying were originally deposited in a river floodplain environment with the creation and subsequent abandonment of migrating meanders, the plants probably growing around the edge of pools in which their remains accumulated. The fossils themselves usually consist of fragments; many reconstructions are therefore speculative, concentrating on the aerial parts, and there is little if any information on underground structures. Close examination of the fossils has revealed though that Gosslingia has the sporangia, the enclosure in which spores are formed, attached laterally along the length of the stem (Fig. 20), while Tarella, which shares many features with Gosslingia, differs in having sporangia distributed in two vertical rows on opposite sides of the stem. Tarella also has prominent swellings on the surface of the stems, although the exact nature of these structures is unclear.

A species unique to Craig y Fro is *Krithodeophyton croftii*, which has bare stems divided into two branches bearing two vertical rows of terminal fertile spikes,

FIG 21. Capel Horeb Quarry, another important site for early vascular plant fossils, including *Cooksonia hemisphaerica*, the world's oldest known vascular plant. (Alan Bowring)

consisting of alternating sporangia and sterile bracts. It seems to be in the order Barinophytales; it is the only member of the order to have been described from Britain and the earliest known example in the world. The barinophytales were one of the early groups of plants that adapted to the land environment during the Devonian, but which disappeared soon after, leaving no evolutionary successors.

Other fossil plants recorded from the site include *Sennicaulis hippocrepiformis* and *Hostiniella beardii*, and together with the plants above they form what is known as the Senni Beds flora. Also present here, and at Llanover Quarry to the south of Abergavenny, is *Dawsonites arcuatus*, one of the world's earliest examples of a trimerophyte, which is the group thought to be ancestral to the seed-bearing plants and thus flowering plants. A primitive fern, *Dawsonites* died out before the beginning of the Upper Devonian. Further species associated with this flora include *Drepanophycus spinaeformis*, *Sporogonites exuberans* and *Sciadophyton steinmanni*.

Another quarry important for a number of early vascular plant fossils is Capel Horeb Quarry near Llandovery (Fig. 21), with the first being described by Heard in 1939. Since then more plant fossils have been described, including *Cooksonia hemisphaerica*, the oldest plant with a vascular system known in the world. The site has also yielded important animal fossils, Murchison visiting in 1834 to collect new species of brachiopods and mussels which helped him to develop the Silurian system. Even though Capel Horeb Quarry is such an important site, it has been inaccessible for many years through the reluctance of the previous owner to allow people access. It has recently been purchased, however, by the British Institute for Geological Conservation and the quarry face cleared of vegetation, with the support of the Countryside Council for Wales. There are also plans to open up the site for public access.

The invasion of the land by plants was a pivotal time in the history of the planet, and recent experiments undertaken by a team led by Timothy Lenton at Exeter University have suggested that these first plants to take root on dry land may have cooled the Earth enough to bring on a series of ice ages (Lenton *et al*. 2012). As the plants spread across the continents they extracted minerals from the rocks they grew on and brought levels of atmospheric carbon down, causing temperatures to drop markedly. This scenario could explain glaciations that saw ice sheets advance during the Ordovician period, between 488 and 444 million years ago. At this time the continents were clustered around the South Pole and stretched as far as the Equator.

As the plants grew, they dissolved silicate rocks, such as granite, to release calcium and magnesium ions. These ions combine with atmospheric carbon and wash into oceans, where they precipitate as carbonate rocks. This process alone might have caused temperatures to fall by around 5 °C. In another parallel process, plants extracted phosphorus and iron from rocks, and as the plants died these elements would have found their way to the sea. The rise in nutrients there was likely to have fuelled the growth of plankton, which captured carbon as they grew and ultimately carried it to the seabed when they died, where it formed rock. The scientists assumed that 15 per cent of the Earth's land mass was covered with early plant life, but even with 5 per cent land coverage, the cooling effect would have been substantial. Although plants are still cooling the Earth's climate by reducing the atmospheric carbon levels and have a central regulatory role in the control of climate, they cannot keep up with the speed of today's human-induced climate change. It would take millions of years for plants to remove current carbon emissions from the atmosphere.

CARBONIFEROUS ROCKS

During the Carboniferous period Britain lay on the Equator and so the climate was tropical. As global sea levels rose at the start of this period, the former river plains were flooded to form a shallow sea which extended across much of

FIG 22. *Lithostrotion*, a genus of rugose coral which which was abundant in the early Carboniferous. Often the original limestone is replaced with quartz, and since this is more resistant to weathering than the surrounding limestone rock, fossils of these corals commonly weather out of natural outcroppings, such as here in the limestone pavement at Ogof Ffynnon Ddu (Gareth Ellis)

what is now South Wales. Corals lived in these warm seas, and among the most interesting fossils to be found in the Beacons are *Lithostrotion* spp., common carboniferous corals whose intricate internal detail is often beautifully preserved (Fig. 22). Each polyp secreted a hard, circular corallite about 1 cm across. These rugose corals are not closely related to modern corals since they became extinct in the Late Permian mass extinction 252 million years ago, when 97 per cent of the species that have left a fossil record disappeared. At this time global temperatures were extremely high and together with the effects of huge volcanic eruptions the severe conditions devastated enormous numbers of marine and terrestrial species. Brachiopods, a type of shellfish, also thrived in the Carboniferous, and the limestone we know today was formed from the shells and skeletons of these animals, both large and small. In time these shallow seas once again received sand and mud carried by rivers from the mountains to the north. Later the resulting river deltas were colonised by plants, and dense swampy forests grew across them, which would eventually form the coal measures.

FOSSIL FISH

The first fossil fish to be discovered in Wales were found by Edward Lhuyd on the Blorenge. In a letter to Dr Tancred Robinson, a Yorkshire physician and naturalist, headlined 'Usk in Monmouthshire, June 15 1697', he records his finds as follows (Gunther 1945):

> *The most considerable discoveries, since my last, were some new species of Glossopetrae and Siliquastra, (the first Ichthyodontes, I suppose, that ever were observ'd in Wales) on the top of a high mountain called Blorens near Aber Gavenni. The Siliquastra were smaller than the generality of those I had observ'd in other countries. Of the Glossopetrae we found one pretty large; but all the rest very small; all black or atrorubent. The same place afforded also some variety of fossil shells, and plenty of Cuthbert's beads, which were very small in comparison of what are found throughout the north of England. We also found there a large Testaceous body, not to be compar'd as to its figure with any sort of shell yet describ'd: Together with some embossed representations of pieces of the skeletons of Eels, or some lesser fish. All these were in limestone.*

When fossilised shark teeth were first discovered embedded in terrestrial rocks, on mountains such as the Blorenge, far from the sea, their origin was a complete mystery. Pliny the Elder, the great Roman naturalist and compiler of the encyclopaedic *Natural History*, believed that they fell from the sky during lunar eclipses. They were later thought to be the tongues of serpents that Saint Paul had turned to stone while visiting Malta, which is how they came to be called *glossopetrae*, 'tongue stones'. *Atrorubent* means dark red. Lhuyd, who struggled to understand how the various animal and vegetable remains could 'be placed in their subterranean repositories by the Noachian flood', a scheme his judgement rejected, described a number of fish teeth found on his travels according to a classification he had developed. Those triangular in shape with serrated edges he called *Glossopetrae*, those round, elongated and pointed he called *Plectronitae*, angular ones were called *Rhombisci* and flattened pod-shaped teeth were called *Siliquastra*. Cuthbert's beads are fossilised portions of the stems or columnals of Carboniferous crinoids or 'sea lilies'. In Northumberland they were collected at Lindisfarne and strung together as a necklace or rosary, becoming associated with St Cuthbert, who was a monk on Lindisfarne in the seventh century.

In a later letter to John Ray, the 'father of English natural history', Lhuyd continued to puzzle over how marine fossils could be found in terrestrial situations and gave more examples he had personally seen in the Beacons. In the cave located beneath Carreg Cennen castle and in Porth yr Ogof cave:

> *Such marine fossils have been observ'd on ye sides or walls within our limestone caves; & are even some times found sticking to the roofs of them, for I have gathered the Cuthbert Beads or Entrochi, which are vertebrae of sea stars, from ye roof of a cave called Lhygad lhwchwr near Kerrig Kennan Castle in the County of Carmarthen: and on the sides (as well as bottom) of a noted cave calld Porth Gogo at Ystrad Velhte in Brecknockshire, I have observed several remains of cockles half worn by the swift current of the River Melhte wch runs through this cave and polishes its limestone. Now although I can readily grant that the Deluge might have cast marine bodies into these & any other caves: yet can I not allow that it could ever fasten them to their polite roofs & sides: and that they should be sunk so deep from the top, is the difficulty of the former objection. To this may be added that such limestone caves are for ye most part wainscoted (as it were) with a stony crust of stalagmites wch is of no very old date: but owing to the continued dropping or distillation of the caves, in wch if any marine-like bodies are found, as I can assure you the Entrochi are, I leave it to your self & other unprejudiced observers to consider of their origin.*

GLACIATED KARST

The limestone with its pavements, caves, dry valleys and swallow holes, or sinkholes, is known as a karst landscape, after the Kras plateau region of eastern Italy and western Slovenia (Kras is *Karst* in German, for 'barren land'). During the Quaternary period, the most recent geological time period spanning the last two million years, cooling of the global climate led to much more extensive glaciation, as ice spread to lower altitudes and latitudes. Areas of limestone such as those in the Beacons, which were previously covered by glaciers, are known as glaciated karst. Characteristic features of glaciated karst include bare rock scarred with multiple straight, parallel grooves, which represent the movement of the sediment-loaded base of glaciers, and limestone pavements, which have been created by the scouring of ice sheets during the last glaciation.

Many of these landscapes have been subject to a number of glaciations over the last two million years, but evidence from the more ancient glacial episodes is seldom preserved on the eroded surfaces. Along the most northerly part of the outcrop the limestone exists as a steep cliff or scar, above a gentler slope underpinned by Old Red Sandstone.

LIMESTONE PAVEMENT

Following their exposure by glaciers, the action of water has subsequently widened the cracks in the pavements to form a complex pattern of crevices, known as grikes, between blocks of weathered limestone called clints (Fig. 23). There is a total of less than 3,000 hectares of limestone pavement in the United Kingdom, with the largest areas occurring in North Yorkshire and Cumbria. The pavements in the Brecon Beacons are the most southerly examples in Britain, and their rich and diverse wildlife is described in a later chapter.

Wales has less than 100 hectares of limestone pavement, and the Brecon Beacons contain a significant proportion of the resource, but until 2009, when the National Park Authority published a comprehensive survey (Ellis 2009), there was no clear understanding of its extent. Previous surveys left areas of pavement unrecorded, even though they were adjacent to surveyed sites. Since limestone pavement is a term used to describe both a geological formation and a habitat type, a geologist might classify any area of exposed, weathered limestone as pavement, whereas a biologist would consider an area to be pavement on the presence of certain species, indicative of the warmth, shelter, humidity and calcareous soils found here. Even this survey cannot be described as complete though, since several known outcrops remain to be visited. Other areas undoubtedly exist, particularly

FIG 23. Limestone pavement at Ogof Ffynnon Ddu, the best example of this habitat in South Wales. (Jonathan Mullard)

wooded pavements, or remnants of pavement within forestry plantations. The most significant outcrops have all been mapped and recorded, however.

The limestone outcrop in the Beacons originates from the Lower Carboniferous period, known as the Dinantian. It is sometimes referred to as the 'north crop' to distinguish it from a parallel outcrop, the 'south crop', which defines the southern rim of the South Wales coalfield. The sequence consists of five distinct limestone beds, sandwiched between limestone shales as shown in Table 1. Limestone pavements occur on each of the limestone beds, and this contributes to the different weathering, jointing and solution patterns now visible.

With only a few exceptions, the pavements that have formed are characterised by patterns of close jointing producing numerous small clints with frequent, though often narrow, grikes. This gives the pavements a 'shattered' appearance, quite different from the solid pavements of northern England. The close jointing is a result of the pressures and stresses created by faulting activity along the Neath and Cribarth disturbances and the numerous cross-faults. These minor fracture planes are distinct from joints, faults or bedding planes and have resulted in the rapid weathering of the post-glacial exposures. Low temperatures and high rainfall, typical of the Welsh uplands, have assisted the weathering process, the freezing of trapped water splitting clints apart.

Variations in the structure of pavements are the result of both the grain size of the limestone bed and the frequency of close jointing, which is itself, as described above, related to the proximity and orientation of substantial faults. Weathering or solution features on individual pavements are rarely consistent, and different formations can be found on similar beds within the same locality. The pattern and frequency of bedding and joint planes within the exposed rock in turn affects the way the limestone is dissolved by rainwater. Fine-grained rocks that have smooth

TABLE 1. The limestone beds that outcrop in the Brecon Beacons.

DINANTIAN LIMESTONE	Upper Limestone shales
	Penwyllt Limestone
	Penderyn oolite
	Dowlais (Cil-yr-ychen) Limestone
	Llanelly formation
	Abercriban oolite
	Lower Limestone shales

Adapted from Barclay et al. (1988). The diagram represents only the sequence of the limestone and does not indicate the relative thickness of the beds.

fracture planes which allow water to penetrate easily are more susceptible to being dissolved than coarse-grained and fine-grained rocks with corrugated fracture planes that limit the penetration of water. In many locations vertical fractures have been a significant factor in both the physical and chemical weathering of the rock.

It is clear that almost all of the limestone outcrops in the Beacons have been disturbed, or damaged, by human activity. Stone walls and sheep folds around Ystradfellte, Blaen Nedd and Pant Mawr, in particular, have clearly been constructed from weathered limestone; either from pavements or from low vertical limestone exposures. Compared to other pavements in Britain, the pavements here are more fractured and fragmented, and while the presence of microfractures has accelerated natural erosion the breaking and removal of stone for human use has undoubtedly been one of the main causes of the present state of the feature. The geologist T. N. George noted in 1926 that 'The rock, owing to its purity, has been quarried extensively for lime-burning, but this practice is now discontinued, except at Landebie and Kidwelly, where the kilns are conveniently situated at which a railway crosses the limestone outcrop. It is, however, still quarried to a fair extent as road-metal.' Today the influence of the lime industry on the landscapes and social history of Wales is often overlooked. Its use has enabled farmers to transform acid soils into productive farmland, and as mortar and whitewash it was until recently a key element of the building industry. Lime and limestone are also crucial for iron and copper smelting, industries which have helped make Wales world-famous (Schlee 2013). Because of the continuing economic value of limestone, there are still several quarries in the Beacons. These larger quarries have replaced the older small-scale workings, many of which are still visible.

QUARRIES AND KILNS

The remains of more than 171 lime kilns, used for the production of agricultural lime, can be found around the limestone pavements at Blaen Nedd and Ystradfellte. Major limekilns can also be found elsewhere in the Beacons, such as in Henllys Vale in the valley of the Afon Twrch (Fig. 24). In the surrounding countryside the exposed faces of small quarries, a flat limestone surface marking a change of bedding, the quarry floor, and numerous vegetated piles of waste rock material can be clearly seen. The area of pavement has therefore been reduced over time, together with the height of exposed rock above the ground surface, smooth features still visible on clint tops indicating the immediate post-glacial ground surface. The high frequency of jointing may have reduced the value of the limestone for building purposes, but will have certainly facilitated the removal of fragments.

FIG 24. The former lime kilns of Henllys Vale, located next to the Afon Twrch. (Harold Grenfell)

Similarly on Mynydd Du there is an area of limestone workings at Herbert's Quarry near Brynamman. Here Dyfed Archaeological Trust is working with the National Park Authority, which owns the site, to find out more about the area and to conserve the industrial remains. The project, called Calch after the Welsh word for lime, aims to make the site more accessible and enable both visitors and local people to explore the area. One of the features of the site is the existence of large areas of tufa, a porous rock formed as a deposit from springs or streams. Because of this feature Herbert's Quarry has been designated as a Regionally Important Geological Site (RIGS).

Tufa is often found in cave systems, or above ground around natural springs, but conditions at Herbert's Quarry have led to it being formed over large areas. Water running through the spoil tips left behind in the lime-making process absorbs calcium hydroxide, making it very alkaline. As it reaches the surface this alkaline water reacts with carbon dioxide from the air, and the calcium hydroxide turns into solid calcium carbonate. Normally, the alkaline waters release carbon dioxide when they reach the surface, which increases the alkalinity, but reduces the solubility of the carbonate, which is therefore deposited. As this process has continued at the quarry, the calcium carbonate has created a variety of impressive mineral formations (Figs 25, 26).

FIG 25. Herbert's Quarry has been designated as a Regionally Important Geological Site, because of the large areas of tufa found there. (Duncan Schlee/Dyfed Archaeological Trust)

FIG 26. An example of the impressive tufa formations at Herbert's Quarry. (Duncan Schlee/Dyfed Archaeological Trust)

SINKHOLES

The Brecon Beacons has a greater density of sinkholes than anywhere else in Britain. Some of these occur in areas that, at first sight, are not limestone. Sinkholes form when a portion of the rock below is eroded away and although in areas such as Mynydd Llangynidr and Mynydd Llangatwg the surface rock is gritstone, the limestone is not far below the surface. The collapse of sections of cave within the limestone leads to craters appearing at the ground surface (Fig. 27). Large sinkholes resulting from this process occur by the A4059 road, north of Penderyn and just beyond the junction of the road leading to Ystradfellte. Some of these collapsed sinkholes are over 60 m across and 2 m deep and form entrances into underground caverns. Sinkholes formed as a result of this process are actually quite rare in Britain, as caves are generally quite stable structures.

Most sinkholes form instead by the process of suffosion, where loose, unconsolidated material overlies fissures and joints in the underlying limestone, and material is washed into these fissures and into the caves beneath. Suffosion sinkholes tend to develop gradually (over months or years) as the covering sediment slumps into open fissures in the underlying limestone, creating a void which migrates towards the surface, eventually creating a sinkhole.

FIG 27. Sinkholes highlighted by snow on Carnau Gwynion, Ystradfellte. The Beacons has the greatest density of sinkholes in Britain. (© Crown copyright: Royal Commission on the Ancient and Historical Monuments of Wales)

Solution sinkholes form by the uneven dissolution of the underlying limestone, creating a broad saucer-like sinkhole, while others occur where a stream sinks underground, creating a blind valley.

FOLDS AND FRACTURES

The Old Red Sandstone has been raised and slightly tilted by earth movements, but the Carboniferous rocks have been not only been tilted and uplifted, but also folded and fractured – and numerous fractures and faults stretch across the south of the National Park, interrupting the continuity of the outcrops. Because these disturbed rocks form weak zones, valleys created by running water run along the faults. Craig y Dinas and Bwa Maen at Pontneddfechan are spectacular examples of rocks lying on or near major faults which have been moved from near horizontal to vertical positions. From Pontneddfechan the zone of disturbance can be traced through the faulted ridges near Penderyn, along the side valleys of the Taf Fawr and Taf Fechan.

Craig y Dinas, or Dinas Rock, is a high promontory which lies between the Afon Mellte and its tributary, the Afon Sychryd (Fig. 28). It derives its name from the presence of Iron Age earthworks on its summit (*dinas* in Welsh signifying a defensive site or city), and it is supposed to have been one of the last places the fairies lived in Britain. There are a few short caves in and around Dinas Rock, including Ogof Pont Sychryd, Ogof Bwa Maen and Will's Hole. The last named is also known as Arthur's Cave, and it extends to just under 400 m in length. It is one of the many locations reputed to be the place where Arthur's knights lie waiting for a call to defend Britain. The present-day landscape, however, is the result of the extraction of limestone and the nearby mining of silica rock. The Dinas Rock Silica Mines, just to the east of Dinas Rock itself, used to provide large quantities of very pure crushed sandstone destined for the manufacture of refractory bricks for furnace linings. A system of tramways, aerial cableways and inclines were used to transport the material from the mines to the valley below. These bricks came to be known as 'Dinas Bricks' and, in at least one of the countries to which these bricks were exported, Russia, the word *dinas* came to mean 'firebrick'. The former limestone quarry immediately adjacent to Dinas Rock is now a car park managed by the Forestry Commission, and it is a popular site. Its dramatic appearance makes Dinas Rock a tourist attraction, while its steep slopes also attract rock climbers.

The formation of rock known as Bwa Maen, literally the 'stone arch', is an extraordinary tightly folded block of limestone, which can best be seen in winter

FIG 28. Dinas Rock, a spectacular example of rocks lying on, or near, major faults which have been moved from near horizontal to vertical positions. (Jonathan Mullard)

FIG 29. Bwa Maen, meaning 'stone arch', is a tightly folded block of limestone in the Sychryd Gorge. This spectacular feature of the Fforest Fawr Geopark is even more clearly seen in winter when the trees have lost their leaves. (Jonathan Mullard)

from near the end of the Sychryd 'all-ability trail' when the vegetation has died back (Fig. 29). Bwa Maen, which has itself recently been cleared of vegetation by the Countryside Council for Wales, is one of a number of geological structures which together form the Neath Disturbance – an ancient weakness in the earth's crust which extends from Swansea Bay to Hereford. It is responsible for a number of significant landscape features along its 100 km length, including the Vale of Neath, a deep valley incised by a glacier along the line of weakness. The feature was created by a continental collision during the Carboniferous period which formed the supercontinent known as Pangaea.

The Cribarth or Swansea Valley Disturbance and the Carreg Cennen Disturbance have a similar origin. The Cribarth Disturbance crosses the river near Craig y Nos Country Park, and the tightly faulted and folded limestone here has created steep buttresses on either side of the river: Cribarth and Craig y Nos to the west and Craig y Rhiwarth to the east. Craig y Rhiwarth is now a nature reserve managed by the Brecknock Wildlife Trust. It has rich limestone plant communities, including one of the finest ash *Fraxinus excelsior* woods in Britain.

FIG 30. The Afon Twrch, which is slowly cutting its way through the strata of Mynydd Du. (Alan Bowring)

NAMURIAN ROCKS

The Namurian stage of the Carboniferous period lasted from 326 to 313 million years ago. Rocks of this age found in the Beacons consist of the Twrch Sandstone and the overlying Bishopston Mudstone Formation. The Twrch Sandstone is named after the Afon Twrch (Fig. 30), which, cutting through Mynydd Du, reveals these rock strata where the thickest seams occur, while the Bishopston Mudstone is named after the Gower village where they were first recorded. The Twrch Sandstone is a hard-wearing rock which gives rise to prominent features in the landscape, such as Tair Carn Uchaf ('upper three cairns'). This is a flat ridge 482 m above sea level marked by the three large Bronze Age round barrows that give the mountain its name (see Fig. 47).

The rocks of the Bishopston Mudstone Formation consist of both mudstones and thin sandstones. The spectacular waterfalls around Ystradfellte were formed where rivers flow over the edges of some of these sandstone layers, wearing away the softer mudstones underneath. The siting of individual falls is closely linked to the presence of faults, aligned from the northwest to the southeast, which have brought the different rocks together.

COAL MEASURES

Along the very southern edge of the Brecon Beacons, rocks of the Carboniferous coal measures outcrop, but the sequence from the younger coal measures to the older Old Red Sandstone is interrupted by major fault lines, disturbances which complicate the interpretation of the geological sequences. Dense swampy forests containing giant horsetails and ferns thrived in the oxygen-rich atmosphere of this period, and their fossilised remains can be found in abundance in the coals, mudstones and sandstones which together comprise the coal measures. The first person to compile a detailed geological map of part of the South Wales coalfield was Sir William Edmond Logan, one of the leading geologists of the nineteenth century. In the course of his work mapping the coalfield he discovered two fossilised trees beneath the waterfall at Henrhyd, and these are now displayed outside Swansea Museum (Fig. 31). William Logan subsequently established the Geological Survey of Canada in 1842 and became its first director. The highest mountain is Canada is now named in his honour.

FIG 31. The largest fossil tree discovered by Sir William Edmond Logan beneath Henrhyd waterfall in the Nant Llech valley, now located in front of Swansea museum. (Harold Grenfell)

The coal measures are traditionally divided into three units, of which only the older two, the Lower and Middle Coal Measures (also known as the Lower Westphalian) are found within the Beacons. The base of the Lower Coal Measures in South Wales is defined by the Farewell Rock, a thick sandstone which occurs widely across the coalfield, although it is in fact several different sandstones that all occur at around the same point in the sequence of rocks. The Farewell Rock is said to have been named by ironstone miners who worked the coal measures deposits which overlie this strata. Digging below this bed would yield no further iron ore and so, on reaching it, they could bid 'farewell' to further riches. The name was subsequently adopted by miners in search of coal, which occurs in the same strata. The stream-bed, bank and cliff exposures along the lower sections of the Nant Lech are one of the best localities in Britain for the study of this important sequence of Carboniferous sedimentary rocks. Several distinct fossil beds are also exposed here, characterised by plants such as *Neuralethopteris schlehanii* and *Lyginopteris hoeninghausii*. The beds also contain abundant remains of neuralethopterid plants, particularly *Neuropteris jongmansii* and *N. rectinervis*, seed plants with fern-like fronds which are characteristic of floras of this age. These key outcrops along the valley are maintained in a condition that enables researchers to re-examine the evidence, and they are often used as a teaching resource.

GLACIAL LANDSCAPES

Glaciers develop from the accumulation of perennial snow, which, when it is thick and dense enough, creates movement by internal deformation and sliding at the base. This movement carries the ice from the relatively cold environment where snow accumulates to warmer environments where it begins to melt. Glaciers act a conveyor belt, carrying debris from the top of the glacier to the bottom, where

FIG 32. Maen Grwydr on Mynydd Du, an Old Red Sandstone boulder deposited on a limestone pavement by a glacier retreating down the Swansea Valley. (Alan Richards)

it is deposited. As the ice moves, it erodes the underlying material by abrasion and removal of blocks. Abrasion leaves behind striated surfaces and produces finely ground rock particles, while block removal generates larger boulders and leaves fractured surfaces, mostly facing in the direction of the glacier's flow. One of the best examples of these larger boulders is Maen Grwydr on Mynydd Du, an Old Red Sandstone boulder which was deposited on a limestone pavement by a retreating glacier flowing down the Swansea Valley approximately 12,500 years ago (Fig. 32). Other similar boulders can be found in the same area.

There is considerable interest in the landscapes associated with the glacial period. Among the most spectacular are the various moraines (accumulations of unconsolidated glacial debris) associated with the very last glacial episode, known as the Loch Lomond Stadial, approximately 13,000 to 12,000 years ago. One of the most accessible of these is a distinctive crescent-shaped hill about 1 km long, a short distance to the west of Llanfihangel church and the Skirrid Mountain Inn (Fig. 33). The Llanfihangel moraine is considered to be the finest example in South Wales of a terminal moraine, formed at the extremity of the ice cap. Over much of the region clear evidence for the limits of the Late Devensian ice sheet is absent, so this moraine provides important information on this aspect.

When the site was first notified as a Site of Special Scientific Interest in 1976, it was thought that the glacier came from the Vale of Ewyas to the north. Research over the last couple of decades, however, has suggested that it was

FIG 33. The steep slope of Llanfihangel Crucorney moraine, viewed from the churchyard. It is the finest example in South Wales of a terminal moraine. (Jonathan Mullard)

a huge wedge of ice spreading from the Usk Valley to the south. During 2010 geologists from the British Geological Survey investigated the site, drilling a series of boreholes to make a cross-section of the different sediments and undertaking a survey to produce a map showing the subtle patterns in landforms left by the glacier and its meltwaters. The size and shape of the terminal moraine is determined by whether the glacier is advancing, receding or at equilibrium. The longer the glacier stays in one place the more debris will accumulate in the moraine. Alongside this work a programme of fieldwork has produced a detailed geomorphological map. Understanding the soils and drift deposits in the area will also provide information on the way the landscape responded to historic climate change during a period of global warming, melting glaciers and sea level rise, with obvious parallels to the changing world we live in today.

The Afon Honddu rises at the Gospel Pass and flows south from Capel y Ffin to Llanfihangel, there to be deflected to the northeast by the moraine to join the Monnow at Alltrynys, but prior to the last glaciation the Honddu probably flowed south along the valley now occupied by the Afon Gafenni to join the Usk at Abergavenny. The southwest-to-northeast alignment of both the Honddu and the Monnow appear to be related to the course of the Neath Disturbance, an ancient geological weakness, which runs through the valley to the north of the Sugar Loaf and on towards Hereford.

Other substantial moraines in the Usk Valley include the Nevill Hall/Llanfoist moraine south of Abergavenny and the Usk moraine, which is believed to represent the furthest advance of an Usk Valley glacier. Other recessional moraines, often noticed as a series of transverse ridges running across a valley behind a terminal moraine, and which are created during temporary halts in a glacier's retreat, can been seen along the length of the Usk Valley, for example at Llangetty, and in the Tawe Valley at Craig y Nos. Much of the lower ground here at Craig y Nos is covered with glacial till, unsorted sediments deposited directly by the glacier.

At Cwm Llwch, in the shadow of the highest peaks of the Beacons, there is a striking 25 m high terminal moraine that also probably formed during the Loch Lomond Stadial (Fig. 34). The prominent shape of the moraine, which wraps around the northern and eastern sides of Llyn Cwm Llwch, contrasts markedly with the smoother, but rockier, contours of the slopes beneath Corn Du. Cwm Llwch is just one of a number of spectacular glacial cirques along the north face of the Old Red Sandstone. The moraine was first mentioned by W. S. Symonds in 1872, and later T. Mellard Reade (1894–95) wrote that 'the sun has traced out this moraine and settled its alignment and position in the larger cwm or valley' (Stephens 1990). Certainly shading is one aspect explaining the huddling of the glacier in the extreme southwestern corner of the escarpment face, but the

FIG 34. The conspicuous shape of the terminal moraine wrapped around Llyn Cwm Llwch. (Jonathan Mullard)

extensive upland slope to the southwest, from which snow could have drifted in to the cwm, is another factor. In addition the curvature of the headwall would have tended to protect snow in its lee from the scouring action of the wind. Similarly, Llangorse Lake owes its existence to the moraine deposits left in the area between Llanfihangel Talyllyn and Talgarth.

Two kilometres south of Cwm Llwch, at the head of Cwm Crew, is the site of yet another glacial moraine, created by a glacier which occupied this hollow approximately 11,000 to 10,000 years ago. The direction of the ice movement here is indicated by the increase in size and extension of the ridges down the valley. Glacial striae, scratches or gouges are also abundant on the surface of the Twrch Sandstone and within Ogof Ffynnon Ddu National Nature Reserve (NNR). As well as indicating the direction of flow of the glacial ice, the depth and extent of weathering of the gouges can also be used to estimate how long the rock has been exposed.

Other glacial features of interest include the so-called pro-talus ramparts, simple landforms created by the presence of long-lived snow banks below rock cliffs. The weathering of the cliffs by frost leads to rock falls, with the blocks rolling down the snow slope to accumulate at its base. Those at the foot of the Mynydd Du scarp are fresh in appearance, as are those situated along the base of the northern slope of the central Beacons, while hybrid forms, combined with landslips, occur at Craig Cerrig Gleisiad National Nature Reserve and, more controversially, at Craig y Fro in Glyn Tarell. Here a low ridge covered with bracken *Pteridium aquilinum* is thought to be a moraine formed by a small glacier which nestled under the cliffs of Craig y Fro at the end of the last ice age. Geologists still debate its exact origins, as there may also have been land slips that contributed to the lumpy ground in this area. The British Geological Survey and others have been sinking bores into the peat and sediment surfaces here in order to research the post-glacial environmental record.

POST-GLACIAL LANDSLIPS

Post-glacial landslips are common throughout the Beacons, and spectacular examples exist beneath Fan Llia above Ystradfellte Reservoir, at the Darren above Crickhowell, at Cwar y Gigfran above Blaen y Glyn and in the east around Ysgyryd Fawr, Cwmyoy and other parts of the Vale of Ewyas. All the major slips have occurred within the Brownstones, the sequence of sandstones and mudstones that forms much of the upper part of the Old Red Sandstone. They date from after the last glaciation, when hillsides that had been over-steepened, or undercut, by ice or meltwater slumped down into the valleys.

Above the church at Cwmyoy a great gouge has been taken out of the mountain, leaving Cwmyoy Graig, the two-part mound above the village which

FIG 35. Cwmyoy church, twisted by severe subsidence. The roof tiles of the church itself are a key site for flat-rock grimmia moss *Grimmia ovalis*. (Jonathan Mullard)

has given the church and village its name, 'the valley of the yoke'. A yoke is a wooden beam with cut-outs for animals' necks, used between a pair of animals to enable them together to pull a cart or plough. Cwmyoy Graig, incidentally, is one of the best sites in Monmouthshire for mosses and liverworts, a number of uncommon species that like rather dry and sunny situations being present here.

The church has been twisted in all directions by subsidence and it is a tribute to the skill of the original masons that it is still standing (Fig. 35). The tower is buttressed in two directions, and leans uphill, the chancel arch leans downhill, and the floors and walls between them buckle alarmingly. The tower is said to lean at an angle greater than the Leaning Tower of Pisa. Cwmyoy church must be one of the few churches, if not the only church, to have its geological history described in a notice – in this case to the left of the church door. This weather-stained note, typed in 1967 by D. Emlyn Evans, Assistant Keeper, Department of Geology, National Museum of Wales, reads:

The church at Cwmyoy in the Vale of Ewyas, Monmouthshire, has suffered appreciably from local subsidence. The main reasons for this appear to be geological, the church having been built immediately below the site of a spectacular landslide. The diagrams show how the valley side above and to the east of the church consists of rocks which dip slightly to the west. These rocks belong to the Brownstone division of the Old Red Sandstone System and are predominately red-brown sandstones separated by occasional beds of marls. During the intensely cold period which occurred at the end of the Quaternary Ice Age, certain processes were initiated which resulted in large scale landsliding on the eastern side of the valley. Ground water percolated down through the cracks or joints in the sandstone until it reached the upper surfaces of the impermeable marls. Repeated diurnal and seasonal freezing and thawing caused large blocks of sandstone to be eased along the water-lubricated and sloping marl surfaces. Massive sections of the eastern valley sides were induced to slide out of position and tumble down the slopes. In the slide above the church a huge section was dislocated and despite the weathering of thousands of years, still retains in its core the undisturbed bedded sandstone. The sketches show, however, how the rock in the front of the slide fell into the valley and gave rise to mounds of large and small fragments which have subsequently been weathered and largely disintegrated. The whole mass has gently settled with minor subsidences occurring at frequent intervals in the past. Similar crumbling and weathering of rock material has taken part in the gorge which occurred in the heart of the slide and the diagram attempts to show how the weathered debris now fills part of this original cavity.

The church was built upon the lower slopes of the slide debris and as this material slowly disintegrated and settled the building has been subjected to a long series of minor disturbances. Since the more modern buildings in the near vicinity show no signs of any subsidence it could well be assumed that the sub-surface material immediately beneath the church now appears to be at rest. The structural dislocations which still persist must obviously be referred to the civil engineers.

In the same picture frame is the line diagram, referred to in the text, showing the process in action.

Ysgyryd Fawr, often anglicised to The Skirrid or Skirrid Fawr, is also known as Holy Mountain or Sacred Hill. Ysgyryd is a word describing the hill's shape, signifying that which has shivered or been shattered. Its distinctive shape comprises a long ridge oriented nearly north–south, with a jagged western side resulting, as at Cwmyoy, from ice-age landslips. The upper slopes of the hill are composed of Devonian-age sandstones of the Brownstones Formation, which overlie weaker marls and mudstones of the St Maughans Formation, a situation which has contributed to the instability of the hill's steep flanks.

There is a rich mythology attached to the mountain, including a distinctive stone known as the Devil's Table. According to legend, part of the mountain is said to have been broken off at the moment of the crucifixion of Jesus. There was a local tradition that earth from the Skirrid was holy and especially fertile, and it was taken away to be scattered on fields elsewhere, on coffins, and in the foundations of churches. Pilgrimages were made, especially on Michaelmas Eve, to the summit. John Britton in *The Beauties of England and Wales, Or, Delineations, Topographical, Historical, and Descriptive* (1810) noted that:

> *Various have been the conjectures respecting the cause of this horrid yawning chasm. Ignorance, ever ready to cut the knot it is unable to untie; and credulity, as ready to credit the surmises of superstition, have trumped up the legendary story, that the mountain was rent asunder by the earthquake which happened at the crucifixion of the Saviour: hence it has obtained the appellation of Holy Mount, a name under which it is best known among the inhabitants of the county.*

This legend is recorded on the sign of the Skirrid Mountain Inn, one of the oldest pubs in Wales with a history dating back over 900 years (Fig. 36).

Another impressive set of landslips can be seen at Black Darren and Red Darren (*darren* signifies 'edge' in Welsh) on the eastern side of Hatterall Ridge, west of Longtown (Fig. 37).

Much more recently there have been a number of slope failures in the Beacons as a result of heavy rain, and new mudflows can often be seen scarring the steeper slopes of the mountains. These mudflows typically involve a few cubic

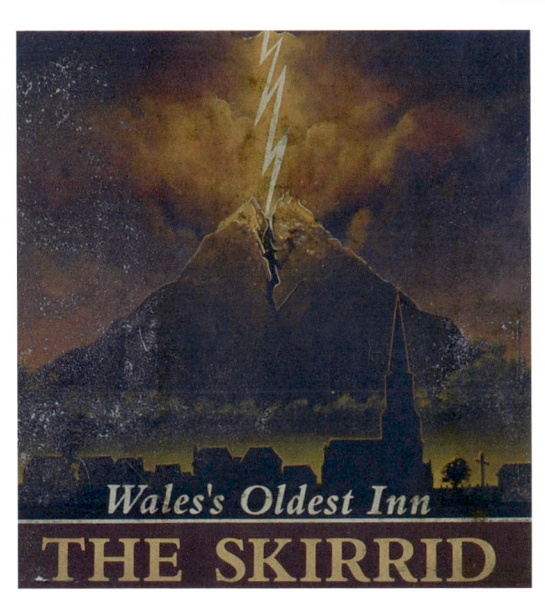

GEOLOGY AND SCENERY · 53

FIG 36. The suitably weathered sign outside the Skirrid Mountain Inn, illustrating the legendary origin of the landslip on Ysgyryd Fawr. (Jonathan Mullard)

BELOW: **FIG 37.** Black Darren, an impressive landslip on the English side of Hatterall Ridge. (Jonathan Mullard)

metres of sand and mud, but on occasions they can be much larger. As occurred during the winter of 2008/09, frost action may be responsible for preparing the ground for these sudden collapses of soil.

SOILS

Like nearly all British soils, the soils in the Brecon Beacons are relatively young, as they have only been formed in the last 12,000 years since the glaciers retreated. Their nature is strongly related to geology and altitude, the geology determining the materials in which soils develop, while the altitude influences microclimates and so determines many of the processes that control soil development. Soils thus develop as a result of the interplay of five factors: the parent material, climate, flora and fauna, topography, and time. Almost certainly the most important of these factors is climate, since soils produced from the same parent material under different climates differ, sometimes quite markedly. Soils also develop very slowly, and in Britain it has been estimated that it takes about 400 years to produce 10 mm of soil. The distribution of plant species is also affected by soil temperatures, which vary with altitude. Annual and biennial species, for instance, are generally less tolerant of extreme conditions and are found below 300 m, while a high proportion of perennial species, which are better adapted for survival in extreme conditions, are recorded above this height. Texts concerning Welsh soils, such as *Soils and Their Use in Wales* (Rudeforth 1984), emphasise agriculture and forestry, but it is possible to provide 'a more general and approachable account of the land of Wales by looking at soil in relation to ecology, landscape and land use' (Hartnup 2011). The National Soil Resources Institute at Cranfield University develops this theme, providing an easily searchable non-technical guide to British soils at www.landis.org.uk/soilscapes.

The National Soil Map, however, is drawn at too small a scale to provide detailed information on soils in the Beacons. The only detailed studies and soil maps that exist were published by the Rothamsted Experimental Station in 1980 and cover an area a few kilometres east of Llandeilo. Although they represent only a small percentage of the region, these studies do include most of the soils that are to be found here. On the Old Red Sandstone, for example, land below about 350 m is covered with well-drained brown earth soils, known as the Milford and Eardiston series (Fig. 38). As might be expected, the topsoil and subsoil are red in colour and are relatively fertile, being among the best agricultural soils in the area. The Eardiston series is coarser in structure than the Milford, and is more common in the east. At higher altitudes, over the well-drained sandstones, podzolic soils have developed. Podzolisation occurs in Wales under conditions of high rainfall and cool summers; it involves the leaching of iron, aluminium, and some other compounds from the topsoil and their accumulation lower down in the soil profile, where they sometimes form an 'iron pan'. These soils, like all podzols, are very acidic and often shallow and stony.

Wetter areas on the sandstone usually indicate the presence of till, unsorted glacial sediments, or, less commonly, springs and seepage zones. The soils in till include, at lower altitudes, the Fforest series, a surface-water gley soil. This is a seasonally waterlogged slowly permeable soil containing relatively little organic matter. It is cultivable with care, being more useful for grasslands than arable, but needs careful management to avoid puddling and poaching by stock. In hollows in the same areas the soils are similar, but are stagnohumic gley soils, known as the Wenallt series. This series, in contrast, is generally too wet for cultivation, often giving rise to mires, fens and other similar vegetation types. The proportion of Wenallt soils increases at higher altitudes, where they may occupy large tracts of wet moorland with occasional drier areas, or wetter parts where the peaty tops are thick enough to be classified as peat soils. The most extensive peat soils occur on the summit plateau of the Brecon Beacons themselves and on the eastern Black Mountains. There are wide tracts of blanket peat on Waun Lysiog and Waun Wen, between the Cantref/Llwyn-on and the Pentwyn/Pontsticell reservoirs, and around Rhos Dirion, Pen y Manllwyn and Waun Fach on the summit ridges of the Black Mountains. One of the major benefits of these deep peat soils is their ability to absorb the copious rainfall and release it gradually into the streams, rivers and reservoirs. Unfortunately, however, many areas of peat have been degraded by overgrazing and recreational activity.

FIG 38. An arable field near Talybont on Usk. These well-drained brown earth soils, known as the Milford and Eardiston series, are red in colour and are relatively fertile, being among the best agricultural soils in the Brecon Beacons. (Jonathan Mullard)

The moorland soils nearly all have peaty tops, the commonest soil being known as the Wilcocks series, which is a stagnohumic gley soil, similar to the Fforest series, but without the reddish colouration derived from the sandstone. In fact these soils, which used to be called peaty gley soils, have grey stony subsoils below the peaty topsoil. Much of the wet, undulating moorland of Mynydd Du and the Brecon Beacons is covered with them. The steeper areas, however, contain islands of drier soils, mainly humo-ferric podzols known as the Anglezarke series. These drier areas are scattered across the moorlands, with larger areas around Garreg Lwyd, Foel Fraith and Cefn Carn Fadog in Mynydd Du and on Mynydd Llangynidr. Many of the limestone soils, in contrast, are very shallow, forming thin topsoils over rock, and are called humic rankers when they are non-calcareous, having been leached of their free carbonates.

Within the patterns determined by geology, there are alluvial soils laid down by the rivers that cross the area. There is surprisingly little though in the way of large tracts of poorly drained alluvium such as that found in Snowdonia or Pembrokeshire, which is probably to do with the size of the rivers, and the amount of fine-textured material in their catchments, rather than being related to rainfall. Only the valley south of Llangorse Lake has extensive alluvial gley soils, and these are mainly pelo-alluvial gley soils dominated by the very heavy Fladbury series. More common, however, are floodplains where the soils, despite occasional flooding, are not waterlogged frequently enough to have developed gley characteristics. These are known as brown alluvial soils, and if flooding is infrequent, for example on land protected by flood banks, they make excellent agricultural soils. There are large areas of this soil, mainly the reddish Lugwardine series, along the length of the Usk from Brecon to Abergavenny, and between Tretower and Cwmdu, along the Rhiangoll. Other significant stretches can be found in Cwm Crai, around Glyn Tawe and Craig y Nos on the upper Tawe, and south of the Llwyn-on Reservoir.

ROCKS AND PEOPLE

Many of the archaeological and historical sites in the Beacons have been constructed from the rocks in their immediate vicinity, and this pattern was continued during the Industrial Revolution, resulting in numerous tramways, limekilns and other structures that are now being reclaimed by nature. In some locations geologists, botanists and archaeologists compete for priority on the same site! It is therefore worth looking at the activities of people in the Brecon Beacons over the millennia, and the legacy they have left us, in more detail.

CHAPTER 3

Creation and Loss

THE WILDLIFE OF THE BRECON BEACONS, and indeed the whole of Wales, has been influenced by repeated glaciations over the last 2.6 million years. The growth and retreat of the ice sheets drove migrations of plants and animals, changing the structure of communities through the various glacial and interglacial cycles, but for the most part, as described in the previous chapter, the area was swept clean by the ice sheets. Some species, especially cave invertebrates buried deep below the ice, survived the repeated glaciations, but the vast majority of the species found today are post-glacial colonists. In the present interglacial period the growing human population has had a considerable effect on the wildlife of the Beacons, with dramatic changes in habitats and reductions in the range and abundance of individual species. In order to understand the current distribution of species it is therefore necessary to review how they re-established in the area following the end of the last glaciation, and consider the impact of people up until the present day.

Much of the information available has been derived from palaeoecology, the reconstruction of ancient ecosystems using data derived from fossils, and the Beacons have played an important role in the development of this approach. Key study sites include Llangorse Lake, the Brecon Beacons themselves, Waun Fignen Felen, a small upland bog on Mynydd Du (Fig. 39), and Traeth Mawr. The peat at these sites has preserved pollen grains, together with the remains of plants and beetles, which allows detailed histories of the various species to be developed. Over the last ten years or so these palaeoecological studies have provided a baseline for monitoring vegetation change, greatly improving our understanding of the natural character, or otherwise, of the communities found here and providing a mechanism for measuring the passage of post-glacial time.

FIG 39. Waun Fignen Felen, a small upland bog on Mynydd Du, is a key site for the study of microfossils. The photograph was taken as the National Park Authority began to restore eroded areas of peat. (Graham Motley/Countryside Council for Wales)

Traeth Mawr, in particular, contains a sequence of peat and clay deposits, and analysis of the pollen in these has provided a detailed record of climatic change over the last 14,000 years. It is a classic example of a 'dead-ice' hollow formed when a glacier melts and withdraws from an area, leaving a block of ice which is subsequently covered by earth and rock (Walker 1982). As the ice melts the ground above it subsides, forming a kettle or hollow, which in the case of Traeth Mawr was once occupied by a large lake that eventually became completely infilled. Very few open areas of water now remain, although there are numerous small pools on the surface of the bog.

From the Roman period onwards there are written records to draw on, and these, although some of the early records are fragmentary, provide a clear narrative about how the landscape has changed over the centuries.

AFTER THE GLACIERS

At the height of the last glaciation the Brecon Beacons were completely covered by the ice sheet, but following its retreat pioneer vegetation communities developed which were dominated by grasses together with docks and sorrels *Rumex* spp. and *Artemesia* species, including mugwort *A. vulgaris*, sagebrush *A. tridentata*, sagewort

A. frigida and wormwood *A. absinthium*, which were the principal constituents of these steppe landscapes. As the climate became warmer they were followed by the establishment of scrub communities dominated by juniper *Juniperus communis*. When the temperature dropped sharply again, between 12,600 and 11,400 years ago, this juniper scrub was replaced by open scrub tundra, with dwarf birch *Betula* spp. and willow *Salix* spp. Glaciers reformed and advanced in many upland areas in Wales including the Brecon Beacons during this time, the last cold period of the Pleistocene, which is known as the Younger Dryas after mountain avens *Dryas octopetala*, a species that is prominent in the pollen records of this period. Today the only Welsh records of mountain avens are from Snowdonia. Herbs such as meadow rue *Thalictrum flavum* and members of the carnation (Caryophyllaceae) family were also abundant in the Younger Dryas. Various mechanisms, involving changes in ocean circulation, changes in atmospheric concentrations of greenhouse gases or haze particles, and changes in snow and ice cover, have been invoked to explain these sudden regional and global changes. It seems likely, however, that phenomena such as the Younger Dryas only occur in a 'glacial' world with much larger ice sheets and more extensive sea ice.

Whatever the exact cause, the Younger Dryas coincided with the loss of many large mammals in Wales, including the woolly mammoth *Mammuthus primigenius*, which was probably hunted to extinction. The fauna of this period is usually associated instead with an arctic fauna characterised by reindeer *Rangifer tarandus*. Small mammals typical of these cold, dry grassland environments included mountain hare *Lepus timidus*, steppe pika *Ochotona pusilla*, arctic lemming *Dicrostonyx torquatus*, Norway lemming *Lemmus lemmus*, tundra vole *Microtus oeconomus*, narrow-headed vole *Microtus gregalis* and water vole *Arvicola amphibius*, the only one of these mammals still to be found in the area today (Fig. 40).

FIG 40. The water vole is the only mammal in the Beacons surviving from the arctic fauna of the Younger Dryas, between 12,600 and 11,400 years ago. (John Windust)

The transition to the present interglacial period around 11,500 years ago was marked by an abrupt rise in maximum summer temperatures, of 7–9 °C over a few decades, and by 10,000 years ago temperatures were close to those of today. This rapid increase in temperature enabled woodland species, such as birch and juniper, to rapidly migrate into the area and establish themselves again as key elements of the flora.

THE BOREAL

During this warm period, known as the Boreal, woodland extended high into the Beacons, with first Scots pine *Pinus sylvestris* and then oak *Quercus* spp. and elm *Ulmus* spp. replacing the birch woodland, except at high elevations. Hazel *Corylus avellana* was also particularly abundant in the area at this time (Walker 1982). By 9,000 years ago all the major tree species were present, with the exception of alder *Alnus glutinosa*, which arrived later – the expansion of alder woodland, in the early to mid Holocene, being a major feature of the changing composition of forests in Wales. At Llangorse Lake pollen records show that the species arrived in the Beacons 8,700 years ago, accompanied by the decline of pine and elm and the expansion of oak woodland in response to increasingly wet conditions.

FIG 41. The Boar on the Hill, a sculpture at the National Botanic Garden of Wales created by artist Michelle Cain, with volunteers from the British Basketmakers Association. Wild boars were a key component of the post-glacial woodlands in the Brecon Beacons. (Jonathan Mullard)

The woodland mix at this time was completed by the arrival of warmth-loving species such as lime *Tilia* spp. In the higher parts of the Brecon Beacons, however, such as the Black Mountains, birch remained the dominant species.

In the early post-glacial period Britain still formed part of the European mainland, and this new forest was populated with animals from refuges in Italy, Spain and the Balkans, including red deer *Cervus elaphus*, roe deer *Capreolus capreolus*, elk *Alces alces*, wild boar *Sus scrofa* (Fig. 41) and aurochs *Bos primigenius*. Small numbers of red deer and roe deer are still present in the Brecon Beacons today though the elk, wild boar and aurochs have long disappeared. Predators of these species included wolf *Canis lupus*, brown bear *Ursus arctos*, lynx *Lynx lynx* and wildcat *Felis sylvestris*. Inland waters such as Llangorse Lake would have supported beaver *Castor fiber*, otter *Lutra lutra* and fish such as pike *Esox lucius*. Even today, as described in Chapter 8, Llangorse is renowned as a haunt of pike.

The early pollen records show periods of woodland retreat that are not readily linked to climate change, but are marked instead by layers of charcoal and the stone tools of Mesolithic hunter–gatherers. Some of the best evidence for Mesolithic people altering the composition of the vegetation in the Beacons is from Waun Fignen Felen, where stone tools were found under the upland peat, which must therefore have formed afterwards. Heathland vegetation and the accumulation of peat began around 9,000 years ago, and there is circumstantial evidence to suggest that the heathland was maintained by burning, perhaps as a deliberate strategy to concentrate game animals and assist hunting. Similar evidence is known from other upland sites in Wales. There is speculation that the rapid expansion of alder across the British Isles at this time may also have been facilitated by people. Alder is a species that needs light and is not adapted to colonising woods with closed canopies. It has been suggested, therefore, that woodland clearance in this period may have provided the openings that alder required before it could spread.

These Boreal woodlands did not therefore consist of an unbroken canopy. Localised open areas were present as a result of burning, diseases, exposure to wind and the actions of grazing animals, all of which would have contributed to producing a woodland mosaic. The openings may have been the first locations of agriculture, as there is evidence for small-scale arable cultivation in temporary clearings before the extensive decline in elm and the beginning of the Neolithic period (Simmons 2003). This decline in elm is one of the most obvious vegetation changes of the present interglacial period, and over the years several competing explanations have been put forward, including the impact of people, climate change and disease. The current consensus is that it was the result of all three factors acting together. The disease was transmitted by the beetle *Scolytus scolytus*, which inhabits clearings, hedges and isolated trees rather than dense primary forest. It has been suggested that the clearance of woodland associated with the adoption of farming created the ideal conditions for the beetle to move to new areas, carrying elm disease with it (Parker *et al.* 2002).

HOLOCENE

The generally cooler conditions of the late Holocene, around 3,000 years ago, encouraged the spread of beech *Fagus sylvatica* to Britain from mainland Europe. The species moved northwards and westwards, arriving in Wales 1,000 years ago (Birks 1989). Like alder, beech required openings in the forest in order to be able to colonise the area, and these were probably created by both the changing climate and the activities of people as described above. Woodland management skills were certainly in use, and there is evidence from many sites in Britain that coppicing was commonly practised. Probably the most visible evidence of human activity in this period is the Neolithic chambered tombs that were built for the collective burial of the dead.

There are nine Neolithic tombs located in and around the Black Mountains. Together, with at least four other sites just outside the area, they form what is known as the 'Black Mountains Group' within a larger regional grouping of tombs, the Severn–Cotswold group. The construction of these monuments was made possible by the development of agriculture and the permanent occupation of land. As well as being burial sites they may have also served as territorial markers, identifying the ownership or occupation of a particular area. It is thought that some tombs were deliberately made to look old, to provide an increased sense of establishment for the community. The best-preserved, and most fully excavated, sites are Penwyrlod and Gwernvale (Children & Nash 2001).

Penwyrlod, near Talgarth, was discovered in 1972 when stone quarrying revealed human remains. This is the largest of the group, being 55 m in length and 25 m across at the broadest end, where it would have stood 3 m high. Excavations at the time of discovery examined and recorded the disturbed areas and obtained an overall plan of the site. Finds included flint tools, pottery and worked stone. The skeletal remains of 17 people were identified, together with a 74 mm long piece of sheep femur, with three small holes, which has been identified as a possible bone flute, or pipe. If this is the case it is the earliest known musical instrument in Britain. Today the chambered tomb is an overgrown mound, covered in summer with rosebay willowherb *Chamerion angustifolium*, supporting a number of large pedunculate oak trees *Quercus robur*, which, although picturesque, are undoubtedly damaging the remains of the structure (Fig. 42).

Gwernvale, previously partly covered by the A40, was also excavated in the 1970s, when the line of the road was altered (Fig. 43). There is far less left of the original structure than at Penwyrlod, but a group of large stones, representing the remains of one chamber, are situated on the highway verge at the entrance of the drive to the Gwernvale Manor Hotel, around half a kilometre to the northwest of Crickhowell. The outline of the original cairn, which is illustrated on a small interpretive panel, is marked by a number of low concrete posts. Interestingly, the excavation established that the cairn was built where there had been earlier activity, beginning in the Mesolithic and ending in the Neolithic before the construction of the monument. This earlier activity was probably domestic, but a rectangular timber structure, identified from post holes within the area of the eastern forecourt, suggests that ceremonial activities took place here before the tomb itself was built.

The cairn was originally around 45 m long with a forecourt at the broader eastern end and four chambers within the mound. Each of the chambers would

FIG 42. Penwyrlod chambered tomb, the largest of the Neolithic chambered tombs in the area, which contained the earliest known musical instrument in Britain. The results of the quarrying in 1972, which severely damaged the site and removed a large amount of the original mound, can be seen to the right of the photograph. (Jonathan Mullard)

FIG 43. Gwernvale Neolithic chambered tomb, now on the highway verge at the entrance to the Gwernvale Manor Hotel, near Crickhowell. (Jonathan Mullard)

FIG 44. The head of the Sorgwm Valley and Mynydd Troed viewed from Cockit Hill. The remains of the chambered tomb are visible as a low mound, free of bracken, just above the large stone in the foreground. (Jonathan Mullard)

have been used for communal burial, and there is evidence that the entrances to the chambers, in the sides of the cairn, were blocked after each successive interment. The final blocking of the chambers and the obscuring of chamber entrances, forecourt and the outer walls of the cairn was achieved by covering the monument with stones. Few human remains were found during the excavation, since much of the tomb had been disturbed and robbed in the past. Agricultural activities were indicated by finds of quern stones for grinding corn, the presence of charred emmer wheat and fragments of animal bone, including red deer, domesticated cattle, sheep and pig. Other finds included Mesolithic and Neolithic flint tools, such as arrowheads, knives, scrapers and axes, and Neolithic pottery.

Another important tomb, Mynydd Troed, is situated at the head of the Sorgwm Valley, with extensive views down the valley to the southeast and across Llangorse Lake to the southwest (Fig. 44). Today it is difficult to recognise the impressive structure it must once have been, as the remains consist of a low, roughly oval, mound with three stones of a chamber visible on the northeast side. A small excavation in the 1960s to recover environmental information showed that it had been built in an area of heathland, within open woodland dominated by oak.

Around 3000 BC the megalithic tombs ceased to be used and were sealed up and abandoned. Gwernvale, for example, was sealed around 2500 BC. Burial practices changed, with round barrows taking the place of the chambered tombs and cremation being adopted as well as burial.

BRONZE AGE

Despite the woodland clearance during the Neolithic period, pollen records from upland South Wales indicate that this was relatively limited compared with the major changes to the forest that took place later (Chambers 1983). Across Wales much of the available evidence indicates that in the Bronze Age, and certainly by the early Iron Age, 2,550 years ago, much of the extensive woodland cover in areas such as the Beacons had been destroyed. The result was a largely deforested upland landscape, with isolated stands of oak, birch and hazel in less accessible places – perhaps in many ways a scene not dissimilar to much of the landscape today.

The most distinctive monuments in the Brecon Beacons from the late Neolithic and early Bronze Age are the standing stones and stone circles. Their precise function will probably never be known, but many prehistoric sites, including stone circles, are aligned to specific phases of the sun and moon. How open the landscape actually was at this time is open to conjecture, but the careful placing of the monuments in relation to one another suggests that even at this

FIG 45. Maen Llia, the most impressive standing stone in the Brecon Beacons, which was visited by Alfred Russel Wallace in 1841. The mosses covering its surface include squirrel-tail moss *Leucodon sciuroides*, a relatively uncommon moss which often grows on base-rich rock outcrops, stone monuments or gravestones. (Jonathan Mullard)

early date the views were extensive. There are over 30 standing stones surviving in the area, the most impressive being Maen Llia (Fig. 45). This massive sandstone block at the head of the Llia Valley stands 3.7 m above ground level and is 2.7 m wide and up to 0.8 m thick. It has been estimated that between a quarter and a third of the stone is below ground. It is clearly visible from some distance down the valley, suggesting that it might have been a territorial marker. Wallace visited in 1841, recording that 'These strange relics of antiquity have always greatly interested me and this, being the first I had ever seen, produced an impression which is still clear and vivid' (Wallace 1905).

Other similar stones include Carreg Waun Llech, located on common land off the Llangynidr to Beaufort road. This is a slab-like stone 2.6 m high, 1.25 m across and 0.4 m thick, which stands alone on the edge of an area of peat bog.

Seven stone circles occur in the Beacons, six grouped together in the west and one on the northern flank of the Black Mountains above Hay on Wye. One of the most interesting is Cerrig Duon, which is situated on a level platform to the west of the Tawe, near the old Trecastle road from Tafarn y Garreg. The site is dominated by a nearby standing stone, the 1.8 m high Maen Mawr, which lies 9 m

FIG 46. The lichen-covered Maen Mawr, an outlier of the Cerrig Duon stone circle, looking towards the Tawe Valley. (Jonathan Mullard)

outside the circle (Fig. 46). Behind Maen Mawr are two smaller stones, and it has been suggested that the three stones are aligned on the rising of one of the major stars, Arcturus, in 1950 BC. There is a similar arrangement of an outlying stone, with two smaller stones set behind it, at one of the two circles at Nant Tarw, near its confluence with the Usk.

About 800 m to the north of Cerrig Duon, but invisible from it, another large standing stone has its long axis pointing towards Maen Mawr. It measures 2 m high, 1.4 m wide and 0.25 m thick and is thought to be a pointer to guide people to the site. The complex of stones also includes an avenue of smaller stones, about 45 m long, which follows the easiest line of approach from the river below and ends 15 m to the west of the circle. Also associated with Cerrig Duon is the monument known as Saith Maen. The name means 'seven stones', but two have fallen over. Varying in height from 1.7 m to 0.5 m, they form a row 13.7 m long and are aligned to the southwest in the direction of the circle.

Blaenau, or Pen y Beacon, stone circle in the Black Mountains, immediately adjacent to the small car park at the base of Hay Bluff, was originally thought to be the remains of a burial chamber, only the large upright slab and the stubs of a few adjacent stones being recognised as prehistoric. At a later date, however, it was realised that the low stones to the northwest were also part of the same monument, and together the stones make up an ellipse with a long axis of 30 m. There is a definite entrance on the southeast side which was marked by flanking portal stones, a rare feature in Welsh circles. Another uncommon feature is a cupmark on the base of the remaining portal stone – a small round depression 7 cm across and 3 cm deep, ground into the stone. These prehistoric monuments often seem to be on ancient routes across the mountains, the modern road from Hay to Llanthony, via the Gospel Pass, passing both the stone circle and Twyn y Beddau round barrow.

ROUND CAIRNS

The stone equivalent of the round barrow, round cairns, are one of the most common prehistoric features in the Welsh uplands and occur throughout the Beacons in various types and sizes. They seem to have evolved around 2000 BC and continued in use for 700 years, throughout the Early Bronze Age. The actual burials take a variety of forms, both cremations and inhumations being found in pits below the cairn, or sometimes in a stone chamber within the body of the cairn. Cremations were sometimes placed in earthen ware pots, often placed upside down within or under the mound. It is thought that a covering, possibly of leather, would have been tied over the mouth of the pot to prevent the cremated bone from spilling out. The change from the mainly communal burial practice in the Neolithic to individual burial in the Late Neolithic and Early Bronze Age is an interesting one, suggesting an increase in the importance of the individual. This is also reflected in the provision of grave goods; those found in Wales, however, are generally no more than a flint tool, a few arrowheads, or some beads.

The classic situation for a Bronze Age cairn is on a hill summit or ridge, or sometimes on a 'false crest', the mound standing out on the skyline. Often they occur in groups, stretched out along a ridge in 'cairn cemeteries'. A good example of a cairn cemetery in the Beacons is Cefn Esgair-carnau, a group of seven cairns situated on a low ridge in the southeast of Ffowrest Fawr to the north of the A4959. The low stony mounds range from 8 m to over 18 m in diameter and are constructed entirely of Old Red Sandstone blocks, which were probably collected as surface stone. Most have been disturbed in the past and this is indicated by a central hollow where the cairn has been mined, presumably in the search for valuables. The largest cairn of the group, at the northeast end, is situated just below the crest of the ridge, but when viewed from the other side of the Hepste, to the north, it appears to be on the skyline. This position on a false crest is almost certainly deliberate.

CREATION AND LOSS · 69

FIG 47. The three cairns on Tair Carn Uchaf, viewed from the top of the southwest cairn looking towards the other two. (Nigel Davies)

Two groups of large cairns, Tair Carn Isaf and Tair Carn Uchaf, constructed this time of gritstone, are situated at the western end of Mynydd Du (Fig. 47). Like Cefn Esgair-carnau these have all suffered considerable disturbance in the past, especially Tair Carn Isaf.

At the transition between the Bronze Age and the Iron Age, around 800 BC, there is some evidence that a number of upland areas such as the Brecon Beacons were abandoned in response to the deteriorating conditions associated with climate change (Chambers 1982), resulting in the recovery of birch and hazel woodland. By the end of the Bronze Age, however, the upland areas of the Beacons, like most of the Welsh uplands, were covered by extensive blanket peat (Caseldine 1990).

IRON AGE

Once it had been cleared of trees during the Bronze Age, the upland heather moorland was used by Iron Age people for common grazing, but there is also some evidence for arable cultivation. Indeed the general pattern of the upland landscape we know today probably originated in this period. The archaeological evidence for the Iron Age period, however, is poorly understood. This is partly because of a lack of radiocarbon dates for the monuments, but the recently developed technology of cosmogenic dating, which can be applied to stone surfaces, may in due course provide us with more accurate dates. Some standing stones, cairns and hut circles which are currently thought to date from the Iron Age may well turn out to be older. The first hillforts in Wales may in fact be Bronze Age in origin.

The largest concentration of hillforts is found west of Brecon, on either side of the Usk Valley, and includes Pen y Crug, Slwch Tump, Coed Fenni-fach, Twyn y Gaer and Garn Goch. In the far west of the Beacons, situated on a hilltop near the village of Bethlehem in Carmarthenshire, Garn Goch is a striking example of a fortified settlement and is one of the largest, if not the largest, in Wales, commanding impressive views over the surrounding countryside. There are two forts on the same hill, both of similar construction, with a small gap dividing the lower fort (Y Gaer Fach) from the main summit where the larger settlement (Y Gaer Fawr) sits. Dated to around 300 BC, Y Gaer Fawr measures 700 m by 200 m and is surrounded by the original stone ramparts, which are over 5 m thick (Fig. 48).

A number of factors contributed to the pattern of distribution of hillforts in the Brecon Beacons, but generally the very highest ridges are avoided as they would have presumably been very exposed, would have been some distance from a water supply, and the surrounding land would have been less suitable for cultivation.

FIG 48. The impressive stone rampart of Y Gaer Fawr, part of Garn Goch, one of the largest Iron Age hillforts in Wales. This artificial habitat supports a rich invertebrate community, particularly spiders. (Jonathan Mullard)

ROMAN PERIOD

The inhabitants of the hillforts probably belonged to a tribe known as the Silures, who, aided by the terrain, resisted the invading Roman army for around 25 years. It was not until AD 79 that the whole of Wales was conquered by the Romans. They were defeated several times in battle by the Silures and abandoned the attempt to build permanent forts, building temporary camps instead to protect their troops during the campaign. There are two well-preserved examples of these temporary camps at Y Pigwn on the summit of Trecastle Mountain. Today only the grassy ramparts remain, but when they were built they protected thousands of soldiers.

The country was eventually garrisoned by a number of regiments consisting of 500 or 1,000 men, housed in permanent forts linked together by metalled roads. One of the best examples of a Roman fort can be seen at Y Gaer, to the west of Brecon, which has the characteristic rectangular plan, with an earthen bank and ditch. At a later stage a stone wall was added in front of the bank and part of the wall and towers can still be seen today (Fig. 49). Excavation of the interior of the fort revealed that the barracks were of wood, but the administrative buildings, the commandant's quarters and the granary were all rebuilt in stone at the same time as the walls. The garrison at first consisted of 500 cavalry recruited in Spain, but its size was reduced in the late second century, and around AD 200 it seems to have been withdrawn altogether.

Well-engineered roads linked the forts together, so that the countryside could be patrolled and garrisons could support one another. Eventually, following the end of Roman rule, the roads become covered in grass and many have vanished altogether. The Roman invasion was essentially a military one; there are no Roman towns in the area, and only two villas are known, one at Llanfrynach and one at Llys Brychan, to the south of Llangadog.

Just south of the Beacons, on the banks of the Usk, lay the Roman legionary fortress of Isca, now modern Caerleon. The site was the permanent base of the Second Augustan Legion in Britain from about AD 75, but it was not until around AD 90 that it was decided to provide the legion with a stone amphitheatre (Knight 2010). It has been estimated that the timber grandstand above the stone walls contained 6,000 seats, roughly the full complement of the legion. Here, as well as the fights between gladiators or condemned criminals, the local forests supplied wild boars, wolves or deer for the slaughter, the latter being 'hunted' on horseback. Sometimes even bulls or cows were used. The remains of brown bears have also been found at the site. It is likely that bears roamed the forests of the Beacons throughout the Roman period and were present until around AD 1000, when they were finally exterminated. The last local bears may therefore have

FIG 49. The southern entrance of Y Gaer, one of the best examples of a Roman fort in Wales, with a characteristic rectangular plan. Today the nutrient-poor soil on the top of the northern walls supports large numbers of cowslips, creating an impressive sight in the spring. (Jonathan Mullard)

met their end in the amphitheatre at Isca. The final British stronghold for the species appears to have been in Scotland, and this is supported by the claim that Caledonian bears were taken to Rome for fighting (Lovegrove 2007).

BRYCHEINIOG

It is unclear exactly when Roman rule ended in the Brecon Beacons, but in the fifth and sixth centuries the princedom of Brycheiniog developed, ruled by a dynasty of Irish ancestry. The physical remains from this period consist of a dozen or more gravestones which can be found on the moorland to the south, or in churches or graveyards in the Usk Valley. It has been suggested that they represent an eastward movement of people from an Irish colony in Dyfed, but it is more likely that people moved up the Usk Valley, occupying the fertile region around Brecon and spreading onto the moorland to secure summer grazing. It has been suggested that they were responsible for the refortification of Y Gaer, and that they used the Roman roads to access the moorlands, as some of their gravestones were set up beside them.

One of the best-known of these gravestones is the 3.4 m high stone known as Maen Madoc, which stands beside the Roman road of Sarn Helen near Ystradfellte (Fig. 50). The letters carved into the face of the stone are difficult to read as weathering and lichen growth have taken their toll, but the Latin inscription *Dervaci filius Ivsti ic iacti* translates as 'Here lies Dervacus, son of Justus.' Originally right alongside the road, it was re-erected a short distance to the west in 1940.

The early Celtic church was an important unifying feature for much of this period, but while traces of pre-Norman monastic settlements have survived the timber buildings themselves have disappeared, leaving no trace except for post holes. Monastic stone buildings are also rare, but they may have been based on

FIG 50. The physical evidence for the princedom of Brycheiniog consists of gravestones such as Maen Madoc, which is situated on moorland adjacent to Sarn Helen, the best-preserved Roman road in the Beacons. (Alan Bowring)

FIG 51. Maen Du holy well with its corbelled stone roof, situated to the north of Brecon castle, just off the public footpath from Brecon to Pen y Crug. (Jonathan Mullard)

corbelled vaults similar to those found in early Irish oratories. This building style was later used for well-head structures, such as Maen Du holy well with its corbelled stone roof, which supplied Brecon Castle with water (Fig. 51). The rectangular doorway is inscribed 'W.W. 1754', but this probably represents a rebuilding or repair of a much earlier structure.

The Maen Du Conservation Group looks after the well and the surrounding area and aims to enhance it for wildlife. The pond fed by the well supports great crested newt *Tritus cristatus*, while lesser spotted woodpecker *Dendrocopos minor*, and typical woodland birds such as treecreeper *Certhia familiaris* and goldcrest *Regulus regulus* have been recorded from the small area of woodland surrounding the well-head. The work here has been supported by the Amphibian and Reptile Conservation Trust and Brecon Town Council, who own the land.

CRANNOG AND LOG BOATS

With the collapse of Roman rule came a revival of power centres based on easily defended sites. The now ancient hillforts were reoccupied, and occasionally new structures were constructed. This situation prevailed for hundreds of years. In the tenth century, for example, an artificial island, or *crannog*, was built about

40 m from the northern shore of Llangorse Lake (Fig. 52). Known as Ynys Bwlc, it was excavated between 1989 and 1993 by Mark Redknap and Alan Lane from the National Museum of Wales. The crannog was also the site of one of the earliest Channel 4 *Time Team* excavations. These investigations revealed that the crannog was made of brushwood tied in bundles and placed on the lakebed, with hardwood beams and a ring of radially split oak piles holding down this rather buoyant foundation. Tree ring data indicate that the trees were felled between 889 and 893, and construction took place very soon afterwards. Red sandstone boulders had then been placed over the brushwood to create a stable platform about 25 m across.

The crannog, unique in England and Wales, was first recognised in the late 1860s by two local antiquarians, Edgar and Henry Dumbleton, after the level of the lake had been lowered by the cutting of a new channel for the Afon Llynfi. The brothers were inspired by the English publication of Ferdinand Keller's excavations of Swiss 'lake villages' in 1866, and by excavations of Irish crannogs. Records suggest the crannog once supported a royal hall, linked with a monastery near the modern parish church. Gerald of Wales recorded of Llangorse that 'those who lived there sometimes observed it to be covered with buildings or rich pasture lands, or adorned with gardens or orchards', while a sixteenth-century manuscript refers to local people seeing 'sometime, great peeces of Tymber and fframes of houses ffleeting upon the water'. There seems little doubt that some of these early observations, though embellished through time, relate to the remains of timber planks on the crannog.

FIG 52. The crannog on Llangorse Lake once supported a royal hall, which was linked with a monastery near the modern parish church in Llangorse village. (Jonathan Mullard)

FIG 53. The modern 'crannog' on the north side of Llangorse Lake. (Jonathan Mullard)

No original floor or surfaces survive today, and the nature of any structure is unclear. A local businessman has, however, created a modern crannog near the boat launching area on the northern side of the lake (Fig. 53). This differs considerably from the original, being a very small hut resting on a platform supported by timber piles – though it does provide an excellent viewing area across the lake to Ynys Bwlc.

The *Abingdon Chronicle*, a manuscript of the Anglo-Saxon Chronicles, records that in AD 916 (when the king was Tewdwr ap Elised, king of Brycheiniog) Aethelflaed, Lady of Mercia, sent an army into Wales to revenge the murder of Abbot Ecgberht. The Mercian contingency destroyed 'Brecenamere' and captured the king's wife and 33 others. The attack on the mere probably refers to the crannog. A crannog is a characteristically Irish type of site, and this, together with discoveries of luxury Irish-style artefacts, created some speculation. It is interesting to note that the origin-legend for the kingdom of Brycheiniog claims descent from an eponymous founder Brychan, son of a Welsh mother Merchell and an Irish king Anlach.

A log boat, hewn from a single trunk of oak using axes, chisels and gouges, was discovered in 1925 submerged in the lake, to the east of the crannog, by Thomas Jenkins, a local carpenter. The marks of the tools used to construct the boat can still be seen on the surface of the timber. A second log boat was found in the lake in 1990. Though the boat was no longer complete, five fragments were reassembled to form approximately half of the bottom of a square-ended vessel some 0.70 m in width and 4.6 m long. Log boats, such as these, were used on the lakes and rivers of Britain from the Neolithic through to the medieval period.

NORMAN INVASION

The Norman invasion caused two centuries of warfare in the Brecon Beacons. In 1088 Bernard Newmarch, a baron who had come from Normandy with William I, moved up the Wye Valley from Hay into Brycheiniog. Like the Romans before them the Normans built their control points in valleys and passes and aimed to contain the hill land. Newmarch advanced along the Talgarth Gap, building the first castles at Hay, Bronllys and Talgarth in 1088 and Brecon in 1091–93. From Brecon he then moved down the Usk Valley, building castles at Pencelli, Blaenllynfi, Tretower and Crickhowell. Similarly the Towy Valley, like the other Norman invasion routes, was dominated by its castles. Most of these were motte and bailey castles, built of earth and wood, but they were eventually replaced by castles of stone. The early castle in Hay, adjacent to the church, was replaced in the late twelfth century by a new structure at the other end of the town (Fig. 54).

FIG 54. The Jacobean manor adjacent to the remains of the twelfth-century castle at Hay. The buildings are currently being conserved by the Hay Castle Trust. (Jonathan Mullard)

MEDIEVAL PERIOD

The Norman invaders brought their manorial system with them, and in the lowland areas cultivation was organised in common fields. The strips of arable and meadow associated with these fields could still be seen around Bronllys and Talgarth until the middle of the nineteenth century. Many of the former extensive manorial open fields in the area have now been lost, following the enclosure movement in the later eighteenth and earlier nineteenth centuries. The Welsh system had similar features, and in the hills Welsh manors and their customs continued long after the English pattern was imposed on the lowlands. The manorial tenants worked on the lord's demesne, the land he retained for his own use, growing wheat, oats, barley and buckwheat in the common fields, tending his herds and gathering his hay. More independent people living in the hills paid money and food rents, rather than providing feudal services. These food rents of flour, meat, butter and cheese came from small common fields and from flocks of sheep, which moved up to the common pastures on the hills in the summer.

The Welsh freemen often lived in farms on the hillsides, but there were also Welsh bondsmen's hamlets clustered around the Welsh lord's manor house, the

FIG 55. The wooded summit of Coed Fenni-fach, in which the manorial tenants had rights to cut trees for the erection and repair of houses and hedges. The conifer plantations are a relatively recent addition. (Jonathan Mullard)

bondsmen tending the lord's land and his flocks like the manorial tenants of the Normans. This pattern of settlement imposed over a thousand years ago by the Norman and Welsh manorial tenure continues to dominate the landscape of the Brecon Beacons today. The higher mountains are still uninhabited and remain as unenclosed common pasture, while on the lower slopes and in the lowlands the settlement pattern consists of scattered hill farms and small hamlets. Larger villages, which originated as clusters of farms on the English manorial pattern and a few formerly fortified boroughs, dominate the lowlands of the Llynfi and Usk valleys.

Between 1100 and 1350 the valleys and lower hillsides would have been farmed as meadow and arable, while the woodland was cleared to provide building timber. The manorial tenants had housebote and heybote rights, that is rights to cut trees for the erection and repair of houses and hedges, in the lord's woods, and for centuries exercised these rights near Llandovery and in Coed Fenni-fach to the west of Brecon (Fig. 55).

The period was far from peaceful, though, and the tenants were often ordered to fell woodland, because it provided cover for thieves and Welsh revolts. The cultivation of the valleys and the use of the common hill pastures gradually expanded until several outbreaks of the Black Death between 1349 and 1413 reduced the available labour force and the lord's mills, crops, manor houses and castles were destroyed in the Glyndwr Revolt between 1400 and 1412.

In the fifteenth century the lords of the manors let part of their demesne land to farmers who enclosed it with hedges, and the common field system, in which people tilled scattered strips and lived in a cluster of farms, gradually gave way to one in which farms were scattered and surrounded by their own fields. Some farmers expanded their landholdings and became prominent Tudor squires. In Brecknock the prominent Tudor families included Games of Newton, the Prices who bought Brecon Priory in 1542, and the Vaughans of Tretower (Fig. 56).

MEDICINAL PLANTS

In Wales a characteristic group of plants grow on, or close to, castles, abbeys and other ancient settlements, such as Tretower. Many of these species have medicinal or other properties, suggesting they were deliberately cultivated at these sites and have survived as relicts until the present day (Conolly 1994). Two main habitats are involved, the ruins themselves and land nearby, and the species concerned may be either rare and of limited occurrence in Wales, or found more widely. Species of limited occurrence on the walls include plants such as vervain *Verbena officinalis*

FIG 56. Picard's Tower and the adjoining manor house at Tretower, one of the best examples of a fortified manor house in Wales. (Jonathan Mullard)

FIG 57. Part of the reconstructed medieval pleasure garden or herber at Tretower Court, with the fountain at the centre. (David Robinson)

and wild clary *Salvia verbenaca*, both of which are well-known medical herbs. A herb tea made from the leaves of wild clary is said, for example, to improve the digestion. Other non-native species found much more widely in these situations include red valerian *Centranthus ruber*, Aegean wallflower *Erysimum cheri* and ivy-leaved toadflax *Cymbalaria muralis*. They often grow alongside native species such as thale cress *Arabidopsis thaliana*, common whitlowgrass *Erophila verna*, southern polypody *Polypodium cambricum*, shining crane's bill *Geranium lucidum*, rue-leaved saxifrage *Saxifraga tridactylites* and pellitory-of-the-wall *Parietaria judaica*.

In 1991 Cadw, the Welsh historic environment body, decided to enhance the setting of Tretower Court by recreating a fifteenth-century pleasure garden (Fig. 57). Situated to the south of the complex, it includes railed and terraced enclosures, flower beds, turf benches and gravel paths. Small medieval gardens or herbers such as these were generally square or rectangular and surrounded by hedges or walls. Often divided into four equal sections, they had a fountain or basin in the centre and beds or containers of herbs, flowers, roses and small trees. Plants in the recreated herber at Tretower include yarrow *Achillea millefolium*, chamomile *Chamaemelum nobile*, feverfew *Tanacetum parthenium* and periwinkle *Vinca minor*.

Some species found in the immediate vicinity of a site, or otherwise close to human habitation, such as vervain, deadly nightshade *Atropa belladonna* and white horehound *Marrubium vulgare*, are considered native, especially in southern England, but in Wales they are rare and closely tied to ancient human settlements – doubtless as a result of a tradition of keeping herbal remedies close at hand. Tansy *Tanacetum vulgare*, for instance, occurs on the tops of old farmyard walls and elecampane *Inula helenium* in hedges or orchards. Species of wider occurrence in these situations include black horehound *Ballota nigra*, common mallow *Malva sylvestris*, hemlock *Conium maculatum*, Alexanders *Smyrnium olusatrum* and white dead-nettle *Lamium album*. It may seem strange including white dead-nettle in this list, but it is comparatively rare in the far west of Britain and in Wales it is never found far from habitation and is characteristic of castles and abbeys. Even today it is used as a dermatological remedy (Conolly 1994).

Exactly when these plants were introduced remains open to debate. There is considerable macrofossil evidence for many of these medicinal plants from England but little from Wales, and this is mostly of Roman or medieval date. Deadly nightshade has been recovered from Roman Caerwent and Carmarthen and there are wide-ranging records from Roman and medieval sites in England. Vervain has also been recorded from Caerwent along with fennel *Foeniculum vulgare*, but this is about the limit of Welsh records, and vervain is absent from most of the Brecon Beacons. More research on this aspect of the area's botanical history is needed.

HISTORIC PARKS AND GARDENS

It is now recognised that high-status medieval buildings, such as castles and manor houses similar to Tretower, stood in landscapes which had been altered to improve the setting of the buildings. Castles in particular were rarely just constructed for warfare; they were also symbols of authority and power, which could be increased by the setting they were in. While the herbers located close to the main buildings added to their status, on a much larger scale features such as lakes, deer parks and approach roads were also created to enhance the standing of the owner of a castle or manor, or impress visitors on their way to the main gate.

There are a number of large country houses on the better farmland in the Usk and Wye valleys, set within parks and gardens that were originally designed to impress. These include, apart from Hay Castle and Tretower Castle and Court, Abergavenny Priory Deer Park, Abercynrig, Buckland House, Craig y Nos Castle and Country Park, Ffrwdgrech, Glangrwyney Court, Glanusk Park and Penmyarth, Gliffaes, Llanfihangel Court, Lllangattock Park, Llwynywermod, Penpont, Plas Llangattock, Treberfydd, Trefecca Fawr and Trewyn. All these houses and their associated landscapes represented another phase in the

FIG 58. The boundary bank and ditch of Abergavenny Priory Deer Park on the Sugar Loaf. (Jonathan Mullard)

allocation of land. For the most part ordinary people were not allowed into these protected areas, which were for the pleasure or utility of the owners.

Substantial portions of these designed landscapes remain today. The boundary bank and ditch and original boundary walls of the deer park that belonged to the Benedictine priory of Abergavenny, for example, covers around 240 hectares on the southeast flank of the Sugar Loaf, between the Rholben and Deri ridges, at the head of the Afon Cibi valley. The boundary bank, ditch and, in places, wall follow the summit of the ridges, enclosing a roughly rectangular area containing open moorland, oak woodland and pasture on the valley floor (Fig. 58).

Other medieval parks in the area included the three parks in Crickhowell manor. The Park of Philip Montaine, which is described as either 5 or 10 acres of woodland in Llanbedr, has not been located, but the boundaries of Belfountain Park in Llangenny, containing a number of ancient oaks, are easily recognisable today (Fig. 59). The largest of the three parks was Killelan, now known as Llangattock Park.

Many of the surviving parks contain ancient trees that are rich in wildlife due to the plant and animal communities associated with wood decay and the bare surfaces of trunks, bough and roots. As described in Chapter 10, however, few surveys of these have been undertaken.

FIG 59. The ancient oak trees of Belfountain Park in Llangenny, one of the surviving medieval deer parks of Crickhowell manor – though no deer remain today. (Jonathan Mullard)

SHEEP AND CATTLE

The development of large-scale sheep rearing, which began after the Norman invasion, has, as described by John Raven and Max Walters in their New Naturalist on *Mountain Flowers* (Raven and Walters 1956), been 'responsible, more than any single factor, for imposing a stamp of uniformity upon large areas of mountain vegetation' (Fig. 60). They go on to say that:

> *It is difficult to overestimate the effect of ... sheep grazing on the British mountain flora. The immediate reaction of any Scandinavian botanist visiting British mountains is surprise at the extent of the uniformity and floristic dullness. Whole communities of plants, containing many characteristic mountain species, are in Britain represented by the merest fragments clinging to relatively inaccessible rock-ledges where the almost ubiquitous sheep cannot penetrate. From the point of view of the mountain flora, sheep ... have the effect of greatly accentuating the contrast ... between the main, floristically dull, mountain communities, and those of unstable rock ledges on cliffs and steep slopes.*

In contrast to the present situation, in previous centuries cattle were an important part of the agricultural economy in upland Wales – certainly until the Enclosure movement of the eighteenth century. The Welsh word for shepherd (English 'sheepherd') is *bugail*, with the first element *bu* cognate with *buwch*, cow; in other words, they were cattle herders. As early as the Middle Ages cows, originally derived from forest animals, were mainly associated with forests and the uplands. Immediately south of Llanthony Priory lies Bugle Bridge, which carries the road over the River Honddu, and a field marked on the 1840 tithe map as Bugley Meadow. Both Bugle and Bugley are probably anglicised versions of *bugail*. Interestingly, the meadow contains earthworks that probably indicate the site of the priory's sheepcote on the bank of the Honddu, providing access for sheep dipping and washing (Procter 2011). Monastic estates in upland areas would have required a large sheepcote down in the valley for housing the flock during the winter months (Fig. 61). In the early sixteenth century the priory had 438 acres (177 ha) of land in demesne, stocked with cattle and sheep and including rabbit warrens and fish weirs (Rhodes 2002).

When cattle dominated the uplands these animals would have been moved under the pastoralist practice of transhumance, whereupon the stock would have been herded to lower pastures for the winter. This pattern of livestock farming is practised today in central European alpine pastures, but in centuries past something very like it would have been a feature of upland farming in Wales. The capacity of grazing land, i.e. how much stock an area of land could support in the lean winter

CREATION AND LOSS · 85

FIG 60. The 'almost ubiquitous' sheep grazing below Cwm Llwch, with the sheep-covered slopes of Twyn y Dyfant in the background. There are several hundred sheep, showing as white dots in the background, just in this one view. (Jonathan Mullard)

FIG 61. The monastic estate associated with Llanthony Priory had large flocks of sheep which occupied a sheepcote during the winter months. (Jonathan Mullard)

months, would have also limited the number of cattle. This lack of sheep and the seasonality of limited grazing land would have resulted in more floristically rich uplands, particularly on the Carboniferous limestone and other relatively base-rich rocks. Most of the population of the village remained in the valleys throughout the year and farmed the surrounding land for grain and hay. In the spring the herdsmen took the animals up to the middle pastures on the mountain slopes. In the summer, pigs were left in the middle pastures while the rest of the animals were moved to the high pasture. At the end of September the animals were moved back to the lower pastures and cattle were stabled, or slaughtered, in the following month. Sheep and goats were stabled in December, unless the winter was mild, then they remained at the middle pastures with the pigs (Barker 1985).

PEAT AND BOG OAK

For many centuries people living in the Brecon Beacons, as elsewhere in Wales, cut peat for fuel. The activity reached a peak in the area during the seventeenth century when 10,000 'loads' of peat per year were removed from the common at Mynydd Illtyd (Owen 1969). It seems probable that these were the same as the loads of 60–100 pounds (27–45 kg) carried during the eighteenth century by the poor from Borth Bog, near Aberystwyth, to be sold there for 4–7 pence (Davies 1814). This implies that not far short of 500 tonnes of peat were removed annually, a significant amount which must have had an impact on the wildlife of the area. During the eighteenth century people in Fforest Fawr also had the right to cut turf for burning without charge, a right exercised from 'time immemorial'.

It was not always just peat that was removed from these bogs, but also the bogwood preserved within them, which was widely used for the making of roofing timbers. Bogwood is the collective term for the sub-fossil roots, stumps and stems of trees found in peat bogs and fens. It occurs in many parts of Wales where local site factors and fluctuating climatic conditions have combined to permit the spread of wet moorland plants and the accumulation of peat deposits on formerly wooded areas. The particular anaerobic conditions prevailing in bogs inhibit the decomposition of wood, which is frequently preserved in a modified sub-fossil state in the peat (Linnard 1984).

This abundant source of free fuel was generally abandoned after the disastrous wet summer of 1816, which caused 'the last great subsistence crisis in the Western world', with its failed corn and peat harvests (Evans 2002). The conditions were caused by a combination of a historic low in solar activity together with a 'volcanic winter' event, caused by a succession of major volcanic eruptions including the 1815 eruption of Mount Tambora in Indonesia, the largest known eruption in over 1,300 years. Unable to dry the cut peat, people living in the Brecon Beacons turned to coal as a reliable source of heat – and from then on the importance of peat as a fuel declined.

INDUSTRY AND THE LANDSCAPE

Coal had been an important fuel since the sixteenth century when the iron industry spread from its origins in the Weald of Kent to other areas with coal, iron ore, limestone, plentiful timber and fast-flowing watercourses. The southern areas of the Beacons had these resources in abundance, and around 1600 the first forge was built on the banks of the Afon Clydach. The woodlands of the

FIG 62. The water balance tower in the Blaenavon Industrial Landscape World Heritage Site. The tower was used to lift pig-iron up the bank to meet a tramway, which passed through a tunnel 2,400 m long, to convey it to forges on the other side of the mountain. (Jonathan Mullard)

Clydach Gorge provided charcoal, and coal and ironstone outcrops were worked in small drift mines, or in surface patches, the precursors of modern opencast workings. By the eighteenth century there were also forges on the Afon Honddu at Brecon, at Llandyfan on the Loughor and at Glangrwyne near the confluence of the Grwyne and Usk. These forges occasionally used pig-iron sent from larger ironworks to the south and eventually succumbed to competition from iron works at the head of the valleys. Before coke replaced charcoal the demands of the forges and the ironworks had caused considerable destruction to the accessible woodlands in the area. At Blaenavon, within the space of only a few decades the landscape changed from that of a sparsely populated moorland area into a busy industrial community (Fig. 62). Miners dug for iron ore and coal on the exposed mountaintop, changing its appearance completely.

The Industrial Revolution had other effects on the landscape. People migrated from rural areas such as the Brecon Beacons, and this migration left in its wake abandoned farms and cottages and untended marginal land. Its influence was felt throughout the area and can be seen most clearly in the upper valleys of the Black Mountains, where the overgrown remains of settlements are scattered across the slopes.

THE VICTORIANS

The Brecon Beacons were not immune to the needless destruction of wildlife that occurred in the Victorian period, and birds suffered especially badly. One of the themes in Phillips's *The Birds of Breconshire* (1882) is the destruction of birdlife in the area:

> *Our grand old Beacons are, to a great extent, destitute of bird life ... Most of the rarer species are getting rarer still; in these days of cheap guns any but the most ordinary bird is at once shot down ... Many birds that once were common are now but seldom seen, and if seen are usually shot, and so generally perish, I regret to say, unobserved and unrecorded; for instance, the Kite, Milvus regalis still nests in a few secluded parts of this county, yet in England, in most counties, it is extinct, and probably will be so here in the course of a few years.*

It is difficult today to appreciate the numbers of birds that were present in the area, and indeed throughout Britain, before the slaughter of the Victorian period. Phillips's concerns, for instance, did not extend to carrion crows *Corvus corone*, which he regarded as 'one of the commonest birds in the county, and one we can well do without ... by far the best way to kill them is to trap them with an egg and a common gin trap.'

Around 1860 'that careful observer of nature' Mr John Lloyd of Dinas, Brecon, referred to the gradual decrease of red kites *Milvus milvus* and other birds in poetry (Phillips 1882):

Well I remember, in my boyish hours,
Gazing with rapture on the fan-tail'd Kite,
As, hovering full o'er Brecknock's ivied towers,
Slowly he wheeled his solitary flight.

Now 'mid the landscape he is seen no more,
Fanning his broad wings in the noontide sun,
Scared from his circuit on that 'customed shore,
By prowling keeper armed with trap and gun.

Hence with each year more dull our woods become,
The tapping Woodpecker, the chattering Pie,
Now rarely heard: the whooping owl is dumb,
The Raven calls not to his mate on high.

A 'copious pamphleteer and versifier', Lloyd became a member of the London County Council, which he helped to establish; while in Brecknock he campaigned for the removal of turnpike gates and championed the cause of the commoners.

Thankfully the populations of a number of highly visible species, such as the red kite, have recovered to some extent, and the feeding station at Llanddeusant now attracts over 50 red kites and buzzards *Buteo buteo* every day (Fig. 63). Set against such gains, however, there has been a continuing and dramatic decline during the last century in many populations of plants and animals. Even though the Victorians killed large numbers of birds and mammals in the Beacons, and probably collected large numbers of ferns as part of the so-called 'fern craze', the generally low-intensity farming meant that many species we now accept as rare were once common and abundant, and those that are present today in reasonable numbers were even more abundant. As George Monbiot (2012) has written:

Researching the history of ecosystems, it is not long before you make an arresting discovery. Great abundance of the kind that exists in the tropics – or existed until recently – was once almost universal. With a very few exceptions, every major ecosystem had a megafauna; every major ecosystem witnessed vast migrations of

FIG 63. Red kite, one of many species decimated throughout Britain during the Victorian era, which can now be seen in numbers at the red kite feeding station at Llanddeusant. (Harold Grenfell)

mammals, birds or fish; every major ecosystem possessed an abundance of animal life orders of magnitude greater than current abundance in the temperate nations. In some cases the ecosystems these life forms created were a world apart from those we now know.

A DIMINISHED INHERITANCE

The Brecon Beacons we know today, like the rest of the British uplands, are largely unnatural, with a reduced range of wildlife. It is a diminished inheritance, degraded acid grasslands with an impoverished flora and fauna covering large areas where once there would have been a rich and varied mosaic of habitats including heath, blanket bog, scrub and woodland. In some places forestry, farming, water management, energy supply and recreation have also shaped the landscape quite dramatically. Across the Beacons as a whole, however, there remains a rich variety of wildlife and, while it is not as abundant as it once was, there is much to interest both the naturalist and the general visitor.

Chapter 4

Mountains and Moorlands

Mountains and moorland make up one of the largest habitats in Britain and contain some of our most spectacular scenery, and the Brecon Beacons are no exception. Though they may seem wild, as described in previous chapters, these moorland habitats have been largely created by people, and today only the tops of the mountains, natural rock faces, scree slopes and some of the wetter bogs are still near-natural habitats.

COMMON LAND

The Beacons contain one of the largest areas of common land in Wales, with 62 registered commons wholly or partly in the area, covering a total of 32,467 hectares. The commons are a remnant of the medieval manorial economic system under which crops were grown on areas with better soil and the poorer land was used for other purposes, including grazing animals. All common land has an owner, and the term *common* refers to the rights that certain people hold 'in common'. The majority of the commons in the Beacons are owned by private estates or companies, but in 1965 the Eagle Star Insurance Company gave the central area of the Beacons to the National Trust, and the National Park Authority has since acquired other commons in order to protect them. Such acquisition does not affect a common's legal status, and grazing rights continue to be exercised, either by individual graziers or by commoners' associations (Fig. 64). Common land grazing is part of the farming tradition, and until recently many farms relied on hill grazing for their financial viability. The number of active commoners is, however, in permanent decline, making it difficult to continue to maintain the commons in their current state. The Brecon Beacons Commoners' Association is an active member of the Welsh Commons Forum, which is working to support the continuation of common grazing.

There are a number of legally defined rights, including grazing or pasture, estovers (the right to gather litter, firewood, bedding, etc.), turbary (peat cutting), piscary (fishing rights), pannage (the right to turn out pigs to eat beech mast or

FIG 64. Welsh mountain ponies, now classified as a rare breed, grazing on common land near Hay Bluff. (Jonathan Mullard)

FIG 65. Commoners on Mynydd Illtyd common still cut and bale bracken each autumn for use as animal bedding during the following winter. (Jonathan Mullard)

acorns) and common in the soil (the right to dig gravel, sand etc. for use on the commoner's holding). All these rights involved the ability to take advantage of the natural products of the land in question and 'were the residue of rights that were much more extensive, rights that in all probability are older than the modern conception of private property. They probably antedate the idea of private property in land, and are therefore of vast antiquity' (Hoskins & Stamp 1963). In many cases people depended on their rights for their survival in that they allowed them to obtain fuel and feed their animals, and even provided some of their own food. The graziers on Mynydd Illtyd common, adjacent to the Mountain Centre, still cut and bale bracken each autumn for use as animal bedding during the winter (Fig. 65). Bracken is also cut regularly on the northern part of the Black Mountains near Hay on Wye.

In most situations today only the grazing rights are really pursued. Sheep are the main grazers, with Welsh mountain ponies, and occasionally cattle, on a few commons. Native ponies existed in Wales prior to 1600 BC, and references to such animals can also be found in medieval Welsh literature. They developed into a hardy breed, suited to the harsh climate, limited shelter and sparse food available in the uplands. The Welsh mountain pony is now, however, classified as a rare breed and there are fewer than 1,000 registered breeding mares left in Wales. Its survival relies entirely on the dedicated breeders who belong to Hill Pony Improvement Societies, of which there are just a handful remaining. The societies believe it is vital for these ponies to run on the hills, as they have done for centuries, if the breed is to maintain its hardiness, characteristics and type.

The sheep are mainly Welsh mountain sheep, which are well adapted to the exposed and often harsh conditions. Unfortunately they will eat almost anything, grazing both coarse and fine grasses, heather, shrubs and trees, including holly *Ilex aquifolium* and ash. This heavy grazing by sheep, latterly in response to agricultural subsidies, has, as described in Chapter 3, had a marked influence on the vegetation of these upland areas and led to the decline in the extent of dwarf shrub vegetation and the development of extensive areas of species-poor acid grassland, dominated by mat-grass *Nardus stricta*. Sheep have also impoverished the so-called terricolous lichen flora, which grows directly on the soil (Fig. 66). Sheep do not eat lichens, which they are unable to digest, but their trampling breaks up the lichen mats, reducing their abundance and cover. A complete cessation of grazing, however, results in the lichens being shaded out by vascular plants.

Areas of wetter ground where purple moor-grass *Molinia caerulea* is a dominant feature of the vegetation tend to be avoided by sheep once the grass has developed into tussocks and, particularly in dry springs, these tussocks can be a fire risk. Sheep grazing and a reduction in grazing by other animals can also result in

FIG 66. The terricolous lichen flora, such as this on the slopes of Carreg Goch above Dan yr Ogof, is especially vulnerable to heavy trampling by sheep. (Jonathan Mullard)

the spread of gorse. This is particularly noticeable on Mynydd Illtyd, where there were formerly more ponies present on the common. Many of the more interesting upland species remain only because they have clung on at a few sites that are protected from grazing, either because of unusually low stocking rates, or because they are on inaccessible ledges or in crevices.

HISTORIC RECORDS

Centuries ago the situation was very different, and the mountains were rich in wild plants. Mynydd Myddfai, for example, to the north of the Usk Reservoir, is the focus for the famous legends of the Lady of the Lake in Llyn y Fan Fach, ancestress of the hereditary Physicians of Myddfai (Meddygon Myddfai), a medical dynasty that lasted over 500 years. The methods of these herbalists in the twelfth century were very simple, just single herbs or combinations of two or three different varieties, usually in the form of an infusion or poultice. They used around 175 locally grown herbs, local plants from the mountains, which is perhaps a reflection of how floristically rich Welsh uplands such as Mynydd Myddfai were before intensive grazing by sheep.

Emerging from the depths of the lake and marrying a local man, the Lady of the Lake returned to the water after 'three causeless blows' had been struck, taking the sheep, cattle, goats and horses that she had brought with her as a dowry. On several occasions, however, the Lady was said to have resurfaced to meet her three sons near the banks of the lake, and once she accompanied them home as far as a place which is still called Pant y Meddygon, 'The Dingle of the Physicians', where she pointed out

FIG 67. Pant y Meddygon, 'The Dingle of the Physicians', on the slopes of Mynydd Myddfai, once famed for its medicinal plants but now just another area of acid grassland. The Physicians Well, a small spring, is situated nearby. (Jonathan Mullard)

to them the various plants and herbs which grew in the dingle, and revealed their medicinal qualities. *The Red Book of Hergest*, a large vellum manuscript written shortly after 1382, is one of the most important medieval manuscripts written in the Welsh language and contains a collection of these herbal remedies, which were associated with Rhiwallon Feddyg, the eldest son and founder of the Physicians of Myddfai. It is now held in the Bodleian Library in Oxford, on behalf of Jesus College. Research into these remedies might well provide an indication of the plants and herbs found in the dingle at that time. Unfortunately today Pant y Meddygon is mainly just another area of upland acid grassland (Fig. 67).

Such was the reputation of the Myddfai physicians across Europe that personnel and medicine from the village were freely exchanged with the medical school in Salerno, Italy, which reached the height of its expertise between the tenth and thirteenth centuries. Through this link this small Welsh settlement would have had access to the medical writings of Hippocrates and Galen, along with Arabic texts such as those by Avicenna, the Persian scholar whose many writings included *The Canon of Medicine*, a standard medical text of the time.

Apart from the notes of the physicians, the earliest botanical record we have for the mountain flora of the Beacons comes from 1698, in a letter from Edward

Lhuyd to Dr Richard Richardson, the leading expert at that time on mountain plants. Interestingly, Lhuyd had the *Red Book of Hergest* 'on loan' from Jesus College for many years and must have studied it in detail before his visit. His letter dated 'Hay in Brecon. Sept 19. 1698' states that:

> We searched this summer the high mountain by Brecknock called *Y Vann uwch deui*, but found nothing in it new, nor any great variety of rare plants. The most choice were Sedum alpinum ericoides [purple saxifrage *Saxifraga oppositifolia*], in abundance; Argemone lutea [Welsh poppy *Meconopsis cambrica*]; Rhodia Radix [roseroot *Sedum rosea*]; Muscus cupressiformis [alpine clubmoss *Lycopodium alpinum*]; and about half a dozen more of the common Snowdon plants.

We must not take Lhuyd's comments to indicate that Pen y Fan was not botanically interesting too seriously, as many of the plants common to him we would now regard as rare.

Purple saxifrage is one of the hardiest arctic-alpine flowers found in Wales, growing in extremely cold and inhospitable mountainous areas (Fig. 68). It flowers early in the year, often among lying snow. As described in previous chapters, at the end of the last glaciation tundra vegetation, similar to that found currently in the Arctic Circle, became established and plants like the purple saxifrage thrived. Within a few thousand years, however, many arctic species were out-competed by faster-growing, more competitive plants, and became

FIG 68. Purple saxifrage, one of Wales's most hardy arctic-alpine flowers, was recorded by Edward Lhuyd in 1698 on 'the high mountain by Brecknock called Y Vann uwch deui'. (Graham Motley)

extinct across most of Britain. Relicts of these arctic plant communities survived in a very few north-facing, high-altitude areas, such as these steep cliffs in the Beacons, where the soil is thin and rocky and the cold temperatures and shade prevented other plants from flourishing.

Similarly, in 1695, Dr Nicholas Roberts, then vicar of Llanddewi Felfre in Pembrokeshire, but also ex-headmaster of Queen Elizabeth Grammar School at Carmarthen and someone who knew the Beacons well, commented in a letter to Lhuyd (Roberts 2010):

> This County [i.e. Carmarthenshire] does afford a great many naturall, as well as Artificiall rarities, among ye former, that of gardh Mathvey [Myddfai] (or ye garden of Mathvey, a famous Physician) upon ye top of a mountain wch abounds with an infinite variety of medicinate plants, not found elsewhere in this countrey.

Pant y Meddygon and Pant y blodau, also on Mynydd Myddfai, were just two areas likely to have supported a much richer diversity of vegetation than they do today. One can imagine that in the very early medieval period, when the Myddfai medicinal texts were compiled, the vegetation was even more varied. Even today, vestiges of such vegetation survive on the nearby crags of Craig Cwm Clyd and, more famously, on the high cliffs overlooking Llyn y Fan Fach, where woodland plants co-exist with arctic-alpines on the more exposed rocks. This pattern would also have been applicable to the other upland massifs of Carmarthenshire such as Mynydd Mallaen, from where another Lhuyd correspondent, again a vicar, this time William Price of Cynwyl Elfed, sent a specimen of juniper to him. Juniper, as a wild plant, is now extinct in Carmarthenshire, the last plant being seen at Llyn Brianne, near Ystradffin, some 40 years ago. It has been exterminated from most of the Welsh uplands, including the Beacons, by overgrazing.

In terms of both the variety of plants and the structure of the vegetation, the Brecon Beacons were once more varied than they are today. These rich habitats would have supported larger bird communities, with feeding areas and nest sites much more abundant than they are today. It is likely that whinchats *Saxicola rubetra* and other birds of the moorland edge were more common, with black grouse *Tetrao tetrix* occupying the wood fringe and areas rich in bilberry *Vaccinium myrtillus*, and even ring ouzels *Turdus torquatus*, summer visitors to the Beacons, would not have been restricted to the few rocky sites to which they are now very much, and very precariously, confined (Fig. 69). Ring ouzels are known to have been in decline across Wales since at least the 1970s, due to a combination of factors, including climate change.

FIG 69. Ring ouzels, summer visitors to the Beacons, are now found only in a few rocky areas but were once much more widespread. (Steve Wilce)

CURRENT VEGETATION COMMUNITIES

As described previously, the relentless overgrazing by sheep, along with poor management of burning and damage by heather beetle *Lochmaea suturalis*, has produced large areas of upland acid grassland of relatively little value for wildlife (Fig. 70). One naturalist commented to the author that 'In general the sheep's-fescue-covered uplands provide testament only to total environmental destruction.' Alongside sheep's fescue *Festuca ovina*, mat-grass is usually present as a rank sward with numerous tussocks, between which wavy hair-grass *Deschampsia flexuosa*, heath bedstraw *Galium saxatile*, heath rush *Juncus squarrosus* and tormentil *Potentilla erecta* can be found. Some stands also contain green-ribbed sedge *Carex binervis* and heath wood-rush *Luzula multiflora*. In addition, there are often small quantities of bilberry, and this vegetation often occurs as a mosaic with dry dwarf-shrub heath. On less well-drained soils the vegetation is dominated by heath rush, with abundant haircap mosses *Polytrichum* spp., often with bog-mosses *Sphagnum* spp. and occasionally common sedge *Carex nigra* and purple moor-grass. The boundary between upland and lowland acid grassland can be difficult to define; in this book the mountain wall, the drystone wall marking the upper limit of enclosure, or an elevation of 300 m, is used as an approximate line.

FIG 70. Upland acid grassland on Cefn Esgair-carnau, viewed from the road from Brecon to Hirwaun. These large expanses of grassland are of relatively little value for wildlife. (Jonathan Mullard)

Where the acid grassland has received increased nutrients in areas favoured by livestock, such as tracks, boundaries, field entrances and feeding stations, semi-improved acidic grassland has developed. Here common bent *Agrostis capillaris* and sheep's fescue tend to be the dominant species, frequently with one or more of the following: annual meadow-grass *Poa annua*, smooth meadow-grass *P. pratensis*, perennial ryegrass *Lolium perenne*, soft-rush *Juncus effusus*, stinging nettle *Urtica dioica*, chickweed *Stellaria media* and creeping thistle *Cirsium arvense*.

The slopes to the north of Bannau Sir Gaer and Fan Brycheiniog are the location for the remarkable corkscrew, or spiral, rush *Juncus effusus* forma *spiralis*. It has been known in the area for many years and indeed one of the localities where it occurs is called Pant Brwyn Trorum, the 'hollow of the twisted rushes' (Fig. 71). David Davies, the palaeobotanist from Gilfach Goch who did so much to improve our understanding of the Welsh Coal Measures fossil flora, collected specimens from this site for the National Museum of Wales on 19 July 1933 and his specimens are still in the herbarium there (Fig. 72). Corkscrew rush usually grows in discrete populations, separate from the normal form of soft-rush, and within the population the degree of spiralling varies considerably from slightly

FIG 71. Pant Brwyn Trorum, the 'hollow of the twisted rushes', to the north of Bannau Sir Gaer and Fan Brycheiniog. (Jonathan Mullard)

OPPOSITE: FIG 72. The specimen of corkscrew rush collected by David Davies in 1933. (National Museum of Wales)

curved stems to stems with six to eight turns. The most striking feature of the plant is its open habit, with the stems prostrate to ascending but never erect. The stems are straight or slightly spirally coiled, but plants in the wild never have stems tightly coiled like a corkscrew, as do the cultivated versions. The status of the spiral rush is debatable. Henderson (1992) reported that the seedlings have spiralling stems so it is a distinct genotype and its occurrence in the wild suggests that it deserves recognition as a botanical variety or form. It is quite likely that corkscrew rush grows elsewhere in the Beacons, and the author would be interested to hear of any other localities for this species.

On the plateau areas and the broader ridges of the higher summits of the Black Mountains and the three commons, which comprise the Brecon Beacons proper, dry modified bog can be found. This is associated with areas of current or past peat erosion, possibly due to air pollution over the last couple of hundred years, taking the form of isolated islands of peat surrounded by acid grassland, and appears to be a remnant of former expanses of blanket peat. The vegetation consists mainly of tussocks of hare's-tail cottongrass *Eriophorum vaginatum*, often

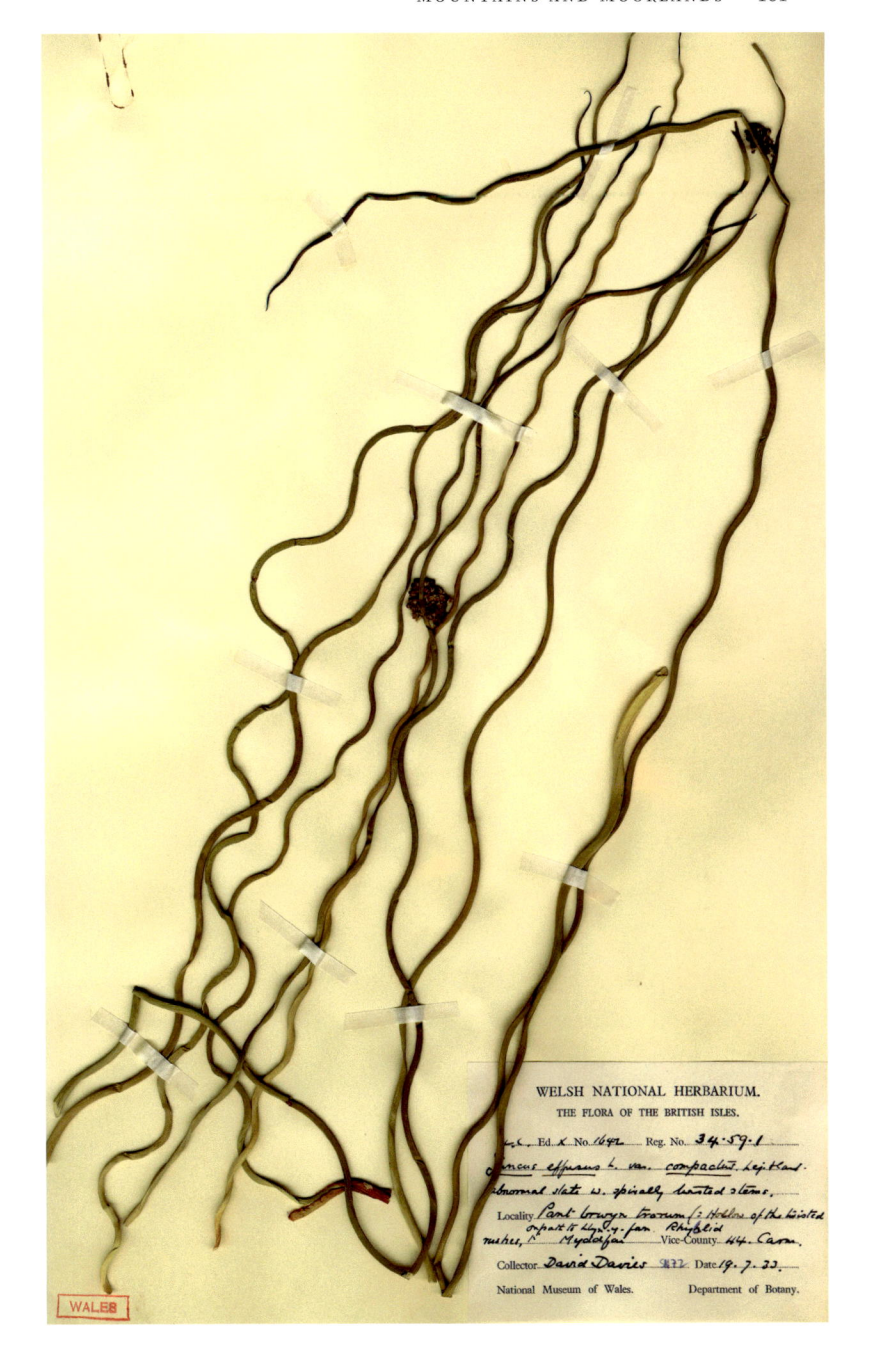

WELSH NATIONAL HERBARIUM.
THE FLORA OF THE BRITISH ISLES.

Ed. X No. *1642* Reg. No. **34·59·1**

Juncus effusus L. var. *compactus* Lej & Court.
abnormal state w. spirally twisted stems.

Locality *Pant Lowyn Troenen (= Hollow of the twisted*
on path to Llyn Ly-fan Rhyfelid
nr hes, C. Myddfai Vice-County *44. Caer.*

Collector *David Davies* 9672 Date *19. 7. 23*

National Museum of Wales.   Department of Botany.

WALES

with common cottongrass *E. angustifolium* and wavy hair-grass. A small area of dry bog on Mynydd Llangatwg contains bog rosemary *Andromeda polifolia*. Bog rosemary is only found in bogs where peat is accumulating, so this plant is probably a remnant from an earlier period in the area's history. It is a small shrub growing to 10–20 cm (rarely to 40 cm) tall with slender stems. The leaves are evergreen, with a superficial resemblance to those of the unrelated rosemary *Rosmarinus officinalis*, whence its name. Where there are small surface pools these contain cottongrass, feathery bog-moss *Sphagnum cuspidatum* and cow-horn bog-moss *S. auriculatum*.

Large expanses of the upland commons are dominated by purple moor-grass growing on a substrate of thin peat, alongside heath rush and mosses such as common haircap *Polytrichum commune* var. *commune*. In wetter areas common cottongrass and hare's-tail cottongrass and bog-mosses occur. Acidic flushes occur frequently and most are species-poor, being dominated by rushes *Juncus* spp. and recurved sphagnum *Sphagnum fallax*. Some, however, contain a wider range of species, including star sedge *Carex echinata*, carnation sedge *C. panicea*, yellow sedge *C. viridula* ssp. *oedocarpa*, common marsh-bedstraw *Galium palustre*, purple moor-grass, velvet bent *Agrostis canina*, bog stitchwort *Stellaria alsine*, common cottongrass, sharp-flowered rush *Juncus acutiflorus*, bulbous rush *J. bulbosus* and sweet vernal-grass *Anthoxanthum odoratum*. Less commonly bog asphodel *Narthecium ossifragum*, bog pondweed *Potamogeton polygonifolius*, round-leaved sundew *Drosera rotundifolia*, ragged robin *Lychnis floscuculi*, opposite-leaved golden-saxifrage *Chrysosplenium oppositifolium*, marsh pennywort *Hydrocotyle vulgaris*, marsh violet *Viola palustris* and round-leaved crowfoot *Ranunculus omiophyllus* can also be found in these flushes.

ERODED PEAT

Two initiatives have been set up in the Beacons to restore areas where erosion has exposed the bare peat. The first of these is at Waun Fignen Felen, which, as mentioned earlier, is a key site for the study of microfossils. Here work is being carried out to slow down erosion by surface water, wind and rain and trap the remaining peat. This allows water to drain through the peat, leaving silt which provides the conditions for cottongrasses and mosses to become established.

The second project is on the side of Pen Trumau in the Black Mountains, where a fire in 1976 left an erosion scar covering around 70,000 m^2. Ever since then the peat has been steadily eroding, and it has been estimated that 6,125

FIG 73. An aerial view of the Woollen Line on Pen Trumau in the Black Mountains created by local artist, Pip Woolf, with the help of volunteers. The photo was taken in Sept 2011 by Mark Fisher of the Black Mountains Gliding Club (Mark Fisher)

tonnes of carbon have been lost to date. An innovative project led by a local artist, Pip Woolf, has, however, started to restore the area (Babbs 2013). With the support of local farmers, together with around 500 volunteers, felt mats were made from local wool and carried up to the site where they were pinned in place using hand-made pegs, forming a 300 m long 'woollen line' (Fig. 73). Heather seed was attached inside pockets within the wool, with the aim of helping to protect the peat while the vegetation re-established itself.

Hand-making felt was, however, time consuming and none of the heather germinated. The project is therefore now focusing on constructing wool 'sausages'. These were first used to fill erosion channels, and more recently they were laid in a line along the top of the eroded area. The ultimate aim of the project is to encourage new vegetation on the eroded areas, and although planting heather seed failed, planting grass is proving more successful. In 2012 volunteers collected seed and cuttings from cottongrass and wavy hair-grass and after growing them on planted them out on the mountain. The project is continuing today, creating a piece of landscape art through a community conservation project.

UPLAND HEATH

Despite the heavy grazing, significant areas of dry dwarf-shrub heath still remain, notably on the Black Mountains and the Blorenge (Fig. 74). Much of the heather *Calluna vulgaris* here is mature, while stands elsewhere show varying degrees of modification by grazing. There are three different forms of heather produced by grazing: carpet heather, which consists of very short, intensively grazed plants in a close carpet; topiary heather, fairly mature plants which have been grazed to produce rounded bushes; and drumstick heather, mature plants which have become degenerate before being subjected to a high, or increased, intensity of grazing. Surprisingly, sheep find heather rather inedible, the most preferred types of vegetation being swards of sheep's fescue and common bent. As a consequence, grasses are often very closely grazed – and this, in turn, encourages the spread of other unpalatable species such as mat-grass, heath rush and, more locally, soft-rush. The grazing of heather by sheep tends to occur in the absence of more appetising vegetation, especially during the winter months. Flocking behaviour, the cessation of shepherding, the location of supplementary feeding sites, the effect of adverse weather and the timing of grazing may all

FIG 74. Despite the heavy grazing and frequent fires, significant areas of dry dwarf-shrub heath with heather and western gorse still remain on the Blorenge. (Steve Smith)

have marked influences on the grazing effect of sheep on heather. Even where the overall stocking density on a site is low, much of the grazing may be taking place in a few localised areas (King & Varney 1994).

Upland dwarf-shrub heath is dominated by the following species, alone or in various combinations: heather, bilberry, crowberry *Empetrum nigrum* and western gorse *Ulex gallii*. For some reason bell heather *Erica cinerea* is very rare in the Beacons, occurring only on the southern boundary of the area. On the Black Mountains and the Blorenge, cowberry *Vaccinium vitis-idaea* is locally abundant in the dry heathland, but further west it is confined to the crags. At least two distinct types of upland heath exist: dry heath is dominated by the dwarf shrubs described above which thrive on dry often rocky soils, while wet heath is found on damper soils and, in addition to some of the above species, supports plants which require more moisture. The most common of these are deergrass *Scirpus cespitosus*, purple moor-grass and cross-leaved heath *Erica tetralix*. The exact species mix within these two broad ecological communities depends on climatic and environmental factors and current management practices.

This dry open heathland can be of exceptional importance for lichens. *Peltigera polydactyla*, for instance, is a common lichen found on these dry heaths in the Beacons, but other significant lichens occur on rock surfaces. The British uplands have two groups of lichen species of outstanding conservation interest, those species found in western oceanic areas and those found on calcareous rock at high altitudes. In the Brecon Beacons a community of crustose lichens on damp, and often soft, calcareous rock is dominated by *Staurothele succedens* and *Thelidium papulare*. Other species present on this substrate include *Opegrapha dolomitica* and *Verrucaria viridula*.

SPECIES-RICH LEDGES

The steep cliffs are mainly inaccessible to sheep, and it is here that most of the interesting plants can be found. The area around Bannau Sir Gaer and Llyn y Fan Fach, in particular, is well known for the arctic-alpines that grow on the Old Red Sandstone cliffs, which have been designated as an Important Plant Area by Plantlife, the national wild plant charity. Together the species-rich ledges on the precipitous north-facing cliffs of Craig Cerrig Gleisiad, Craig Cwm Llwch, Craig Cwm Sere, Graig Cwm Cynwyn and Craig Cwareli support an outstanding range of plants, at or close to the southern edge of their range in Britain. These include, in addition to the purple saxifrage and roseroot noted by Edward Lhuyd in 1698 (Fig. 75), rock stonecrop *Sedum forsteranum*, dwarf willow *Salix herbacea*, serrated

FIG 75. Roseroot on the cliffs at Craig Cwm Sere, a species first noted in the Beacons by Edward Lhuyd in 1698. (Graham Motley)

wintergreen *Orthilia secunda*, northern bedstraw *Galium boreale* and cowberry, along with ferns such as Wilson's filmy-fern *Hymenophyllum wilsonii*, oak fern *Gymnocarpium dryopteris* and beech fern *Phegopteris connectilis*.

The more acidic ledges often support great wood-rush *Luzula sylvatica*, while the damper, richer ones may have smooth lady's-mantle *Alchemilla glabra*, water avens *Geum rivale*, meadowsweet *Filipendula ulmaria*, cowslip *Primula veris*, early-purple orchid *Orchis mascula* and occasionally lesser meadow-rue *Thalictrum minus*.

The hawkweeds *Hieracium* spp. are also very sensitive to grazing and so, like the plants mentioned above, tend to be confined to the ledges that the sheep cannot reach. They are also an extremely diverse group of plants, mainly due to the fact that they are apomictic: that is, their seed does not need to be fertilised since they receive their DNA directly from a single parent plant. This means that all new plants are direct copies of the original and even the smallest hereditary mutations result in an independent lineage, known as a microspecies. Summit hawkweed *Hieracium cacuminum*, for instance, is known historically from six sites but the plant has only been rediscovered at three of these. It has been estimated that there is a world population of fewer than 250 plants, the main populations being below Pen y Fan (Fig. 76) and also at Craig y Fro on the western side of the A470 just north of the Storey Arms. The writer and naturalist Peter Marren (2012)

FIG 76. Joe Daggett (National Trust) and Tim Rich (National Museum of Wales) searching for summit hawkweed on the slopes below Pen y Fan in the summer of 2004. (Graham Motley)

considers that hawkweeds are 'botanists' plants which few others know about or care about. On the other hand, they are part of the genetic diversity that we as a nation are committed to preserve … They form a kind of genetic fine-tuning, lending uniqueness to certain hills, valleys and headlands.'

The nearby Craig Cerrig Gleisiad (Fig. 77), a dramatic, ice-carved, northeast-facing valley and National Nature Reserve, with cliffs up to 150 m high, even has its own species of hawkweed, Craig Cerrig Gleisiad hawkweed *Hieracium neocoracinum*. Like most of the hawkweeds this is a very rare endemic plant, confined in this instance entirely to the reserve. The hawkweed was first found by Augustin Ley in 1895, and it occurs in at least two places on the cliffs. In 1975 there were estimated to be 60 plants in one population, but further surveys in 2003 in 2003 revealed 147 plants at the same place, although it was also present at the second site. The population increase is probably due to the plant colonising bare ground created by a landslip and a reduction in grazing pressure.

Many of the plants found on these cliffs survive by growing in pockets of soil in cracks and crevices. They are generally small and often hug the rock by means of creeping stems or by adopting a cushion shape to minimise their exposure to strong winds. Scrubby wind-blasted hawthorn *Crataegus monogyna* and rowan *Sorbus aucuparia* also cling on to these precipitous slopes. While the soil, derived

FIG 77. Craig Cerrig Gleisiad National Nature Reserve, which has its own species of hawkweed. Like the other north-facing cliffs, this area is rich in plants more typical of the mountainous areas of North Wales, northern England and Scotland. (Jonathan Mullard)

from the sandstone, is often acidic, the lime-rich mudstones weather to produce immature soils and rock rubble of a more alkaline nature which is suitable for these plants. The flushing effect of water running down the cliffs also contributes to the development of alkaline conditions.

MOSSES AND LIVERWORTS

While the arctic-alpines and endemics, like the hawkweeds, are often seen as the key botanical species, the area is less well known for its impressive suite of mosses and liverworts, more typical of the mountainous areas of North Wales, northern England and Scotland. Craig Cerrig Gleisiad itself has records of well over 100 different bryophytes, many of which, like the other upland plants, are at their southern British limit. Undoubtedly the most important habitats though for mosses and liverworts are the cliffs below Bannau Sir Gaer and the central Beacons, at Craig Cerrig Gleisiad and Pen y Fan. As described previously, the cliffs are quite variable in that some beds are softer than others, eroding comparatively quickly and producing fine-grained soils, whilst other beds are harder, weathering to form crags and screes. The base content of the rocks also varies between beds, creating niches both for plants suited to calcareous soils and for plants that cannot tolerate alkaline conditions. Most of the crags have extensive expanses of acid rock, punctuated by small areas with base-enriched sandstone.

The typical flora of this habitat has been described as an assemblage of rather dull-coloured bryophytes, including the liverworts white earwort *Diplophyllum albicans* and notched rustwort *Marsupella emarginata*, and dusky rock-moss *Andreaea rothii* ssp. *falcata*, broom fork-moss *Dicranum scoparium*, wry-leaved tamarisk-moss *Heterocladium heteropterum*, heath plait-moss *Hypnum jutlandicum*, swan's-neck thyme-moss *Mnium hornum*, nodding thread-moss *Pohlia nutans*, alpine haircap *Polytrichum alpinum*, elegant silk-moss *Pseudotaxiphyllum elegans*, narrow-leaved fringe-moss *Racomitrium aquaticum* and green mountain fringe-moss *R. fasciculare*. More localised species include alpine rock-moss *Andreaea alpina*, black rock-moss *A. rupestris*, alpine ditrichum *Ditrichum zonatum*, mouse-tail moss *Isothecium myosuroides*, donnian silk-moss *Plagiothecium denticulatum* var. *obtusifolium* and sickle-leaved hook-moss *Sanionia uncinata*. These acidic strata also support large numbers of liverworts, including tumid notchwort *Lophozia ventricosa*.

Areas enriched by alkaline runoff have a much more diverse flora, including several bright green or orange mosses that give these areas a more vivid appearance. The most basic outcrops, for example, have large cushions of summer-moss *Anoectangium aestivum* and frizzled crisp-moss *Tortella tortuosa*, both of which are a highly visible bright yellow-green, together with darker patches of fine distichium *Distichium capillaceum* and verdigris tufa-moss *Gymnostomum aeruginosum*. In addition there is often a glaucous-green mat of narrow mushroom-headed liverwort *Preissia quadrata* in the cracks between rocks. A variety of small liverworts, including the almost filamentous hairy threadwort *Blepharostoma trichophyllum*, can be found growing through some moss cushions.

Groups from the British Bryological Society visited the north-facing cliffs in 1963, 1965 and 1978, but it was not until 1981, when the Nature Conservancy Council undertook a survey to establish what plants grew on the cliffs and the communities present, that there was a wider appreciation of their importance. The survey, which involved abseiling down parts of the cliff and sampling and describing the vegetation on the ledges, recorded a number of species, including twisted grimmia *Grimmia torquata* and Griffith's oedipodium moss *Oedipodium griffithianum*. Following the publication of the survey the Beacons have frequently been visited by bryologists, and finds include narrow-lobed earwort *Scapania gymnostomophila*, a small liverwort new to Wales, and Russow's bog-moss *Sphagnum russowii*. Many of the recent records, including the stunning red leskea moss

FIG 78. Red leskea moss, an important arctic-alpine species discovered by Sam Bosanquet from the Countryside Council for Wales on a crag above the Afon Tawe. (Graham Motley)

Orthothecium rufescens, have been generated as a result of additional work by Sam Bosanquet and Graham Motley from the Countryside Council for Wales (Fig. 78). As Sam told the author:

> One of my most heart-stopping moments was spotting this species on a crag above the Afon Tawe whilst 'mossing' with Graham Motley. It involved a moss I recognised instantly, with an adrenaline rush similar to finding desert wheatear on the Gwent coast; unlike some rarities, where the eureka moment comes after hours of careful microscope work. We had covered most of the major sandstone crags in the Brecon Beacons for our survey report and were 'mopping up' minor sites in summer 2006. After arriving at the crag, Graham worked along one level of outcrops and I worked another, so I was on my own when I noticed some dark, shiny red moss patches on a rock face by the waterfall. No other British moss looks like Orthothecium rufescens, so I yelled for Graham to come and look at what I'd found and scrambled up to the rock face, where I was confronted by several spectacularly glossy patches of the Orthothecium. The nearest known population is over 100 km to the north, on Cadair Idris, making this one of the Brecon Beacons' most important southern outliers, akin to purple saxifrage. That it grows on a minor crag, rather than one of the known hotspots such as Craig Cerrig Gleisiad or Bannau Sir Gaer, just goes to show how continuing widespread recording, instead of 'honeypotting', can reap rewards.

INVERTEBRATES

There are not many invertebrate records from the Welsh uplands, but a preliminary survey of the Brecon Beacons National Trust Estate carried out in July 1981 revealed a typical assemblage of upland species, including click beetles, dung beetles, ground beetles and molluscs.

Like the other invertebrates, the beetles are not generally conspicuous and the majority have to be actively searched for around the base of plants, or beneath stones. Species recorded from the Beacons include *Patrobus assimilis*, a small (7–10 mm) long black beetle which is widely distributed in mountainous areas of the British Isles, and northern dung beetle *Aphodius lapponum*, a common beetle which feeds on sheep dung at altitudes over 300 m. The Minotaur beetle *Typhaeus typhoeus* though is often the main large dung beetle found in these locations (Fig. 79). It excavates underground chambers for its larvae, filling the shafts with dung for them to feed on. The adults overwinter in burrows as pairs, and the best time to see this impressive beetle is on mild days from September through to March, when they emerge to feed.

Also present is *Otiorhynchus nodosus*, a spectacular large blue-black weevil, which until the late 1960s was regarded as a rarity in Wales, but occurs on most of the high ground in the country. Another attractive upland beetle, which is occasionally quite abundant under stones and moss, is the black, often metallic-looking, click-beetle *Hypnoidus riparius*. Click beetles are named for their ability to flip into the air in order to right themselves when upside down; it is this

FIG 79. A male Minotaur beetle, a large dung beetle often found in the uplands, on the slopes below Llyn y Fan Fach. The males use the long horn-like extensions on the thorax to compete for females. (Graham Motley)

mechanism that produces the familiar click. The larvae of *H. riparius* develop in soil, but the adults are semi-aquatic, being found underneath stones at the edges of montane watercourses. Predominantly a northern and western species, it is less common in Wales. Another click beetle, *Ctenicera cuprea*, can also be common on the moorland in summer. It comes in two forms, the usual copper-coloured one and a completely purple one. This beetle is a predominantly northern insect, with few records south of a line from the Wash to the Severn estuary. Although there are a few species which are widespread throughout the British Isles, many click beetles are either rare or very locally distributed, with some found only in one or two locations nationwide and others known only from historic records.

For reasons that are not clear, the summit of Pen y Fan has an unusually varied community of ground beetles including, amongst others, *Leistus rufomarginatus*, a very distinctive 'black' beetle with red legs, antennae and palps (normally a lowland woodland species!); *Olisthopus rotundatus*, a metallic bronze and brown ground beetle that is widespread on high ground; *Nebria salina*, found mainly under stones on mountain summits; *Dyschirius globosus*, found on most types of moist ground, particularly the bare peat around the summit; *Clivina fossor*, a widespread species of arable cultivation and mountain summits, where it occurs on well-drained peaty soils; and *Pterostichus madidus*, yet another 'lowland' species, which lives under stones and grass tussocks.

There is still much to discover about Welsh mountain spiders, but the money spider *Meioneta gulosa* is thought to be at its southern limit in the Brecon Beacons, being widely distributed north of a line between the Beacons and Yorkshire. It is a small spider, only 1.6–2.2 mm long, which can be found beneath rocks. In areas covered with frost-shattered angular rock, numerous individuals of this species may be found 'ballooning' together in fine weather, and this aerial dispersal probably accounts for many of the lowland records. *M. gulosa* has also been found amongst shingle at the side of upland streams. Mature specimens of both sexes are usually found between May and August, but little is known about its life cycle. The species is very local and scarce, but paradoxically, like many rare species, it is often abundant where it does occur. In some areas recreational pressure may be a threat, but in the long term climate change may adversely affect this and other montane invertebrates.

The species-rich rock ledges support species such as the aphid *Nasonovia saxifragae*, an arctic rarity which, as its scientific name suggests, feeds on mossy saxifrage *Saxifraga hypnoides*. Until it was found in the National Trust's 1981 survey, this aphid had only previously been recorded in Britain from Cumbria and Perthshire. Also associated with the rich vegetation on the cliff ledges is the gold spot moth *Plusia festucae*. In contrast to the aphid it is reasonably common throughout the whole of Britain, the larvae feeding on a variety of plants associated with damp habitats.

Other species recorded from the north-facing crags, which are an excellent habitat for invertebrates, include the beetle *Nebria gyllenhali*, often associated with stony margins near to running water. This is a large, very elongated species, which occurs in various colour combinations, including dark yellow wing cases with green tips and a green thorax, or completely green or purple. In amongst mosses, in areas of running water, nematode worms, earthworms, springtails, spiders, moth flies, biting midges and the riffle beetle *Elmis aenea*, a common water beetle, have been recorded. On this flushed vegetation can also be found two common slugs, the grey field slug *Deroceras reticulatum* and the large black slug *Arion ater*. In addition, this wet vegetation can provide a refuge for unexpected species. In 1970, for instance, Peter Dance from the National Museum of Wales, a mollusc expert, found dwarf pond snail *Galba truncatula*, a species that normally lives in shallow freshwater habitats, 'just below the summit of Pen y Fan at 2,700 feet', the highest recorded altitude for this species in Britain. Dry ledges in these relatively lime-rich areas are inhabited by rounded snail *Discus rotundatus* and the two-toothed door snail *Clausilia bidentata*, a small cylindrical snail commonly found in rock crevices.

On the slopes of Tarren yr Esgob, overlooking Capel y Ffin in the Black Mountains, dedicated searching during daylight, under stones and among moss, will reveal Britain's rarest woodlouse, *Armadillidium pictum* (Fig. 80). Known from only two other sites in Wales, at Coed Aberedw and Bachawy Gorge, Radnorshire, it is found on, or near, screes that are rich in tufa. There are also four known sites in England and, as all these sites are remote and isolated from human habitation,

FIG 80. Britain's rarest woodlouse, *Armadillidium pictum*, can be found on the slopes of Tarren yr Esgob in the Black Mountains. (Paul Richards)

it seems probable that *A. pictum* is part of our native fauna. In Europe, by contrast, it is a common species, mainly found in forests, several metres above the ground under loose bark, or in holes in rotting wood. Experience at Tarren yr Esgob suggests that it is also capable of burrowing to considerable depths, supporting European observations that it can be collected at depths of 1–2 m in the soil of dry woods.

The Black Mountains are also one of the most southerly outposts for upland moths in the British Isles, providing a habitat for a number of interesting species such as the scarce silver y *Syngrapha interrogationis*, galium carpet *Epirrhoe galiata* and grey mountain carpet *Entephria caesiata*. Other moths found in the area include the emperor moth *Saturnia pavonia*, a widespread but never very common moth found mainly on heathland and moorland. It is a very large insect, the female having a wingspan of up to 10 cm, although the male is smaller, with large feathery antennae. During the day, males can be seen flying swiftly about and are often mistaken for butterflies. The females rest in low vegetation, releasing a scent to attract the males. The fully grown caterpillar is green with black hoops, containing yellow wart-like spots, and feeds on moorland plants such as heather (Fig. 81).

FIG 81. Emperor moth caterpillar feeding on heather on the Blorenge. (Graham Motley)

Also found in the same habitat is the heather fly *Bibio pomonae*, which is easily recognised because the upper leg segments are bright red. It is often abundant on the mountains in late summer, hovering over the heather. Sometimes it occurs in such large numbers that, on occasions, walkers have visited the Countryside Council for Wales's office in Abergavenny to complain about it.

THE SILURIAN

The rarest moth found in the Black Mountains is the Silurian *Eriopygodes imbecilla*. A small brown moth that frequents gullies and hollows on high moorland, its colour varies from tawny to reddish brown, with the female being darker and smaller than the male. A paler kidney mark on the forewing and two wavy cross-lines help to identify the species (Fig. 82).

For many years, since its discovery in 1972, the Silurian moth had been thought to be restricted in Britain to a small area of upland at around 500 m above sea level near to Abertillery, a few kilometres to the south of the Black Mountains. Michael Majerus, author of the New Naturalist volume *Moths* (2002), considered that the Silurian was an 'established arrival', which had migrated to Britain and become a permanent resident at an unknown date. The relatively remote location suggested that it had been present some time before it was found. Outside Britain it is found, across Europe and Asia, in wet meadows and peaty areas, often close to streams and springs.

The moth appears to fly well after midnight at the end of June and the beginning of July, although it can also be found flying in hot afternoon sunshine. Larvae

FIG 82. The rare Silurian moth. A photograph taken at night in July 2011. (Dave Grundy)

FIG 83. Caterpillar of the Silurian moth, found in darkness on the Hatterall Ridge in April 2012. (Dave Grundy)

were not discovered in Britain until 2005, when it was found to be feeding on bilberry, a common plant throughout the Black Mountains. In view of this it is something of a mystery why the Silurian is so rare. For many years, searches for likely breeding sites in the area had been unsuccessful, although single moths had occasionally been found in neighbouring valleys – blown, it was thought, from nearby mountaintops. In July 2011, however, it was decided to organise an intensive search for the moth. Preliminary surveys indicated that habitat similar to the Abertillery site existed at the top of the Hatterall Ridge, above Llanthony Priory, and moth enthusiasts Dave Grundy, Robin Hemming and Dr Norman Lowe therefore decided to visit and set up a number of ultraviolet light traps and stay there all night.

A few days before the survey was planned, a single Silurian was found much further down the mountain, just below the Hatterall Ridge, possibly blown there by strong winds. Consequently, excitement was running high when the group made the long journey to the Hatterall Ridge site. Although the weather was cold, ten moth traps were set up, four on the Welsh side of Offa's Dyke and six on the English side. By one o'clock in the morning, it was very cold and wet and it seemed that no moths were flying. Spirits were low, but shortly afterwards an examination of one of the Welsh traps revealed a single Silurian, and five minutes later a second flew in. The other traps were then visited and a further three Silurians were discovered in one trap on the Herefordshire side of the border. Still more were found at intervals, and by 03:40, when the last one was found, a total of 11 Silurian moths had been recorded, all males.

When they finally found it, the moth behaved very oddly in the trap, running round in circles, and they wondered if this was the reason for its scientific name *imbecilla*, which loosely translates as 'idiot'. Where the moth does occur it can be numerous, and as many as 50 individuals have been recorded in one trap per night. Interestingly, almost all arrive late in the night, mostly in the two hours before dawn. Despite this, like the scarce silver y, the species is also occasionally seen flying across areas of heathland on sunny afternoons.

The find generated publicity in the local and national press, some of it inaccurate, with claims, for example, that the species had not been seen for 35 years. In fact a single moth had been recorded coming to a light in a house located in the Black Mountains in July 1999 and the species continued to be recorded and collected at its original site to the south, occurring quite extensively over an area of 4 km². The first authenticated British record of the Silurian was of a single male found in a light trap on 29 July 1972 in a gully at Blaentillary Quarry, to the west of Blaenavon. Despite many searches the species was not seen again until 26 June 1976, when a colony was found, confirming the moth as resident in Britain.

During April 2012 the team again organised a number of expeditions to the Hatterall Ridge to try to find the larvae. As Dave Grundy related to the author, 'It's an interesting experience in darkness, at over 2000 feet, in a bitter northerly wind and sleet, searching for caterpillars in bilberry on your hands and knees!' Despite these rigours the team was successful in finding a number of the Silurian caterpillars (Fig. 83). Like the moth itself, the larvae are not brightly coloured, but there is now indisputable evidence of breeding at this site, expanding the known range of the species. The main threat to the Silurian is from moorland fires and changes in grazing levels. Low-intensity grazing is likely to be beneficial, however, as it allows the food plants to thrive.

MOLLUSCS

Despite abundant moisture, upland grasslands are generally poor in mollusc species. The acidic soils rule out calcicolous species, and the lack of decaying plant matter, which offers both food and shelter, probably prevents even the calcifuge hollowed glass snail *Zonitoides excavatus* from being abundant. The only readily encountered molluscs are the slugs, and then only at night or in damp weather, including snow; they have a remarkable ability to squeeze into soil and crevices in sunshine or drying winds. Upland slugs in the Beacons include the large black slug, the orange-staining dusky slug *Arion subfuscus* and the tiny hedgehog slug *Arion intermedius*. These can subsist on decaying vegetable matter,

FIG 84. The darker, upland, form of tree slug near Llyn y Fan Fawr. (James Turner/National Museum of Wales)

although they supplement their diet with live plants and animal remains. All these species can live above 900 m in British mountains, the montane forms often being noticeably darker in colour than lowland populations.

Perhaps more surprising is the occurrence of the tree slug *Lehmannia marginata* on cliffs and boulders many kilometres from trees (Fig. 84). Woodland populations of this species, a lichen feeder that shows no interest in live plants, climb far into the canopy of tall trees to feed at night. By day they return to the ground or to tree boles to replenish the great quantities of water lost in the mucus that records their route – these gelatinous animals literally cannot move without leaking. The darker individuals found, for example, above 600 m on the crags above Llyn y Fan Fawr, and even above the original tree line (the species has been found at the summit of Snowdon) must feed on the saxicolous lichens and algae available around their refuges (Dance 1972).

Their dark colour has led to confusion with other species elsewhere, including the ash-black slug *Limax cinereoniger*, the largest European land mollusc, which can reach 30 cm in length. This huge species is celebrated as an ancient woodland indicator in much of England, where it is rare, but it is remarkably numerous in woods in the Beacons. During the day it is usually found under dead wood on the woodland floor, but at night it can be seen on tree trunks. The ash-black slug, like the tree slug, also occurs in formerly wooded areas, a juvenile being found at 520 m on Craig Cerrig Gleisiad in 2012. The wetter, milder, climate of Wales allows several mollusc species to have broader habitat ranges than in eastern Britain, so whether such populations are relicts of former woodland cover, like some of the plants occurring nearby, or later arrivals that were somehow dispersed, is not known.

Most lime-loving molluscs are naturally confined to the limestone, but at least one, the rock snail *Pyramidula pusilla*, has been spread further on the quarried stone used in drystone walls. The pavements at Ogof Ffynnon Ddu support a few species, but the areas in the eastern Beacons and Black Mountains are richer and support a number of species that barely penetrate into Wales. The lapidary snail *Helicogona lapicida* occurs more widely on these eastern cliffs where it manoeuvres its flat, sharply keeled shell deep into crevices, emerging only at night or in wet weather. It is thought to be absent from the limestones at Carreg Cennen in the west of the Park, despite an outlying population in the ruins of Dryslwyn Castle (Rowson 2010). Such species are often remarkably local, being absent, even as old empty shells, from apparently suitable habitat. The large chrysalis snail *Abida secale*, for example, occurs on scree on Darren Cilau on northern Mynydd Llangatwg, yet has not been found elsewhere in the Beacons or even at the almost adjacent Craig y Cilau National Nature Reserve (Alexander & Harper 2007). The British fossil record of snails is very good, and evidence shows that the large chrysalis snail, in particular, flourished in the open landscape left by the retreat of the glaciers, only to have its spread checked by the establishment of forests. The rarity of such species in the western Beacons might be explained by these isolated populations being the result of tentative secondary dispersals after the initial forest clearances, rather than relicts of the earlier pre-forested landscape.

SNOW WILDLIFE

Despite the comparatively mild climate, most winters usually see significant falls of snow in the Brecon Beacons (Fig. 85). The number of days of snowfall and snow cover varies enormously though from year to year. After a good fall, especially on a weekend, there are often people snowboarding and skiing on the slopes above the footpath to Pen y Fan. Winter sports were once so popular here that until about 1980 an occasional rope tow operated in the area, but the fact that the snow is unreliable, combined with the advent of dry ski slopes and the availability of cheap flights to Europe, means that comparatively few people now use the area. When snow occurs, however, the landscape is transformed. Roland Mathias, one of the key figures of Welsh writing in English, describes, in his short story *The Eleven Men of Eppynt*, which was based on the deep snowfalls of the 1947–48 winter, 'the Beacons hanging like a candelabra of snow lamps out of the sky, flushed with rose from the perfunctory sun'.

There are other reasons why the snow in the Beacons might be flushed with rose, however, as Alan Bowring, Geopark Development Officer for the National

FIG 85. Fan Brycheiniog and Bannau Sir Gaer under snow. (Harold Grenfell)

FIG 86. Watermelon snow, probably caused by the alga *Chlamydomonas nivalis*, on boulders in the Afon Sychryd. (Alan Bowring)

Park Authority, found on Christmas Eve 2010. He left the office early to visit the Sychryd Gorge between Dinas Rock and Bwa Maen, in order to take some pictures of the snow that had fallen and, though the area is often crowded with people, on this day he had the place to himself. As he came to the end of the 'all-ability trail' he noticed a red colour in the gloom. His first thought was that it was blood, since this is a location where there have been various accidents. It clearly wasn't blood, so Alan then had the idea it might be a pinkish powder left by one of the activity groups as a trail marker, but it seemed to be dispersed through the body of the snow in a way that powder would not be. It then occurred to him that it looked like the pink-coloured snow he had seen at first hand on the slopes of Mount Hood in Oregon when he was on holiday there 15 years earlier, where it is called 'watermelon snow', as it has the slight scent of a fresh watermelon.

Alan's previous sighting, however, had been at an altitude of 3,000 m in the Cascades Range – and this was a wooded valley on the edge of the South Wales coalfield, so he was hesitant at first about assuming that this was also watermelon snow. The coloration extended over several snow-covered boulders, and snow would have been lying on them for a few weeks in this shaded spot, where the winter sun doesn't really penetrate. Alan took a few photos in the gloom to show other people, but didn't dare to step down onto the snow and ice-covered boulders in the bed of the gorge to take a closer look as he was on his own and did not want to risk an accident. He subsequently shared the photographs with colleagues, having checked on the internet, and thought there was at least a chance that it might be watermelon snow (Fig. 86).

Watermelon snow is caused by the alga *Chlamydomonas nivalis*, a species of green algae containing a secondary red carotenoid pigment (astaxanthin) in addition to chlorophyll. The pigment protects the chloroplast from intense visible and also ultraviolet radiation, as well as absorbing heat, which provides the alga with liquid water as the snow melts around it. Unlike most species of freshwater algae, it is cryophilic (cold-loving) and thrives in freezing water. Algal blooms may extend to a depth of 25 cm, with each cell measuring about 20–30 micrometres in diameter, about four times the diameter of a human red blood cell. It has been calculated that a teaspoon of melted snow contains a million or more algal cells. In spring increased levels of light stimulate germination and the resting cells release smaller green flagellate cells which travel towards the surface of the snow, where they lose their flagellae and form thick-walled resting cells. They may also act as gametes, fusing in pairs.

Many species feed on *C. nivalis*, including protozoans such as ciliates, rotifers, nematodes and springtails. Snow algae have been reported from permanent and semi-permanent snowbeds in all continents, but the only previous British

FIG 87. Snow flea, a type of scorpion-fly, the adult of which lacks wings, on rocks below Llyn y Fan Fach. This is a female, with the projecting orange-coloured ovipositor at the rear. (Graham Motley)

records of this species were from the Cairngorms. Although the ravine was too inaccessible for anyone to collect the sample needed for identification, and a number of other members of the genus could cause similar snow coloration, the current consensus is that *C. nivalis* is present in the Beacons and is only detectable in extremely heavy snow.

Other insects present in snow, and only active in winter, include snow fleas *Boreus hyemalis* (Fig. 87). They are not often encountered, because few naturalists search moss or snowfields in midwinter. The species has, however, been recorded by Graham Motley and Sam Bosanquet from rocks below Llyn y Fan Fach, while they were on one of their 'mossing' trips. It is not actually a flea, but a type of scorpion-fly. The adults appear in the winter when the temperature can be too cold for insects to fly, so they crawl and jump rather than using wings; the male wings are modified into curved spines used in mating. The adults will often move between breeding areas by walking across the open snow, hence their common name. Exactly how they manage to jump up to 5 cm without muscular hind legs is not obvious. The head has a very long downward-projecting beak, which has biting mouthparts at the end, a feature characteristic of scorpion-flies. Females have a projecting ovipositor at the rear which has an orange tinge. In some respects the snow flea looks like a small bush-cricket, but the antennae are not nearly as long. The body is also stout, unlike the narrow body of a true scorpion-fly. Larvae live in a channel in the soil just underneath mosses and pupate at the end of the burrow. Like the adult they are predatory and active during late spring and the summer.

Springtails are also present in these conditions. On top of Mynydd Du in February 2012 there was a glazing of ice everywhere, but despite the cold, springtails were wandering across the remaining snow drifts. These species, which are normally found in leaf litter and soil, work their way to the surface of the snow, probably feeding on small particles of debris that have collected there. Many eventually work their way back down to the soil, but some become trapped and die.

CRAIG Y CILAU

At Craig y Cilau National Nature Reserve the acid rocks give way to one of the limestone cliffs, though even here they are present, as Old Red Sandstone occurs at the base and Millstone Grit above. Centuries ago this was the scene of large-scale quarrying, and sections of the cliff have been excavated for the limestone, a key ingredient in iron making, although other areas of the reserve remain in their natural state (Fig. 88). Due to the presence of the limestone, and because the steep and inaccessible nature of the rock faces limits the grazing, it is one of the most outstanding botanical sites in Wales, the cliffs supporting many scarce plants, with at least 250 species being recorded.

It is perhaps best known for its five rare endemic whitebeams, described in Chapter 10, but it is equally important for hawkweeds. Craig y Cilau hawkweed *Hieracium cillense* (Fig. 89) and Llangattock hawkweed *H. asteridiophyllum* are

FIG 88. Craig y Cilau National Nature Reserve, a spectacular limestone escarpment on Mynydd Llangatwg near Crickhowell and the location of many rare plants. (Jonathan Mullard)

FIG 89. Craig y Cilau hawkweed, a very rare endemic Welsh hawkweed confined to limestone cliffs in and around the National Nature Reserve. (Jonathan Mullard)

equally rare endemic Welsh hawkweeds confined to the limestone cliffs in and around Craig y Cilau (Rich 2002). As a result of their rarity they are unusual amongst hawkweeds in Britain in that there is detailed information available on their population sizes. A survey in June 2000 found 659 specimens of Craig y Cilau hawkweed and 512 Llangattock hawkweeds. Compared with a previous survey carried out in 1975, there were more individuals of Craig y Cilau hawkweed and fewer of Llangattock hawkweed – but the differences are probably due to the problems of recording. Both species are regarded as Critically Endangered, but they are probably not at significant risk. Seed from both species has been deposited in the Millennium Seed Bank and plants are being cultivated at the National Botanic Garden of Wales. As hawkweeds are palatable to sheep, a reduction in stocking levels might allow them to spread.

Other important plants found here include angular Solomon's seal *Polygonatum odoratum*, mountain melick *Melica nutans*, maiden pink *Dianthus deltoides*, hutchinsia *Hornungia petraea* and the most southerly British population of alpine enchanter's-nightshade *Circaea alpina*. Despite its rather imposing name, alpine enchanter's-nightshade is low-growing, thin-leaved and small-flowered. The flower also lacks nectar, with the pollen being released while the flower is still a bud, so that it falls onto its own stigmas. The plant tends to spread vegetatively through subterranean runners and forms large clones, while the fruit has hooked hairs and catches on passing animals or people. Open screes below the cliffs are the favoured habitat of the limestone fern *Gymnocarpium robertianum*, with large stands also occurring below the cliffs of Darren Fawr to the north of Merthyr Tydfil.

Natural limestone outcrops at Craig y Cilau, Foel Fawr, Cwm Taf Fechan, the Blorenge and elsewhere support a rich array of tiny rock-bristles, *Seligeria* spp., almost all of which are designated as nationally scarce, or rare. All are minute mosses, with shoots only 2 mm tall and leaves less than 1 mm long. Their main habitats are shaded limestone rocks, cliffs, boulders and crevices. Acuteleaf small limestone moss *Seligeria acutifolia*, Donn's rock-bristle *S. donniana* and small limestone moss *S. pusilla* grow on permanently damp limestone where there is a little bit of water seepage. Triangular or trifid rock-bristle *S. patula* requires more constant flushing of vertical limestone faces and is often encrusted with calcite and algae. It is restricted in South Wales to Craig y Cilau and the Blorenge, with most British populations being found on the limestone in northern England.

Alongside this latter species the very wettest, most permanently flushed limestone face at Craig y Cilau is the only location for Irish rock-bristle *Seligeria oelandica* in Britain; disjunct from northwest Ireland and Scandinavia and perhaps an indication that parts of Craig y Cilau (like the Benbulben range in Ireland) protruded from the ice sheets during previous glaciations. Irish rock-bristle is a very distinctive, exceptionally rare species. Its shoots are 5–15 mm long and almost black, and the leaves are about 1 mm long, spearhead-shaped, narrowing more or less abruptly to a stout point. The capsules are common, wide-mouthed, shaped like a top and held clear of the leaves on a straight and very stout seta. Unusually, the column of tissue in the centre of the capsule persists, with the lid remaining attached to it for some time after the capsule has opened. Both triangular rock-bristle and Irish rock-bristle are extremely tiny plants and look like grubby blackish smears on the rock. A related species, bentfoot rock-bristle *S. campylopoda*, grows on limestone pebbles embedded in the woodland floor on Gilwern Hill and the Blorenge and is otherwise only known in Britain from the Lower Wye Valley.

CARREG CENNEN

As described in Chapter 2, the western end of the limestone is marked by the high crag of Carreg Cennen, a massive and imposing outlier of limestone, over 100 m high, crowned by the ruins of probably the most spectacularly situated of all Welsh castles (Fig. 90). High above the Afon Cennen, a tributary of the Towy, the first masonry castle on this site was probably the work of the Lord Rhys, one of the Welsh Princes of Deheubarth, in the late twelfth century, but the castle we see today was constructed by John Gifford, who was handed the fortress by Edward I in 1283. The end of the castle as a fortress came in 1462, during the War of the Roses, when it was demolished by 500 Yorkist men with picks and crowbars, as it had been a Lancastrian hideout. The crag also gives its name to the Carreg Cennen Disturbance, an ancient weakness in the Earth's crust which extends from Carmarthen Bay to Sennybridge and beyond.

Carreg Cennen is the only known location of a particular community of sun- and limestone-loving lichens in South Wales. This is dominated by the white crustose lichen *Aspicilia calcarea*, which is abundant on sunny, exposed, slightly nutrient-enriched limestone, where it can form extensive and conspicuous white colonies which exclude most other species. The tops of the castle walls are covered in it, as are some nearby rock surfaces. The other main component of this lichen community, which can contain up to 20 other species, is the common yellow lichen *Caloplaca citrina* agg.

The limestone cliffs are also renowned for the rare plant species which occur here, and there are stable or increasing populations of the rare spiked speedwell *Veronica spicata* ssp. *hybrida* and wild chives *Allium schoenoprasum* (Fig. 91) – hence

FIG 90. Carreg Cennen castle, perched on a limestone crag above the Afon Cennen. The tops of the walls are covered with white crustose lichen. (Jonathan Mullard)

FIG 91. The massive crag of Carreg Cennen derives its name from the wild chives that occur here, *carreg* being Welsh for stone or rock and *cennan* a generic name for the leek family. (Richard Pryce)

cennen, a generic Welsh name for the leek family (*carreg* is Welsh for stone or rock). Like most perennial bulbs, chives lies dormant during winter, producing new leaf growth in early spring. The plants flower profusely in early summer, and seed may germinate immediately, or during the autumn and following spring. Bulb reproduction also occurs, which results in clumps. In rocky depressions where plants are stunted, flowering is much less common, and in some populations reproduction is predominantly asexual.

Spiked speedwell is a clump-forming perennial whose striking deep violet-blue flowers are carried in a pyramidal spike, which can, with care, usually be seen growing on the vertical rock face below the castle. The fact that it occurs at Carreg Cennen is of particular interest because, although it is widely distributed in Europe, it has a disjunct distribution in Britain, with widely separated populations. Divided into two subspecies, the form which occurs here is nationally scarce, occurring in only 15 locations in Wales. All the known sites are on basic rocks, or in areas with base-rich drainage water and where there is no natural woodland, due to the steepness, or shallowness, or instability of the soil. For this reason it is

FIG 92. Pal y Cwrt, below Banwen Gwythwch at the eastern end of Mynydd Du, an important area of species-rich limestone grassland and scree. (Jonathan Mullard)

considered that this subspecies, along with many of the associated species in their
scattered sites, represents the relics of once widespread late glacial steppe-tundra
vegetation, most of which, as described in Chapter 3, was lost under closed forest.
In 12 of these Welsh locations grazing, by sheep or rabbits *Oryctolagus cuniculus*,
plays an important role in maintaining the populations because it suppresses
competitors and maintains an open habitat. At Carreg Cennen, however, the
cliff ledges, while inaccessible for the most part to grazing animals, are sparsely
vegetated and provide an excellent habitat for the plants.

UPLAND LIMESTONE GRASSLAND

Upland calcareous grassland is one of the scarcest grassland types in Wales, with
nearly three-quarters of it occurring in the Brecon Beacons. This habitat is found
only where the limestone outcrops as a thin band across the area and in isolated
outcrops elsewhere. Nowhere is the difference between upland acid grassland and
limestone grassland more clearly demonstrated than at Pal y Cwrt, below Banwen
Gwythwch at the eastern end of Mynydd Du (Fig. 92). Here, within a few metres of
the single-track road, tormentil and other plants typical of acid conditions give
way to a short species-rich turf of sheep's
fescue and herbs such as wild thyme
Thymus polytrichus, salad burnet *Sanguisorba
minor*, bird's-foot-trefoil *Lotus corniculatus*
and common rock-rose *Helianthemum
nummularium*.

While the rare plants at Carreg Cennen
are mainly confined to the cliffs and can
sometimes be difficult to see, the summit
grassland contains species similar to
those found at Pal y Cwrt. Given the high
level of sheep grazing, these can rarely
be found in flower, but in the autumn
the tightly grazed grassland around the
castle supports an exceptional variety
of grassland fungi, including golden
spindles *Clavulinopsis fusiformis*, crazed
cap *Dermoloma cuneifolium*, lilac pinkgill
Entoloma porphyrophaeum and toasted,
glutinous, crimson and persistent waxcaps

FIG 93. Persistent waxcap, a common
component of waxcap grasslands.
(Graham Motley)

(*Hygrocybe colemanniana*, *H. glutinipes*, *H. panacea* and *H. persistens*, respectively) (Fig. 93). These are the most distinctive and visible components of the grassland fungi, being brightly coloured mushrooms which are commonly seen in the autumn, and grasslands that support these fungi are known as waxcap grasslands. At other sites such as Cwm Clydach the rare rose spindles *Clavaria rosea* can be found (Fig. 94). Between 2003 and 2005 the Countryside Council for Wales funded a survey, which showed that Wales was one of the richest areas in Europe for grassland fungi. A feature common to all sites with diverse waxcap populations is that they are grazed or mown regularly and that there has been no recent fertiliser application. Another consistent feature of habitats in which waxcaps occur is the presence of moss, usually springy turf-moss *Rhytidiadelphus squarrosus* in Wales.

There are 51 species of *Hygrocybe* found in Britain, more than in any other genus of grassland fungi. The presence of the waxcap community is dependent on very low nutrient levels associated with grazing by sheep, cattle or other livestock. This low nutrient level is critical, because even the application of low amounts of organic or inorganic fertiliser will completely alter the fungal flora. Although the sheep affect the flowering plants they are in fact recommended for grazing waxcap grasslands, with 12 of the top 15 Welsh sites being sheep-grazed (Rotheroe 2001, Evans & Holden 2003), but other livestock can also give good results.

FIG 94. Rose spindles, a rare species found in waxcap grasslands in the Beacons – here on grassland in Cwm Clydach. (Graham Motley)

One of the richest locations for calcareous grasslands is Ogof Ffynnon Ddu. The grassland here contains a number of rarities including mountain everlasting *Antennaria dioica*, autumn gentian *Gentianella amarella*, mossy saxifrage and great burnet *Sanguisorba officinalis*, while on the plateau above is the best example of limestone pavement in South Wales.

LIMESTONE PAVEMENT

Limestone pavements are a rare, and often attractive, feature in the countryside with great importance not only for their geomorphological features, as described in Chapter 2, but also as habitats for wildlife. The unique conditions on limestone pavements support many different plants and animals.

Limestone pavement vegetation may also contain unusual combinations of plants, with woodland and wood-edge species well represented in the sheltered grikes, while the clints support plants of rocky habitats, or are often unvegetated. Nationally and locally rare species recorded from the pavement at Ogof Ffynnon Ddu include soft-leaved sedge *Carex montana*, lily-of-the-valley *Convallaria majalis*, hairy greenweed *Genista pilosa* and mountain melick. Other plants found here include hairy rock-cress *Arabis hirsuta*, lesser meadow-rue, wood anemone *Anemone nemorosa*, hart's-tongue fern *Phyllitis scolopendrium*, black spleenwort *Asplenium adiantum-nigrum*, green spleenwort *A. viride*, small scabious *Scabiosa columbaria*, mossy saxifrage (Fig. 95) and herb-Robert *Geranium robertianum*.

Some areas of limestone pavement at Ogof Ffynnon Ddu have been fenced off to exclude stock and allow some of the rare plant species to flourish, but even

FIG 95. Mossy saxifrage on the limestone pavement at Ogof Ffynnon Ddu. (Jonathan Mullard)

here occasional grazing may be required to control the build-up of leaf litter and to prevent the vegetation becoming rank. Grazing is an important aspect of the management and conservation of pavement vegetation. It keeps tree and shrub species in check, preventing the area reverting to woodland and protecting the open aspect of the pavements, whereas high stocking rates result in overgrazing, which reduces the diversity of the grike vegetation and prevents species from spreading out onto the surface of the pavement and into the surrounding grassland. Winter grazing also inhibits the growth of ivy *Hedera helix*, which the sheep will eat since it is one of the few green plants available at this time of year. Cattle are generally preferable to sheep, as they are reluctant to go onto the pavement surface and will do less damage, but light sheep grazing helps to maintain the species diversity in grass swards on open pavements with wide grikes.

Lying amongst pastures to the west of Ystradfellte are a number of limestone pavements, the majority of which have characteristically distinct clints separated by deep grikes up to 1 m in depth. A few of the pavements have a broken surface and were at one time thought to be largely destroyed – but it seems that these fragmented pavements in fact represent a different structural form. The other pavements in this area of the Beacons are considered to be only 20–30 per cent intact. The pastures are separated by drystone walls, and the stone for these was probably obtained from the pavements. All the pavements are grazed by stock, mainly sheep, and this has been sufficiently low in intensity to allow hazel scrub to remain, along with specimens of hawthorn, blackthorn *Prunus spinosa* and guelder rose *Viburnum opulus*. Other species which can be found within the grikes here include ivy, honeysuckle *Lonicera periclymenum*, burnet rose *Rosa pimpinellifolia*, apple rose *R. villosa* and stone bramble *Rubus saxatilis*. The uncommon rose-moss *Rhodobryum roseum* grows here and in similar habitats near Penderyn, at Cadair Fawr, around edges of the limestone blocks. This moss usually occurs as scattered stems in short grassland in open woodland, heaths, sand dunes and chalk grassland. A favoured habitat is on and around the large nests of yellow meadow ants *Lasius flavus*.

Pavements with more herb-rich floras contain species such as bearded couch *Elymus caninus*, cow parsley *Anthriscus sylvestris*, false brome *Brachypodium sylvaticum*, enchanter's-nightshade *Circaea lutetiana*, broad-leaved helleborine *Epipactis helleborine*, hemp-agrimony *Eupatorium cannabinum*, meadowsweet, wood avens *Geum urbanum*, cow-wheat *Melampyrum pratense*, small scabious, wood sage *Teucrium scorodinia* and zigzag clover *Trifolium medium*. Both cow-wheat and zigzag clover are unusual species to find on limestone pavements, but the plants usually occur at the base of hazel bushes where they are protected to some extent from grazing.

The nationally uncommon species found here include hairy rock-cress, brittle bladder-fern *Cystopteris fragilis* and yellow archangel *Lamium galeobdolon* ssp. *galeobdolon*. The last of these is characteristic of Welsh limestone pavements, but is rarely found in this habitat elsewhere in Britain (Ward & Evans 1975). Occasional species recorded from the area include lords-and-ladies *Arum maculatum*, green spleenwort, rustyback *Ceterach officinarum*, hard shield-fern *Polystichum aculeatum*, wall lettuce *Mycelis muralis*, cowslip, mossy saxifrage, small scabious and more rarely limestone fern, lily-of-the-valley and globeflower *Trollius europaeus*.

Common species, which are frequent or abundant, on these Ystradfellte pavements are false oat-grass *Arrhenatherum elatius*, wall-rue *Asplenium ruta-muraria*, maidenhair spleenwort *A. trichomanes*, spear thistle *Cirsium vulgare*, male-fern *Dryopteris felix-mas*, bluebell *Hyacinthoides non-scripta*, red fescue *Festuca rubra*, herb-Robert, dog's mercury *Mercurialis perennis*, wood-sorrel *Oxalis acetosella*, hart's-tongue fern, bracken, sanicle *Sanicula europea*, stinging nettle and dog-violet *Viola riviniana*. In addition there are occasional records of ramsons *Allium ursinum*, lesser burdock *Arctium minus*, lady-fern *Athyrium felix-femina*, harebell *Campanula rotundifolia*, glaucous sedge *Carex flacca*, marsh thistle *Cirsium palustre*, cock's-foot *Dactylis glomerata*, broad-leaved willowherb *Epilobium montanum*, cleavers *Galium aparine*, limestone bedstraw *G. sternei*, cow parsnip *Heracleum sphondylium*, polypody *Polypodium vulgare*, selfheal *Prunella vulgaris*, dandelion *Taraxacum officinale* agg. and valerian.

Most limestone pavements in the Beacons are on the open hill and devoid of trees, but there are wooded examples north of Ystradfellte, largely covered in dense ash and hazel (Fig. 96). These are botanically poor, but on a nearby hillside another area of pavement with some hazel scrub has a rich flora. In other areas the limestone rock is only just exposed and the grikes are filled with soil. These areas and isolated areas of remnant pavements are often botanically uninteresting, as they tend to occur on moorland and are grazed in preference to the less palatable habitats around.

All the relatively intact areas of pavement support a wide range of invertebrates, with grikes being the most important area for invertebrates, such as weevils, and the nationally scarce cranefly *Dactylolabis sexmaculata*, which has been recorded from several sites in the Beacons. Intense grazing though has a detrimental effect on the larvae of this species. Moss cover on shaded clint tops provides valuable shelter for invertebrates such as snails, rove beetles and woodlice. Butterflies can often be found basking on the exposed limestone, and the pavement and grassland at Ogof Ffynnon Ddu is a good area for dark green fritillary *Argynnis aglaja*.

FIG 96. Limestone pavement and hazel scrub at Carn y Goetre above Ystradfellte. (Jonathan Mullard)

UPLAND SCREE

Scree slopes, formed from angular rocks that have fallen from the cliffs above, are an important habitat and are widespread around the upland edge (Fig. 97). Formed by ice expanding existing cracks in the rock and eventually breaking away large blocks, they obviously reflect the geology of the cliffs above. Quarrying and the construction of roads and railways have also enlarged these natural areas and created new areas of scree. Naturally formed screes represent some of the least disturbed habitats in Britain, with only atmospheric pollution and climate change affecting the more inaccessible sites. The continuing erosion and landslips along the scarps of most of the upland areas produce some of the most characteristic landscapes in the Beacons, including the spectacular landslips at Cwmyoy and Skirrid described in Chapter 2. Over time some of these screes and boulder fields may become covered in scrub, grassland, heathland or bog, while erosion, or burning, will expose them again.

Since material falling from the cliffs is sorted down the scree, the upper parts will consist of finer material while the lower parts are often dominated by rocks and large boulders. Scree slopes created by quarrying or other activities do not exhibit this selection by size to the same extent, but the size of the debris is one of the most important environmental factors that determine which species occur

FIG 97. Limestone scree slopes below the cliffs of Darren Fawr, the largest and most spectacular of the Brecknock Wildlife Trust's reserves, viewed from Penmoelallt Community Woodland. (Graham Motley)

here. The dimensions of the blocks are influenced both by the rock type and the rate of erosion. The Carboniferous grits tend to be harder and tend to form the largest blocks, although some of the Old Red Sandstone beds can also form large block screes, as seen at the Darren just northwest of Crickhowell. The screes in the west of the Beacons, such as those on Mynydd Du, are almost pure silica and as a result are very hard, smooth and angular.

The screes with the largest blocks are the ones that have the deepest recesses, and particularly where these occur on shady slopes rare humidity-demanding bryophytes occur. The great variation in environmental conditions over short distances that occurs in areas of scree results in a correspondingly high diversity of lichens and bryophytes. Access to light, the angle of the slope and the amount of available moisture are important factors in determining which species are present. Unstable exposed scree of a small size may be a suitable habitat for vascular plants, but in the areas of larger boulders, where there is no soil accumulation, lichens, mosses and pioneer plants predominate.

Notable lower plant communities found in the Beacons include submontane lichens that are rare in Wales, but which commonly occur in the Scottish Highlands, such as *Umbilicaria cylindrica*, *U. torrefacta*, *U. proboscidea*, *Pseudephebe pubescens*, *Cetrariella commixta* and *Cornicularia normoerica*. Liverworts and mosses found amongst the blocks of Millstone Grit scree on the Blorenge (Fig. 98) include trunk pawwort *Barbilophozia attenuata*, greater whipwort *Bazzania trilobata*, rock fingerwort *Lepidozia cupressina*, western earwort *Scapania gracilis* and smaller white-moss *Leucobryum juniperoideum*. Some of these are at, or close to, the edge of their range in Britain. Woolly fringe-moss *Racomitrium lanuginosum* can also be very abundant in some areas of scree. In contrast, dusky fork-moss *Dicranum fuscescens* is widely scattered, although it may be masked by the abundant rusty swan-neck moss *Campylopus flexuosus* when it is not fruiting. Base-rich sandstone boulders provide a habitat for fringed extinguisher-moss *Encalypta ciliata* (which is rare in this habitat, occurring most frequently on cliff ledges), thickpoint grimmia *Schistidium crassipilum* and Bamberger's crisp-moss *Tortella bambergeri*, which is most abundant on isolated Old Red Sandstone boulders (Fig. 99). The Brecon Beacons are a stronghold for this species, which was described as new to Britain by Sam

FIG 98. Graham Motley, Senior Conservation Officer for the Countryside Council for Wales, searching for mosses in scree on the western side of the Blorenge. (Jonathan Mullard)

FIG 99. Bamberger's crisp-moss occurs on Old Red Sandstone boulders across the Brecon Beacons, yet generations of botanists appear to have overlooked it. The species was only added to the British list in 2006. (Graham Motley)

Bosanquet in 2006. It is almost always found alongside frizzled crisp-moss, but tends to grow in less exposed positions on a block than the latter – although tufts of the two species are often immediately adjacent to each other. In such situations, the differences between the two species are readily apparent (Bosanquet 2006).

Few mosses are able to grow on the silica screes on Mynydd Du, but crustose lichens such as *Rhizocarpon geographicum*, *Parmelia saxatilis*, *Fuscidea cyathoides*, *F. lygea* and *F. kochiana* are abundant. Between the rocks, where humus has built up, *Cladonia* spp. can be prominent and, in some areas of scree, Vesuvius snow lichen *Stereocaulon vesuvianum* is abundant. Common in upland areas on siliceous rocks, the snow lichen is a spectacular and easily recognised species with grey or white branches.

Many of the areas of larger scree are inaccessible to grazing animals and are unmanaged, while on the finer screes grazing may keep the vegetation in check. The inaccessibility of scree to grazing animals provides a refuge for

FIG 100. Slender cruet-moss growing on the remains of a sheep skull in Pal y Cwrt Quarry. (Sam Bosanquet)

many plants that are sensitive to grazing, including numerous local and rare species and sometimes species normally confined to cliffs spread into the screes. Occasionally sheep become trapped amongst the larger boulders and die, creating the ideal conditions for slender cruet-moss *Tetraplodon mnioides*, which grows on sheep bones (Fig. 100). Slender cruet-moss belongs to a group known as 'dung mosses' which grow on animal remains including dung, bones and regurgitated pellets from birds of prey. They are unique among seedless plants, since they rely on insects rather than wind for spore dispersal. When flies land on their capsules, attracted by odours that mimic those of dung and carrion, the sticky spores at the mouth of the capsule become attached to the flies and are carried away by them. Other members of this group recorded from the Beacons are cruet collar-moss *Splachnum ampullaceum* and round-fruited collar-moss *S. sphaericum*, although they are generally rare, having declined over the past century because of drainage and improvement of lowland fields and the reduction in cattle grazing.

Ferns can be prominent in some areas of scree, and some scarce species can be found including oak fern, beech fern and the even rarer parsley fern *Cryptogramma crispa* found at Craig Cerrig Gleisiad. In the central Beacons, lemon-scented fern *Oreopteris limbosperma* can be frequent amongst screes made up of relatively small rocks. Open screes below limestone cliffs are also the favoured habitat of the limestone fern, with large stands occurring below the cliffs of Darren Fawr (Fig. 101). There are also very large populations at Craig y Cilau, with smaller numbers on Gilwern Hill and the Blorenge. Interestingly, limestone fern also occurs in Old Red Sandstone screes at Tarren yr Esgob near Hay on Wye. The scree slope at Darren Fawr is also home to the rigid buckler-fern *Dryopteris submontana* and one of only two Welsh sites for this nationally scarce species. Both species can tolerate high light levels and moderate summer droughts. They are also deciduous and have bluish, rough-textured fronds, which seem to be adaptations to increasing the light-reflecting ability of the upper surface of the fronds on the brightly lit limestone surfaces (Page 1988).

Areas of scree are also particularly valuable for invertebrates, and the abundance of spiders found here is, in part, a reflection of the size and shape of the debris and the way the rocks have accumulated. There have been no detailed studies of the invertebrates associated with scree, and this is a subject worthy of further investigation, especially as these animals provide a food source for birds such as ring ouzel and wheatear *Oenanthe oenanthe* which nest amongst the boulders.

FIG 101. Limestone fern is frequently found on the open screes below limestone cliffs, as here at Darren Fawr. (Graham Motley)

BIRDS

While wheatears are associated with the lower scree slopes of the valleys, the ring ouzels breed in the vicinity of the crags, along with ravens *Corvus corax*, kestrels *Falco tinnunculus* and peregrines *Falco peregrinus*. The number of species breeding in the uplands is fairly small, however, compared with similar habitats in northern Britain. Peregrines are still under threat from persecution and theft so their nesting sites have to remain secret, but they can readily be seen on the high crags and moorland areas. Mid Wales has one of the highest density of ravens in Europe, and the Beacons are no exception (Fig. 102). Ravens are quite shy and wary of humans but can be approached with care. If you observe them for a while it will not be very long, if they are in a playful mood, before you see them deliberately flying upside down – they just love to fly. Ravens clearly have a sense of fun, and a nature programme on the radio once described ravens in the

FIG 102. Raven on a fence post in the Beacons. Abundant sheep carrion and the provision of food for lambing flocks in spring has contributed to a rise in their numbers. (Steve Wilce)

FIG 103. Merlins often nest on the edges of upland conifer plantations. They are elusive birds, however, and nests are often difficult to locate. (Roy Blewitt)

Brecon Beacons taking advantage of a period of wintry weather by sliding down an icy slope on their backs! One of the largest roosts in the Beacons is in a conifer plantation on Allt yr Esgair near the village of Bwlch, about 11 km southeast of Brecon.

Dry dwarf-shrub heath is a crucially important habitat for upland birds such as red grouse *Lagopus lagopus*, golden plover *Pluvialis apricaria* and merlin *Falco columbarius* (Fig. 103). The red grouse that breed on the Blorenge are the most southerly natural population in Britain, but there is concern about the condition of the habitat here and the grouse are struggling to survive in the face of sometimes intensive recreational pressures. In December 2011 a group of eight volunteers began monitoring the grouse population on the Blorenge as part of the Forgotten Landscapes project set up by the Blaenavon Industrial Landscape World Heritage Site. The project is carrying out controlled burning of the heather to create a mosaic of different-aged heather plants, and this will benefit red grouse. The volunteers are part of a bigger group, the World Heritage Site Volunteer Rangers, who carry out a variety of conservation projects, ranging from drystone walling to stock fencing and planting of reed beds.

Common land is also important for common sandpiper *Actitis hypoleucos,* curlew *Numenius arquata* and wintering red kite, along with fieldfare *Turdus pilaris* and redwing *T. iliacus.* In the summer, skylark *Alauda arvensis* and meadow pipit *Anthus pratensis* are abundant and take advantage of the diverse mosaic of grassland and shrub habitats. Some of these areas are also important for lapwing *Vanellus vanellus,* a bird which is rapidly declining in Wales, and rock pipit *Anthus petrosus* has also been occasionally recorded. Flocks of feeding barn swallow *Hirundo rustica*, swift *Apus apus* and house martin *Delichon urbicum* are also frequently seen. Land around the summits on Mynydd Du is covered by boulders and rocky outcrops, and this habitat is favoured by dotterel *Charadrius morinellus* in late April and early May. This enigmatic wader, slightly smaller than the golden plover, is the biggest birding 'prize' of the uplands. They are only seen for odd days, passing through from their wintering grounds in north Africa to their breeding grounds in Scandinavia, and although dotterel have been seen by walkers on the slope between Pen y Fan and Corn Du, as in 2011, you could search forever and never find one.

A number of these birds are also found in the ffridd, the transition between the upland and lowland zones. This specific, and very Welsh, habitat deserves a chapter to itself.

CHAPTER 5

The Ffridd

In many parts of the Brecon Beacons, as in the rest of the Welsh uplands, there is a distinctive area of land on the lower hillside where the moorland meets the relatively fertile farmland. A complex mosaic of acid grassland, heathland, exposed rock, flushes and mires, it is a classic Welsh habitat, traditionally grazed by horses and cattle, and known as ffridd (pronounced 'freeth'). In North Wales ffridd usually refers to unenclosed land, whereas in South Wales it sometimes refers to enclosed land. The term coedcae (wood–field) is used instead to denote unenclosed ffridd, but in practice the terms are often used interchangeably. For simplicity, in this chapter both unenclosed and enclosed land will be referred to as ffridd. Found almost exclusively on slopes, particularly those areas that cannot be effectively farmed because of their steepness, or the fact that they contain rocks or scree, it may also develop on areas of former conifer plantations. Enormous areas of ffridd in Wales have been improved during agricultural intensification, and this makes the remaining areas in the Beacons especially important.

Generally neglected by naturalists, the habitat has been little studied. It is often characterised by gnarled, sheep-pruned hawthorn bushes, with isolated holly trees, amongst moss-covered boulder scree surrounded by bracken (Fig. 104). Many sites contain small areas of trees and scrub, with other typical species including western gorse, common gorse *Ulex europaeus*, broom *Cytisus scoparius*, bramble, wild rose *Rosa canina*, rowan, elder *Sambucus nigra*, blackthorn and a number of willow species. These small stands spread by suckering or seed dispersal caused by roosting birds. Individual bushes may be very old, and their presence is probably a result of a relaxation in grazing or previous woodland cover. As it contains a number of semi-natural habitats, it is noted for its dynamic nature

FIG 104. Ffridd below Craig y Castell on the northern slopes of Mynydd Llangatwg (Jonathan Mullard)

and often displays successional stages in the development of woodland from grassland and heathland. Some sites are also periodically burned by farmers, or commoners, to reduce the extent of gorse and improve the quality of grazing. In the absence of this heavy grazing and burning the ffridd would probably develop into woodland, such as that at Coed Nant Menascin, which is dominated by sessile oak *Quercus petraea*, the commonest type of woodland in Wales.

Areas of ffridd also support the main populations of plant species such as ivy-leaved bell flower *Wahlenbergia hederacea* and upright vetch *Vicia orobus*, while the bracken also creates a canopy for woodland flowers such as dog-violet. In general, bracken stands are species-poor, except where they protect a relict woodland flora. Common dog-violet is the food plant of dark green fritillary caterpillars, and this species occurs at low densities in the Beacons, the adults being highly mobile (Fig. 105).

The dark green fritillary is single-brooded, with the adults on the wing from early June until mid-August. The eggs are laid singly either on the food plant or more usually on a nearby plant, dead leaves, or dead bracken. Immediately after hatching, the larvae enter hibernation amongst dead grass or leaf litter and only begin feeding on the first warm days of spring. When the weather is cool the caterpillars bask on dead leaves or dead grass, while in warmer weather they remain concealed, feeding on violets.

FIG 105. The dark green fritillary is the most widespread fritillary found in the British Isles. (Harold Grenfell)

Grazing by cattle and horses serves to break up the bracken and litter, allowing the female butterflies to reach the violets beneath the bracken. It also provides suitable germination sites for the violets themselves. At the same time sufficient bracken litter is retained to capture the warmth and raise the temperature of the surroundings, which assists the development of the caterpillars in the spring. Unlike cattle and horses, however, sheep selectively graze the violet flowers that the butterflies feed on. They also do not trample the bracken litter sufficiently to create the right conditions for the caterpillars. Although some reduction of sheep numbers has taken place in recent years, sheep are still stocked at a relatively high level, and this has implications for the future of these butterflies.

Up to 40 invertebrates in Britain feed on bracken, including a sawfly *Aneugmenus* spp., a planthopper *Dytroptis pteridis* and the caterpillars of map-winged swift moth *Pharmacis fusconebulosa* and brown silver-line moth *Petrophora chlorosata*. A fairly common moth over much of Britain, this latter species can be disturbed in the daytime by walking through the bracken. The number of insects feeding on the bracken increases as the growing season progresses due to the decreasing levels of toxin, and the production of nectaries in the spring, food for ants, which in turn may kill any herbivorous insects in the vicinity. Unfortunately bracken is also a favoured haunt of the sheep tick *Ixodes ricinus*, which can carry Lyme disease. This is caused by an infection from the bacterium *Borrelia burgdorferi*, itself transmitted by a bite from the tick, a blood-sucking parasite. Ticks, however, seem less of a problem in the Beacons than in some other areas of Wales. Climatic factors such as drought or prolonged cold weather can affect tick populations and activity significantly, which may also affect the incidence of Lyme disease from year to year.

Studies have suggested that ant predation, by *Myrmica* species and *Formica lemani*, appears to have played a significant role in determining the structure of British bracken-feeding insect communities. Distasteful fluid in the circulatory system of sawfly caterpillars, for instance, which exhibit reflex bleeding when attacked by ants, may have evolved in response to selection from ant predation, while other species may accidentally possess characteristics, evolved in response to a variety of selective forces, that also reduce the impact of ants. An absence of external foliage-feeding butterflies and moths early in the spring, a high proportion of sawfly species, and gall-formers and leaf-miners may all be characteristics of the bracken herbivore community which have been influenced by ant predation. The effectiveness of aggressive wood ants in protecting bracken from attack by other invertebrates is in no doubt.

BIRDS OF THE FFRIDD

Bracken can be an important breeding habitat for moorland birds, and the ffridd supports a wide variety of species. A study of breeding bird communities in areas of ffridd in Wales, including the Brecon Beacons, which was based on data collected in the mid-1980s, recorded a total of 62 bird species (Fuller *et al.* 2006). Unsurprisingly, given the mixture of habitats present, these included species typical of moorland, grassland, scrub and woodland. Few species, however, were widespread or numerous, and only 14 species were recorded at more than 25 per cent of the sites.

By far the most abundant and indeed ubiquitous species recorded was meadow pipit (Table 2). Tree pipit *Anthus trivialis*, wheatear, whinchat, chaffinch *Fringilla coelebs*, yellowhammer *Emberiza citrinella* and willow warbler *Phylloscopus trochilus* were also abundant. Considerably more species, including most of the scrub and woodland species, were associated with bracken-dominated sites than with grassland or moorland sites. The density of trees on the site was found to be a key factor in determining the breeding birds present, including wren *Troglodytes troglodytes*, dunnock *Prunella modularis*, robin *Erithacus rubecula*, mistle thrush *Turdus viscivorus* and garden warbler *Sylvia borin*. Another cluster of species was more associated with areas of scattered trees and bracken such as tree pipit, redstart, blackbird, great tit *Parus major*, magpie *Pica pica*, chaffinch, linnet *Carduelis cannabina* and yellowhammer. The importance of trees and bushes for many bird

TABLE 2. Common breeding birds associated with ffridd in the 1980s.

Species	Number of sites	Relative abundance
Meadow pipit *Anthus pratensis*	116	1108.0
Tree pipit *Anthus trivialis*	94	311.5
Wheatear *Oenanthe oenanthe*	92	334.0
Whinchat *Saxicola rubetra*	85	289.5
Chaffinch *Fringilla coelebs*	77	155.5
Yellowhammer *Emberiza citrinella*	73	168.5
Willow warbler *Phylloscopus trochilus*	62	149.0
Skylark *Alauda arvensis*	52	79.5
Linnet *Carduelis cannabina*	51	115.0
Redstart *Phoenicurus phoenicurus*	50	72.5
Pied wagtail *Motacilla alba*	40	43.5
Wren *Troglodytes troglodytes*	35	32.0
Carrion crow *Corvus corone*	33	57.5
Blackbird *Turdus merula*	31	29.5
Cuckoo *Cuculus canorus*	26	21.0
Blue tit *Cyanistes caeruleus*	21	16.5
Magpie *Pica pica*	20	24.0
Great tit *Parus major*	17	22.0
Dunnock *Prunella modularis*	16	16.0
Robin *Erithacus rubecula*	16	12.0
Mistle thrush *Turdus viscivorus*	13	15.5
Raven *Corvus corax*	11	12.0
Jay *Garrulus glandarius*	10	6.0
Buzzard *Buteo buteo*	10	8.0
Ring ouzel *Turdus torquatus*	10	12.0
Garden warbler *Sylvia borin*	9	6.5

The top 30 species recorded across 118 study sites, ranked by the frequency of occurrence (i.e. 116 = recorded on 116 out of 118 sites). Relative abundance is the sum across all sites of the mean of two counts. Adapted from Fuller *et al.* (2006).

species is hardly surprising, but it is interesting that the very low densities of trees that characterise the ffridd have such an effect on the richness of bird species.

The ffridd is also significant for birds in a wider context because it provides foraging habitats for birds of prey nesting in nearby woodlands, or on moorland, such as merlin. The cuckoo *Cuculus canorus*, a well-known brood parasite, is also attracted to the ffridd, since the females lay their eggs in the nests of birds such as meadow pipits and dunnocks. The Punchbowl, along with the Skirrid, is one of the best places in the Beacons to hear and sometimes see the cuckoo.

It is worth noting that the study summarised in Table 2 is based on historical data, and there have almost certainly been some substantial changes in bird communities in the ffridd since the 1980s. Some areas continue to retain large populations of key species such as whinchat, but continued heavy grazing by sheep may have altered the structure of vegetation and bird communities in many areas. A re-survey of the ffridd, not only in the Brecon Beacons, is long overdue. In particular there is a need to identify the preferred vegetation structures for birds such as tree pipit, whinchat, stonechat *Saxicola rubicola* and yellowhammer, in order to obtain a better understanding of the implications of grazing pressure, and bracken and scrub control, on habitat quality.

WHINCHAT

The whinchat is one of the most distinctive summer visitors to the Welsh uplands, and Steve Smith, Assistant Area Warden for the eastern end of the National Park, has been studying them enthusiastically since 1986. The study area is a relatively small section of bracken-covered ffridd and the associated moorland, including Mynydd Garn Clochdy, Mynydd y Garn Fawr and the Blorenge. The main objective of the study is to obtain a greater understanding of whinchat breeding biology and habitat requirements, and Steve traps an average of 250 young whinchats each summer (Fig. 106). He also makes efforts to trap and re-trap the adult breeding population within the study area in order to determine the survival rate, and between 1999 and 2001 an average of 95 birds were trapped

FIG 106. Steve Smith, Assistant Area Warden for the National Park Authority, traps and rings an average of 250 young whinchats each summer as part of his long-term study of the species' breeding biology. (Steve Smith)

annually. The whinchat overwinters in central and southern Africa, and adult males typically arrive back in the study area in the last week of April. Traditional territories are re-established and singing then commences in order to defend chosen sites and to attract the females, which arrive a few days later.

Whinchats nest in rough vegetation, in locations near to bushes, trees or fence lines which they can use as song posts. The ffridd is therefore an ideal habitat, given the scattered bushes and trees found here. Hillsides with few trees, or those which are heavily wooded, have lower numbers of birds. Data gathered by Steve between 1986 and 1994 showed that bilberry is the favoured nesting site, being used in 65 per cent of cases, while only 12 per cent of nests were found in bracken. The bracken in the study area is comparatively sparse, especially at nesting time, which results in very little cover for the nest, unlike the protection provided by bilberry. Interestingly, the majority of the nests face south or east, perhaps to ensure warmth from the morning or midday sun. The females lay eggs from the middle of May onwards, and the young are born around the first week of June. The young are in the nest for around 13 days, though a well-fed brood may leave the nest as early as eight days if they are disturbed. There is a small resurgence in nesting activity from early to mid-July. Most of these late nests are replacements for earlier failures, though a few are second clutches, and the nesting season is effectively over by the end of July. Table 3 summarises some results from the study.

On the Blorenge there is a stable population and a good breeding success rate, but nationally the whinchat is becoming scarcer, with the population receding from its southern outposts. National surveys show that whinchat numbers in Britain more than halved between 1995 and 2008. The cause of this dramatic decline is unknown, although substantial recent rises in losses of eggs and chicks in the nest would seem to be a factor. It has been proved that sparrowhawks *Accipiter nisus* have a significant impact on the species, especially in those areas of ffridd close to conifer plantations, where the sparrowhawks nest (Smith & Laurence

TABLE 3. Whinchat breeding success on the Blorenge, 1998–2001.

Year	Pairs	Nests	Eggs	Young	Fledged	Success (%)
1998	35	28	163	151	135	83
1999	40	36	196	185	165	84
2000	40	30	151	148	122	81
2001	33	26	149	140	124	83
Average	37	30	165	156	137	83

Adapted from Smith (2001).

2002). This study involved searching old and new sparrowhawk nesting sites, and 15 rings involving six species were found, some in the nest itself, some in pellets and some buried in the leaf litter. Eleven of the rings had originally been fitted to whinchats in the study area.

In addition to the whinchat, many other African migrants are also showing acute declines, including species as diverse in their breeding habits as yellow wagtail *Motacilla flava*, wood warbler *Phylloscopus sibilatrix* and nightingale *Luscinia megarhynchos*, so it is reasonable to assume that the conditions on their wintering grounds, or on migration, are also contributing to the decline in breeding numbers. As a result of this reduction the whinchat has recently been moved from the green to the amber list, indicating that it is of conservation concern.

WARBLERS

On a routine expedition to find whinchat nests during the summer of 1998 Steve Smith discovered Dartford warblers *Sylvia undata* breeding in the area. This was the first record of the species for Wales, and family parties could be seen until December 1998. The following year a male bird held territory in the same locality, but nothing came of it after a heavy fall of snow during April. Apart from a record of a single bird spending the whole of November on the Blorenge, Dartford warblers were not recorded again until the spring of 2005 when one pair nested successfully. The following summer three pairs bred and Steve ringed some of the nestlings (Fig. 107). Sadly, following a number of cold winters, there have been no further sightings. In Britain as a whole, Dartford Warblers have suffered from severe winters, the population dropping to a few pairs in the 1960s, since when it has gradually recovered, increasing in both numbers and range.

In June 2011 a Marmora's warbler *Sylvia sarda*, a very rare vagrant to Britain, held territory on the Blorenge for around 10 days before disappearing; this was the first record for Wales. Named after the Italian naturalist Alberto della Marmora, the species breeds only on the islands and islets of the western Mediterranean, notably Corsica, Sardinia and the Balearic Islands. Wintering in north Africa, it is usually a relatively short-distance migrant, so it was an amazing bird to find in the Beacons. The warbler was highly visible, often sitting out in the open and singing. Over 1,000 people were lucky enough to see the bird, a first-summer male, but several local breeding species deserted their nests because of the disturbance. These small, long tailed, large-headed birds are very similar in appearance to Dartford warblers, but Marmora's warblers are grey above and below, lacking the brick-red underparts of the Dartford warbler.

FIG 107. Dartford warbler nestlings on the Blorenge in the summer of 1998. (Steve Smith)

Adult males also have darker patches on the forehead and between the eye and the pointed bill. Immature birds can be confused with young Dartford warblers, which are also grey below, but Marmora's have a paler throat.

REPTILES

The ffridd is also an ideal habitat for reptiles, common lizard *Lacerta vivipara* frequently occurring in these upland edge habitats. Adders *Vipera berus* are less common than might be expected, with most records from the Blorenge and areas to the south (Fig. 108). As noted elsewhere in Britain, a small percentage of adders on the Blorenge are melanistic, i.e. almost totally black. Often these black adders are mistaken for non-native species, but it is usually possible to see the darker diamond pattern, within the overall coloration, that is distinctive of adders. It has been suggested that melanistic snakes are better suited to colder climates than normally coloured individuals because of their higher thermoregulatory efficiency, but more prone to predation because they are easier to see. Studies have disproved this, however, and there seems to be no obvious difference in range or extent of predation between the two forms.

Although it is Britain's most widespread snake, the adder, like the whinchat, is in decline nationally – and this is also the case in the Beacons. As a result the Amphibian and Reptile Conservation Trust has set up a long-term national surveillance programme, collating data from many sites, to monitor trends in adder populations. Further research is urgently needed to understand what is

FIG 108. Male adder curled up on a tussock of common haircap moss on the Blorenge. (Chris Hatch)

happening. The best time to see adders is after their springtime emergence from winter hibernacula. At this time of year adders are at their most visible, lying out, sometimes in aggregations. Mating takes place in April or May, and female adders incubate their eggs internally, rather than laying shelled eggs like the grass snake *Natrix natrix*, giving birth to live young in August or September.

Although adders have a very wide range of habitats, they tend to prefer open grounds such as moorland and grassland, as prey is often abundant in these locations. Grass snakes, in contrast, are often found around ponds, lakes or slow-running rivers where frogs *Rana temporaria* and toads *Bufo bufo* live.

CHAPTER 6

Rivers and Waterfalls

THE BRECON BEACONS ARE THE SOURCE of more than 25 rivers and streams, including significant river systems such as the Usk, Tawe, Twrch, Nedd, Mellte, Hepste, Cynon, Taff, Rhymney and Ebbw, and the mountains are of strategic importance to South Wales as a water-supply catchment. The key role of the area in this respect has been recognised for centuries, the poet Michael Drayton (1563–1631) writing in his 'Poly-Olbion', a topographical poem describing England and Wales:

> *Brecknock, long time known a county of much worth,*
> *Unto this conflict brings her goodly fountains forth,*
> *For almost not a brook of Morgany or Gwent*
> *But from her fruitful womb do fetch their high descent*

Some of these rivers, including the Afon Hepste, Afon Mellte and Nedd Fechan, wind down deep tree-lined gorges over a series of dramatic and famous waterfalls (Fig. 109). Particularly attractive to visitors is the walk behind the curtain of water at Sgwd yr Eira near Ystradfellte. Other parts of the rivers are much less visited, but are still an important habitat and support an enormous range of wildlife. The watercourses form large linear ecosystems that act as migration routes and key breeding areas for many nationally and internationally important species. Although most are still relatively natural the original hydrology of some has been transformed, as described in Chapter 8, by the storage and release of water from reservoirs. Reservoirs change the upstream part of the river and prevent the free movement of fish and other species, while downstream river processes are altered since there is no longer a natural flood cycle.

FIG 109. The wooded course of the Afon Mellte near Craig y Ddinas, one of a number of short but important rivers within the catchment of the River Neath. It is renowned for the impressive waterfalls along its length. (Jonathan Mullard)

FLASHY RIVERS

Peak water flows from upland areas like the Brecon Beacons can be very intense, as a result of the generally impermeable nature of the rocks, the steep gradients and the often heavy rain, the average annual rainfall being 1,366 mm. Upland river flows can change very rapidly, with periods of severe flooding often following periods of very low water (Fig. 110). While the extensive bogs and mires, which cover large areas of the catchments, act as surface-water reservoirs, slowing the discharge into river systems and stabilising the flows, as indeed do the many artificial reservoirs in the area, these river systems are still 'flashy'. Sometimes the effects can be extreme, as recalled in a note by a local landowner, Cyril Powell, in the early 1960s:

> *A day in the History of the Hamlet of Glyntawe in the parish of Defynog in the year of our Lord 1907.*
>
> *It was a Sunday in the mid-summer of 1907, over 55 years ago. The morning started fine and very warm, but in the afternoon the black clouds started to gather portending a storm. The clouds banked up in thick, dark ominous layers over the Wern, Penwyllt and Fan Gyhirych and, as we subsequently learned, over most of*

FIG 110. The Afon Haffes, a tributary of the Afon Tawe near Glyntawe, is a typical high-energy watercourse with large boulders and rapidly changing flows. (Jonathan Mullard)

> *North Breconshire. Sometime in the afternoon the thunder started rolling and kept at it for some hours. The rain came down over Penwyllt in torrents mixed with hailstones, some as large as acorns. The same must have occurred over Waun Byfre and Fan Gyhirych and the Carmarthen Fans. All this naturally oozed down into the Upper Tawe Valley.*
>
> *Someone looking out of the windows of Craig y Nos Castle heard the sound of rushing waters and soon saw a red wall of water rolling down the [Tawe] river bed. He had the presence of mind to telephone down the valley to Abercrave and Ystradgynlais to warn them of what was coming. I understand that a lot of bathers were warned only just in time. The fields of Rhongyr Uchaf and the lower hills of the Gelli were soon flooded to a depth of 7 feet. The cows of Rhongyr Uchaf, which were grazing quietly on the field, were caught in the flood, panicked and made for home on the other side of the Tawe, thus wading right into the middle of the big flood, and were carried away one after the other down the valley, some as far as Abercrave.*

The high energy of the river systems, the mobile substrates and the wide fluctuations in temperature and flows in these upland rivers create demanding conditions for the associated flora and fauna. There is a limited number of truly aquatic plants that thrive in the larger tributary streams and main rivers, the most common of these being greater water-moss *Fontinalis antipyretica,* which is usually attached to stones, rocks or waterside trees. This is the largest aquatic moss found in Britain, with shoots 5–8 mm wide and plants often exceeding 15 cm in length. In their middle and upper reaches the rivers are rich in floating and submerged plants, including river water-crowfoot *Ranunculus fluitans* and water-milfoils *Myriophyllum* spp. River water-crowfoot is especially adapted to fast-flowing water and, unlike common water-crowfoot *Ranunculus aquatilis* it has no floating leaves. Instead, the leaves are found under the water and are split lengthways into long strands. This prevents the leaves from being damaged by strong currents, because the water can pass straight through. The crowfoot provides a valuable habitat for freshwater invertebrates such as shrimps, snails, insect larvae and nymphs. Britain has more than 20 per cent of the world population of this plant, the species needing a stony substrate with shallow, swift-flowing and clean oxygen-rich water (Fig. 111).

Many of these macroinvertebrate species exhibit a similar range of adaptions to the plants. Mayfly nymphs of the genera *Ecdyonurus* and *Heptagagenia* are dorsally or ventrally flattened, allowing them to crawl under rocks and boulders, where they are protected from fast-moving water.

FIG 111. The white flowers of river water-crowfoot in the emergent Afon Sychlwch below Llyn y Fan Fach (Jonathan Mullard)

Fish stocks are also relatively restricted, with brown trout *Salmo trutta*, Atlantic salmon *Salmo salar* and European eel *Anguilla anguilla* dominating. Other species that regularly occur include the three lamprey species, brook lamprey *Lampetra planeri*, river lamprey *L. fluviatilus* and sea lamprey *Petromyzon marinus*, along with bullhead *Cottus gobio*, minnow *Phoxinus phoxinus*, allis shad *Alosa alosa* and twaite shad *A. fallax*. The species that spawn in these upland watercourses all tend to lay small numbers of eggs and provide a high degree of care to them. Trout and salmon, for instance, deposit their eggs in carefully excavated nests or redds, while bullheads lay eggs in nest sites under stones, with the male guarding the nest until the fry have hatched. Similarly, lampreys work in pairs, sometimes having the assistance of a second female, to dig out a redd in the stony riverbed, usually about 1 m in diameter and 15 cm deep, where the eggs are deposited. This is in contrast to fish species that occupy lower-energy watercourses, which deposit large numbers of eggs with a reduced degree of care.

SINKS AND RESURGENCES

Most of the rivers behave 'normally', but once water reaches the Carboniferous Limestone things change, with water both entering and leaving caves and underground watercourses. The Afon Giedd is a prime example, since although there are two separate rivers of the same name occupying the same valley, they are not connected. The addition of dye to the rivers in 1970 revealed that the waters of the upper Giedd, which rises on the southern slopes of Fan Brycheiniog and flows southwest for about 3 km until it sinks into the Carboniferous Limestone outcrop at Sinc y Giedd, eventually re-emerges in the caves at Dan yr Ogof and does not contribute in any way to the lower Giedd (Fig. 112). This separate river rises further down the valley and flows for about 6 km to where it joins the Afon Tawe at Ystradgynlais in the Swansea Valley.

Similarly the Afon Llwchwr emerges fully formed as a powerful surge from the base of a limestone rock face at the dramatic resurgence known as Llygad Llwchwr – the 'eye of the Loughor' (Fig. 113). A notched weir constructed outside the resurgence once facilitated the extraction of water, but that sold by the Beacons Natural Water Company now comes from boreholes nearby. The force of water issuing from Llygad Llwchwr is tremendous, large quantities emerging from a 1.2 km-long cave system, the extent of which is not fully known, although surface water entering the ground at Sinc Ger y Ffordd (literally the 'sink by the road') beside the A4069 several kilometres to the east is known to make its way to this location.

FIG 112. Sinc y Giedd, where the Afon Giedd, the main source of the water emerging from Dan yr Ogof caves, sinks into the limestone. (Alan Bowring)

FIG 113. Llygad Llwchwr – the 'eye of the Loughor'. The notched weir constructed outside the resurgence once facilitated the extraction of water. (Harold Grenfell)

FIG 114. The swallow hole of Pwll y Felin in flood conditions (Alan Bowring)

Other dramatic resurgences include Pwll Du, or the 'black pool', beside the Nedd Fechan, which can be viewed by walking upriver along the footpath from the car park at Pont Melin Fach. In contrast, locations where watercourses disappear underground include the extraordinary swallow hole of Pwll y Felin beside the minor road between Penderyn and Ystradfellte (Fig. 114). In wet weather the stream delivers water into this large crater faster than the cave beneath can take it away, so it can fill to the brim.

THE USK

In the space available it is not possible to describe all the rivers and streams in the Brecon Beacons in detail, but the Usk is one of the largest rivers in Wales and since many of its features can be found on the other watercourses it serves as a good example of what can be found along their banks by the inquisitive naturalist. From its source in a large expanse of rough boggy ground situated on Mynydd Du to where it meets the Severn Estuary near Newport the main channel of the Usk is over 120 km long and drains a catchment of nearly 1400 km². The upper reaches of the river divide the area in two as it flows eastwards along the

FIG 115. The aqueduct near Glanusk farm that takes the Monmouthshire and Brecon canal over the Usk, the canal following a parallel course to the river. (Jonathan Mullard)

northern scarp of the Brecon Beacons before turning south towards Abergavenny. The headwaters of the Usk and some of its 13 tributaries are regulated by flows out of reservoirs, notably the Usk, Cray, Talybont and Grwyne Fawr dams. Some of the river's flow is diverted at Brecon to feed the Monmouthshire and Brecon Canal, which follows a parallel route until it reaches Abergavenny (Fig. 115). Water is also abstracted from the river and nearby boreholes for the public water supply and returned as treated sewage, a reduction in the flow occurring between the abstraction point and the return discharge. In general, however, water quality is excellent and the main river exceeds the requirement for both drinking water and salmon and sea trout.

Once past the dams, the Usk is an almost entirely natural river, since it has not suffered engineering works, such as flood-bank construction and channel straightening, which have impoverished habitats in other British rivers. Below Trecastle there are rapids and waterfalls and, in places, the river has cut down to the bedrock, forming a deep channel between marginal rock shelves. Near Brecon the valley broadens out and the river begins to meander across a flood plain, creating gravel shoals and earth cliffs with localised areas of braided channels, backwaters and oxbows. Further downstream at Llangynidr it has cut south through the Black Mountains scarp, exploiting a major fault line, to form a steep-sided gorge. The channel here is characterised by boulders, exposed rock platforms and deep channels and pools. Finally, between Crickhowell and Abergavenny, the Usk meanders across a flood plain, creating gravel shoals, earth cliffs, backwaters and oxbows.

VEGETATION

The headwaters of the Usk and the other rivers contain fairly acidic water, which supports a number of characteristic upland species, including bulbous rush, alternate water-milfoil *Myriophyllum alternifolium*, floating sweet-grass *Glyceria fluitans* and a number of filamentous algae. Marginal plants include marsh marigold *Caltha palustris*, meadowsweet, lesser spearwort *Ranunculus flammula*, rushes *Juncus* spp. and a range of characteristic mosses and liverworts, such as yellow fringe-moss *Racomitrium aciculare*, claw brook-moss *Hygrohypnum ochraceum*, long-beaked water feather-moss *Rhynchostegium riparioides*, overleaf pellia *Pellia epiphylla* and water earwort *Scapania undulata*. Further down the channel the water becomes less acidic and is largely shaded by alder and rusty willow *Salix cinerea* ssp. *oleifolia*. Species found on the banks include lady-fern, remote sedge *Carex remota*, brook-side feather-moss *Amblystegium fluviatile* and fox-tail feather-moss *Thamnobryum alopecurum*. Aquatic species are scarce here, but alternate water-milfoil and the red alga *Hildenbrandia rivularis* occur occasionally.

As the river becomes wider the channel is less shaded and aquatic species become more frequent. Riverside rocks and boulders here are covered by a rich flora of mosses such as smaller lattice-moss *Cinclidotus fontinaloides*, fox-tail feather-moss and St Winifrid's moss *Chiloscyphus polyanthus*, together with liverworts such as great scented liverwort *Conocephalum conicum* and star-headed liverwort *Marchantia polymorpha* ssp. *polymorpha*, the filamentous red alga *Lemanea fluviatilis*, which is actually blue-green to olive in colour, and lichens of the genera *Verrucaria*. Until recently, most British naturalists would have regarded great scented liverwort as one of the most straightforward liverworts to identify, as it is large and conspicuous. Recent research though has shown that there are in fact two species of the liverwort in Europe, both of which occur in Britain (Szweykowski et al. 2005). These are the typical *C. conicum* and a second plant which has been described as a new species *C. salebrosum*. Whether the 'new' species occurs along the Usk has not yet been determined. The nationally scarce river pocket-moss *Fissidens rivularis* and beck pocket-moss *F. rufulus* have been frequently reported on rocks, which are rarely exposed above water level, from these reaches.

Marginal vegetation along the river is dominated variously by reed canary-grass *Phalaris arundinacea*, branched bur-reed *Sparganium erectum*, common spike-rush *Eleocharis palustris* and lesser pond-sedge *Carex acutiformis* with a variety of other species including brooklime *Veronica beccabunga*, water forget-me-not *Myosotis scorpioides*, water mint *Mentha aquatica*, hemlock water-dropwort *Oenanthe crocata* and yellow cress *Rorippa* spp. Blunt feather-moss *Homalia tricholmanoides*, tufted feather-moss *Scleropodium cespitans*, endive pellia *Pellia endiviifolia* and crescent-cup liverwort *Lunularia cruciata* also occur in this section of the river. Characteristic riverbank plants include common knapweed *Centaurea nigra*, meadowsweet and comfrey *Symphytum* spp., stinging nettle and great willowherb *Epilobium hirsutum*. Trees are also abundant, and the riverbanks are frequently lined with willows and alder. In addition, there are larger areas of woodland adjacent to the river dominated by these species, or by sycamore *Acer pseudoplatanus*, pedunculate oak and ash. The immediate edge of the river is kept free of dense woody growth, however, by regular flooding.

Steep slopes or rock outcrops adjacent to the river support a range of interesting plants including two nationally scarce hawkweeds, Stenström's hawkweed *Hieracium stenstroemii* and long-bracted hawkweed *H. cinderella*, which occur around Llangynidr. The nationally scarce bramble *Rubus iscanus*, named after the Isca (Usk), is found at the confluence with the Afon Crawnon. Also located in this area is the rare endemic Brecon dandelion, which is known only from limestone cliffs, walls and the banks of lanes in the area. Another uncommon dandelion, Degelius's dandelion *Taraxacum degelii*, occurs on rocks upstream around Fenni Fach. This is more widely distributed than Brecon dandelion, occurring in Mid Wales, by the sea in North Wales and at other locations across Britain. Dandelions are taxonomically complex, with some botanists dividing the group into about 34 macrospecies and about 2,000 microspecies, approximately 235 of the latter being recorded in Britain and Ireland. This can lead to confusion about exactly how many species there are in a particular area. *Taraxacum vachellii* (named after Eleanor Vachell, 1879–1948, an outstanding amateur botanist from Cardiff) was, for instance, thought to occur alongside Brecon dandelion near the Crawnon but is now a *nomen confusum*, i.e. a confused name, and is no longer accepted as a species.

OXBOWS

Meandering in a wide flood plain near Pencelli, the Usk has produced a range of habitats of interest for their wildlife. There are old river channels, shingle banks in various stages of colonisation, eroding earth banks, pools and riffles, which are reconnected to the main river during flooding (Fig. 116). The highly active, mobile nature of the main channel, in addition to frequent, severe flooding with deep and fast flows, is a significant factor in determining the species that can survive here. Old channels contain both marsh and open water, supporting a number of plant communities, dominated variously by floating sweet-grass, amphibious bistort *Persicaria amphibia*, broad-leaved pondweed *Potamogeton natans* and Canadian waterweed *Flodea canadensis*. A wide variety of aquatic and emergent species are present in these areas including local rarities such as greater spearwort *Ranunculus lingua*, pink water-speedwell *Veronica catenata*, lesser marshwort *Apium inundatum* and wood club-rush *Scirpus sylvaticus*.

There are also extensive deposits of shingle and silt banks, some of which are sparsely vegetated with species such as water-pepper *Persicaria hydropiper*, redshank *P. maculosa* and silverweed *Potentilla anserina*. More stable areas support communities dominated by stinging nettle, creeping thistle and other tall herbs such as mugwort and hemlock. Thickets of willow scrub have developed locally along backwaters and on islands. At Pencelli these thickets are dominated by a particularly diverse range of willows, including crack willow *Salix fragilis*, osier *S. viminalis* and the locally scarce almond willow *S. triandra*, the last of these

FIG 116. Old river channels on the Usk near Pencelli viewed from the slopes of Allt yr Esgair, with the snow-covered slopes of Pen y Fan in the distance. The oxbows, pools and riffles provide a range of habitats for wildlife. (Jonathan Mullard)

represented by the largest stand of the species known in the area. The ground beneath the willows is dominated by stinging nettle and other tall herbs, such as bittersweet *Solanum dulcamara* and cleavers.

Adjacent areas of seasonally flooded grassland are characterised by creeping bent *Agrostis stolonifera* and marsh foxtail *Alopecurus geniculatus*, which provide important feeding areas for migrating wildfowl and waders, including wigeon *Anas penelope*, curlew, lapwing, jack snipe *Lymnocryptes minimus* and green sandpiper *Tringa ochropus*.

INVASIVE PLANTS

The catchments of the Usk and the other rivers in the Beacons are under threat, however, from at least three species of invading plants: giant hogweed *Heracleum mantegazzianum*, Japanese knotweed *Fallopia japonica* and Himalayan balsam *Impatiens glandulifera*. These species are aggressive colonisers that represent a significant threat to any river system, but these problems are more severe on a river such as the Usk, which is of high conservation value. The plants are shade-tolerant, have dense vegetation and form a canopy well above the height of the native flora. Areas where the species are allowed to colonise rapidly lose their original diversity, as nothing can out-compete them or survive in the environment underneath.

The Usk has the dubious distinction of having the worst infestation of giant hogweed of any Welsh river, and the situation is being tackled by the River Usk Giant Hogweed Partnership, a consortium set up by a number of organisations, as the task is too large for one body alone. Principal partners include the National Park Authority, the Countryside Council for Wales, Keep Wales Tidy, Monmouthshire County Council, the National Trust and Newport City Council. The area most badly affected by hogweed is the stretch in the Beacons between Glanusk Park and Abergavenny (Fig. 117). The plant is a native of the Caucasus Mountains between Russia and Turkey and was originally introduced in Britain as an ornamental in the late nineteenth century. Giant hogweed is a perennial and can grow up to 5 m tall with leaves reaching 1 m across. Each plant can produce more than 50,000 seeds every year, and those seeds can remain viable for 15 years. The control programme aims to stop the seed production at the upper extent of the infestation, preventing the seeds entering the Usk and spreading the problem further downstream.

The spread of Japanese knotweed also results in habitat loss and shading of the river course. The success of this species is due to its tolerance of a very wide range of soil types. Its rhizomes can survive temperatures of $-35\,°C$ and can extend 7 m horizontally and 3 m deep, making removal by excavation extremely difficult. The plant is also very resilient to cutting, vigorously re-sprouting from the roots. The most effective method of control is by herbicide application during the flowering stage in late summer or autumn.

Himalayan balsam (Fig. 118) is reputed to be the tallest annual plant found in Britain, growing up to 3 m tall. A native of the western Himalayas, it was introduced in 1839 and is now recorded throughout the country. It grows rapidly,

ABOVE: **FIG 117.** Giant hogweed on the banks of the Usk in Castle Meadows, Abergavenny. The plant is about to come into flower. (Graham Motley)

FIG 118. Himalayan balsam on the Usk near Christ College, Brecon. (Jonathan Mullard)

spreads easily, out-competes other vegetation and readily colonises new areas. Himalayan balsam is also relatively shade-tolerant. When the plants die down in winter they leave large bare areas that are sensitive to erosion. The seedpods are dehiscent and explode when touched or shaken, expelling the seeds up to 7 m from the parent plant. The seed is transported by water but can also be carried in mud by animals and people. In contrast to Japanese knotweed, however, the Himalayan balsam is shallow-rooted and is easily removed. It is therefore controlled by grazing or by cutting or pulling before it sets seed.

SHINGLE INVERTEBRATES

Shingle banks on the Usk are also invaded by Himalayan balsam, and this is having a damaging effect on the species present in this habitat. There are many sparsely vegetated shingle and sand banks and gravel islands downstream of Brecon, which are only covered when the river is in flood (Fig. 119). Some of the best stretches of shingle are between Pencelli and Talybont-on-Usk. Although these areas may appear to be just lifeless sand and gravel, this apparently barren habitat supports a unique group of invertebrates (Drake *et al.* 2010).

The shingle banks are especially important for a number of predatory beetles, known unsurprisingly as river shingle beetles. Six species in particular are more or less exclusively associated with these exposed areas and have a restricted, patchy and generally western distribution in Britain. Most species also appear to have suffered declines in populations during the twentieth century. It is an unstable habitat, with the shingle either dry or inundated by rapidly rising water levels, and the beetles feed on carrion, material washed down the river and larvae emerging from the water.

Species known from the Usk include *Bembidion testaceum*, a predatory ground beetle with a dark head with a greenish reflection, and reddish-brown wing cases. Although this species is easily confused with other related *Bembidion* species, and old records may not be reliable, it is clear that it once had a wide, yet scattered distribution in England and Wales, reaching up into southern Scotland. *B. testaceum* is now known only from four areas, two in northern England, one in South Wales on the Usk and the fourth on the Welsh Borders. It appears to be tied to catchments with hard rock geology that erodes to produce coarse sandy sediments. The beetle undergoes larval development and pupation through summer, emerging in late summer to find sites for overwintering as a first-year adult. It is one the most enigmatic and poorly researched beetle species associated with these exposed riverine sediments. It is a very difficult species

FIG 119. A partially vegetated area of shingle on the Usk near Abergavenny, covered with soapwort *Saponaria officinalis*. (Graham Motley)

to find in the field, as it occurs in very low numbers, requiring a lot of searching, and even when found it readily flies off if disturbed, being one of the most active of the *Bembidion* beetles. Additionally, it is very difficult to identify in the field as the only reliable characteristics differentiating it from other species of its genus require higher levels of magnification and better lighting conditions than those available when using a hand lens.

Another river shingle beetle, *Lionychus quadrillum*, easily recognised by the yellow spots on the black wing cases, was long considered to be a very localised and largely coastal species. The species has suffered losses of many of its former coastal populations, mostly through loss of suitable habitat due to the construction of coastal defences and agricultural intensification. In recent years though the species has also been shown to be well established inland in association with shingle and sand banks at a number of sites on a number of Welsh rivers, including the Usk. Other ground beetles found on shingle banks in the area include *Meotica anglica*, a tiny and probably much overlooked species which appears to be largely subterranean and is rarely seen on the surface of the substrates that it inhabits.

While beetles have been studied in exposed riverine sediments for around 20 years, there is still much to learn about their ecology. The Countryside Council for Wales, English Nature and the Environment Agency have therefore recently funded a number of further studies in order to improve our understanding of these species and their conservation needs. Paul Sinnadurai, Senior Ecologist with the National Park Authority, is undertaking a PhD on the ecology of the beetles on the exposed shingle and sand bars of the Usk, and this should add to our knowledge of these areas.

While beetles continue to receive attention, naturalists are now also starting to study the flies that occur in this specialised habitat. Three flies are particularly dependent on such areas: the southern silver stiletto-fly *Cliorismia rustica*, northern silver stiletto-fly *Spiriverpa lunulata* and the cranefly *Rhabdomastix laeta*. All three species have been recorded from the Brecon Beacons. There are particularly strong colonies of southern silver stiletto on the Usk, but compared to the northern silver stiletto, the males of which perform aerial 'leks' where several individuals dance together, their silver bodies glinting in the sunlight, the adults of the southern species are secretive and hard to find (Drake *et al.* 2010). The larvae of these flies on the other hand, are relatively easy to find, because stiletto-fly larvae are very different from the larvae of other flies, being smooth, shiny and dry-skinned. They are active predators, 'swimming' through loose dry sand in search of prey, which they subdue with venom within seconds.

The geology of the river has a large impact on the fauna present. Some of the best rivers for both beetles and flies, like the Usk, have sand within the sediments, derived from eroding uplands or from sandy terrain – but sand alone is not sufficient, since many sandy lowland rivers lack the diversity of species found in upland rivers.

As well as beetles and flies, larger areas of shingle also support species such as the scarce wolf spider *Arctosa cinerea* (Fig. 120). This is probably under-

FIG 120. The wolf spider *Arctosa cinerea* is found in areas of shingle on the Usk. (Fritz Geller-Grimm)

recorded because of its specialised habitat and the need to turn over many rocks before finding a specimen, but it seems to be locally abundant on certain sections of the Usk.

PEARL MUSSELS

Around 200 years ago the river bed in the Usk and other Welsh rivers would have been covered in places with freshwater pearl mussels *Margaritifera margaritifera*. Freshwater pearl mussels have been recorded in Wales for more than 400 years and some rivers, such as the Conwy, supported substantial populations with hundreds of thousands of mussels and were historically famous pearl fisheries. William Camden (1551–1623) recorded that pearls traded in Britain and Ireland were to be found in the large black mussel which were peculiar to the rapid and stony rivers of Wales, northern England, Scotland and some parts of Ireland, recording that 'Those who fish for pearls, know partly by the outside of the mussels whether they contain any, for such as have them are a little contracted or distorted from their usual shape.'

Between 1926 and 1936 a group of Scottish pearl fishers paid annual visits to Wales during July and August, when the water was low and fishing was relatively easy. The group travelled widely in England and Wales and covered the rivers in rotation, retaining the services of an advocate to challenge any cases against them in the courts to prevent them fishing, but the outcome of the action was often immaterial. By the time judgment was given, sufficient time had elapsed to allow them to 'clean up' the river in question (Jones 1973). Few mussels remain today, and it is estimated that there has been a 90 per cent decline in Welsh populations in the last 100 years. Although pearl fishing is now illegal, the level of the populations at most, if not all, of the sites still reflect the impact of this historic activity. Furthermore, there is recent evidence to suggest that pearl fishing is still occurring at a low level in practically every British and Irish river (Young *et al.* 2000). This illegal activity will have a serious effect on the small remaining populations.

Pearl mussels were reported from the Usk in 1921 by the pearl fisherman Alfred Yates, but there were no further records until 1992 when Graham Oliver from the National Museum of Wales found six live adult mussels downstream of Brecon, in the riffle water below the bridge at Llansantffraed (Fig. 121). These were unfortunately removed and added to the museum's collections. In 1997 the National Museum resurveyed all Welsh rivers for the Countryside Council for Wales but could not find any more mussels in the Usk. To all intents and purposes the Usk population is now extinct. A single dead shell was, however, found low down in the Usk in 2012, suggesting that some adults survive somewhere in the river. The few mussels that have been found are old, with no evidence of juveniles, so if there are any mussels left in the river they are not breeding and hence slowly and inevitably dying out. This sadly mirrors the situation in most Welsh rivers. They are still found in the Dee and the Wye and in nine other rivers but are believed to have already become extinct in the Ogwen, Taf and Gwyrfai – although, as with the Usk, there may be isolated individuals still surviving on these watercourses.

The freshwater pearl mussel is one of the longest-lived invertebrates known, and individuals living in colder northern rivers can be up to 120 years old. They live buried, or partly buried, in coarse sand and fine gravel in clean, fast-flowing rivers and streams, drawing in water through their exposed siphons to filter out the minute organic particles on which they feed. In locations where the species was formerly abundant, it is possible that this filtration helped to clean the water (Zuiganov *et al.* 1994).

Mussels grow up to 140 mm in length, burrowing into sandy substrates, often between boulders and pebbles. The larval, or glochidial, stage is spent attached to the gills of salmonid fishes, thereby allowing the species to move upstream. Each female ejects between one and four million glochidia in a sudden, highly synchronised event, usually over one to two days. Almost all the glochidia die, but a few are inhaled by juvenile salmon or trout. At this stage they resemble tiny mussels, but their shells are held apart until they encounter a suitable host, when they snap shut onto the host's gill filaments. Larvae attach themselves during mid to late summer, and the following spring they drop off the fish and settle in the riverbed gravel. They then spend between five and seven years living within the gravel before emerging as filter-feeding mussels.

The reliance on other species to complete its life cycle make the freshwater pearl mussel particularly vulnerable to adverse conditions. Declines have been caused by historic pearl fishing, acidification, siltation and declining salmonid stocks. A number of organisations, however, are now working together to tackle pollution in the rivers and moving mussels to hatcheries to create breeding stocks. Eventually it is hoped that new populations can be created in the rivers.

FISH

For centuries the Usk has been regarded as one of the finest salmon-fishing rivers in Britain – as shown by the three salmon portrayed on the historic coat of arms of the town of Usk. In fact it has a higher deposition of salmon eggs than any other

RIVERS AND WATERFALLS · 171

ABOVE: **FIG 121.** A shell of one of the six freshwater pearl mussels collected by the National Museum of Wales in 1992. Old mussels such as this are typically eroded, since they live in acidic water that dissolves the shell. The specimen was probably well over 50 years old but could have been as much as 80 or 90. (James Turner/National Museum of Wales)

LEFT: **FIG 122.** Fishermen with a very large salmon caught in the Usk at Brecon on 20 October 1917. (Brecknock Museum)

river south of Cumbria and has recently been rated as the best fly-fishing water in Wales for salmon and one of the top ten salmon rivers in Britain, the catch in 2004, 2007 and 2008 exceeding 1,000 fish. Populations are still at a low level, however, compared with catches from the late 1960s, when over 2,000 fish were regularly caught in a single season, and are a fraction of the great catches of the late 1800s. Over 3,500 fish were caught, for example, in 1879, and even in 1917 some very large fish were being caught in the Usk at Brecon (Fig. 122).

The decline was caused by a range of problems including barriers to fish migration, pollution, acidification and habitat degradation. In the Usk catchment, the most significant sources of diffuse pollution and siltation are from agriculture, including fertiliser runoff, livestock manure, silage effluent and soil erosion from ploughed land. Water abstracted from the river for the Brecon canal can also reduce the depth of the river downstream of the off-take weir. The subsequent reduction in the salmon population caused by these factors meant that fishing also contributed to the problem. Rainfall and river flow are critical in determining how far fish will travel, with high water suiting the Abergavenny to Brecon area while lower flows confine consistent sport to the river below Abergavenny. In wet years, for example, large numbers of fish can be found upstream of Brecon, but in most years the best of the salmon fishing is to be found from Crickhowell downstream. There is now though a strong catch-and-release culture on the Usk, promoted by the fishery owners and the Wye and Usk Foundation, which works to improve and protect the habitats and fish stocks of the two rivers.

The Usk's fame as a trout fishery can be ascribed largely to the abundance and diversity of fly life on the river. The so-called upwinged flies found on the river include mayflies such as the large dark olive *Baetis rhodani*, small dark olive *B. scambus*, medium olive *B. vernus*, southern iron blue *B. niger*, March brown *Rithrogena germanica*, olive upright *R. semicolorata*, blue-winged olive *Serratella ignita*, yellow may dun *Heptagenia sulphurea*, large brook dun *Ecdyonurus torrentis* and autumn dun *E. dispar*. Large yellow sally stoneflies *Chloroperla torrentium* hatch in good numbers in summer, and the trout sometimes rise steadily to take them even in the midday sun, while evenings bring good hatches of caddisflies, or sedge flies.

These riverflies are a vital link in the aquatic food chain, providing food for a range of birds as well as fish. Over the last few decades, however, there has been a widespread decline in the numbers of riverflies in British rivers. As well as the effects of light pollution, mentioned in Chapter 1, they are also affected by artificially high nutrient levels and diffuse pollution from farmland. Excess nutrients also produce algal growths, which overwhelm vegetation and reduce water oxygen levels. The southern iron blue, for example, is a widespread species but its populations have declined by as much as 80 per cent in recent decades due to the pressures on its habitat. The larvae are found mainly in aquatic vegetation and are narrow-bodied with a black band across their tail and six pairs of plate-like gills, whereas the adult fly is small, with two tails and small oval hindwings (Fig. 123). The Riverfly Partnership is working to conserve rare and threatened riverfly species, such as the southern iron blue, and their habitats.

FIG 123. The southern iron blue is one of the many upwinged mayflies found along the river. Numbers have declined markedly across Britain but it remains abundant on certain stretches of the Usk. (Stuart Crofts/Buglife)

Other important migratory species found in the river, such as the river lamprey, twaite shad and allis shad – which, like the salmon, swim upriver to spawn and go through their juvenile stages in the river – are also present in numbers that reflect a healthy and sustainable population supported by good-quality habitats. Allis shad is thought to be rare, with no recent records in the Usk, but twaite shad is relatively common. The Usk is one of only four sites in the UK where a known breeding population of twaite shad occurs (the Rivers Wye and Tywi are the other Welsh sites). As the main channel is largely unmodified and a variety of aquatic habitats are present, including good-quality spawning gravels and deep pools used for cover by adults and fry, there are ideal conditions for this species. Twaite shad are recorded only infrequently above Crickhowell Bridge, however, as they are held back by the barrier created by the footings of the bridge (Fig. 124). The structure is considered to be the most significant barrier to fish migration in the catchment, and the reduction or removal of the effect of this barrier is a high priority.

Shad are members of the herring family, and it is difficult to distinguish twaite shad from allis shad, since both fish have streamlined bodies covered with distinct, large, circular scales with a toothed edge on the lower margin, and an adipose membrane which partially covers each eye. Twaite shad are usually smaller than allis shad, which measure 30–50 cm, but the only reliable way of separating the two species is to examine the gills: twaite shad have only 40–60 gill-rakers (comb-like structures that are used to filter zooplankton) on the first gill arch, whereas allis shad have 90–130.

Twaite shad return from the sea to spawn in the Usk in spring, usually between April and June (Fig. 125). Adults spawn at night with a great deal of noisy

FIG 124. Crickhowell Bridge was built over the river Usk in 1706 and remains one of the finest bridges in the area, but the footings and the step downstream of the bridge are considered to be a significant barrier to fish migration. (Jonathan Mullard)

FIG 125. Twaite shad spend most of their lives in the sea, but return to fresh water to breed. Their annual return to the Usk, usually between April and May, gives their alternative name of 'May fish'. (Alan Parfit)

splashing, in a shallow area near deeper pools, in which the fish congregate. The same spawning sites tend to be used year after year. The eggs are released into the water column, sinking into the small spaces between coarse gravel or cobbles. The majority of adults die after spawning, though British populations appear to have an unusually high proportion of repeat spawners, up to 25 per cent. After hatching, the fry develop and slowly drift downstream. Breeding success seems to be highest in warm years; high water flows between May and August may result in fry being washed prematurely out to sea.

Relatively little information is available on the freshwater habitat requirements of allis shad. It lives in coastal waters and estuaries but migrates into rivers to spawn. Like twaite shad, allis shad do not readily traverse obstacles to migration such as dams or weirs, and this has been a major cause of their decline. Unlike twaite shad, almost all adults die after spawning.

The most widely distributed species in the Usk include chub *Leuciscus cephalus*, roach *Rutilus rutilus* and dace *Leuciscus leuciscus*, which, together with the bullhead, are the most widely distributed fish along the river. Large numbers of eels also migrate up the river with spring tides. In addition, the Usk supports an exceptionally healthy population of river lamprey. This is a migratory species, which grows to maturity in estuaries around Britain and moves in winter into fresh water to spawn in rivers and streams. The larvae spend several years in silt beds before metamorphosing and migrating downstream to estuaries and the sea. Spawning in British rivers starts when the water temperature reaches 10–11 °C, usually in March and April, in areas of small stones and gravel in flowing water. The nest, which may be constructed by up to a dozen or more adults, is an oval depression 30–70 cm across and 2–10 cm deep. Spawning of each female may take place over several days, and the whitish eggs immediately adhere to sand particles when they are laid and mostly become embedded in the nest substrate. There is a high mortality at this time from various fish, birds and mammals, and all lampreys die after spawning.

After hatching, the lamprey larvae immediately start to drift downstream and burrow in suitable silt beds. The main food of the larvae is fine particulate matter, predominantly microorganisms. After metamorphosis, in July or September, at 3–5 years of age, the young adults move during the night to estuaries. River lamprey juveniles are often found in association with juveniles of the other two species and have been recorded throughout the Usk, but Brecon weir was a major restriction to their migration route until the construction in 2002 of a fish pass. Some reaches of the Usk are more suitable for some species than others: for example, the Senni has important populations of brook and river lampreys and salmon, but is not used by shad due to its small size and distance from the estuary.

CRAYFISH

The distribution of the native white-clawed crayfish *Austropotamobius pallipes* in Britain is largely determined by geology and water quality, the species occurring in areas with relatively hard, mineral-rich waters over calcareous and rapidly

FIG 126. An adult male white-clawed crayfish. (Oliver Brown, Environment Agency Wales)

weathering rocks (Fig. 126). The watercourses in the Beacons are therefore an ideal habitat for them, but the species is disappearing rapidly, due to a fungal disease *Aphanomyces astaci*, to which it is highly susceptible. The fungus is spread by the invasive signal crayfish *Pacifastacus leniusculus*, a North American species first introduced to Europe for aquaculture during the 1960s. The story, although less publicised, is similar to the impact of grey squirrels *Sciurus carolinensis* on red squirrels *S. vulgaris* through the parapox virus. The signal crayfish is highly invasive, digging extensive burrows into soft riverbanks and causing bank erosion with subsequent silting. Since the white-clawed crayfish requires well-oxygenated clear water, this alteration of the habitat, combined with disease, pollution and habitat loss, has had a considerable impact on the distribution of the native species. It is now only found regularly in two streams in the area, one a tributary of the Usk and the other a tributary of the Wye. It may also be present in Llwyn-on Reservoir, since a recently moulted individual was found in 2001 in the Taf Fawr, which feeds the reservoir and the smaller Cantref Reservoir higher up the watercourse.

Crayfish are the largest, most mobile freshwater invertebrates and have a critical role in freshwater communities, since as a 'keystone species' they determine the type and number of other species present. White-clawed crayfish are largely nocturnal, although they can occasionally be seen on warm summer evenings, foraging in the shallows as dusk approaches. They are omnivorous, consuming blanketweed *Cladophora* spp., willow moss *Fontinalis* spp. or vascular plants such as river water-crowfoot and water-cress *Nasturtium officinale*, alongside insect larvae, snails and small fish. The crayfish themselves are eaten by a large number of predators including fish such as perch *Perca fluviatilis*, chub, trout, pike and eel, and, particularly when water levels are low, by mammals such as brown rats *Rattus norvegicus* and otters, and birds including grey herons *Ardea cinerea* and crows *Corvus* spp. Water voles also prey on crayfish and may be attracted to the bait in traps used for recording work, where they will drown if trapped under water.

In the autumn the female attaches the egg cluster (around 100) to the underside of her abdomen (Fig. 127) and overwinters in a burrow with her brood until late spring or early summer when they hatch into miniature crayfish, but without their tail-fans. At this stage they are immobile and so continue to cling to the female's abdomen, until they moult into a second stage – when they develop a hairy tail-fan enabling them to become mobile and active. After a second moult they develop an outspread tail-fan and have the appearance of mature crayfish. Juvenile crayfish may undergo seven or more moults during their first year, but upon reaching maturity after 3–4 years they only moult once a year. Adults may grow to a length of 12 cm and reach a wet weight of 90 g, although they are often much smaller.

FIG 127. A 'berried' female white-clawed crayfish, collected for brood stock from a tributary of the Rhymney. Females overwinter with their eggs glued to the underside of the abdomen. (Oliver Brown, Environment Agency Wales)

Signal crayfish have also been shown to have negative effects on other native freshwater fauna and flora. A recent study of signal crayfish in Scottish rivers recorded as much as a 40 per cent decline in invertebrate density and significant impacts on community structure (Crawford *et al.* 2006). They also have impacts on larger vertebrate species by direct predation, for example the consumption of amphibian eggs, and through competition for food and refuges, particularly with the juvenile stages of overwintering salmon (Griffiths *et al.* 2004) and bullheads (Guan & Wiles 1997). The Environment Agency has carried out research into potential methods of controlling the signal crayfish, and is currently investigating the use of pheromones to lure it into traps. It has been shown that there is an inverse correlation between the number of signal crayfish and the number of fish species, including bullhead, that live on or near the beds of rivers. Signal crayfish affect bullheads through competition for shelter and food, in addition to predation of bullhead eggs and adults by larger individuals.

BIRDS

Bullheads are caught by a number of birds, particularly grey heron and kingfisher *Alcedo atthis*, as well as dipper *Cinclus cinclus*, which take a relatively high proportion of bullhead in Welsh streams (Ormerod & Tyler 1991) – though they have nowhere near the impact on bullheads that signal crayfish have. The kingfisher and dipper are the two classic birds of the rivers and streams in the Beacons, the dipper preferring fast-moving rocky stretches of water, while the kingfisher occupies areas of slow-moving water with overhanging willow. The dipper is an important species, as its presence as a breeding species is a good indicator of the health of the river systems. Its invertebrate prey is very sensitive to changes in water quality, especially acidity which is the main cause of poor water quality. There is little information about dippers on the Usk, but a survey in 1993 identified ten dipper territories on the Mellte, eleven on the Nedd Fechan, three on the Hepste, and one on the Pyrddin. Dippers are particularly well adapted to their environment, the bird's plumage being dense and water-repellent, allowing them to dive and select prey from the river bed (Fig. 128). Their blood also carries more oxygen than other birds of their size, allowing them to stay under the water longer. Even their call is pitched so that it can be heard above the noise of the river.

The watercourses of the Black Mountains also hold good populations of dippers, and those on the Grwyne Fawr and its major tributary the Grwyne Fechan have been monitored by Jerry Lewis, a local birdwatcher, since the late 1970s. During that time, the number of pairs on the two rivers has fluctuated

FIG 128. The fast-flowing watercourses in the Brecon Beacons are an ideal habitat for dippers, which feed on small bottom-feeding fish such as bullheads and insects including caddisfly and mayfly larvae. (Peter Beasley)

between 17 and 39 but the long-term trend has been downward. Although there have been slight reductions in the average clutch and brood sizes during the period, these have not been sufficient to account for the long-term decline, the reasons for which are not fully understood. The river flow seems to have changed, however, partly as a result of changing rainfall patterns, but mainly through the speed with which the falling rain becomes a flash flood. New roads constructed through the forests have changed drainage patterns and reduced the capacity of the ground to hold the water, so that within just a few hours of the rain falling, the rivers are in flood. In addition, the water sometimes contains a lot of sediment, particularly when forest operations on the hillside have disturbed the ground. The overall effect is to make dipper survival, especially of newly independent young birds, that much more difficult. Conversely, in the dry periods the river flow is considerably reduced. As dippers feed almost exclusively on aquatic invertebrates, it is the surface area of water at times of low flow that ultimately determines the number of territories. Low flows mean less surface area, fewer aquatic invertebrates and ultimately fewer dipper territories.

The Usk, together with the other rivers and streams in the Brecon Beacons, supports a range of breeding birds that are associated with watercourses, including grey wagtail *Motacilla cinerea* and sand martin *Riparia riparia*. Birds that nest on the shingle banks along the watercourse include little ringed plover *Charadrius dubius*. Particularly important areas for little ringed plover include the stretch of river between Brecon and Talybont and the River Wye below Glasbury. Although these birds are quite resistant to disturbance, utilising active gravel pits and sewage farms as well, it is important to avoid the areas of shingle where they nest between March and July. The eggs and young birds are so well camouflaged that they could easily be trodden on. Little ringed plover are also protected under the Wildlife and Countryside Act 1981, and disturbance would be an offence.

FIG 129. The Usk and the Wye are the most important rivers in Wales for the kingfisher. The black lower mandible on this bird indicates that it is a male. (Steve Wilce)

Most sand martins breed in a hole excavated in a near-vertical earth or sand bank, so colonies are scarce between Crickhowell and Talybont and above Brecon, where the riverbanks are mainly rocky and often heavily wooded. They are found instead in areas where the river has broadened out and is surrounded by flat meadows. Here the water flows much more slowly and steep banks or river cliffs build up as a result of meandering and general erosion. Bank erosion may also be accelerated by cattle feeding and trampling along the edges of the banks. The erosion and eventual collapse of banks containing whole colonies of sand martins is a fairly common occurrence on the Usk, and the subsequent movement of colonies from one year to the next is a major factor influencing the distribution of sand martins on the river. Colonies are also susceptible to predation by badgers *Meles meles* if there is a dry access route beneath the nest holes. The sand martin overwinters in the Sahel, on the southern side of the Sahara desert, and is one of the earliest migrant species to appear in spring. Autumn roosts are a regular feature of the return trip; the well-known roost at Llangorse Lake generally holds between 500 and 3,000 birds a year, with an exceptional estimate of 10,000 in August 1979.

Rivers with soft earth banks suitable for excavating nesting tunnels and an abundant supply of small fish also attract kingfishers, and the Usk and its tributaries are one of its strongholds in Wales (Fig. 129). The 'blue [bird] of the riverbank', which is the literal translation of the Welsh name for the kingfisher, *glas y dorlan*, is a frequent sight, fishing from the banks of the river, particularly on the stretch immediately to the south of Brecon. The kingfisher has two broods a year of around six or seven eggs, but kingfisher populations in Britain have tended to decline after a recent run of hard winters, to which the bird is particularly susceptible.

In addition, the Usk is one of the most important areas in Wales for mute swans *Cygnus olor*. Most of the breeding pairs in South Wales can be found here, along with a summer flock of immature and non-breeding birds, which arrive each year in June and July and leave again in September and October, probably for the Severn Estuary. There is an interchange of birds between Talybont Reservoir, Llangorse Lake and the Usk, with around 100 birds overwintering each year at Llangorse. The population has increased recently, perhaps due to better protection and the ban on the sale of lead fishing weights. The mute swan is Britain's largest bird and one of the heaviest flying birds in the world, and this limits their distribution as they need stretches of water that are large enough for their take-off runs. They also rarely nest at heights greater than 300 m. Historically an indigenous species that was semi-domesticated in the medieval period, it has reverted to the wild state, although many of the Welsh birds are still closely associated with artificial ponds and castle moats.

OTTERS

The upper reaches of the Usk are one of the best areas in Wales for otters and may have acted as a refuge between the 1950s and 1970s, when otter populations declined rapidly across Britain due to the pollution of watercourses, especially by endocrine-disrupting chemicals, including organochlorine pesticides and polychlorinated biphenyls. Otters had almost died out in the Brecon Beacons before the decline was halted as a result of national and international legislation to protect the species and the positive management of habitats. The remnant population in the Usk probably acted as a source for the recolonisation of southeast Wales. Otters can now be found on every watercourse in the Brecon Beacons, and it is not unusual to come across breeding pairs with accompanying cubs. They can even be found in Brecon, Crickhowell and Llangynidr, where the Usk flows through the towns.

In April 2011 a young otter was released back into the Usk a year after she was found, wounded, in a house. The owner, Mrs Banks, heard a sound coming from under the stairs one morning and was surprised to find an otter staring back at her when she shone a torch into the darkness. The six-month old female was emaciated and suffering from bite wounds and an infected foot. Tempted out of her hiding place and into a cat box with a trail of prawns, she was handed over to the RSPCA, which nursed her back to health. Apparently it is not unusual for otters to go into houses when they are in a bad condition. Not so long ago, however, otters were actively hunted.

The Brecknock County Naturalists' Trust, as the Brecknock Wildlife Trust was once called, played a key role in conserving the otter and ending otter hunting, which was eventually banned in England and Wales in 1979. In 1968, pending the results of the Mammal Society's national survey of the otter population, the Trust called for a halt to the killing of the remaining otters in the area. Letters from the Trust's chairman, David Kyle, were sent to 177 owners of fishing rights and owners of land adjoining the Usk and its tributaries asking them to deny access to the Hawkstone Otter Hounds Association. In response 115 owners supported the Trust's policy of ending the hunting of otters, with only seven refusing directly. The Mammal Society, however, felt that the information gained from otter hunts was important, and that the number of otters killed by hunts had little effect on total numbers. This may have been true, but hunting, and the associated disturbance, was an added pressure on the species at a time when their numbers were very low.

Other nearby Trusts cooperated with the Hawkstone Otter Hounds, but the Brecknock Trust stood firm, actively monitoring the movements of the

Association. The Afon Llynfi enters the River Wye just east of Aberllynfi (Three Cocks), and on 15 October 1970 it was the scene of a hunt recorded by the Trust. The eyewitness report reads as follows and gives a real flavour of how otters were hunted at the time:

> 10.45 Hunt lorry seen at Three Cocks Hotel.
> 11.30 Lorry and five cars move off to Lynfi bridge on A438. Hounds put in water and worked upstream to bridge by Bronllys castle, then a short way up Dulais brook, then back again to the Llynfi, continuing upstream.
> 13.00 Hounds called up by long calls on horn. Lunch by bridge on minor road, first turning left after de-restriction sign on Talgarth–Llangorse road.
> 13.45 Hounds worked upstream to Llynfi bridge on minor road between Llangorse Halt and Llangorse–Talgarth road.
> 15.30 Hounds taken by lorry to Llynfi bridge and put in downstream.
> 15.45 Baying from hounds and men seen hurrying through the trees suggests that an otter may have been found.
> 16.15 Hounds had not yet arrived at new bridge between Three Cocks and Llsywen. Observer walked back upstream, expecting to meet them, but hounds had been taken back to lay-by by AA box, where there were no vehicles at 17.00. Some evidence of grass trampling by stream, some five minutes walk from AA box.
> 17.20 No lorry at Three Cocks, but several cars recognised and man in red coat seen through hotel window.
> 17.30 Observer left Three Cocks.

It seems that only the Brecknock Trust was keeping such records, the other Trusts relying on reports from the Hawkstone Otter Hounds Association itself. One such Trust noted in its newsletter that 'It is only fair to recognise the fact that in our region the Hunt, far from meriting the title of otter's enemy number one, is now playing a useful part in the task of assessing the present status of the otter and is thereby furthering the cause of its conservation.' Having sent this newsletter extract to the Brecknock Trust, the Hawkstone Otter Hounds wrote in 1971:

> Perhaps you appreciate from this how much better it would be for all those concerned (including the otter) if your Trust was included amongst those with whom we co-operate ... As you know we are trying very hard to assist the Mammal Society in its survey. It is, of course, impossible to do this unless we are allowed to 'draw' the rivers in our country. It was interesting to note that on many occasions when we found an otter there was little or no visible sign of one, even to the most experienced eye – prior to the hounds finding it.

Unsurprisingly the Trust did not agree with the argument that otters needed to be hunted in order to conserve them and stood firm, as did the landowners who had promised the Trust that they would deny access.

The following year, 1971, the Trust noted with some relief that, following every effort to protect their holts, five otter cubs had been successfully reared from two holts on the Usk and a further two cubs reared on the Wye. By 1976 the otter was increasing in the Usk catchment and the Hawkstone Otter Hounds Association had been disbanded.

The main threat to otters is now road deaths, especially along the A40 next to the River Usk near Brecon. Otters are highly susceptible to being killed on roads, with 60 per cent of all recorded violent deaths in the UK being attributed to road accidents (Woodroffe 2001). Trunk and A-roads account for 57 per cent of these casualties, although they comprise only 13 per cent of the road network (Philcox et al. 1999). The majority of road casualties (over 50 per cent) occur within 100 m of a watercourse during high water levels (Highways Agency 1998), since during floods otters are reluctant, or unable, to swim under bridges or through culverts, because of strong currents and high flows. Accidents may be increased where drainage ditches run alongside the road, as otters can be attracted onto the carriageway (Grogan et al. 2001). Records of otter road casualties and other otter deaths have been kept systematically in Wales and parts of England since 1980, with many carcasses collected for autopsy (Simpson 1998, Bradshaw & Slater 1999, Liles & Colley 2000). From 1980 to 2000 a total of 261 otter road deaths were recorded in the Environment Agency Wales region (which includes part of some English counties along the Welsh border), and of these 39 were pregnant or lactating females and cubs.

The diet of otters varies, but fish generally comprise over 80 per cent, with other prey including birds, amphibians, molluscs, crustaceans and small mammals. Otters generally favour riparian habitat, although they may travel several kilometres over land to reach water bodies or to cross between river catchments. In Britain they tend to be largely nocturnal where they occur in freshwater habitats. Male otters have been known to travel up to 30 km overnight in search of food or potential mates, lying up during the day at any number of resting sites (Woodroffe 2001).

BATS

The river and bankside trees support large populations of flying insects, which provide an important food source for several bat species, including Daubenton's bat *Myotis daubentoni*. Daubenton's bat has its stronghold in the National Park in the Usk and Wye valleys, but the various populations do not appear to cross the catchment boundaries. The bats emerge at twilight to hunt for insects over the water, which are often eaten while the animal is still in flight. The majority of known summer colonies are in humid, more or less underground sites near water. These may be tunnels or bridges over canals and rivers, or caves, mines and cellars.

The Usk Valley is also the main location in the Beacons for the lesser horseshoe bat *Rhinolophus hipposideros*, a rare bat confined in the British Isles to Wales, western England and western Ireland (Fig. 130). East of Brecon, however,

FIG 130. Lesser horseshoe bats forage mainly in broadleaved woodlands, taking prey from branches. (Melvin Grey)

they seem to be absent, even though the habitat appears to be suitable. A study of lesser horseshoes in Monmouthshire showed that they mainly foraged in broadleaved woodlands, as well as in other woods and areas of high habitat diversity (Bontadina *et al.* 2002). These riverside habitats are therefore ideal foraging areas for the bats, which feed amongst the vegetation, rarely flying more than 5 m above the ground, and frequently circling over favoured areas, taking prey from branches. Their diet consists mainly of mosquitoes, craneflies, gnats and midges. Large items of prey, such as craneflies, are often taken back to a temporary night roost or sometimes dealt with whilst the bat hangs in a tree. Insect remains are often found in these temporary night roosts, which include porches and tunnel entrances.

Lesser horseshoe bats are one of the National Park Authority's conservation success stories, due to its work in protecting roost sites. The bats are particularly sensitive to disturbance, especially in their nursery and winter roosts, and these sites need to be protected. The total Welsh population has been estimated to be in excess of 10,000 individuals and appears to be stable, but the number of lesser horseshoes in Wales could be increased by protecting potential roost sites, such as old buildings, and protecting and improving hibernation sites and habitats used for foraging (Warren & Witter 2002).

Particularly important sites for lesser horseshoes include a coach house and nearby ice house at Buckland, between Talybont and Llangynidr. Until 20 years ago these sites were unknown, and they were only found by chance. In June 1985 Phil Morgan, now running a wildlife consultancy, was manning a display on bats at Brecon Carnival when a woman came to him to ask for advice about a problem with bats at a nearby mansion. She was a nurse working at the property, which was at that time run as a home for ex-servicemen. She was concerned about a population of pipistrelles *Pipistrellus pipistrellus sensu lato* living in one of the third-floor sash windows and wanted some advice, as her daughter, who sometimes stayed with her, was scared of bats. Phil duly arranged to visit with John Messenger, a renowned bat expert, who was then working for the Nature Conservancy Council. When they arrived they did indeed find a maternity colony of pipistrelle bats in the frame of the sash window, and they were also pleasantly surprised to find a brown long-eared bat *Plecotus auritus* maternity colony in the loft spaces of the main house.

Phil and John had arranged several other visits that day, so having dealt with everyone's concerns they were keen to get off to the next site on their list. Then, as Phil explained to the author, 'We were literally going out the front door when the caretaker, who had shown us around, said, "Mind you there could be bats in the old coach house up the road." Our interest was aroused, and despite being in something of a rush, we asked if we could take a look. The caretaker went off to find the keys, and it took so much time that if he had said he couldn't find them, we would have probably have taken to our heels and left.' Fate intervened again, though, and the caretaker found the key and they wandered up the track to the coach house. When they got inside, they were met with old copies of newspapers dating from England's World Cup victory in 1966 – it literally had been that long since anyone had gone inside – but they were also somewhat taken aback by the sight of a large number of lesser horseshoe bats, perhaps around 300 individuals.

The rest is conservation history. The following year the ice house behind the coach house was found to be the hibernation site for the lesser horseshoe bats, although many of these bats may relocate to other associated winter roosts during particularly cold weather. The ice house also acts as a day and night-time roost for smaller numbers of bats at other times of the year. The site was notified as a Site of Special Scientific Interest and subsequently became part of the Usk Bat Sites Special Area of Conservation. Today it is leased by the Vincent Wildlife Trust, a charity which works to safeguard the future of rare mammals, and several species of bat occupy the site, including greater horseshoe bats *Rhinolophus ferrumequinum*. When Phil and John revisited the ice house in December 2010 they counted an incredible 841 lesser horseshoe bats and one lone greater horseshoe bat in hibernation. The site certainly has something special about it – but there might not be any bats there today without that lucky visit in 1985.

In order to ensure a healthy future for lesser horseshoes along the Usk, the Vincent Wildlife Trust has also recently launched the Our Beacons for Bats project, which aims to develop a network of landowner and community 'bat custodians' within the Usk Valley. By developing the initiative the Trust hopes to raise awareness of the importance of this species in the Usk Valley and to ensure local people are aware of their ecology and environmental needs. It will teach local people to identify bats in the field, and help them to promote the conservation of lesser horseshoes within their area. There are also plans to work with local communities to identify important landscape features used by the bats, in order to help inform decisions on land use.

SMALLER RIVERS

As well as large watercourses like the Usk there are a number of smaller rivers in the Beacons, and these are also rich in wildlife. A typical example is the Afon Honddu, which rises near the Gospel Pass at the head of the Vale of Ewyas, down

FIG 131. The Afon Honddu flowing down the Vale of Ewyas is typical of the smaller watercourses in the Brecon Beacons. (Jonathan Mullard)

which it flows, passing southwards to Llanfihangel Crucorney before turning northeast to join the River Monnow (Fig. 131). The smaller rivers and their feeder streams make up most of the total channel length within a river basin, and they often provide habitats for organisms which may be found nowhere else in the watercourse (Meyer & Wallace 2001). Since their catchments are relatively small they can be greatly influenced by small-scale variations in the local environment, and as a result these small rivers are some of the most varied freshwater habitats to be found in the Beacons. The close relationship between terrestrial and aquatic systems in these small channels also means that they are important sources of sediments and nutrients for downstream habitats.

Slower-flowing rivers are also usually more shaded than the larger rivers and often have a rich fauna of dragonflies and damselflies. Typical species found here include the banded demoiselle *Calopteryx splendens*, which is locally abundant on these smaller rivers, preferring sites with a moderate or slow flow of water over a muddy bed and abundant waterside vegetation. They are easily recognised, as the male has wings with a broad, dark iridescent blue-black band across the outer part (Fig. 132).

FIG 132. Male banded demoiselle on the Afon Honddu near Pont Rhys Powell. (Jonathan Mullard)

WATERFALL COUNTRY

The waterfalls on the rivers Nedd, Nedd Fechan, Pyrddin, Sychryd, Mellte and Hepste can be divided into two groups: the Clun Gwyns, Sgwd y Pannwr and Sgwd yr Eira on the Mellte and Lower Hepste, and Sgwd Gwladus, the Horseshoe Falls and the Upper and Lower Ddwli on the Nedd Fechan. The area has been a tourist destination for centuries, and its attractions were summarised by William Condry, author of *The Natural History of Wales* (1981):

> Scenically there are few limestone districts more delectable than that part of the Brecon Beacons National Park which lies at the head of the Vale of Neath where streams with delightful names – Hepste, Pyrddin, Mellte and Nedd – have gnawed deeply into the rocks. First cutting shadowy ravines across a soft limestone band and then falling beautifully over hard steps in the Millstone Grit, these waters have created a unique land, as long alluring to tourists as it has been to naturalists.

The area attracts 160,000 visitors a year, and over 100 adventure activity companies rely on 'Waterfall Country' as a key element of their businesses. Given the recreational pressures on the area, the National Park Authority, Forestry Commission Wales and the Countryside Council for Wales have produced a management plan, the overall aim of which is to identify ways in which the organisations can successfully manage the area to allow wildlife, visitors and local people to co-exist, without damaging this very special place.

Whilst each of the waterfalls has its own particular origins, there are certain aspects which are common to the formation of many of the main falls. All have a cap rock of one of the bands of erosion-resistant sandstone, and most are associated with one of the faults that run from north-northwest to south-southeast. During successive glaciations the Vale of Neath has been gouged out by ice so that its floor is hundreds of metres lower than it would have been originally. This has resulted in the various tributary rivers of the Nedd cutting down into their beds to form the deep gorges characteristic of the area. Where much older faults have brought the two rock types into conjunction, down-cutting by rivers in the mudstone has normally left a projecting lip of the sandstone over which the waterfalls flow. With continued fracturing of the underlying exposed mudstones and their removal, the stresses on the protruding sandstone above lead to its collapse. Severe weather conditions, high flow rates and severe frosts accelerate the process. By this process the waterfalls migrate slowly upstream at a rate which can be determined by the distance between the current location of each individual fall and the fault, which often lies some metres downstream. It has been estimated, for example, that Henrhyd waterfall in the Nant Llech valley was initiated up to 20,000 years ago, and in that time the waterfall has retreated up the valley around 50 m, the gorge below it lengthening at the same time.

Henrhyd Falls near Coelbren is the highest waterfall in South Wales (Fig. 133). Here on the Nant Llech, which translates as 'slab stream' (presumably a reference to the sandstones across which it flows), a 27 m-high waterfall plunges over the edge of the sandstone known as the Farewell Rock into a deep pool. Close to Craig y Nos Country Park and Dan yr Ogof caves, the waterfall attracts up to 5,000 visitors per year.

Sgwd yr Eira on the Afon Hepste provides a good example of the erosion process, which continues to this day, as shown by the problems experienced with loose rock in 2008, when access to the site was temporarily closed. A public footpath runs behind this waterfall, making it one of the most popular tourist attractions in South Wales. The site is at its most spectacular when the river is in flood, following a few days of heavy rainfall (Fig. 134).

The high humidity of the wooded valleys has a strong influence on their botany, with trees and rocks supporting a range of plants usually confined to the Atlantic coast. Overall, their botanical diversity is outstanding, with more than 600 species of plants recorded. Boulder screes, cliff faces, grassy banks, springs, seepages, decaying logs and mature trees provide some of the specific habitats required by lower plants which prefer conditions that are subject to little

FIG 133. Henrhyd Falls, at 27 m the highest waterfall in South Wales. (Jonathan Mullard)

FIG 134. Sgwd yr Eira, which translates as 'fall of snow', after several days of heavy rain in March 2010. (Jonathan Mullard)

change over time. The waterfalls and adjoining areas influenced by spray can be particularly rich in lower plants, with ferns being especially prominent. Species found here include royal fern *Osmunda regalis*, hay-scented buckler-fern *Dryopteris aemula*, Tunbridge filmy-fern *Hymenophyllum tunbrigense* and Wilson's filmy-fern.

Wilson's filmy-fern is a small plant that superficially resembles a tuft of moss rather than a fern. The individual leaves are very thin and transparent, and divided into parallel-sided, toothed segments. This species is frequent in western Scotland, the English Lake District, North Wales and southwest Ireland (Page 1988), and the main factor controlling its distribution appears to be the number of rainy days per year (Richards & Evans 1972). It occurs alongside the Tunbridge filmy-fern, which grows as relatively pure stands on the steep cliffs, whereas Wilson's filmy-fern tends to occur amongst mosses. Tunbridge filmy-fern is less widespread and abundant in the British Isles than Wilson's filmy-fern and has a fragmented distribution, which is presumably a relic of a more continuous past (Fig. 135). Once established, the fern grows outwards in all directions and increases at a rate of about 7–25 mm per year, sometimes reaching 1 m or more in diameter. The populations are dynamic and there seems to be a cyclical pattern

FIG 135. Tunbridge filmy-fern has a patchy distribution across the British Isles, but the waterfalls of the Brecon Beacons provide an ideal habitat, as it requires deep shade and humid conditions. (Graham Motley)

of succession, where colonisation is followed by the gradual build-up of a mat of bryophytes, including the filmy-fern itself, which eventually fall off the rock surface under their own weight, leaving bare rock as a potential site for the cycle to start again. Most sites where the species occurs have a long history of continuous or dynamic tree cover, the filmy-fern re-colonising from local refuges after periods when the canopy has been open.

Beech fern is also abundant on the wet cliffs, growing alongside the rarer green spleenwort. Green spleenwort is a strong calcicole; that is, it is present only where there are lime-rich soils, and it is a particularly good indicator of such sites. It is also more of an alpine species than the related maidenhair spleenwort, being usually found only at altitudes above 300 m. Like many plants in the gorge it is able to tolerate deep shade and high humidity, which enables it to occupy deep crevices and recesses beneath large fixed boulders. Chris Page, the author of *Ferns* in the New Naturalist series (1988), noted that the fronds of green spleenwort typically turn their pinnae perpendicular to the incident light, which clearly gives the plant an 'efficient light-catching ability in the unusual depths of these dank, dark recesses'.

Over 150 species of mosses and liverworts have been found in the gorges alongside the ferns, including the liverworts greater whipwort, Hutchins' hollywort *Jubula hutchinsiae*, matchstick flapwort *Odontoschisma denudatum*, Heller's notchwort *Anastrophyllum hellerianum*, fingered cowlwort *Colura calyptrifolia*, autumn flapwort *Jamesoniella autumnalis*, horsehair threadwort *Sphenolobopsis pearsonii* and straggling pouchwort *Saccogyna viticulosa*. Mosses include Holt's mouse-tail moss *Isothecium holtii*, transparent or yellowish fork-moss *Dichodontium denudatum*, Haller's apple moss *Bartramia hallerana* and scarce turf-moss *Rhytidiadelphus subpinnatus*. Also present on these wet rocks are Brown's four-tooth moss *Tetradontium brownianum*, a rare specialised moss of overhanging sandstone rocks, which is usually found only by actively searching for it in deep shade, and Curnow's pocket-moss *Fissidens curnovii*. Another shade-loving moss, Welsh pocket-moss *Fissidens celticus*, can be found nearby on bare patches of soil that have been eroded by flood water.

There are also good communities of lichens, and five nationally scarce species have been identified in past surveys: the bright yellow mustard powder, or gold dust, lichen *Chrysothrix chlorine*, which can be locally abundant on the drier cliffs, and *Micarea pycnidiophora*, *M. stipitata*, *Phyllopsora rosei* and *Polyblastia allobata*. Other lichen species known to occur include *Enterographa hutchinsii*, *Micarea alabastrites* and *M. hedlundii*.

WALLACE

In June 1846, Alfred Russel Wallace decided to walk with his brother from Neath to Pen y Fan and back via Sgwd Gwladus and Cwm Porth 'to see if I could find any more rare beetles and to show my brother the waterfalls and other beauties of the upper valley.' In his autobiography *My Life*, published in 1905, Wallace remembered that:

> Starting after an early breakfast we walked to Pont-nedd-fychan, and then turned up the western branch to the Rocking Stone, a large bounder of millstone-grit resting on a nearly level surface, but which by a succession of pushes with one hand can be made to rock considerably. It was here I obtained one of the most beautiful British beetles, Trichius fasciatus, *the only time I ever captured it.*

This discovery led to Wallace's very first scientific publication, a very brief note in *The Zoologist* for 1847 recording this striking but rare scarabaeid beetle, known as the bee beetle *Trichius fasciatus* because the body is very hairy and resembles that of a bumblebee (Fig. 136). This note was in response to a previous submission that no specimen of the beetle had been caught for over 20 years.

> Capture of Trichius fasciatus *near Neath – I took a single specimen of this beautiful insect on a blossom of* Carduus heterophyllus *near the falls at the top of Neath Vale. –Alfred R. Wallace, Neath.*

FIG 136. Bee beetle, the 'beautiful insect' which Alfred Russel Wallace captured near Pontneddfechan. (Roger Key)

The editor of *The Zoologist* at the time, E. Newman, added the derogatory note, 'The other insects in my correspondent's list are scarcely worth publishing.' Lewis Weston Dillwyn, a noted Swansea landowner and naturalist, did, however, include in his volume on the flora and fauna of the Swansea area a list of beetles collected by Wallace in the Beacons, though by the time it appeared he was on his way to South America on the first of his collecting expeditions and probably never saw it. Wallace's beetle collection was said to be in Neath Museum, but despite many efforts since to locate it, the collection has never been found. Wallace himself only returned for a brief visit to Wales towards the end of his life.

The bee beetle has two main strongholds in Britain, the Scottish Highlands and South Wales. The larvae develop in dead hardwood and emerge as a spectacular beetle often found on thistle heads, such as melancholy thistle *Cirsium heterophyllum*, as recorded by Wallace, where they are somewhat lethargic and easily observed. Being up to 15 mm long it is easily noticed, although often the head is buried in the flowers and all that is visible are the unmistakable pale brown and black wing cases. It is recorded from May to July, which fits Wallace's sighting in June.

MINOR WATERFALLS

As well as the big, dramatic and much-visited waterfalls there are countless other small waterfalls in the Beacons on many of the streams and rivulets that cascade down the mountainsides. None of these have been studied by naturalists in any detail even though they are often quite accessible. Like the larger falls, small waterfalls also create areas of increased humidity and this can lead to the development of important communities of mosses and liverworts in the spray zone. In cold weather these smaller waterfalls also freeze more easily than

FIG 137. The small waterfalls that cascade across Craig y Fro Quarry froze in March 2013, creating a spectacular sight. (Jonathan Mullard)

the larger ones, creating a surface of ice behind which water continues to run (Fig. 137). During the very cold spring of 2013 many of these developed impressive sheets of ice, which were colonised by numerous springtails and mites.

UNDERGROUND WILDLIFE

The plants and animals described in the preceding pages are not the only species to be found along the watercourses. The sinks and resurgences, mentioned earlier, form the entrances to a vast network of caves that exist in the limestone; many of them excavated by the rivers and streams themselves. Despite the absence of light, a surprising variety of wildlife can be found along the underground channels but it is rarely encountered by most naturalists, due to the difficulties of access. It is also often disregarded by cavers, whose main interest is exploration, though awareness is growing in certain sections of the caving community. As a result there are now a number of excellent websites with both photographs of the caves themselves and the wildlife to be encountered there. These often elusive and under-regarded species are the subject of the following chapter.

Chapter 7

Cave Systems

CAVES HAVE BEEN DESCRIBED AS 'NATURAL MUSEUMS', as they preserve important archaeological evidence and deposits that provide information about past environments, and although several thousand kilometres of cave tunnels have been explored across the world it is certain that more remain to be examined. Along with the deep ocean, they represent some of the last unknown places on Earth – and it is partly for this reason that caving has become such a popular recreational activity. The limestone belt stretching across the Brecon Beacons contains some of the most important cave systems in Europe. They include Britain's deepest cave, Ogof Ffynnon Ddu, which is 308 m deep, several of the longest, such as Ogof Draenen, which has 70 km of passages, and the largest known passage, the Time Machine in Ogof y Darren Cilau.

People have been visiting the caves in the Beacons for hundreds of years, and in Egwlys Faen, one of the main caves under Craig y Cilau, drawings and messages in the cave can be found dating from at least 1787, when someone called Frederick J. Fredericks carved his name into the rock. Since the limestones that occur in South Wales represent just one layer in a huge depositional basin, with the cave-bearing strata exposed by the activity of rivers and streams at a number of isolated sites, it has been difficult to build up a clear picture of the relationships between the caves. Explorations over many years have therefore been necessary in order to improve our knowledge of the area. Quarrying of the limestone has also helped to expose some of the cave entrances, such as those under Craig y Cilau National Nature Reserve on Mynydd Llangatwg.

The majority of the caves can only be accessed by experienced cavers with local knowledge, or with the assistance of guides, so comparatively few naturalists have explored them. Of the five caves that are easily accessible the largest is the extensive Dan yr Ogof system in the Swansea Valley where, at the National Showcaves Centre, thousands of people visit the commercially developed caves. The Centre is one of Wales's most popular tourist attractions and was recently voted 'Britain's finest natural wonder'. Only the first section of the cave system at Dan yr Ogof is open to the public, the natural limestone bridge in Bridge Chamber marking the end of the showcaves; only cavers are allowed to penetrate further. Beyond this point there are around 17 km of passages, many of them large and magnificent chambers decorated with stalactites and stalagmites deep beneath Mynydd Du. The Centre also includes two nearby caves, Cathedral Cave and Bone Cave, and together with Dan yr Ogof they provide a good introduction to cave habitats. A few kilometres further east visitors can also investigate Porth yr Ogof, where the Afon Mellte disappears underground, one of many caves intimately associated with the river systems as they cross the limestone (Fig. 138). If not properly equipped it is dangerous, however, to venture further than the entrance of this cave, and following heavy rain the cave floods quickly, so great care is needed. Finally, a small cave underneath Carreg Cennen castle, which may once have served as a water supply, can also be entered by visitors to the site.

Although it is not a show cave, the impressive entrance of Porth yr Ogof is visited by a large number of people each year; indeed only Dan yr Ogof itself

FIG 138. Porth yr Ogof, just north of Ystradfellte. Here the river Mellte disappears underground into the largest cave entrance in the Brecon Beacons, re-emerging several hundred metres downstream at the Blue Pool. (Jonathan Mullard)

attracts more visitors. Despite the dangers, the Entrance Chamber and the dry Right Hand Series are often explored by adventurous visitors, and the cave is also very popular with both novice and experienced cavers. The word *porth* means gateway in Welsh, and Porth yr Ogof is best translated as 'gateway to the cave'. The first reference to the site seems to have been by the naturalist and antiquary Edward Lhuyd in the letter to John Ray, discussed in Chapter 3, about its many visible fossils. Lhuyd called it Porth Gogo, and this suggests that the present name for the cave was used by tourists in the seventeenth century. Other names mentioned by early travellers are Porth Mawr, 'great gateway', perhaps more appropriate since the main entrance is the largest cave entrance in the Brecon Beacons (though there are 15 entrances and exits to this cave in total), and Cwm Porth Cavern, but these fell into disuse long ago.

Notable visitors in the early nineteenth century included the Reverend Richard Warner of Bath, the Reverend John Evens, and Benjamin Malkin. Their writings vary in accuracy but make interesting reading. Warner walked up the Mellte Valley from the Hepste, and on arriving at the entrance wrote that he:

> *perceived the River Felddta, like the classical Alpheus, rolling its stream through a vast subterranean cavern, which it had entered a quarter of a mile above. Had the water been low, we might have pursued its gloomy course through the windings of this natural excavation, for nearly one hundred yards, to an aperture on the left hand, where it quits its secret bed and again emerges into day; but the floods preventing us, we continued our walk to the valley, in which it first shrinks from the light and hides its head in the rock.* (Standing & Lloyd 1970)

Just as the size of Porth yr Ogof was sometimes exaggerated in early writings, it was also inaccurately portrayed by several nineteenth-century artists. Strangely, some of these show the river flowing out of the main entrance, instead of into the cave.

ORIGIN OF THE CAVES

Water, indeed, is the key to understanding the origin of the caves in the Beacons. Although it cannot penetrate solid limestone it is able to flow through cracks in the rocks. Caverns in the rock form principally by means of a simple chemical reaction in which hydrogen ions from groundwaters, acidified with dissolved carbon dioxide, act on the relatively insoluble carbonate ions in the limestone to produce soluble bicarbonate ions, which are then washed away. It has been estimated that the process makes the limestone 25 times more soluble than it would be in pure water, and the result is holes in the rock. This first stage of cave formation, known as initiation, creates the openings through the rock that permit the flow of groundwater. Although cave formation is determined totally by the geology, the water starts to influence the development of the cave soon after the initial openings are created. As the limestone fissures are enlarged the permeability of the rock increases and the fissures and caves are drained so that they contain air-filled spaces and a water table is established. Below the water table the openings remain submerged and the cave therefore develops differently above and below the water level. In particular, the water flow becomes more turbulent and there is increased erosion due to mechanical abrasion by sediment from the surface.

The main stage of cave development is enlargement, when the small initial fissures expand in size. As the cave system evolves it increases in complexity as individual passages are abandoned in favour of new routes at lower levels. The timescales for cave formation are long, and the initiation phase can take tens of millions of years, while the enlargement of a cave passage to 1 m in diameter can take up to 10,000 years. The caves form along both bedding planes – the layers of rock themselves – and along vertical fractures. Since most of the rocks in the Beacons slope gently towards the South Wales coalfield, many caves follow this southward dip, but they also extend east–west across it until they emerge in one of the major valleys carved through the limestone.

Enlargement is followed by degradation. This is the terminal phase, and it may take one of three forms: the cave collapses, or it is filled with sediment, or it is removed by a lowering of the overlying surface. In a complex cave system all three processes take place simultaneously in passages at different depths and positions in the limestone. Enlargement and sediment infilling can also take place at the same time in a single passage. Wall and roof collapse is a widespread feature in caves, modifying the profiles of passages and contributing to cave enlargement where fallen blocks expose new surfaces to attack by water. Major collapses ultimately block the passages, however, since the fallen material occupies a larger volume than the undisturbed rock.

Calcite deposition is common in caves where saturated percolation water issuing from fissures loses carbon dioxide to the cave air and deposits calcium carbonate to regain equilibrium, forming stalactites and stalagmites. These are known as speleothems, deposits of minerals that form into structures and line the insides of a cave. Stalactites are the formations that hang from the roofs of caves, while deposition on the cave floor creates tall stalagmites or rounded bosses, the profiles of which relate to saturation levels and drip rates. Some may take thousands of years to form, while others can grow quite rapidly. In Dan yr Ogof the Dagger, a massive flat stalactite, was damaged in the 1940s when the

FIG 139. Straw stalactites on the roof of Cathedral cave in Dan yr Ogof. (Jonathan Mullard)

tip was broken off, and measurements have since been made on a regular basis to determine how fast the formation is growing. The results suggest that one cubic millimetre is being added to the structure every 10 years, highlighting the extremely long periods of time it takes for these structures to form. Stalactites and stalagmites are of considerable scientific value since caves are very long-lived landforms that preserve valuable evidence of past events on the Earth's surface.

On the roof of Cathedral Cave in Dan yr Ogof are thousands of tiny straw stalactites, delicate tubes of calcite through which the water drips (Fig. 139). If the tubes are blocked by an impurity, or inconsistent crystal growth, then the water breaks through to the outside of the straw and starts flowing along the outside surface to form a stalactite.

Flowstones are formed when films of water moving across walls of the cave lose dissolved carbon dioxide through agitation and can no longer hold minerals in solution; thin layers of these deposits then build on each other, becoming more rounded as the deposit gets thicker. These deposits sometimes grade into thin sheets known as curtains where they extend across overhanging portions of the wall. Some are translucent, while others have brown and beige layers and are known as 'cave bacon'. One of the best known examples of these is the Flitch of Bacon, a curtain formation in Dan yr Ogof that has been stained red by iron oxide (Fig. 140). Though flowstones are among the largest of speleothems, they

FIG 140. The Flitch of Bacon, a curtain formation in Dan yr Ogof that has been stained red by iron oxide. (Jonathan Mullard)

can still be damaged by a single touch, oil from human fingers causing water to avoid the area, which then dries out.

The climate of a cave is controlled by a large number of factors including cave volume, the shape of passages and their cross-sectional area, and the number, size and relative elevation of cave entrances. Even small changes in cave microclimates can lead to the loss of suitable habitats for species such as bats. Cave temperatures do not generally exhibit the variation that occurs in the external environment, however, and in many cases the mean annual surface air temperature approximates to the deep cave temperature. External conditions, conduction through walls, the exchange of latent heat by condensation or evaporation and air movements all have an effect on cave temperatures. Air movement may be caused by chimney effects, the adjustment of the cave atmosphere, changes in atmospheric pressure, the resonance of air in large chambers, the entrainment of air by flowing water or changes in the volume of the cave due to flooding. The apparent frequency of lightning strikes near cave entrances and measurements of the ionisation of cave air suggests that it has particular electrical properties. It has been suggested that the precipitation of substances in solution from condensation droplets attracted to electrically conductive sites may be a factor in the formation of stalactites and stalagmites. The moisture levels of the cave atmosphere may also be changed by alterations in the vegetation cover above the cave (Mullard 2006).

CAVE EXPLORATION

Modern, systematic, cave exploration in the Brecon Beacons can be said to have begun in the 1840s when Thomas Jenkins of Llandeilo took a rope ladder and collapsible coracle into the opening at Llygad Llwchwr, where, at the west end of the Mynydd Du, the Afon Llwchwr emerges dramatically from the limestone. Jenkins was a polymath, known as the 'Leonardo of Llandeilo', who collected fossils, constructed boats and violins, conducted chemical and electrical experiments and had a great interest in astronomy. Exploring caves with collapsible coracles was just another sign of his inquiring mind (Jenkins 1986).

Dan yr Ogof was first explored by two local brothers, Tommy and Jeff Morgan, in 1912, using candles and primitive equipment. They named the cave after their farm Dan yr Ogof ('beneath the cave') and, uncertain about what they would discover, armed themselves with a revolver. The brothers' initial explorations were halted by a large lake, which they later managed to cross using a coracle, eventually crossing three more lakes in the same way, ending at a small passage. This passage, known as the Long Crawl, was first negotiated by Eileen Davies, a member of Swansea University Caving Club, in 1963, although it is claimed that it was explored by Peter Ogden of the same club the previous October. Exploration has been continued by later cavers, who have extended the known passages to the present 18 km length, including some areas that can only be reached by cave diving. In the Swansea Valley the South Wales Caving Club and its precursors worked first at Dan yr Ogof between 1936 and 1939 and then Ogof Ffynnon Ddu from 1946 to 1953. The Cave Research Group had some very competent surveyors, and Lewis Railton (1907–71) in particular set the benchmark for cave survey and presentation with the publication of his survey of Ogof Ffynnon Ddu (Railton 1953). With Arthur Butcher, Railton set out a clear and well-defined basis for a range of techniques and presentation standards.

Ogof Ffynnon Ddu ('cave of the black spring'), located in the upper Swansea Valley, was discovered in 1946 through digging by Peter Harvey and Ian Nixon, members of the Wales Caving Club, who were intrigued by springs of water that surged from the rock after heavy rainfall. The system is famous for its intricate maze-like structure and its impressive main stream passage. Major extensions were discovered in 1967 and the top entrance opened out. The trip from the top to the bottom entrance is considered a classic route, the 80.5 km of passages providing everything from enormous chambers and striking formations to wide chasms and torrential river passages. The cave is decorated throughout with many different calcite decorations, of which the most well known are The Columns, which are around 2 m high, and The Trident, which at 5 m is the longest stalactite in Britain.

The exploration of Mynydd Llangatwg, an impressive scarp overlooking the Usk Valley, began in 1957 with the breakthrough at Ogof Agen Allwedd. The cave is another long cave (32.5 km) and certainly the longest cave system on the Llangattock escarpment, where Ogof y Darren Cilau is also found. There are several round trips that can be followed within the system, but all trips start via the short entrance series and first boulder choke, which is mostly easy caving. Some newly discovered passages in Ogof Agen Allwedd contain particularly fine formations of stalactites and stalagmites.

Major extensions to the cave systems in the Brecon Beacons were discovered between 1960 and 1980, when a complex system of apparently unconnected caves

FIG 141. A school party preparing to enter Eglwys Faen below Craig y Cilau National Nature Reserve. (Jonathan Mullard)

gradually emerged with discoveries in Ogof y Darren Cilau and Eglwys Faen (Fig. 141), two cave systems in the Llangattock escarpment near Crickhowell, and Ogof Craig ar Ffynnon. Ogof Craig ar Ffynnon ('rock and fountain cave') can only be entered from its resurgence in the Clydach Gorge; it is about 7 km in length and renowned as one of the most well-decorated caves in Britain. The cave contains some early short crawling sections (and an arduous and uncomfortable boulder choke) and some wet passages with prolific quantities of mud, before it develops into a series of large sections abundantly decorated with mud and calcite formations. The most spectacular of these is the Hall of the Mountain King, a large cavern adorned with flowstone. Beyond the well-decorated section the cave continues in a long series of low passages, and it is thought that the cave eventually connects to the Llangattock System through Ogof y Darren Cilau. Since November 2007, access to the cave has been controlled by the Mynydd Llangatwg Cave Management and Advisory Committee, and a key must be obtained to gain access through the door.

In addition to the Time Machine, which as mentioned above is the largest cave passage in Britain, Ogof y Darren Cilau is also notable for a set of pure white stalactites called the White Company (Fig. 142) and a branching helictite known as the Bonsai Tree. A helictite is a formation found in limestone caves that changes its axis from the vertical at one or more stages during its growth. It has a curving or angular form that looks as if it has grown in zero gravity. Helictites are probably the result of capillary forces acting on tiny water droplets, a force which is often strong enough at this scale to defy gravity. They are typically radically symmetrical, but can be easily crushed or broken.

The most recent phase of cave exploration in the Beacons commenced in 1994 with the discovery of Ogof Draenen ('hawthorn cave') located at the southern extremity of the limestone above Blaenavon. Twenty years later the exploration of the caverns by caving clubs is still progressing, and the known system now exceeds 70 km – making Ogof Draenen the longest cave system in Wales and the second-longest in Great Britain, second only to the Easegill Caverns in Yorkshire. The cave was known only as a small entrance on a steep hillside until several years of digging broke through into a major passage. It was then explored at unprecedented speed. Draenen contains a variety of spectacular decorations and some huge passages (the War of the Worlds section is probably the second-largest cave passage in Britain). Its large size and occasional complexity make the cave a challenge for even experienced cavers. The cave is managed by the Pwll Du Cave Management Group and marker tapes have been laid in many parts of the cave, to help protect the formations, and occasionally the floor, in order to preserve the cave environment.

FIG 142. The White Company, pure white stalactites with helictites, in Epocalypse [sic] Passage, Ogof y Darren Cilau. (Brendan Marris)

IMPACTS ON CAVE WILDLIFE

Most of the important discoveries and extensions to existing cave systems, described above, have resulted from excavations (Hardwick & Gunn 1997), and this can result in passages having their sediment fill partially, or totally, removed and deposited into active watercourses. Although these excavations have increased the known cave resource, the impact on the ecology of the caves is largely unknown. Cave habitats in Britain are poorly researched and understood, there have been no systematic surveys, and few direct conservation measures are in place. Guidelines have, however, been developed to facilitate the sustainable development and conservation of cave and karst environments at national and international scales (National Caving Association 1995, Watson *et al.* 1997). These include the development of voluntary cave conservation plans, the formation of a conservation committee to cover each major cave or area and education and training, including the theory and practice of cave conservation and practical conservation matters. They are difficult to apply though to the ecology of British caves in general because of the dearth of information available on the fauna that utilise, or may be dependent on, subterranean environments. Undoubtedly, however, despite the best efforts of organisations such as the British Caving Association, the wildlife of some caves continues to be affected by the actions of recreational cavers.

Caves are one of the most discontinuous of terrestrial habitats, even more so than islands and mountain peaks, and the populations of terrestrial cave-dwelling animals are restricted to relatively confined habitats. There are therefore a large number of closely related, but geographically isolated, species to be found in the caverns and cavities underneath the Brecon Beacons. The main investigations were carried out in the late 1970s and early 1980s by Geoff Jefferson from the Zoology Department of University College, Cardiff, who also explored the Gower caves. His work, and that of more recent researchers, has been collated by Graham Proudlove, Biological Recorder for the British Cave Research Association, and Andy Lewington, who has developed the *Cave Life of Britain* website (http://cambriancavingcouncil.org.uk/cavelife) and personally taken many high-quality photographs of cave wildlife, a number of which are reproduced here.

In 1975 Ogof Ffynnon Ddu was the first cave in Britain to be declared a National Nature Reserve, in recognition of both its underground features and the surface landscape, and in 2004 Dan yr Ogof was declared the smallest National Nature Reserve in Wales. The new designation, appropriately perhaps for a showcave, was 'sung in' by the Gyrlais Male Voice Choir performing deep underground! Neither cave though was designated for its current wildlife. Many other caves in the Beacons, such as the Minera Caves, Otter Hole and Little Neath

TABLE 4. Designation criteria for caves designated as Sites of Special Scientific Interest (SSSIs) in the Brecon Beacons.

Site	Macroscale interest: geology/hydrology	Microscale interest: cave formations	Clastic sediments*	Minerals	Biology
Dan yr Ogof Caves	1	1	1	x	x
Ogof Ffynnon Ddu	1	1	x	x	x
Little Neath River Cave	1	x	x	x	x
Porth yr Ogof	1	x	x	x	x
Nant Glais Caves	1	x	x	x	1
Mynydd Llangattwg	1	2	1	x	x

1, features of primary importance; 2, features of secondary importance; x, no scientific interest. Adapted from Hardwick and Gunn (1996).
NB: 'no scientific interest' at the time of designation does not mean that there is no scientific interest!
* Clastic sediments are rocks composed predominantly of broken pieces or 'clasts' of older weathered and eroded rocks.

River cave are Sites of Special Scientific Interest for geological reasons, but Nant Glais Caves is currently the only cave system in Britain currently notified on biological grounds, mainly for the unusually large populations of white trout that live there (Table 4). The site includes both the limestone gorge of Nant Glais and the two cave systems that lie parallel to and beneath the stream.

The impacts of cave exploration on their ecology have been mentioned previously, but this is only one of a number of issues that need to be considered in securing their conservation. One of the main concerns is the definition of boundaries. Since all active caves are part of more extensive karst hydrological systems, conservation measures should logically extend to cover the whole catchment, so as to protect the cave from the possible impact of changes in input water quantity or quality. Potentially therefore large areas of land surface with no inherent scientific interest need be designated to effectively conserve caves beneath them or downstream of them.

CAVE FLORA

The information on cave flora is negligible compared to that on fauna, and the earliest information dates from the 1950s when a study was carried out in a number of caves in South Wales, including Porth yr Ogof (Mason-Williams & Benson-Evans 1958). Plants in the cave threshold show a marked zonation controlled by light intensity and the nature of the substrate. Flowering plants near the cave entrance are succeeded by ferns, then mosses, then liverworts and finally in the dim light green and blue-green algae. In the dark zone only fungi and moulds occur, but there are no species found here that are confined to underground habitats. Shade-loving plants growing around the entrances of caves include herb-Robert, wood-sorrel and opposite-leaved golden-saxifrage. Other typical flowering plants of the threshold include ivy, lords-and-ladies, stinging nettle, dog-violet and dog's mercury, which prefers drier conditions. In deep shade some plants, such as dog-violet, have a different form with larger leaves.

Ferns recorded from this habitat include maidenhair spleenwort, wall-rue and rustyback fern. One of the commonest mosses is verdigris tufa-moss, which forms dense cushions in the damp areas and may become encrusted with calcite deposits. Great scented liverwort is also a very common species in cave entrances. It has large thalli, up to 17 mm wide, which often form extensive mats. Another common liverwort of cave entrances is endive pellia. Less common species include hart's-tongue, thyme-moss *Plagiomnium undulatum* and wall feather-moss *Rhynchostegium murale*.

Algae recorded from the entrance of Porth yr Ogof include the blue-green alga (cyanobacterium) *Nostoc muscorum* and other freshwater algae such as *Chroococcus giganteus* and *Synechoccus aeruginosum*. Within electrically lit caves such as Dan yr Ogof, growths of algae, cyanobacteria, mosses and moss protonemia (green filamentous structures arising from an asexual spore of moss) are common. In some cases lichens and ferns also occur locally. All such growths are termed 'lampenflora' because of their association with electric lighting. Lampenflora change the natural appearance of cave features and, if not properly treated, damage features in the cave by the production of organic acids which corrode the surface. Mechanical removal with brushes and water can, however, create more damage. On the positive side, though, lampenflora does provide an additional food source for the animals found in this habitat.

CAVE FAUNA

The comparative lack of research on British cave fauna is reflected in the fact that none of the species currently has any form of statutory protection. Around 75 per cent of cave passages in Britain lie within Sites of Special Scientific Interest, and 11 caves are recognised for their importance for hibernating bats, but, as described earlier, only the citation for Nant Glais Caves mentions any cave fauna. This omission really needs to be addressed.

The effects of the glaciations mean that life in British caves is limited, especially when compared to Europe. Over 100 species of invertebrate animals nevertheless have been recorded as permanently living in British caves, while other species such as bats and moths use caves regularly as temporary shelters. Animals using caves can be divided into different categories depending on the use they make of the cave. Some animals spend only part of their lives in caves (trogloxenes), while others, although occurring elsewhere, are able to live in caves permanently (troglophiles), and some are only found underground (troglobites). In addition to the use they make of the cave, it is also possible to categorise animals based on the type of habitat they occupy, the so-called threshold fauna living in the zone between the entrance and the limit of light penetration and the dark-zone fauna living where there is no natural light.

Although the term *cave* is usually applied to natural openings that are large enough to allow people to enter, these macrocaverns form only a tiny proportion of the total cave habitat, the great majority being mesocaverns, that is holes with a diameter ranging from 1 to 200 mm. It has been estimated that the habitable surface area within limestone mesocaverns must run to at least two or three orders of magnitude more than that within explored caves. It is within these mesocaverns, which are for the most part completely inaccessible to the naturalist, that the majority of the specialised flora and fauna of the caves resides, but to date there have been no studies of this habitat. The communities remain mysterious and under-recorded. Judging by the studies of other cave habitats in Britain, however, it is likely that a wide range of species is present in the mesocaverns, ranging from bacteria and fungi to flatworms, mites, polychaete worms and spiders.

A study of caves in Romania during the early 1980s found that the four main subterranean habitats – caves, the mesocaverns or fissures described above, the network of microspaces that exist between rock fragments at the junction of soil and rock, and the soil itself – are connected through multiple interrelationships within a unique functional system (Decu & Iliffe 1983). Each of these habitats is characterised by a specific fauna, as well as containing fauna common to the other habitats. Despite our limited knowledge, more is known about the cave fauna and soil fauna in the Beacons than about the fauna of the mesocaverns and microspaces, yet it is in these difficult-to-access places that new discoveries will be made.

Many cave communities rely on food being brought into the cave from the surface. This organic debris includes leafs and twigs brought in by surface streams or falling down vertical shafts; it also includes organic matter brought in by visitors, carcasses of animals that have wandered in, and droppings from animals such as bats. In the depths of a cave the communities are concentrated around food sources generated by bacteria, such as the cyanobacterium *Synechococcus elongatus*, which is involved in the conversion of limestone to moonmilk. Moonmilk is a cheese-like mass, consisting of carbonate minerals and a microorganism, which is found sprouting from the cave ceiling or walls, usually near to an entrance. A large range of organisms has been isolated from this peculiar substance, including the bacterium *Macromonas* sp. (probably *M. bipunctata*), and various blue-green algae such as *Synechococcus elongatus* also occur. It is thought that in the darkness they feed by metabolic pathways quite different to the ones they use in the light. Curious encrusting growths known as wall-fungus also occur frequently in the caves, and investigation has shown that they consist of a complex bacterium on the borderline between bacteria and fungi, a species of *Streptomyces*, probably associated with a fungus, *Fusarium* spp.

ANIMALS OF THE THRESHOLD

Many of the animals in the threshold zone are troglophiles, that is animals that live in caves and often complete their life cycle there, although they are not limited to this habitat and are found elsewhere, both above and below ground. Typical cave-entrance communities include the orb-web cave spider *Meta menardi*, the tissue moth *Triphosa dubitata* and the herald moth *Scoliopteryx libatrix*, and an array of flies such as the dungfly *Leria serrata* and the fungus, or cave, gnat *Speleolepta leptogaster* (Mullard 2006). The dungfly is interesting as it becomes infected with a fungus and dies on the walls and ceiling of a cave, often in very large numbers. Where this occurs you know you are near the surface. The common cave gnat is particularly widespread and numerous in the caves, its thin, translucent larvae, up to 14 mm long, living on the damp walls and feeding on microorganisms and fungal material. Like many animals that live permanently in caves the gnat can be found in the deep threshold as well as in the dark zone, but it is only rarely recorded from outside caves and it may be a troglobite. Similarly large numbers of the common mosquito *Culex pipiens* can be seen in the caves from September to April. These are females of the autumn generation which have already mated, but which will not lay their eggs until they have left the cave in spring. The entrance of Porth yr Ogof is a good location to see many of these species.

The tissue moth and herald moth also use cave thresholds as overwintering sites (Fig. 143). The caterpillars feed on vegetation outside the cave, but soon after emerging from the chrysalis the adults fly into the threshold area. Herald moths often become very torpid and can be seen high in the dark zone of the cave covered with beads of moisture, while tissue moths prefer to settle closer to the entrance and lower down. It appears that a period of suspended development is necessary before the ovaries of the female of both species can produce eggs.

LEFT: **FIG 143.** Herald moths use cave thresholds as overwintering sites. (Nick Greatorex-Davies)

BELOW: **FIG 144.** One of Britain's largest spiders, the orb-web cave spider, photographed in Porth yr Ogof with its egg sac. The body length can be up to 13 mm in males and 17 mm in females. (Andrew Lewington)

The orb-web spider is found in the deeper part of cave entrances, trapping insects on their way in and out (Fig. 144). It feeds on virtually any prey and catches both flying and crawling insects, also feeding on woodlice and millipedes, among other animals. The main morphological adaptions of troglobitic spiders are the reduction or loss of eyes, depigmentation and the lengthening of appendages. This adaption to the subterranean environment also affects their life cycle, their embryonic and post-embryonic development, as well as lengthening of their adult lifespan. The spider's eggs are roughly spherical and about 1 mm in diameter, being laid in a compact mass and covered with silk to form a sac. The number of eggs laid depends on the size of the female, with larger cave spiders laying more and sometimes larger eggs. Like lacewings, the egg sacs are placed on stalks to protect them from predators.

One of the easiest places in the Beacons to view the orb-web spider, and indeed the herald moth, is not actually a cave, but a tunnel under the Brecon and Monmouthshire Canal near Llanfoist church (Fig. 145). This tunnel was constructed when the canal was built to allow access for parishioners to Llanfoist wharf. A public footpath passes through the tunnel and is used on a daily basis by both local people and visitors, who probably do not realise that there are large black spiders and their egg sacs hanging just above their heads!

FIG 145. The tunnel under the Brecon and Monmouthshire Canal, near Llanfoist church, is one of the easiest places in the Beacons to see large cave spiders and herald moths. The canal itself forms the boundary of the National Park. (Jonathan Mullard)

Another cave spider, *Metellina merianae*, is found in the threshold of caves, often at the entrance itself where it spins a larger, finer orb web across the passage to catch creatures flying in and out of the cave. The spider is a similar shape to *Meta menardi*, but smaller and brown and grey in colour. In the cracks by the cave entrance the comb-footed cellar spider *Nesticus cellulanus* also often occurs. It is a smaller, paler spider that builds a fine crisscross platform web that is attached to the walls by longer threads that have a sticky 'gum' drop near the base. These probably trap crawling insects, and in this way it avoids competing for the same food as *M. merianae*. Sheet webs by the entrance containing silk tunnels are constructed by *Tegenaria* spp., but the spider is usually well hidden in a crevice behind the web.

There are also a number of 'money spiders' found in the caves, including Britain's only troglobitic spider, *Porrhomma rosenhaueri* (Fig. 146). It is a straw-coloured blind spider, only 2 mm long, and like most of the spiders spends most of its time hiding in crevices. Its webs are often in obscure cracks and crevices in the walls of the cave, and the spiders even harder to spot. The first British record was from Ogof y Ci in 1971 (Hazleton 1972), and in 1979 it was found in Lesser Garth Cave near Cardiff. Ogof y Ci is part of Nant Glais Caves, which as mentioned earlier is the only cave system in Britain currently notified on biological grounds. The spider is morphologically adapted to life within the permanent darkness of the deep cave zone, where it probably feeds largely on springtails. Although cave fauna is undoubtedly under-recorded, sufficient work has been carried out in Britain to suggest that *P. rosenhaueri* is genuinely rare. Its true British status may be impossible to ascertain though, as it may preferentially occupy mesocavernous habitats that are too small for human exploration.

FIG 146. Britain's only troglobitic spider, *Porrhomma rosenhaueri*, in Lesser Garth Cave. (Andrew Lewington)

Nonetheless, it is clear that it has a restricted distribution – and as one of the few members of our palaeotroglobitic fauna it deserves conservation and further study. Palaeotroglobites are species that are thought to have survived the repeated glaciations of the Pleistocene underground, in contrast to neotroglobites, which have colonised the subterranean habitat relatively recently.

Other money spiders include *Lessertia dentichelis* and *Lepthyphantes pallidus*. Apart from caves the latter generally occurs in damp situations in a range of habitats including grassland, wood and heathland. It also occurs under stones on mountains as high as 900 m. All the spiders are predatory, but they do not themselves have many predators in the cave. Young spiders have to shed their exoskeletons five to ten times to grow, and often the discarded remains are mistaken for dead spiders.

Probably the most widespread troglophiles are amphipod crustaceans of the genus *Gammarus*. These 'shrimps' are common in numerous aquatic habitats on the surface and are also frequently recorded in caves, especially after heavy rain. Some species found in cave streams and higher pools filled and emptied by flood water are part of a transitory population that have been washed underground and spend some time in the cave before being washed out of a resurgence. The most interesting specimens though are those found in pools above flood level, in water resulting from percolation through rock cavities, and which have existed in isolation from populations on the surface for some time. *Gammarus pulex* in this situation lose their orange colour, appearing white with white eye facets. Indeed, eyeless *G. pulex* have been found, and it is thought that some populations are in the process of evolving into a new subterranean species.

Birds can also be considered as animals of the threshold, at least at Porth yr Ogof, where dippers have nested high inside the main entrance for many years and do not seem bothered by the number of cavers. In 2006, for some reason, they nested lower down on the opposite wall but the winter floods washed the nest away. It was rebuilt in 2007 in the original position. Several species of birds are known to nest in cave entrances; apart from dipper, other birds recorded from this location in the Beacons include barn swallow, swift, jackdaw *Corvus monedula* and wren.

ANIMALS OF THE DARK

There are two significant factors in the ecology of the dark zone of caves, the absence of light and a remarkably constant environment. Temperature, for instance, usually stays constant at 8 or 9 °C, although it may vary in the vicinity of active stream passages. The lack of light means that the cave community does not have a direct source of energy and that the food chain must generally start outside the cave, and it is noticeable that animals tend to be more numerous in parts of caves which are near the surface. Many cave animals have enlarged sensory systems that allow them to perceive food from some distance away, and to improve their ability to find it they also move continually though their environment.

Deep in the cave live the few true troglobite species, the key ones being the well shrimp *Niphargus fontanus* and a freshwater hoglouse (similar to a woodlouse), *Proasellus cavaticus*, both of which are common in the Brecon Beacons. Like the well shrimp and a number of other inhabitants of the dark zone the freshwater hoglouse is blind and lacks pigmentation. There appear to be two different sizes: an 8 mm-long form found in the caves in South Wales and passages in the Cheddar River Cave and Wookey Hole, and a 4 mm form found above the water table in Mendip caves. It has been suggested that they might be two distinct groups, and genetic studies are planned to investigate this. The larger hoglice are usually found in streams on the underside of stones, on the thin film of water flowing over flowstone and in pools (Fig. 147). They probably feed on the silt and slimy brown film consisting of filamentous bacteria and fungi, and they have the capacity to multiply quickly when food is plentiful. At times in Ogof Ffynnon Ddu populations of up to 80 animals per square metre have been recorded. In turn they are eaten by the well shrimp and some flatworms.

South Wales was subject to repeated glaciations, yet true cave-dwelling crustaceans, such as the well shrimp, are commoner in this area than in any other part of Britain. Two possible explanations have been put forward for this: either

FIG 147. The hoglouse is a truly underground animal, usually found in the water film flowing over flowstone, or on stones in streams. These animals were photographed in Ogof Ffynnon Ddu. (Andrew Lewington)

there has been recolonisation since the last retreat of the glaciers or the animals survived beneath the ice cover. The similarity of the Mendip and South Wales faunas suggests a recolonisation from Mendip. The two areas are not far apart, and in immediate postglacial times they were not separated by water, as the upper part of the Bristol Channel was then dry land. There are some problems with the theory, however, as the two faunas are not identical. The alternative explanation, of survival beneath the ice, also raises further questions, although the Beacons were at times near the edge of the ice sheet and this probably aided survival in that it allowed food from the surface to reach the animals below.

The well shrimp, so named because the first records were from wells, is widespread, living in the flooded parts of caves as well as above the water table, but its true habitat is believed to be the small channels of water in underground rock strata and aquifers (Fig. 148). Their presence in caves is usually the result of the animals being washed out of the fissures in the rock by heavy rain. If conditions are suitable in the cave then stable populations will develop, but if there is insufficient food, or other constraints, then the animals will often move back to their original habitat. The shrimp is an omnivore, ingesting silt to extract organic matter, as well as preying on the hoglouse.

The most important members of the terrestrial communities in the dark zone are springtails, several species of which are commonly found on mud banks. More than 70 species have been found in British caves, but only 15 are widespread, with the most frequently recorded being *Tomocerus minor*. Springtails are rarely studied

FIG 148. The well shrimp is common in caves in the Brecon Beacons, but probably also lives in small water channels in underground rock strata and aquifers. (Andrew Lewington)

in any detail, but a few years ago Julian Carter, Zoological Conservation Officer at the National Museum of Wales, did identify *Folsomia palearctica,* which has few British records, from a new passage found in Dan yr Ogof. Almost nothing is known about the ecology of springtails in British caves, although they appear to be 'base level' consumers grazing on bacteria and microfungi in the sediments. In turn they are prey for various carnivorous mites and beetles. It is not known whether the species found underground are genetically the same as those species found outside the caves, or whether some are isolated in caves and are de facto troglobites but unrecognisable as such. Clearly much work is required, and genetic or molecular studies will be required to answer these questions.

Flatworms are simple white or brown flattened worms and move about their damp habitat by a series of undulations. Both the white *Phagocata vitta* and the grey *Crenobia alpina* are found in Porth yr Ogof. The white *Dendrocoelum lacteum,* also found in Dan yr Ogof, is relatively big for a flatworm, being 14–25 mm long and having a 'pseudo-sucker' to help capture prey such as the hoglouse, with which it is often found. It is not limited to caves though and is widespread in most of Britain, occurring almost anywhere there is water.

The most common snail found in the caves is the cellar snail *Oxychilus cellarius,* although point snail *Acicula fusca,* herald snail *Carychium minimum,* two-toothed door snail, rounded snail, lesser bulin *Ena obscura,* crystal snail *Vitrea contracta,* hairy snail *Trochulus hispida* and furrowed, or strawberry, snail *T. striolata* have also been recorded.

Woodlice, such as the common shiny woodlouse *Oniscus asellus* and the rosy, or pink, woodlouse *Androniscus dentiger,* are often seen near the threshold in Porth yr Ogof and other caves, living on the walls and amongst the rotting plant debris. Other species recorded here include water beetles and non-biting midges *Dixa* spp., commonly known as meniscus midges because the larvae of these aquatic insects live in the meniscus of the water. The water beetles include the New Forest mud beetle *Helophorus laticollis,* which is usually found in shallow, exposed, grassy pools on heathland. Many of these animals have obviously been carried into the caves by the various streams.

Fish also enter the underground stretches of streams, and brown trout is the species most often seen. Some animals appear pale and are often recorded as 'white fish', but although they are in a remarkably blanched condition they darken rapidly if brought into daylight. The caves in the limestone gorge of the Nant Glais, which lie parallel to it and under each bank are, as noted previously, particularly important for their unusually large populations of white trout. Unlike some of their counterparts in other countries these trout are not blind, feeding mainly on crustaceans and insect larvae that they can detect in the absence of

FIG 149. Bullhead in Porth yr Ogof. They are often found in the caves and, unlike trout, their colour is not affected by living in the dark. (Andrew Lewington)

light. White trout also exist in some of the other systems, such as Little Neath River Cave and Ogof Ffynnon Ddu. On discovering the Little Neath River Cave in 1967, for example, the South Wales Caving Club noted that 'there are a number of pale, almost white fish swimming in the sump, but it is unlikely that they are indigenous to the cave' (Norton *et al.* 1967). The dark spots, which in any case tend to be variable in trout, are reduced to almost nothing, although the row of orange-red spots along the lateral line is often retained. Bullheads are also often found in the caves and appear to live there all year round (Fig. 149). Unlike trout, they do not seem to be affected by the dark and their colour does not change.

BATS

Some of the caves in the east of the Brecon Beacons, such as Ogof Agen Allwedd and Ogof Draenen, contain important bat populations, primarily lesser horseshoe bat, which is the commonest bat found in Welsh caves. Edward Lhwyd noted the habits of hibernating lesser horseshoes in Welsh caves in a letter to John Ray in January 1698/9 (Gunther 1945):

> *I know not whether I ever mentioned to you (although you have probably frequently observed it yourself) in what manner the Bats are lodged in the caves during winter. The caves of this country (to mention that by the by) are always*

(I speak of the inland caves), in limestone, and in such places only are all our subterraneous brooks, which in Wales are no great rarity. In these caves the bats choose the driest apartments, where, planting their talons to the roof, they cover their bodies with their wings, and so, hanging perpendicularly in great numbers (but not so as they touch each other) they sleep for some months.

Lesser horseshoes eat half their weight in insects each day, producing large amounts of nitrogen-rich guano, which provides food for beetles and other forms of cave life. An annual survey of the bat population in Agen Allwedd shows that numbers are currently on the increase, and there is no evidence to suggest that cavers cause them undue disturbance.

Ogof Draenen has the largest guano deposits to be found in a British cave. Unfortunately, with the exception of one small chamber, Siambre Ddu, which is located directly above the main Ogof Draenen system, there are now few bats found inside the main cave complex. The entrance has been blocked by a rock collapse and there has been a decline in the local forest cover, as well as a change in its composition. Extensive accumulations of guano from lesser horseshoes though are found in several parts of the system. In places these piles of guano cover many square metres and the heaps can be over 0.5 m high, volumes not found in any other cave system in Britain. Although it is not known when the main Ogof Draenen system was abandoned as a bat roost, six radiocarbon dates from the guano indicate that it was occupied from the Iron Age to the medieval period. As part of the dating process the guano was compared with two modern guano samples, one from Siambre Ddu and one from Agen Allwedd cave, 5 km to the northwest. The latter is currently one of the largest active roosts for lesser horseshoes in Britain and lies close to the present northern limit of the species in Europe. Ogof Draenen appears to have been used both as a summer and a winter roost and, if the largest heap is continuous, it represents the accumulation of around 750 years of guano, at a rate of 0.16 mm per year.

OTHER MAMMALS

Badgers, foxes *Vulpes vulpes* and otters sometimes use a cave entrance for shelter, and badgers, at times, use them as ready-made setts, penetrating quite deep into the systems. Otter spraints are occasionally seen on prominent rocks just inside the entrance to tunnels and caves, including the triangular rock in the entrance to Porth yr Ogof, but the animals are more often encountered in the many lakes, rivers and streams that exist in the Beacons.

Chapter 8

Wetlands

When the glaciers of the last ice age retreated, around 10,000 years ago, they left large deposits of ice behind boulders, gravel and glacial debris. As the temperature continued to rise these deposits melted to create lakes, such as the remote 'myth-laden twins' of Llyn y Fan Fach and Llyn y Fan Fawr, or Llangorse Lake, the second-largest natural lake in Wales (only Bala Lake in North Wales is larger). There is a sense of remoteness and mystery about these water bodies, even the busy Llangorse Lake, so perhaps it is not surprising that they are all the focus of a number of legends, which record them as the haunts of fairies, lost cities and monsters. The original medium for these legends was oral storytelling, and while the great majority of these stories are 'migratory legends' – that is, the basic plot may turn up anywhere provided the physical setting is appropriate – many of the legends associated with these lakes have turned out to have some measure of truth in archaeology or natural history. The associated fens and bogs are also mainly relicts of the ice age and have their own stories to tell.

Natural water bodies are dwarfed though by the reservoirs constructed in the nineteenth and twentieth centuries to supply water to industrial South Wales, the Usk Reservoir being the last to be completed, in 1955. Today the reservoirs are all owned and managed by Dŵr Cymru/Welsh Water, and they are an accepted part of the landscape, with a range of fascinating wildlife. Some, such as the Talybont and Usk reservoirs, are productive trout fisheries, the native brown trout being supplemented by rainbow trout *Oncorhynchus mykiss*. Another artificial habitat is the Monmouthshire and Brecon Canal, which was constructed between 1796 and 1805 to link Brecon to the River Usk near Caerleon, and this too has interest for the naturalist.

LLYN Y FAN FACH

There are many legends associated with Llyn y Fan Fach, 'lake of the small beacon-hill', located under the species-rich cliffs of Bannau Sir Gaer (Fig. 150). Like Llyn Cwm Llwch, at the foot of Pen y Fan, the lake is traditionally thought to have been bottomless, and it has long been associated with fairies. As described in Chapter 4, it is particularly renowned for the legend of the Lady of the Lake, whose sons became the Physicians of Myddfai.

In 2011 Llyn y Fan Fach was named as one of the 1,000 'must-see' sights across the globe by Lonely Planet travel guides – the only place in Wales to make the list. Whether this accolade will make a substantial difference to the number of people visiting this isolated location remains to be seen, but such interest in the lake is not a new phenomenon, for as early as 1695 Dr Nicholas Roberts noted 'Lhan y Vane, a famous fontain resorted to in ye summer time by an infinite number of sick and crazy people' (British Museum Harleian MS 7017). Similarly, the Reverend A. G. Edwards, Warden of the Welsh College at Llandovery, recorded in 1881 (Rhys 1901):

> *An old woman from Myddfai, who is now, that is to say in January 1881, about eighty years of age, tells me that she remembers 'thousands and thousands of*

FIG 150. Llyn y Fan Fach, one of the most southerly examples of a corried lake in Britain and location of the legend of the Lady of the Lake. (Tim Rich)

people visiting the Lake of the Little Fan on the first Sunday or Monday in August, and when she was young she often heard old men declare that at that time a commotion took place in the lake, and that its waters boiled, which was taken to herald the approach of the Lake Lady and her Oxen.' The custom of going up to the lake on the first Sunday in August was a very well-known one in years gone by, as I have learned from a good many people, and it is corroborated by Mr. Joseph Joseph of Brecon, who kindly writes as follows, in reply to some queries of mine: 'On the first Sunday in the month of August, Llyn y Fan Fach is supposed to be boiling (berwi). I have seen scores of people going up to see it (not boiling though) on that day. I do not remember that any of them expected to see the Lady of the Lake.' As to the boiling of the lake I have nothing to say, and I am not sure that there is anything in the following statement made as an explanation of the yearly visit to the lake by an old fisherwoman from Llandovery: 'The best time for eels is in August, when the north-east wind blows on the lake, and makes huge waves in it. The eels can then be seen floating on the waves.'

Eels are still found here, though not often seen by the casual visitor, and it was common practice around 150 years ago for local farmers to fix basket traps under the small waterfalls below the lake at night. It is recorded that some colossal specimens were caught in these traps, with some, so local tradition says, up to 10 feet (3 m) in length. Other species of fish occurring here were small, but had the reputation of being tasty, and this attracted poachers from the mining village of Brynamman on the other side of the mountain.

Llyn y Fan Fach is the source of the Afon Sawdde, and it is also noted as one of the most southerly examples of a corried lake in Britain. Corries are steep-walled semicircular basins, formed at the head of a valley glacier by erosion, often containing, as in this case, a small lake behind a dam of glacial till. Much of the lake was drained during the First World War, in 1916, when conscientious objectors and Irish labourers were housed in huts at the site to construct an earthen dam on top of the natural one. From 1918 until 1993, the lake was used as a water-supply reservoir, the water being treated on site and piped to Llanelli. The original dam was supplemented in the 1930s by an embankment of concrete, reinforced by earth and clay, which raised the natural water level by 3 m. The catchment was also enlarged at this time by diverting water from the upper reaches of the adjacent Nant Sychlwch and Nant Coch, along the contours, via weirs, pipes and a culvert.

The water of Llyn y Fan Fach and the other upland lakes in the Beacons is cold, clear and low in nutrients, and they all support a poor but distinctive flora with characteristic narrow leaves, tough cuticles and either tight rosettes of leaves

FIG 151. Shoreweed forms dense swards around the shelving margins of Llyn y Fan Fach. (Graham Motley)

or long linear leaves, that offer little resistance to wave action. The shores are mostly rocky, and wave action in these exposed situations means that floating-leaved or emergent plants are virtually absent, or restricted to sheltered areas. In the shallow water there is typically a zone of shoreweed *Littorella uniflora*, which forms dense swards around the shelving margins, the plants consisting of tufts of short rigid semi-cylindrical leaves a few centimetres in length growing from a slender creeping stolon (Fig. 151). In deeper water, but often overlapping with the shoreweed, the rare quillwort *Isoetes lacustris* occurs. This too has rosettes with long cylindrical leaves. The non-flowering submerged specimens of shoreweed bear a superficial resemblance to quillwort, the tiny greenish flowers usually only being produced on plants growing above the water.

Quillwort is a submerged aquatic plant that resembles a small spring onion, but it is actually a relative of the clubmosses and ferns. The stem is very short and completely hidden by the expanded whitish bases of the long, narrow, tubular leaves. The leaves vary in length but are normally between about 5 and 15 cm long. It is perennial, with typically two flushes of new leaves each year, in spring and autumn. The plant grows rooted in the mud and is not immediately obvious, but in autumn, after storms and gales have disturbed the water, many plants are uprooted and float to the surface, sometimes collecting in drifts around the margins of the lake.

The Natural History Museum in London has a herbarium sheet of awlwort *Subularia aquatica* collected from Llyn y Fan Fach by H. J. Riddelsdell on 21 July 1902. A printed note attached to the sheet states 'Very small plants, but quite characteristic and in good flower, with fruit well developed on the more forward specimens. Apparently a new record for South Wales province of H. C. Watson.' There have been no recent records and it was probably lost when the natural level of the lake was raised. A small submerged aquatic plant with small white four-petalled flowers and narrow grass-like leaves, it is often found in similar situations to shoreweed. The flowers, which rise above the surface of the water open, while those that remain submersed stay closed and self-pollinate. The seeds are contained inside tiny inflated pods.

In deeper water this community is replaced by an aquatic free-floating form of bulbous rush *Juncus bulbosus* var. *fluitans* which has long branching thread-like stems. Bog pondweed, a typical plant of peaty acid water, is also abundant in certain locations. Stonewort *Nitella flexilis sensu lato* and alternate water-milfoil can also be found occasionally in this zone. In early summer large areas of the lake and the Afon Sawdde nearby are covered with the flowers of river water-crowfoot. Narrowleaf bur-reed *Sparganium angustifolium* also forms floating mats on the lake.

Llyn y Fan Fach has a diverse bottom-dwelling insect fauna which includes mayfly and caddisfly larvae. Although the water is nutrient-poor this rich insect fauna used to support the eels mentioned by the Reverend Edwards, together with trout – both of which were renowned as being of 'superior quality'. George Agar Hansard, the author of *Trout and Salmon Fishing in Wales* (1834) wrote:

> When a strong breeze ruffles the surface of Llyn Van, the rise of the fish is almost incredible, and can be compared only to violent rain, or the effect that would be produced by casting handfuls of gravel upon its surface. We once spent an entire day on its wild, rocky shores, and were, for that period at least, perfectly satiated with sport. The trout threw themselves out of the water in summersaults, by hundreds at once: and the effect was most singular, as their golden spotted sides flashed and glittered in the sunbeams that occasionally broke through the gloom which over-spread the atmosphere.

Even today the walk up to Llyn y Fan Fach from the single-track road passes a trout hatchery, where the fish can be seen leaping out of the water. There are unfortunately no trout occurring naturally in the lake now, although local angling clubs regularly reinstate them.

LLYN Y FAN FAWR

While Llyn y Fan Fach is noted as one of the most southerly corried lakes, Llyn y Fan Fawr, to the east of Fan Brycheiniog, the highest peak of the Mynydd Du range, is regarded as the best example of a corrie lake in South Wales (Fig. 152). As the surface of the lake, which covers 16.5 hectares, lies 605 m above sea level, it is also the highest natural lake in the region. It is drained by a stream known as Nant y Llyn ('stream of the lake'), whose waters flow into the Afon Tawe.

Unlike Llyn y Fan Fach the lake is almost devoid of aquatic plants. The reasons for this are unclear, although the steeply shelving shoreline, dominated by sandstone boulders, is unsuitable for many species. A sandy area close to the outflow, however, has been colonised by shoreweed, while a shallow-water form of quillwort extends to a depth of about 1 m. Llyn y Fan Fawr was included in the Nature Conservancy's *A Nature Conservation Review* (Ratcliffe 1977), and the description of the site seems to indicate that shoreweed and quillwort were once more widespread along the eastern shore. The only other species found at the site is greater water-moss, which occurs occasionally on boulders around the waterline. Greater water-moss is a dark green plant with leaves that are sharply pointed,

FIG 152. Llyn y Fan Fawr, the highest natural lake in South Wales, with the slopes of Fan Brycheiniog behind. (John Light)

ridged, overlapping, and arranged in three rows along the entire length of the stems. The stems grow up to 60 cm long and appear triangular if the leaves are removed.

With the exception of the small, air-breathing, freshwater limpet *Ancylus fiuviatilis* and a few insects, such as the caddisflies *Polycentropus flavomaculatus* and *Sericostoma personatum*, there is little animal life. Perhaps this is the reason why Llyn y Fan Fawr, unlike Llyn y Fan Fach, is not renowned for its fish. A manuscript of the late seventeenth century noted that it 'hathe no fish attaile in't nither will any fish being put into it live, but as soon as they have tasted of this water turne up their silver bellies and suddenly dey' (British Museum Harleian MS 7017).

LLYN CWM LLWCH

Llyn Cwm Llwch occupies a hollow beneath the peaks of Pen y Fan and Corn Du in the central Brecon Beacons (Fig. 153). It is drained by the Nant Cwm Llwch, which empties into the Afon Tarell, which itself enters the River Usk at Brecon. It is a small, roughly circular lake around 150 m in diameter, but with a depth of only 8 m. While it may at first appear to have been excavated from the solid rock by a

FIG 153. Llyn Cwm Llwch lies below Craig Cwm Llwch and is renowned for its abundant invertebrate fauna and large numbers of smooth newts. (Jonathan Mullard)

glacier, the 'lake of the hollow of the lake' (*llwch* being an old Welsh word for lake, related to the Gaelic *loch*) was actually formed, like Llyn y Fan Fach, by a glacial moraine. The moraine, which forms its northern and eastern sides, contrasts with the smoother contours of the slopes beneath Corn Du, while the bottom of the lake consists of boulders, stones and silt derived from the Old Red Sandstone.

The steep banks are grassy with occasional specimens of soft-rush, and bulbous rush has also been recorded from the site. As with the other lakes, plants found around the edge include shoreweed and quillwort. Bog pondweed also occurs here. The rounded leaves float on or just below the surface of the water, while below there is a network of rhizomes and branching stems.

The invertebrate fauna of the lake is abundant, although it only consists of a few species, such as *Gammarus pulex*, the flatworm *Polycelis nigra*, small numbers of the horse leech *Haemopis sanguisuga* and mayfly nymphs of the species *Cloeon dipterum* (Edington 1967). This is the commonest mayfly found in ponds in Britain, but it is unusual among mayflies in being ovoviviparous, the embryos developing inside eggs that are retained within the female's body until they are ready to hatch. Females lay eggs 10–14 days after mating, and the eggs hatch as soon as they hit the water. In some years large numbers of several species of caddisfly larvae can also be found here.

Samuel Lewis in *A Topographical Dictionary of Wales* (1833) noted that Llyn Cwm Llwch contained 'great numbers of the *lacerta aquatica*, or waterlizard' and 'by the peasantry of the surrounding country this pool is believed to be of unfathomable depth'. While the depth might not be unfathomable, the waterlizard, now known as the smooth, or common, newt *Lissotriton vulgaris*, is still abundant in the area and especially noticeable during the spring. Smaller numbers of palmate newts *Lissotriton helveticus* also occur, and like the smooth newts they are well able to survive in these acid moorland waterbodies. Great crested newts have also been recorded here by the Brecknock Wildlife Trust. Only found in ponds during the breeding season between February and June, for most of the year newts come onto land and live in damp places underneath rocks and debris. Common frogs are also present, but there are no fish, which probably accounts for the abundance of invertebrate life.

LLANGORSE LAKE

The Brecon Beacons not only has the highest natural lake in South Wales, but also, in Llangorse Lake, the second-largest in the whole of Wales, covering 153 hectares (Fig. 154). Situated towards the head of the Afon Llynfi between the hills

FIG 154. Llangorse Lake, one of the few naturally nutrient-rich lakes in Wales: the view over the lake from Mynydd Troed, looking southwest towards Pen y Fan. (Jonathan Mullard)

of Mynydd Llangorse and Allt yr Esgair, Llangorse Lake in contrast to the other glacial lakes in the area is relatively low-lying, being only 154 m above sea level. It is also shallow, with depths ranging from 2.5 to 4.0 m. Llangorse Lake is a very popular location for recreation, and the setting of the lake and its large size means that it attracts fishermen, sailing craft, water-skiers, canoeists and outdoor groups – all of which have the potential to disturb both habitats and wildlife. Guidelines have therefore been drawn up by the Llangorse Lake Advisory Group to ensure that water users are aware of the wildlife of the lake and the need to undertake activities in a responsible manner.

Because of Llangorse Lake's long history of human activity it has been known by many different names, in both Welsh and English. These include the lake's original Welsh name, Llyn Syfaddon/Syfaddan, and Brycheiniog Mere. One interpretation of Llyn Syfaddon is that it is derived from the name of a pre-Christian deity, suggesting that the lake may have been the focus of an early pagan cult. The English name is comparatively recent, but will be used here, as it is the one by which it is commonly known.

Llangorse Lake is important as one of the few naturally nutrient-rich lakes in Wales, and it is of national, if not international, significance. Because of this interest it was designated as early as 1954 as a Site of Special Scientific Interest and in 1995 as a Special Area of Conservation under the Habitats and Species

Directive. Naturally occurring eutrophic lakes have fairly high concentrations of nutrients, such as nitrogen and phosphorus, which help plants to grow. However, many of the lakes considered eutrophic, such as Llangorse, were once not so rich in nutrients, but have been affected by human activity. The lake has a long history of eutrophication problems, and the earliest record of an algal bloom dates back to 1188, while the earliest record of large amounts of sediment being delivered to the lake by the Afon Llynfi after heavy rainfall dates back to the mid-1500s (Griffiths 1939). Gerald of Wales also recorded in his description of a journey through Wales that Llangorse Lake had a number of miraculous properties, including sometimes turning green. He noted that the lake was sometimes tinged with red 'as if blood flowed partially through certain veins and small channels', though at other times it was seen as being portentous if 'the large lake and river Leveni [Llynfi] were tinged with a deep green colour' (Thorpe 1978).

The situation became much worse in the 1950s, the period when the use of inorganic fertilisers first became widespread, when the aquatic plants began to decline. This coincided with a switch in the diatom community from non-planktonic to planktonic forms (Bennion & Appleby 1999). The most noticeable change was the decline of a relatively diverse submerged flora, dominated by fennel pondweed *Potamogeton pectinatus* and horned pondweed *Zannichellia palustris*, from at least eight species in 1973 to a monoculture of horned pondweed by 1977. Although the eutrophication processes partly accounted for the decline they did not adequately explain the survival of *Z. palustris* alone, and it is considered that a combination of eutrophication and mechanical disturbance was the prime cause of the problem. In recent years significant efforts have been made to meet water quality targets by reducing the input of phosphorus from agricultural and domestic sources. As Afon Llynfi, the main outlet for water from the lake, is quite small, the water flows through the lake very slowly and any pollutants entering the lake remain there for long periods. Much of the current pollution is in the form of nutrients from the air and the many small watercourses entering the lake. Although it has improved substantially in quality following the diversion of effluent from Llangorse sewage treatment works in 1981 and the construction of Bwlch sewage treatment works in 1992, the levels of phosphorus in the water still remain a concern.

Management decisions to reduce the input of phosphorus were originally based on the widely held assumption that shallow lakes are limited in this nutrient during the summer. A recent study, however, clearly shows that this is not always the case (May *et al.* 2010). Llangorse Lake, at least, is strongly limited by nitrogen over the summer months. As a result, phosphorus released from the sediments cannot be used by the phytoplankton population and accumulates in the water column, causing very high concentrations to occur in late summer. This puts the lake at a high risk of developing algal blooms when nitrogen availability increases, usually in early autumn. The study also found that the hydrology of the lake was strongly affected by subsurface flows, and nutrients and water could be delivered to the lake from areas beyond the surface-water catchment. These findings have serious implications for the successful management of the lake, which currently tends to focus on management of the surface-water catchment only.

Algal blooms still occur today. In June 2012, for instance, water sports on the lake were banned and pet and livestock owners were warned to keep their animals away from the water after toxic cyanobacteria (blue-green algae) were identified (Fig. 155). These extensive and highly visible 'blooms', created when the cyanobacteria reproduce rapidly due to high levels of available nutrients, have the appearance of blue-green paint, or scum, hence their common name. Several cases of human poisoning have been documented in the UK, but a lack of knowledge prevents an accurate assessment of the risks.

Most sources of nutrients within the catchment seem to be diffuse sources, and these can only be addressed through landscape-scale initiatives, better

FIG 155. Cyanobacteria (blue-green algae) blooms on Llangorse Lake in June 2012. (Graham Motley)

animal husbandry and improved management of discharges containing sewage effluent. Catchment sensitive farming would probably be the best approach to this since other measures, such as making the area a nitrate-vulnerable zone, would only address part of the problem. There are also problems arising from the occasional flooding of the meadows around the lake. Although flooding was once encouraged by local farmers as a way of carrying plant food to the pastures 'both in solution and in very finely divided particles' (Griffiths 1939), in these days of intensive agriculture, flooding of the meadows is more likely to carry nutrients from the meadows to the lake. The increasing numbers of Canada geese *Branta canadensis* which graze on the surrounding fields may also move nutrients from surrounding land to the lake.

Despite continuing concerns about eutrophication, however, the quality and clarity of the water is generally good and Llangorse Lake is an outstanding natural feature. Most importantly, the water levels are allowed to change naturally with changes in rainfall patterns and season. Thus, during wetter periods, the surrounding land becomes flooded, which maintains the rich array of transitional habitats between open water and drier ground. These habitats include reed beds, sedge fen, wet woodland and wet and dry grasslands, and the lake has some of the best-developed transitions from aquatic vegetation to dry grassland in Wales. The finest examples occur along the western and southwestern shores, since agricultural activities have truncated the zonation around the northeastern edge, but overall the emergent and terrestrial vegetation occurring here is a very significant feature, alongside the aquatic plants. This wide band of vegetation seems to have been a longstanding feature of the lake, Gerald of Wales noting in the twelfth century that:

> *It is a large, though by no means a beautiful, piece of water, its banks being low and flat, and covered with rushes and other aquatic plants to a considerable distance from the shore.*

AQUATIC PLANTS

The flora of Llangorse Lake is relatively well studied, with some plant records dating back to the seventeenth century. It still supports a wide range of plants, and species characteristic of the area include water-starworts *Callitriche* spp., stoneworts *Chara* spp., curled pondweed *Potamogeton crispus*, shining pondweed *P. lucens*, perfoliate pondweed *P. perfoliatus*, lesser pondweed *P. pusillus*, mare's-

FIG 156. Close to the lake's edge the water surface is covered in the floating leaves and flowers of water lilies along with great duckweed. (Graham Motley)

tail *Hippuris vulgaris*, fan-leaved water-crowfoot *Ranunculus circinatus* and greater duckweed *Spirodela polyrhiza*. The growth of pondweeds is dependent on a variety of factors such as water temperature and turbidity, but in most years there is good growth, with pondweeds, with both thin and wide leaves, mixing with the delicate leaves of water-milfoils, hornworts and water-crowfoots. Various-leaved pondweed *P. gramineus* and long-stalked pondweed *P. praelongus* have not been seen for many years but, if recorded, this would indicate an improvement in water quality. The rare hybrid yellow water-lily *Nuphar* × *spenneriana* also grows here; it is a cross between least water-lily *N. pumila* and yellow water-lily *N. lutea*. Great duckweed *Lemna polyrhiza* also occurs here, with each plant a smooth, round, flat disc up to 1 cm wide (Fig. 156).

Stoneworts are a unique group of algae that grow in fresh or brackish water. Named due to their encrusted appearance, most stoneworts create an external skeleton of calcium carbonate instead of using cellulose like flowering plants consisting of stems with whorls of 'leaves', anchored in the sediment by colourless rhizoids that function like a root. They reproduce sexually via gametes produced by male and female reproductive organs with seed-like 'oospores' that germinate into new plants. Many species require high water quality and clarity for survival, so their presence indicates the existence of a healthy ecosystem. They are special because of their long history, which has been traced back to the Silurian around 440 to 416 million years ago. Many produce lime-shells around their oospores, and these shells, known as gyrogonites, are frequently found as fossils. Stoneworts were much more diverse in prehistoric times, so by studying the species living now it is possible to reconstruct past climates.

Close to the lake's edge the water surface is covered in the floating leaves and flowers of water lilies, while large parts of the lake margin are fringed by dense beds of common reed *Phragmites australis* and tall sedges. There are also patches of lesser reedmace *Typha angustifolia*, branched bur-reed and club-rush *Schoenoplectus* spp. The southern edge of Llangorse Lake has the most extensive reed beds in the Beacons; indeed, Llangors (or Llangorse, the anglicised version of the name) is derived from the Welsh *llan* (church) and cors (reeds, marsh, bog). Scattered amongst these beds are uncommon plants such as flowering rush *Butomus umbellatus*, tubular water-dropwort *Oenanthe fistulosa* and meadow rue. In midsummer the striking flowers of purple-loosestrife *Lythrum salicaria*, bogbean *Menyanthes trifoliata* and water mint add extra interest. Water mint has flowers of varying colour from mauve to blue and pink, which grow in clusters at the end of the stems. The minty aroma is most distinctive when the leaves are crushed or rubbed. In 1698 Edward Lhuyd also recorded awlwort from the lake, writing:

> *In a great lake called Lhyn Savadhan I found a pellucid plant I had never met with before; the leaves are extraordinary thin and transparent, in form not unlike small Dock leaves; but the middle rib is continued beyond the extremity, so that each leaf has a soft prickle at the end: by which note I hope that you will be able to tell me what it is. We found there also the* Hippuris saxea *[Chara spp.], and two elegant sorts of small Leeches, which I suppose not describ'd.*

INVERTEBRATES

The two species of leech noted by Lhuyd were the medicinal leech *Hirudo medicinalis*, which is still found in company with far larger numbers of the common and widely distributed horse leech. The medicinal leech can be distinguished from the horse leech by a dull yellow dorsal stripe on each side of the median line, bearing irregular brown spots, though H. E. Quick (1938) also noted another way of distinguishing them, which is probably not recommended!

Many colour and pattern varieties of the medicinal leech have been recorded, and the most darkly pigmented of these four (examples) needed close inspection to distinguish it from the neighbouring horse leeches. Application to the back of the hand, however, left no doubt, as it promptly adhered and gorged itself with blood, a feat which Haemopis sanguisuga in spite of its name is unable to accomplish.

Numerous other invertebrates found at Llangorse include the two-tone reed beetle *Donacia bicolora*, a small aquatic insect found only on branched bur-reed (Fig. 157). This beetle was previously more widespread, but has been lost from many sites over the last century. It was thought to have disappeared from Wales, the last record being more than 50 years ago at a site near Neath, but in 2006 it was discovered at Llangorse, and this is now the only known site for the beetle in Wales. In a subsequent survey in 2007 a total of 146 individual beetles were counted, many of them mating pairs (Gibbs 2008). The adults are 8.0–11.6 mm long and a greenish-gold colour on the upper side, with a more silvery underside. Later in the season individuals may be blue-tinged, or purple, hence the bicoloured name. Being relatively large and conspicuous insects they are comparatively easy to survey, even at a distance through binoculars. The adults overwinter in tough fibrous pupal cocoons, becoming active from mid-April until August, with most records in June. Eggs are laid at the base of the host plants in early summer, and the cream-coloured maggot-like larvae develop with their rear ends attached to roots under the water. The pupae, which are also attached to the air spaces in aquatic root systems, develop in late summer and late autumn, the adults remaining inside the cocoons until the following spring.

FIG 157. Two-tone reed beetle occurs exclusively on branched bur-reed, and Llangorse Lake is now the only known site for the beetle in Wales. (Roger Key)

FIG 158. Llangorse Lake is an important habitat for the variable blue damselfly, which is uncommon in Britain. (Harold Grenfell)

The lake also provides an important habitat for a wide range of other invertebrates, including the variable blue damselfly *Coenagrion pulchellum* (Fig. 158). The 'variable' lives up to its name: the markings on both thorax and abdomen can sometimes be difficult to interpret, and its similarity to the more widespread azure damselfly *C. puella*, which also occurs around the lake, often leads to confusion over identification. In May 2010 the Brecknock Wildlife Trust dragonfly recorder, Keith Noble, recorded that the fields between Llangorse Lake and Llangasty village hall were full of thousands of damselflies, mostly immature. They seemed to be a mixture of common blue damselfly *Enallagma cyathigerum* and variable damselflies, although some may have been azure damselflies.

BIRDS

During spring, and then again in late summer and autumn, migrating birds including terns, waders, hirundines and warblers stop over to rest and feed. Llangorse Lake is especially celebrated for one very rare species, the aquatic warbler *Acrocephalus paludicola* (Fig. 159). Once widespread and numerous in fen mires and wet meadows throughout the continent, this bird has disappeared from most of its former range. More yellow-brown and streaked than the similar sedge warbler *Acrocephalus schoenobaenus*, it is a specialist of large open sedge and fen mires, which

FIG 159. The aquatic warbler, one of Europe's rarest songbirds, is regularly recorded from Llangorse Lake. (Alan Lowe)

have been much reduced by human pressure in western and central Europe. Its dependence on a specialised and vulnerable breeding habitat means it has become a globally threatened and declining species. Nowadays, its global population of only 10,200–13,800 breeding pairs is confined to fewer than 40 sites in only six countries.

The presence of aquatic warblers at Llangorse is only known as a result of the 'constant effort' ringing carried out by the Llangorse Lake Ringing Group, which was formed in 1978 with the main purpose of monitoring the populations of the resident birds and numbers of passage and summer visitors. The Group now has one of the longest-running data sets in the British Trust for Ornithology's Constant Effort Sites project, for which bird ringers operate the same nets in the same locations over the same time period, at regular intervals through the breeding season, at 120 sites throughout Britain and Ireland. The approach provides valuable information on trends associated with the abundance of adults and juveniles, productivity and also adult survival rates for 25 species of common songbird.

In recent years the Group has ringed about 2,500–3,000 birds annually. The most frequently ringed species is the reed warbler *Acrocephalus scirpaceus*, of which the ten-thousandth individual was ringed in 2011. Other birds found in the reed beds and ringed by the Group include sedge warbler, reed bunting *Emberiza schoeniclus* and roosting species such as barn swallow, sand martin, pied wagtail *Motacilla alba* ssp. *yarrellii*, yellow wagtail and Canada goose. In the summer Cetti's warbler *Cettia cetti* can sometimes be heard singing from the tall marginal vegetation, while hobbies *Falco subbuteo* hunt dragonflies and damselflies above. The thatched hide on the south side of the lake, which was built by students of the Prince's Trust in 2011/12, is an excellent location from which to watch a number of these birds (Fig. 160).

Towards midsummer large numbers of mute swans arrive to moult. As the end of July approaches, the swans begin to moult and for a period of around six weeks they remain flightless (Fig. 161). They have a mixed diet which includes aquatic plants, grass, grains, insects, fish, frogs, worms and molluscs, cropping plants growing on the bottom by reaching down with their long necks. In the process they stir up the bottom and often uproot plants, making food available to other animals and water birds that otherwise could not reach it. Llangorse Lake has been noted

ABOVE: **FIG 160.** The thatched hide on the south side of Llangorse Lake. (Harold Grenfell)

LEFT: **FIG 161.** Llangorse Lake has been noted for its mute swans for centuries. Moulting birds are unable to fly for about six weeks until they have grown new flight feathers. (Jonathan Mullard)

for its swans for centuries, and they are the subject of a poem entitled 'The Swan on Syfaddan Lake' attributed to the fourteenth-century poet Dafydd ap Gwilym, the most distinguished of the medieval Welsh poets, which begins:

> *Fair swan, the lake you ride*
> *Like white-robed abbot in your pride;*
> *Round-footed bird of the drifted snow,*
> *Like heavenly visitant you show.*
> *A stately ministry is yours,*
> *And beauty haunts your young hours.*
> *From God's hand this day you take*
> *Lordship over Syfaddon lake.*

In winter, large rafts of wildfowl such as pochard *Aythya ferina*, tufted duck *A. fuligula*, goldeneye *Bucephala clangula* and coot *Fulica atra* can be seen drifting on the lake, with an occasional smew *Mergellus albellus*. There are also acrobatic displays of thousands of starlings *Sturnus vulgaris* as they prepare to roost each evening. Occasional bitterns *Botaurus stellaris* are also recorded overwintering in the reed beds.

Given the lake's importance for birds, it is probably no coincidence that one of the early Welsh folk-tales is located here. Gerald of Wales records in his topographical work *The Description of Wales* an 'ancient saying in Wales that if the natural prince of the country, coming to this lake, shall order the birds to sing, they will immediately obey him', and he describes an instance of this during the reign of Henry I, when Gruffudd, son of Rhys ap Tewdwr, succeeded in this challenge where the two Normans who accompanied him, Milo, Earl of Hereford and Lord of Brecknock, and Payne FitzJohn, failed. What birds were singing and what time of year it was we are not told, but if it was summer it might well have been reed and sedge warblers that responded to the Welsh voice! In another account though it is recorded that 'the birds, beating the water with their wings, began to cry aloud, and proclaim him' – so perhaps it was the normally 'mute' swans that replied.

FISH

Gerald also commented that Llangorse Lake, which he referred to as Brecknock Mere, was 'a broad expanse of water which is very well known, that supplies plenty of pike, perch, excellent trout, tench and mud-loving eels for the local inhabitants'. Llanthony Priory had the right to take fish from Llangorse Lake and they were carried, still alive and wrapped in wet rushes, over the mountains, along the path still known as Rhiw Pyscod ('fish hill') to stock the fishponds at the monastery. Another path, Rhiw Cwrw, developed to bring the monks' beer from Dore Abbey, in the Golden Valley in Herefordshire! The fishing rights were granted to the monks of Brecon priory, and there is a mid-thirteenth-century reference to the use of a boat. John Leland refers to the stocks of fish in the lake in the early sixteenth century, while a map of 1584 shows two boats drawn up on the bank of the lake, a watermill where the Llynfi joins the southern end of the lake and three eel traps where the river flows out of its northern side. A survey in the seventeenth century entitled *A Survey of a certain Poole or fishing Poole commonly called Llinsavathen* refers to the presence of weirs at which 'good store of Eles taken in potts', while Gibson's 1722 edition of Camden's *Britannia* mentions the use of coracles for fishing. Today the fish population still consists of native species such as perch and eels, with populations of bottom-feeding species, such as bream *Abramis brama*, at population levels that do not affect the aquatic flora. Non-native species, such as Chinese grass-carp *Ctenopharyngodon idella*, which have done so much damage to other aquatic ecosystems, are thankfully absent.

Unfortunately, however, there is no longer a 'good store of Eles' in Llangorse, as eel populations have declined dramatically both here and in other parts of Britain. According to the Environment Agency the number of eels across Europe has declined by as much as 95 per cent in the last 25 years. It is not at all clear why eels are vanishing in such large numbers. One theory is that the shifting of the Gulf Stream means that not so many eels are being swept from the Sargasso Sea, close to Bermuda, where they are born, to the shores of Europe. In 2011 the Environment Agency began a programme of restocking Llangorse with elvers in the hope that the population in the Wye catchment and beyond can be boosted, but it will be a long time before it is clear whether this has been a success.

THE AFANC

The fifteenth-century Welsh poet Lewys Glyn Cothi mentions Llangorse Lake in a poem that includes the earliest known surviving literary reference to the Afanc of Llangorse, a lake monster from Welsh mythology. In the poem, addressed to his friend Llywelyn ab Gwilym ab Thomas Vaughan of Bryn Hafod in the Towy Valley, Lewys suggests that it would be as hard to make him leave his friend's hospitable dwelling as it would be to lure the Afanc away from Llyn Syfaddan. The exact description of the Afanc is hard to pin down, and it is variously described as resembling a crocodile, a beaver, a dwarf-like creature, or a demon. Belief in the Afanc was formerly widespread, and several Welsh lakes are named after the monster, including Llyn yr Afanc, a lake near Betws y Coed. *Afanc*, in modern Welsh, is still used to refer to the beaver.

> *The afanc am I, who, sought for, bides*
> *In hiding on the edge of the lake;*
> *Out of the waters of Syfaddon Mere*
> *Was he not drawn, once he got there?*
> *So with me: nor wain nor oxen wont to toil*
> *Me to-day will draw from here forth.*

The Afanc is still regularly sighted to this day, since the description probably refers to a large pike (Fig. 162). The description 'bides in hiding on the edge of the lake' fits the habits of the fish well. It is an ambush predator, and the body is elongated with large fins set near the tail to increase the surface area pushing against the water during explosive lunges at prey. A pike is usually olive-green and silver in colour with distinct dark striped markings on the flanks to afford good camouflage. Markings vary between individuals and can be used to distinguish

FIG 162. The Afanc of Welsh legend in its modern incarnation. Llangorse Lake is famous for its pike fishing and attracts large numbers of fishermen. (Wil Meinderts /Corbis)

individual fish. Immature pike have yellow stripes along a green body, but as they grow the stripes turn into light spots and the body colour darkens.

Much of the pike's routine movement is achieved by sculling motions of the paired fins on the underside of the body. These fins gently manoeuvre the fish into position for attack. The eyes swivel to stay fixed on the prey and the body tenses into an S shape. As the body unwinds and the pike accelerates forward, the mouth opens to engulf the prey, which is usually captured sideways on. The pike's large bony mouth is armed with rows of teeth, which point backwards and hinge to allow the prey to slide into the gullet, but mean there is little chance of escape. The prey is usually turned so that it is swallowed head-first. Pike feed extensively on fish but include a range of other animals in their diet, including insect larvae, frogs, water voles and sometimes even ducks. In August 1999 Darren Blake, a visitor from Lichfield, was bitten on the left foot by a pike while he was water-skiing on the lake, but this is very unusual and no further incidents have been reported since that date. Presumably the pike mistook the man's foot for a duck or another fish.

The lake is famous for its coarse fishing, particularly pike, and attracts large numbers of fishermen. The largest pike caught by rod in the UK was supposedly caught in Llangorse Lake in 1846 by O. Owen and was said to weigh around 68 pounds (31 kg). The weight of this particular fish is unsubstantiated, however, and, if true, it would have been the largest pike in the world, so the record seems somewhat doubtful. In 1987 though a local man, Mike Tunnicliffe, found the skull of a dead pike in the lake which was 46 cm long. This suggests that the skull belonged to a pike around 1.8–2.4 m in length.

WATER VOLES

In May 2011 more than 200 water voles were released by the Environment Agency Wales near Llangorse Lake in an ongoing programme to try to restore population numbers, the organisation having developed a water vole rearing facility at the Cynrig Fish Hatchery, near Brecon, to enable animals to be bred for reintroduction programmes. Prior to this release the species had not been seen at Llangorse since the early 1990s. The work included creating suitable habitats by clearing and creating ditches adjacent to the lake, removing some vegetation and coppicing trees, as the voles prefer more open wetland habitats away from tree cover. It also involved liaison with landowners regarding a mink control programme.

The water vole is one of the most endangered mammals in Britain, and although once widespread, it can now be found in only a few scattered places.

Predation by the introduced American mink *Neovison vison* has had a severe impact on water vole populations, even causing local extinctions. It is estimated that the population has decreased from an estimated eight million animals in the late 1950s to only around 220,000 in 2004. This may be because the voles' usual way of evading predators, by diving and using burrows with underwater entrances, does not protect them from the mink. Following the release, a survey of the Llangorse area found evidence of the voles almost everywhere there was suitable habitat for them, but continued control of mink will be necessary if they are to survive here in the future.

POOLS

Besides Llangorse Lake and the high-altitude lakes described earlier, other natural waterbodies include the Illtyd Pools, a collection of water and peat-filled hollows on the summit ridge of Mynydd Illtyd created by the extensive peat extraction described in Chapter 3. All are rich in rare plants and insects, and some of the pools, the largest of which is Traeth Bach (Fig. 163), support a number of

FIG 163. Traeth Bach, the largest of a number of pools and peat-filled hollows on the summit ridge of Mynydd Illtyd which are important for rare plants and insects. (Jonathan Mullard)

rare calcicolous plant species, including fen-sedge *Cladium mariscus* and slender sedge *Carex lasiocarpa*, at their only known locality in the Beacons. Other pools here are more acidic, with floating mats of vegetation at their edges, while peat has formed in some hollows to produce 'hummock and hollow' mires with well-developed hummocks of bog-mosses *Sphagnum* spp. and lichens such as *Cladonia impexa*. Water mudwort *Limosella aquatica* appears sporadically in some of the shallower pools, most recently being recorded in the wet summer of 2007 when it was seen growing in some deep wheel ruts by the road that crosses the common. It usually prefers the drying mud of lakesides or reservoirs and, if conditions are right, thousands of plants occur, even though it is nationally rare.

A number of uncommon aquatic insects have also been recorded from the area, whilst the hummocks of the mires support an unusual spider fauna. J. A. L. Cooke, from King's College London, a well-known spider expert of his day, recorded around 50 species of spider here on three day-visits in 1965 and 1966, 14 of these being regional rarities, including *Wackenaera unicornis*, *W. kochi* and *Aphileta misera* (Cooke 1967).

Another important pool is the Brechfa Pool on Llangoed Common. This is a shallow mud-bottomed lake with an adjoining area of periodically inundated

FIG 164. Pillwort in a pool at Twyn y Beddau, north of Hay Bluff. The UK now holds a significant proportion of the global population of this aquatic fern. (Graham Motley)

grassland, which supports a number of rare plants including the rare aquatic fern pillwort *Pilularia globulifera* and pennyroyal *Mentha pulegium*, a short-lived perennial herb of seasonally inundated grassland overlying silt and clay. The majority of the populations are now confined to pools, runnels, ruts and poached areas on heavily grazed land, such as Llangoed Common. Other species found here include orange foxtail grass *Alopecurus aequalis*, which grows on the muddy margins.

Pools at Twyn y Beddau, north of Hay Bluff, also support good populations of pillwort (Fig. 164). Pillwort is declining rapidly throughout its northwest European range, and the UK now has a substantial proportion of the global population, so this site is of high conservation value. The ponds are of varying size and depth and are thought to have been created by bombs dropped in the Second World War. In general pillwort is only present where the pool margins have been heavily poached by horses and sheep. Associated species include lesser marshwort, floating sweet-grass, marsh foxtail and lesser spearwort.

As mentioned in earlier chapters some of the upland areas, particularly around Abercraf and Ystradfellte and on Mynydd Llangatwg and Mynydd Llangynidr, are covered with sinkholes and swallow holes as a result of underground collapses in cave systems. Occasionally these become blocked and pools are formed, which are often visible on aerial photographs as black, or white, holes depending on how the light is reflected. These pools are often quite peaty and acidic and colonised by invertebrates such as black darter dragonflies *Sympetrum danae*. As their name suggests, the mature males are the only black dragonfly found in Britain. Females and immature males have a yellow abdomen and brown thorax marked with a black triangle on top, although some yellow markings remain along the sides of the abdomen and thorax of the adult males. Ultimately these interesting waterbodies become covered in a mat of sphagnum moss and other bog species, but sometimes the 'plug' disappears, probably due to further collapses in the cave system, and the pools drain away.

In contrast to the pools on the open moorland, Ty Mawr Pool, to the north of Llanfrynach, is hidden behind a tall hedge and a row of poplars *Populus* spp. to the north (Fig. 165). It was open to the public until about 15 years ago, but access was subsequently closed because of concerns about safety. An attractive feature, it is well known for its birds, with grey herons, mute swans and coot present all year. It is in fact one of the best breeding sites in the Beacons for coot, nine juveniles being fledged from three nests in 2012. Little grebe *Tachybaptus ruficollis* and tufted duck have also been recorded from the site.

Keeper's Pond, or Pen Ffordd Goch Pond, near Pwll Du on the hill above Blaenavon, was built in the early nineteenth century to provide water for Garnddyrys Forge. The forge was dismantled during the 1860s and the pond,

FIG 165. The secluded Ty Mawr Pool, to the north of Llanfrynach, is one of the best breeding sites in the Beacons for coot. (Jonathan Mullard)

whilst no longer fulfilling an industrial purpose, rapidly became a local beauty spot. It gained the name Keeper's Pond because the gamekeeper of the grouse moors lived in a cottage nearby. There are not many birds on the pond today, as the adjacent car park and encircling paths result in heavy disturbance, but there are sightings of palmate newt, and ten species of damselflies and dragonflies have been recorded from the site. The most abundant of these are large red damselfly *Pyrrhosoma nymphula*, common blue damselfly and common aeshna *Aeshna juncea*. The great diving beetle *Dysticus marginalis* also occurs here. The beetle, as its name implies, is a large insect, the larvae growing up to 60 mm in length, with the adults between 27 and 35 mm long. Both the adult and larvae are voracious predators, feeding on smaller invertebrates, tadpoles and even small fish.

A lesser known pool is Llyn Traeth Bach, to the south of Trecastle, which lies behind a low earth embankment within a naturally boggy hollow. There is no public access other than from the bridleway which runs to the northeast and few wildlife records, other than those which used to be published by the Wetland Bird Survey, the scheme which monitors non-breeding waterbirds in the UK. It used to be a fairly productive site until it was used for shooting and marketed as a coarse fishery, although it is managed less intensively now. Its main claim to fame was for breeding little grebe and black-headed gull *Chroicocephalus ridibundus* and a few snipe *Gallinago gallinago* and woodcock *Scolopax rusticola* in winter. Occasionally it draws in other waterfowl on passage, such as wigeon and pintail *Anas acuta*, but never more than low numbers.

There are not many ponds rich in wildlife in the urban areas, but Penlan ponds, four waterbodies situated in the grounds of the Brecon Leisure Centre, provide an important habitat for five of Wales's six native amphibian species: great crested newt, palmate newt, smooth newt, common frog and common toad (Fig. 166). (The missing sixth species is the natterjack toad *Epidalea calamita*, which was once extinct in Wales but has now been reintroduced at sites in the north of the country.)

Other natural waterbodies marked on the Ordnance Survey maps of the area include the remote Llyn y Garn Fawr on Mynydd Llangynidr, Pwll Gwy Rhoc on Mynydd Llangatwg and Pwll Pant Mawr on Pant Mawr. While they are depicted as small to medium-sized pools with open water, the reality is rather different, Llyn y Garn Fawr being often almost totally dry in summer and Pwll Pant Mawr now just a wet boggy area. Once upon a time they must indeed have been areas of open water, perhaps kept that way by livestock, but natural succession has taken place and they are now disappearing from the landscape. Blaencamlais Pool, to the north of Mynydd Illtyd, is also rapidly becoming a raised mire.

FIG 166. Penlan ponds, behind Brecon Leisure Centre, are an important habitat for five of Wales's six native amphibian species. (Jonathan Mullard)

FENS AND BOGS

Natural succession from open water to raised mire is also evident on Mynydd Illtyd itself, where the basin occupied by Traeth Mawr once contained a large lake but, apart from the pools mentioned earlier, few areas of open water now remain, although there are numerous areas of water on the bog surface (Fig. 167). Two streams drain to the northwest into Cwm Camlais and eventually into the River Usk. This mix of different habitats in a small location is unique, and there is supposedly no other site like it elsewhere in Wales. The intensive peat cutting that occurred in the area in previous centuries, described in Chapter 3, must have played a significant role in shaping this area and creating the variety of habitats that are present today.

Large areas of the bog surface are covered by cottongrass *Eriophorum angustifolium* and hare's-tail cottongrass, with small stands of bilberry. Cross-leaved heath and crowberry occur on the drier tussocks, along with such small herbs as tormentil, heath milkwort *Polygala serpyllifolia* and heath bedstraw, while the intervening damp hollows are typically occupied by species of rush, particularly compact rush *Juncus conglomeratus* and soft-rush *J. effusus* with butterwort *Pinguicula vulgaris*, round-leaved sundew, lousewort *Pedicularis sylvatica* and lesser spearwort. The principal mosses are common haircap moss and bog-mosses, mainly acute-leaved bog-moss *Sphagnum capillifolium* and papillose bog-moss *S. papillosum*. The small pools and watercourses contain common water-crowfoot, water-cress, bottle sedge *Carex rostrata* and species of pondweed *Potamogeton* spp. One large shallow pool is almost completely covered with lesser water-plantain *Baldellia ranunculoides*, which is very striking when it is flowering.

The site also has a number of open pools and runnels containing bog pondweed and marsh St John's-wort *Hypericum elodes*, with greater tussock-sedge *Carex paniculata* in places and a good range of dragonflies and damselflies. This is one of the best sites in the Beacons for these insects. Andrew Peterken from the Countryside Council for Wales recorded 11 species here in one day in July 1995, the dragonflies being common aeshna, golden-ringed dragonfly *Cordulegaster boltonii*, keeled skimmer *Orthetrum coerulescens* and black darter, while the damselflies were beautiful demoiselle *Calopteryx virgo*, emerald damselfly *Lestes sponsa*, large red damselfly, blue-tailed damselfly *Ischnura elegans*, scarce blue-tailed damselfly *I. pumilio*, common blue damselfly and azure damselfly. Andrew was actually looking for southern damselfly *Coenagrion mercuriale* and, although he was not successful on this occasion, the species was subsequently found at the site, together with a number of others, making a total of 21 species for this site alone.

Gors Llwyn, located right on the southern edge of the Brecon Beacons near the village of Onllwyn, is one of the most important lowland bogs in southern

FIG 167. Traeth Mawr on Mynydd Illtyd common, an important bog that was heavily cut for peat in the seventeenth and eighteenth centuries. (Jonathan Mullard)

Wales. Large areas of this habitat are now rare as result of drainage, mining, urban encroachment and agricultural improvement. Even this site is not completely immune to these influences, part of the peat overlying an area of pulverised fuel ash. Despite this it contains one of the few examples of a raised mire, a dome-shaped mass of peat, in South Wales. There is a thriving population of the regionally rare oblong-leaved sundew *Drosera intermedia*. Like other species of sundew, the leaf blades are densely covered with stalked mucilaginous glands which secrete a sugary solution to attract insects.

Much of the mire drains north into an area dominated by common reed with clumps of greater tussock-sedge. In many cases the clumps of tussock-sedge are over 1 m high, and these provide drier areas allowing willow species *Salix* spp. to establish – and willow carr now covers most of the area bordering the main east-flowing drainage stream. A range of woodland species, including royal fern, can be found beneath the tree canopy. The area is not completely covered with peat though and in some parts of the site the vegetation has developed as floating 'lawns' over open water. The more nutrient-rich lawns support an extremely diverse flora, with up to 28 species recorded in an area of only 4 m^2.

Gors Llwyn is a very important site for invertebrates, including a range of ground beetles typical of habitats dominated by purple moor-grass, the commonest species being *Pterostichus diligens*. Other beetles recorded from the site include fen soldier beetle *Cantharis thoracica*, which favours tall fen vegetation, and the leaf beetle *Plateumaris affinis*, which feeds on the roots of reeds. The area is also very good for flies, two nationally scarce craneflies, *Limnophila abdominalis* and *Tipula marginata*, being recorded from the site along with two rare snail-killing flies, *Antichaeta analis* and *Psacadina verbekei*, which parasitise wetland snails, especially pond snails.

Another, smaller, raised mire, Waen Ddu, can be found at the northern end of Craig y Cilau National Nature Reserve. Species found here are much more typical of acid, wet conditions and include round-leaved sundew, along with lesser skullcap *Scutellaria minor* and few-flowered spike-rush *Eleocharis quinqueflora*, which is becoming increasingly rare due to land drainage for agricultural purposes. Another plant that occurs here is bog pimpernel *Anagallis tenella*. Mawn Bwll Du Mawr, a small fenced bog on common land near the Usk Reservoir, is the only site in the Beacons for Magellanic bog-moss *Sphagnum magellanicum*, which is confined to the tops and sides of large hummocks in the older, drier and more acidic parts of bogs. The plant is an unmistakable wine-red colour, though in more shaded areas it has tinges of green.

CALCAREOUS FLUSHES

Calcareous grasslands at Craig y Ciliau National Nature Reserve are an important habitat for a number of rare invertebrates, including Geyer's whorl snail *Vertigo geyeri*, an alpine snail found in northern Europe. Until very recently Geyer's whorl snail was known from just two sites in England and one in Wales. Recent survey work, however, has discovered over 20 further populations, including sites in Scotland and Northern Ireland. All the populations occur in calcareous flushes – small, often weakly flowing, springs of lime-rich water. These generally occur where porous calcareous bedrock is underlain by impermeable strata, which forces the groundwater, rich in dissolved lime, to emerge as a spring. The most important conservation priority for the whorl snail is the maintenance of the hydrological conditions that supply the flush with lime-rich waters. Lowering of water tables or the interruption of water flow could have damaging effects.

Because of its high lime content, any twigs, fallen leaves or other debris in contact with the upwelling water soon become covered in tufa. Calcareous flushes, such as those to be found at Cwm Cadlan National Nature Reserve, are therefore characterised by the deposition of tufa around the spring heads. Since they occur as a chance consequence of landform and geology they are a rare habitat in Britain

FIG 168. Horse leech in a calcareous flush at Cwm Cadlan. They feed on smaller animals, such as midge larvae and snails, but sometimes move onto land in search of earthworms. (Jonathan Mullard)

and indeed throughout Europe. Although upland dry calcareous grassland has a relatively small number of specialist invertebrate species compared with lowland sites, a rich fauna can occur where these seepages, springs and streams are present (Fig. 168). Flushes, in particular, provide very shallow water that supports a diverse semi-aquatic invertebrate community, which utilises the water film, the oxygenated surface layers of silt or water-logged mosses. Where tufa-encrusted substrates occur, additional specialised invertebrates, such as soldier flies, can also be found. Most of these specialist species are rare, due to the scarcity of their habitat. These calcareous flushes therefore provide an important and contrasting 'aquatic' habitat to lakes, rivers, ponds and streams.

Rare examples of the freshwater cyanobacterium *Rivularia haematites* also occur on pebbles and boulders in these relatively uncontaminated natural limestone springs. *Rivularia* is a good example of a modern freshwater stromatolite, forming hemispherical colonies with a radiating filamentous structure and well-defined concentric zones of calcification. Essentially it consists of a 'microbial mat' in which there are layers of precipitated minerals. Fossil stromatolites constitute our earliest record of life on Earth, but there are a number of locations such as this where they are still forming.

RESERVOIRS

During the nineteenth century the expanding populations of Cardiff, Swansea and the South Wales Valleys utilised the Brecon Beacons to provide a convenient supply of drinking water and water for industry. Numerous reservoirs were constructed, ranging in size from the smallest one at Penderyn to Pontsticill Reservoir, which stores 1.5 million cubic metres (3,400 million gallons) of fresh water. The creation of each one was determined by the geology, local stone being used to construct the dams and glacial till dug as 'puddling clay' to waterproof the structures. Upland reservoirs are commonly known as impounding reservoirs, since they are built across river valleys, and those in the Beacons have developed into important areas for wildlife. Today the eight active water storage reservoirs are all owned and managed by Dŵr Cymru/Welsh Water.

The reservoir margins provide an unusual habitat, known as the inundation zone. They are often flooded for much of the year, but occasionally in dry summers they are exposed for months at a time. Conversely the margins can remain under water for several successive years if the rainfall during the summer is high. These ephemeral habitats support a range of specialised plant and animal species that can survive and thrive in situations with frequent water-level fluctuations. The inundation zone is especially important for bryophytes, and the species found here have special adaptations to enable them to survive in the changeable environment. In particular, they have long-lived spores or tubers that are produced in abundance in years when water levels fall, but which can also survive under water for several years until a drop in the water level again allows the plant to germinate. When water levels are low, bryophytes can grow with extraordinary speed, with some species completing their whole life cycle from germinating spore to mature plants, which release their own spores, within two or three months. They can appear in vast numbers, thousands of plants reproducing as rapidly as possible before the water rises again. The species colonise new water bodies by being transported, as spores, on the feet and plumage of ducks and other waterfowl (Fig. 169). Where reservoirs are connected, spores are also likely to be carried by the water flow from locations higher up a valley to those further down.

Reservoirs within the Brecon Beacons have long been known to support significant populations of the liverwort violet crystalwort *Riccia huebeneriana*, a nationally rare species (Fig. 170). It was last recorded at Beacons Reservoir in 1951, but has since been found in the Talybont, Lower Neuadd, Pentwyn, Usk and Cantref reservoirs and is likely to be present in many others. It would be interesting to know where violet crystalwort occurred before the reservoirs were

FIG 169. Talybont Reservoir, an important area for wintering wildfowl, which may transport the spores of the bryophytes on their feet and plumage. (Jonathan Mullard)

built. Many of the mud-bottomed pools on Hay and Mynydd Illtyd commons might be suitable habitats, as might the banks of the River Usk, although the habitat here is probably not peaty enough. Most probably it grew by a few naturally fluctuating pools, and was absent from the rest of the Beacons until the reservoirs were built.

Violet crystalwort grows as tiny rosettes lying flat against drying mud, the edges of the plant becoming purple as they mature. It has been recorded from 34 localities in the UK, but has become extinct at a number of sites, due mainly to water levels being kept artificially high. The chemistry of the mud is important in determining which bryophytes become established, and the natural distribution of the plant is limited by its need for slightly acidic mud. In this respect it is interesting to note that the majority of the sites in South Wales with this species are located on the Old Red Sandstone, which often produces mildly basic red soils and gravels. The Silurian deposits at Usk Reservoir also produce similar red soils and gravels. Violet crystalwort is usually considered less demanding of alkaline conditions than cavernous crystalwort *Riccia cavernosa*, another specialist of water-body margins, which grows around the base-rich Llangorse Lake, and it would be a useful project to measure the pH of the substrates on which these liverworts grow.

At many sites where violet crystalwort occurs, the main colonies are located near inflow streams where silts have built-up to create shallow-marginal gradients. Graham Motley once stopped by the inlet of the Cantref Reservoir when water levels were low and noticed that someone, probably a fisherman, had walked across the muddy margins. The sun had then baked the surface hard, but in the footprint-shaped depressions the mud was slightly shaded and

FIG 170. Violet crystalwort is a nationally rare species of liverwort with significant populations in the reservoirs of the Brecon Beacons. (Sam Bosanquet)

damper and had been heavily colonised by violet crystalwort, with none present on the drier surface mud – producing crystalwort footprints! Unfortunately he did not take any photographs. Presumably fishermen might also play a part in transporting spores of these reservoir species around. Although it is often found on these open muddy areas, it can occur in great quantity under the light shade of emergent vascular plants such as sedges *Carex* spp., amphibious bistort and horsetails *Equisetum* spp. Other bryophytes associated with violet crystalwort include liverworts such as acid frillwort *Fossombronia wondraczekii* and glaucous crystalwort *Riccia glauca*, which grows in bright green rosettes up to 2 cm or more in diameter, and tiny ephemeral species such as spreading earth-moss *Aphanorhegma patens* and delicate earth-moss *Pseudephemerum nitidum*.

Lower Neuadd Reservoir was partially drained a few years ago and only small numbers of violet crystalwort are still present, but there is still some fluctuation in water levels and this may be just enough to allow the species to persist. In 2003 four *Riccia* species were found on the margins here, the greatest diversity of the genus known from a locality in South Wales (Fig. 171). Alongside violet crystalwort can be found what is probably the largest population of purple crystalwort *Riccia beyrichiana* in the area, with glaucous crystalwort and common crystalwort *R. sorocarpa* also occurring. Purple crystalwort appears not to be particular about its habitat requirements, being recorded elsewhere in South Wales from limestone grassland, seasonally flushed grassland on stream and riverbanks and coastal slopes. It is not therefore strictly dependent on fluctuating reservoir water levels for its survival, but it does tend to favour areas that are damp in the winter and dry in the summer.

Three additional species of liverwort – common frillwort *Fossombronia pusilla*, pitted frillwort *F. foveolata* and weedy frillwort *F. incurva* – have also been recorded from reservoir margins. This is a difficult group that can often only be identified with certainty by examining the spores of fertile material, and members of the genus therefore tend to be under-recorded. Common frillwort, as its name suggests, is a relatively common and widespread species of roadside banks, sides of ditches and arable fields, as well as occurring alongside reservoirs, but it is not a regular component of the reservoir-margin flora. In contrast, weedy frillwort is a nationally scarce species, which until recently was known from only a few sites in South Wales. In the past few years the number of known colonies has increased and it has been reported as new to Breconshire. Elsewhere in the region, however, it grows on gritty moorland streamsides and gravely quarry floors, so it cannot be considered a reservoir-margin specialist. Acid frillwort is a rather local, although widely distributed species, which sometimes occurs in abundance on reservoir margins in South Wales, while pitted frillwort was present in abundance at Usk Reservoir in 2010.

FIG 171. Lower Neuadd Reservoir, a key site in the Beacons for crystalworts. Note the inundation zone around the margin. (Alan Bowring)

Other bryophytes which occupy the draw-down zone or margins of reservoirs, particularly mosses, have been neglected by naturalists, possibly because of their small size and the fact that their occurrence depends on water levels and is therefore unpredictable. Recent surveys have, for instance, shown that some bryophytes previously thought to be rare, such as clay earth-moss *Archidium alternifolium*, are actually common on reservoir margins. Other widespread, but sometimes local, species, such as greater water-moss and tree-moss *Climacium dendroides* can be common at the upper margins of some reservoirs. Other species such as Tozer's thread-moss *Epipterygium tozeri*, golden thread-moss *Leptobryum pyriforme*, small-bud bryum *Bryum gemmiferum* and crookneck nodding-moss *Pohlia camptotrachela* have also been recorded, but have their main populations in different habitats.

Rare species include dwarf bladder-moss *Physcomitrium sphaericum*, a Red Data Book near-threatened species confined to seasonally exposed mud at the margins of reservoirs and other water bodies. Although a rare plant, it can sometimes grow in enormous abundance when conditions permit. It was recorded as new to Wales as recently as 2002, when a very large population, numbering many millions of plants, was found at Lower Lliedi Reservoir near Llanelli by Ian Morgan who, although not a bryologist, was aware that the Countryside Council for Wales were recording this habitat and sent a few specimens for identification. A second small colony was discovered in the Beacons, at Pontsticill Reservoir, in 2003. Previously, the species was mainly known in Britain from a small number of sites in northern England and central Scotland, so its occurrence in Wales represents a considerable extension of its range. The moss is dependent on fluctuating water levels, and the plants can only develop and mature during periods of drought or when water has been artificially drained for long periods (Hill et al. 1994). Other populations will probably be found in the near future.

Sessile earth-moss *Ephemerum sessile* is another near-threatened species. Unlike dwarf bladder-moss though it is not confined to reservoir margins, being recorded from other damp habitats such as woodland rides and the wetter areas of heathland. Populations are sparsely scattered throughout England and Wales. It was first recorded at Talybont Reservoir in 1976 and has been found in the past ten years at Llandegfedd, near Cwmbran, and Wentwood Reservoir near Newport. In the Beacons it also occurs on a damp track near Llanthony. Sessile earth-moss is a very small species and may be overlooked to some extent, but reservoirs in South Wales are certainly important for this species. Another related species, serrated earth-moss *Ephemerum serratum*, is a nationally scarce plant that has only recently been added to the local lists. It appears that, in South Wales at least, serrated earth-moss is confined to reservoir margins and dried-out pools and is probably the commonest and most widespread of the mosses found on reservoir margins. It is an extremely small moss, with individual plants less than 2 mm high, and therefore very difficult to photograph properly in the field.

More information is needed about the water levels required by each bryophyte species. Propagules buried in the mud gradually die over time, and ideally they need to be replenished every few years. Although several reservoirs are Sites of Special Scientific Interest, most are notified for their bird populations or habitats and none is specifically notified for bryophytes. Relatively little direct management appears to be required for most of these species, as their survival largely depends on fluctuating water levels, with some species responding best during times of drought or when water levels are low for other reasons. As mentioned earlier, it would seem that the main threat to them is from water levels being kept artificially, or naturally, high for long periods. Water levels at some reservoirs outside the Beacons appear to be kept high for fishing, and this practice would clearly threaten the important bryophyte floras of the reservoirs in the area. At sites known to support threatened species the natural seasonal fluctuations in water levels need to be maintained, and any attempts to stabilise water levels artificially for recreation should be resisted. Bryophytes also need clean water. Runoff of agricultural chemicals, including nitrate and phosphate fertilisers, can kill off many species, as can the extensive felling of conifer plantations, which can also cause large amounts of nutrients to enter lakes and reservoirs.

WINTERING AND PASSAGE BIRDS

Reservoirs are also important areas for wintering wildfowl and passage migrants, such as the occasional visiting osprey *Pandion haliaetus* in spring and autumn. Favoured passage sites for osprey in the Beacons include Talybont and Cantref reservoirs and Llangorse Lake. Sightings from other favoured sites across Wales seem to indicate distinct migration routes. Birds which appear on autumn passage in Monmouthshire are often recorded first at Talybont, or Llangorse, and in spring ospreys seem to move from Llyn Brianne in Carmarthenshire through the Elan and Wye valleys. Most passage birds are recorded in April or May and August or September (Lovegrove et al. 1994). The number of Welsh records has increased over the years in parallel with the expansion in range and numbers of the Scottish breeding population. Ospreys first began nesting in Wales in 2004, near Croesor in the Glaslyn Valley in North Wales, and up to 2012 had fledged 18 chicks. Given this continued expansion, a breeding pair in the Beacons remains a strong possibility.

Steve Wilce of the Brecknock Birds Group, recorded an interesting sighting of ospreys, in April 2012, on the Group's website:

> While watching one osprey sitting in a tree on the edge of Cantref Reservoir, another dived into the water and caught a very large rainbow trout. It couldn't take off with it so it dragged it to the bank and then the other osprey came down to try and steal it. This resulted in an almighty scrap over the fish, both ospreys pulling in opposite directions. The osprey that caught the fish won and managed to fly off with it east over the mountain. I thought it might be headed to the Talybont area, but it must have gone over to Llangorse. (Where it was seen by another member of the Group sitting on the trig point on Mynydd Llangorse eating the fish.) I say this because it came back afterwards still carrying half the fish.

This description is a useful reminder of the large areas these birds can cover, although osprey breeding territories can be quite small. Cantref Reservoir is some 19 km southwest of Mynydd Llangorse, so assuming the bird flew in a straight line between the two points, which it probably did not, it covered around 38 km to escape its companion and eat half a fish!

Wintering wildfowl on the reservoirs include tufted duck, goldeneye, goosander *Mergus merganser* and teal *Anas crecca*.

MONMOUTHSHIRE AND BRECON CANAL

Running alongside the River Usk for most of its 56 km, the Monmouthshire and Brecon Canal is a narrow waterway completely isolated from the rest of the canal system in England and Wales (Fig. 172). Originally built in the late eighteenth century as an industrial transport route for coal and iron, which was brought to the canal by a network of tramways and railways, it has developed into an important habitat for wildlife. It was originally two independent canals, the Monmouthshire Canal, from Newport to Pontymoile Basin, and the Brecknock and Abergavenny Canal, running from Pontymoile to Brecon. Both canals were abandoned in 1962, but the Brecknock and Abergavenny route and a small section of the Monmouthshire route have been reopened since 1970.

In the late 1950s the leisure potential of the route was recognised and a weekly hire firm started in 1961, though rowing boats and canoes had been used on the canal since the early 1800s. Today there are over 400 privately owned boats and over 40 hire boats operating between Brecon and Pontnewydd, a small number in comparison to canals such as the Llangollen Canal, one of the most popular canals for holidaymakers in Britain.

The Monmouthshire, Brecon and Abergavenny Canals Trust was set up in 1984 to campaign for more resources for the canal's maintenance and restoration. The Trust's aim is a fully restored and well-maintained canal running from Brecon to a new marina terminus at Crindau, Newport, but one which is rich in wildlife.

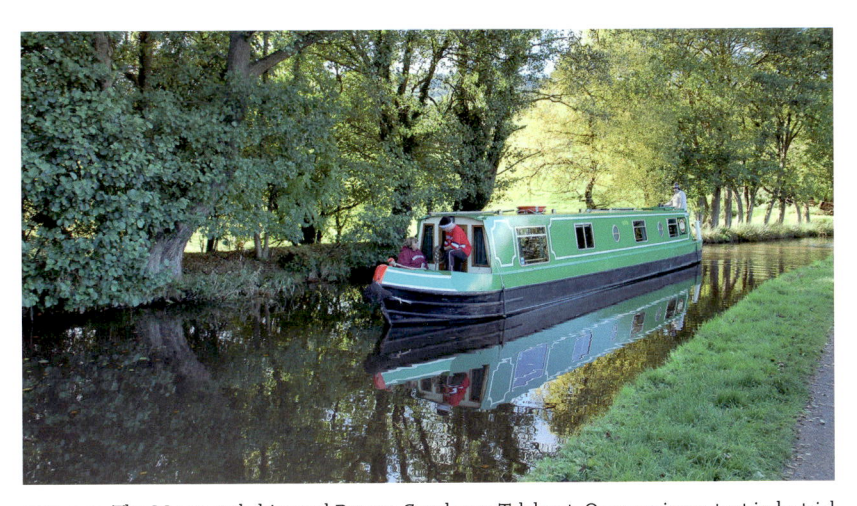

FIG 172. The Monmouthshire and Brecon Canal near Talybont. Once an important industrial route, the canal is now rich in wildlife. (Jonathan Mullard)

Increasing the recreational use of the canal though will undoubtedly have an effect on the plants and animals that utilise the area, and a careful balance will need to be struck between access and conservation if this aim is to be realised. The current importance of the canal for wildlife is a direct result of the relatively low level of disturbance by boats and other recreational users. The more popular canals elsewhere in Britain are of less interest for wildlife, largely because of intensive management and use – there being a negative relationship between the level of boat traffic and the quantity of aquatic and emergent vegetation.

Although water flows through the canal, via locks and sluices, the movement is so small in comparison with the total volume of the system that it can be considered as standing water – in effect a linear pond. Habitats on the Monmouthshire and Brecon Canal include the open water itself, emergent vegetation, meadow-like verges, hedge banks and embankments, and this range of habitats probably supports a wide variety of species. There have been few surveys of the plants and animals along its length, but the 2011 British Waterways wildlife survey resulted in a number of species being recorded by volunteers in the area. Some of the records are obviously likely to be more accurate than others, and some such as 'butterfly' are fairly generic, but overall they provide a fascinating glimpse of the species found along the canal. The results of the national survey, biased towards animals, showed that kingfishers, newts, toads and otters had all been spotted in record numbers on Britain's canals and rivers, and the Monmouthshire and Brecon results were very similar.

Kingfishers are frequently seen along the canal as a bright flash of blue and green as they fly fast and low across the water; as mentioned previously, they also occur on the Usk and Llangorse Lake. Other birds found along the canal include grey heron, mallard *Anas platyrhynchos*, moorhen *Gallinula chloropus* and coot, while fish include roach, perch and pike.

Although the canal does not provide a suitable habitat for otters there is often evidence of their presence. It seems likely that otters visit the canal for fish, which may be easier for them to catch than in the nearby river. Water voles have also been shown to have a strong affinity for these slow-moving watercourses and they were once common on canals across Britain, with large colonies in the adjoining banks, though not where there have been reinforced or piled. Probably the most numerous mammals found along canals though are bats, with several species such as Daubenton's bat, pipistrelle and noctule *Nyctalus noctula* roosting in canal structures such as bridges and tunnels and foraging for insects over the water and towpath.

The canal follows the wooded hillsides along the Usk Valley all the way from Pontnewydd to Brecon and is noted for its picturesque views. These woodlands, however, represent just a small fraction of those in the Beacons.

CHAPTER 9

Woodlands

WOODLANDS IN THE BRECON BEACONS consist of a combination of mainly privately owned broadleaved woodland and the coniferous forests, the majority of which are in the public sector. These coniferous plantations cover in excess of 10,000 hectares, whereas the private woodland comprises a mosaic of much smaller, dispersed farm woodland holdings and some traditional forests managed by estates. Much of the broadleaved woodland is a mixture of oak and ash, often with hazel, hawthorn and other species forming an understorey beneath the larger trees. It is all that remains of the original forests that once covered most of the area and, as described in Chapter 3, they have been extensively modified.

THE TREE LINE

There is little woodland at high altitude, but sufficient evidence remains to confirm that the tree line, the limit at which trees are able to grow, extends from 300 to 600 m according to locality. Since the highest point, Pen y Fan, is 886 m, this implies that, certainly in the current climatic conditions, the highest part of the mountains have never been tree-covered. This is confirmed, to some extent, by the woodland on the slopes of the Punchbowl, a large glacial cwm containing an artificial lake situated on the eastern side of the Blorenge (Fig. 173). The area is dominated by wood-pasture of old beech pollards, some of which are over 200 years old. Ash, downy birch *Betula pubescens*, sessile oak, field maple *Acer campestre* and holly also occur here as part of one of the highest ancient seminatural woodlands in Britain. Oliver Rackham in his New Naturalist *Woodlands* (2006)

FIG 173. The Punchbowl on the Blorenge, considered by Oliver Rackham to be one of the nearest approximations in Britain to a natural tree line. Note the new fenced planting on the slopes to the right. (Jonathan Mullard)

describes the Punchbowl as 'a tract of surrealistic beech pollards … affected by avalanches that roar down from the mountain above' and considers that it is 'one of the nearest approximations in Britain to a natural tree line, as with the tree-limit beeches in the outer French Alps and in the Balkans.' As the area is enclosed from above by the mountain wall, and there are large holly bushes growing from the relative safety of scree at much higher elevations, it would seem that the true tree line is somewhat higher, but it is, as always, affected by the heavy grazing. That said, it is a special place and it does give some indication of what the higher woodland in the Beacons would have been like before the relentless cropping by sheep began.

The Punchbowl is still managed by the Woodland Trust, who own the site, as wood-pasture, with the land being grazed by sheep. As the veteran trees come to the end of their lives, the Trust intends to create replacements for the original pollards by pollarding younger trees within planted areas of beech woodland nearby, the seeds for which have been sourced from the site. Currently these areas are excluded from grazing while the trees become established.

Beyond the tree line, exemplified by the Blorenge, shrub communities predominate, although stunted birch, rowan and Scots pine can also occur, first as scattered clumps and then as individual trees. The 'natural' situation therefore would be a mosaic of tree and shrub vegetation continuing in altitude up to the biological limit of tree growth. Tree lines are transition zones where woodland canopies begin to break up and habitats such as scrub, heath or grassland begin to dominate, and they vary in width and altitude across the Beacons. Woodland, for example, extends over Tarren yr Esgob in the Black Mountains up to around 600 m, but even here the general tree line is well below this. Trees also occur at an altitude of 500 m on the northeast slopes of the Brecon Beacons themselves, but in the more sheltered parts of Mynydd Du the timberline is no higher than 400 m, while on the southwest slopes of Fforest Fawr and Mynydd Du the limit for trees is reached at 300 m, as indicated by dwarf windblown specimens. Since the prevailing winds are from the west and southwest, the southwest-facing slopes are relatively exposed while the sheltered northeast slopes are more favourable for tree growth.

OAK WOODLAND

Pedunculate oak covers some of the steep foothills of the Black Mountains near Talgarth and Abergavenny, but it is generally a species characteristic of rich soils in valleys such as the Wye, Usk and Tawe. These rich, low-lying and generally heavy soils today support the best-quality pastures, damp oakwoods having long ago given way to agriculture. In contrast, woodland dominated by sessile oak once formed the greater part of the natural forest cover. There are still numerous relict woodlands containing sessile oak in the Beacons, and these inevitably occupy the poorer soils, mainly on steep hillsides where drainage is unimpeded.

One of the best examples of sessile oak woodland in the Brecon Beacons is Coed Nant Menascin, an extensive area of semi-natural woodland situated in the steep-sided Menascin Valley to the southwest of Llanfrynach (Fig. 174). Large undisturbed native woodlands such as this are now uncommon in the Welsh countryside, many having been felled or converted to plantations, with the remainder being heavily grazed by livestock. Those, such as Coed Nant Menascin, that are relatively undisturbed support many specialised plants and animals which are well adapted to woodland conditions and which cannot survive in intensively managed or heavily grazed sites. The drier, base-rich soils, particularly towards the head of the valley, support a canopy of sessile oak with occasional specimens of downy birch, hazel, holly and rowan. The ground flora here is extremely rich, supporting species such as wood anemone, bluebell, yellow archangel, yellow pimpernel *Lysimachia nemorum*, dog's mercury, lesser celandine *Ranunculus ficaria*, wood speedwell *Veronica montana*, hart's

FIG 174. Coed Nant Menascin, viewed from the ridge of Cefn Cyff to the west. This is one of the best examples of sessile oak, ash and alder woodland in the Beacons, with a rich ground flora that extends to the upland edge. (Jonathan Mullard)

tongue, lady-fern and false brome, with mosses such as springy turf-moss, neat feather-moss *Pseudoscleropodium purum* and common tamarisk-moss *Thuidium tamariscinum*.

The woods north of Pontneddfechan comprise another very large and diverse example of oak woodland, characterised by holly and hard-ferns *Blechnum spicant*. They extend along a series of deeply incised valleys and ravines along the Afon Nedd, Nedd Fechan, Hepste, Pyrddin and Afon Mellte and contain complex mosaics of sessile oak woodland, ash woodland and transitions to other lowland woodland types. The whole site is biologically rich, with many woodland plant communities represented and extensive bryophyte and lichen communities. Notable species include wood fescue *Festuca altissima and* hay-scented buckler-fern and green spleenwort. As described in Chapter 6, the river valleys and waterfalls are generally well shaded and constantly humid, and as a result they support a rich bryophyte flora that covers large areas of the riverside rocks and cliffs and the trunks of trees.

The Sugar Loaf is also noted for its oak woodland, the site having a long history of being extensively cut for charcoal, and this has produced an even-aged structure. Most trees are on average around 80–100 years old but the trunks of some are probably much older, since they show signs of being coppiced many times in the past.

WOODLAND MANAGEMENT

Strawberry Cottage Wood on the southern edge of the Black Mountains consists mainly of sessile oak, together with some ash. Part of the area is managed as a Nature Reserve by the Gwent Wildlife Trust, but the larger part of the wood forms part of Great Llwygy farm and is now managed by a local community woodland group. Coppicing and pollarding are traditional woodland management techniques that can have numerous benefits to wildlife. Therefore, re-cutting any areas of old coppice and pollards is desirable. Non-native trees and shrubs, such as sycamore, can be invasive and if allowed to spread can seriously alter the character of a wood.

In 2012 Rob Penn, a local resident and writer, spent 12 months working to bring part of Strawberry Cottage Wood, outside the nature reserve, back into management. He was helped by a number of woodland experts as part of a television series, *Tales from the Wild Wood*, which was broadcast on BBC4. He introduced pigs to remove the overgrown bracken and brambles, learnt about coppicing, horse logging, making charcoal and trapping grey squirrels. He also helped fell an ash tree and found out how to market the timber. The aim of the series was to encourage people to manage more of our woods and to manage them better. In keeping with this ethos, although the series is now over, Rob still helps the community group to look after the area.

ASH WOODLAND

Ash is the third most common native tree species in Britain after oak and birch. In the Beacons the most notable areas of ash woodland occur near the confluence of the Taf Fawr and Taf Fechan at Cefn Coed y Cymmer and on the west-facing limestone escarpment of Craig y Rhiwarth on the east bank of the Afon Tawe, above Craig y Nos (Fig. 175). This latter area supports some of the best limestone plant communities in the Beacons, while the ash woodland which covers some of the screes, cliffs, steeper slopes and the sinkhole to the southwest of Pwllcoediog is one of the finest ash woods in Britain. Upland ash woods are amongst the richest habitats for wildlife in the uplands, notable for bright displays of flowers in the spring, some of which are rarities. The ground flora found here

FIG 175. Craig y Rhiwarth above Craig y Nos, one of the finest ash woods in Britain, with a rich ground flora. (Jonathan Mullard)

at Craig y Rhiwarth is no exception and includes lily-of-the-valley, wood spurge *Euphorbia amygdaloides*, wood fescue and short-beaked wood-moss *Hylocomium brevirostre*. Decaying ash logs support other notable mosses and liverworts such as beaked bow-moss *Dicranodontium denudatum* and larger cut notchwort *Tritomaria exsectiformis*, while the shrub layer includes such locally scarce shrubs as buckthorn *Rhamnus cathartica*. As described in Chapter 10, some of the ledges on the cliffs within the reserve provide a refuge for populations of nationally important whitebeams.

Many of these woods are ancient, but ash is a vigorous colonist of open ground and secondary upland mixed ash woodland can form quite rapidly. The future of ash in Britain is now, however, being threatened by chalara dieback, a serious disease of ash trees caused by an asexual fungal organism called *Chalara fraxinea* and its sexual stage *Hymenoscyphus pseudoalbidus*. The disease causes leaf loss and crown dieback in affected trees and usually leads to the death of the tree. Ash trees suffering with *C. fraxinea* infection have been found widely across Europe, including, at the time of writing, in areas to the south of the Beacons. Young ash plants are particularly at risk, with the fungus killing them within one growing season of symptoms becoming visible. Older trees can survive initial attacks, but tend to succumb eventually after several seasons of infection.

ALDER WOODLAND

Alder woodlands often occur on the northeast slopes of the mountains where steep gradients ease off suddenly, leading to the extension of flush margins near streams, but usually avoid the waterlogged areas where peat is accumulating on the southwest dip slopes. Coed Ynys Faen, located 1.5 km north of Llangenny, and one of the most diverse and species-rich alder woodlands in the Brecon Beacons, is however an exception to this rule (Fig. 176). Alder coppice dominates much of the area and exists in a wide range of situations, from the silted and vegetated areas of an old river channel, to steep but heavily flushed slopes. As at Coed Nant Menascin, ash occurs alongside the alder, especially in the dryer areas, while the shrub layer is relatively similar, consisting mainly of hazel with occasional specimens of bird cherry *Prunus avium,* wych elm *Ulmus glabra* and grey willow *Salix cinerea.*

There is a rich and varied field layer, the most widespread and characteristic species being yellow pimpernel, creeping buttercup *Ranunculus repens* and rough meadow-grass *Poa trivialis.* In drier stands of alder, tufted hair-grass *Deschampsia cespitosa* is abundant, along with ferns, particularly lady-fern. Creeping buttercup and opposite-leaved golden-saxifrage form a carpet in free-draining wet hollows, while water mint, marsh valerian *Valeriana dioica* and meadowsweet are abundant

FIG 176. Coed Ynys Faen, adjacent to the Grwyne Fawr, is one of the most diverse and species-rich examples of alder woodland in the Beacons, with transitions to other woodland types. (Jonathan Mullard)

FIG 177. Alder coppice at Coed y Cerrig National Nature Reserve in the southern Black Mountains. (Jonathan Mullard)

on soft soils heavily flushed by base-rich water. On steeper slopes this flushing can cause the ground to slump, and in situations such as this the locally uncommon giant horsetail *Equisetum telmateia* can be found. The wood's rich and varied flora includes records for a number of scarcer plants such as herb-Paris *Paris quadrifolia*, columbine *Aquilegia vulgaris*, rough horsetail *Equisetum hyemale* and sweet cicely *Myrrhis odorata*. The nationally scarce Welsh poppy also occurs here at the extreme southeasterly limit of its native British range.

Coed y Cerrig National Nature Reserve includes an area of wet alder-dominated woodland that was traditionally managed as coppice, together with areas that were managed as grazed fen-meadow, but from which grazing has now ceased and onto which the alder has spread (Fig. 177). Coppicing was traditionally carried out here to provide timber for the charcoal and clog-making industries, but ceased before the 1940s. It was reintroduced in 1994, with small areas being cut on a rotation. Alder can only be harvested in the winter months and needs to be left to season for at least nine months before it can be used. Clogging was therefore a seasonal occupation, and gangs of a dozen or more craftsmen travelled from wood to wood, living a hard, tough life in roughly built temporary shelters. The roughly shaped clog blocks were built into small conical stacks in the open air, so that air could circulate freely between the blocks to speed the drying process, after which they were sent to factories in the north of England to be finally shaped and finished.

NATIVE BEECH WOODLAND

Beech occurs as a native tree in a number of discrete areas of Britain, including southeast Wales, and many of these places, as at the Punchbowl, have a history of common wood-pasture. The open woodland provided shelter and forage for grazing animals, particularly sheep and cattle, as well as timber and other woodland products. After the last glaciation, beech was slow to return to Britain. In fact, it had probably not reached its climatic limits before the original woodlands were cleared. Although it is strictly native only in southern England and South Wales, it has been introduced to woodlands further north and west, which, given time, it might have reached naturally. Numerous documentary references and place names in southeast Wales, from the thirteenth century onwards, include the Welsh word for beech (*ffawydd, ffawydden, ffawyddog*), but beech is not recorded elsewhere in Wales until the eighteenth century, and then only as a planted tree (Linnard 1982). Apart from the Blorenge the only remnants of these native beech woods can be found in Llangynidr Gorge and on the southern edge of the Beacons in Clydach Gorge, the latter being a National Nature Reserve (Fig. 178).

FIG 178. Cwm Clydach, a relic of the native beech woods of South Wales, now a National Nature Reserve. (Harold Grenfell)

The availability of dense woodland in the Clydach Gorge, which provided a resource of timber and charcoal for firing furnaces, is thought to have been an important consideration in attracting industry during the seventeenth and eighteenth centuries. The steepness of the terrain was also an advantage to early ironworking and lime-burning businesses, allowing blast furnaces and limekilns to be strategically sited on the valley sides to facilitate charging of materials above them and withdrawal of the products and waste materials below them. As can be imagined, this exploitation of the area had a fairly drastic effect on tree coverage. Today, however, much of the woodland has regenerated and the lower valley sides are once more extensively wooded. Around two-thirds of the site is still covered by beech woodland, with mature sessile oak and hybrid oaks in the west of the reserve. Many of the beech trees though are old and even-aged, almost certainly an indication of past management, and in recent years a considerable number of them have died and fallen over. The species still regenerates well, however, and in time new trees will grow and fill the gaps. In fact the abundance of standing and fallen dead wood is a characteristic feature of the reserve and it provides an important habitat for a number of plants and animals.

The dense foliage of the beech canopy results in a rather minimal ground flora, but species such as bird's-nest orchid *Neottia nidus-avis* are found amongst the

FIG 179. Yellow bird's-nest, an epiparasite that obtains nutrients from dead vegetation through an association with a fungus, in Cwm Clydach National Nature Reserve. (James Latham)

leaf litter. The short, underground stem and the mass of roots, which resembles a bird's nest, store food until about the ninth year, when the plant first blooms. Unlike most other flowering plants the orchid does not have green leaves; instead it is saprophytic, obtaining nutrients from dead vegetation, prepared for it by a fungus which occupies the matted root system. The uncommon yellow bird's-nest *Monotropa hypopitys*, another plant with no chlorophyll, is also found here (Fig. 179). Until recently it was thought to be saprophytic like the bird's nest orchid, but recent research has shown that it is actually epiparasitic, using *Tricholoma* spp. fungi to extract nutrients from living trees in its vicinity. Yellow bird's-nest is a rather transient plant, sometimes appearing in large numbers, with hundreds of flowering spikes, only to disappear within a few years (Leake *et al.* 2004).

While the shrub layer and ground flora can be quite sparse in the beech woodland, in places where the canopy is more open, hazel and hawthorn are amongst the most frequent species. The ground layer is often a patchy mix of false brome, enchanter's-nightshade, wood avens and bramble. The nationally scarce mosses Spruce's leskea *Platydictya jungermannioides*, chalk feather-moss *Campylophyllum calcareum* and twist-tip feather-moss *Eurhynchium schleicheri* can also be found here. Where the soil is more acidic the shrub layer is rather sparse and the ground layer is naturally species-poor, with scattered patches of tufted hair-grass, common bent, bilberry, bracken, swan's-neck thyme-moss, greater fork-moss *Dicranum majus* and cypress-leaved plait-moss *Hypnum cupressiforme* occur. The more humid parts of Cwm Clydach often have a lush cover of mosses and liverworts, with some western or Atlantic species such as five-ranked bog-moss *Sphagnum quinquefarium* and the liverworts fragrant crestwort *Lophocolea fragrans*, MacKay's pouncewort *Marchesinia mackaii* and straggling pouchwort.

A wide range of woodland fungi have also been recorded from the reserve, including many species restricted to beech woodland and some at their only known Welsh locality. These include uncommon species such as salmon salad *Tremiscus helvelloides*, horn of plenty *Craterellus cornucopioides*, *Cantharellus ferruginascens* and *Russula minutula*, along with giant club *Clavariadelphus pistillaris* and the wonderfully named powdercap strangler *Squamanita paradoxa*. The latter is a rare parasite on the earthy powdercap *Cystoderma amianthinum*, itself a common grassland fungus.

The cliff woodland in Llangynidr Gorge is also notable for the abundance of beech, here at the northwestern edge of its native British range. Other species of southeast Britain which occur in profusion include toothwort *Lathraea squamaria* and early dog-violet *Viola reichenbachiana*. Small-leaved lime *Tilia cordata* is also found here and is colonised by mistletoe *Viscum album*. Wild service-tree *Sorbus torminalis* is present in small numbers.

BIRCH WOODLAND

Like ash, silver birch *Betula pendula* and downy birch are pioneers, often rapidly colonising areas such as forest clearings and heathlands. At Coed Dyfodol Sarnau, for instance, near Sarnau, an ancient woodland site planted with conifers which were felled in 1999, birch now dominates the area. This begins a process of succession which will eventually convert the area into woodland, provided there is no outside intervention in the form of grazing or human activities. Birch are not long-lived trees, rarely exceeding 80 years old, and as a pioneer species they also require fairly high light levels. As other slower-growing tree species grow up around them, the birch will be shaded out, giving way to oak woodland in a natural succession. Birch woods have a very diverse invertebrate life, supporting over 300 different species of insects and mites, including two closely related species of leafhoppers, *Oncopsis flavicollis* and *O. subangulata*, which are restricted to birches. This rich insect life in turn attracts a variety of birds, particularly willow warblers and chaffinches. Birch also has a number of fungi associated with it, including fly agaric *Amanita muscaria*, and a variety of bracket fungi.

The downy birch found in Cwm Sere, just to the north of Pen y Fan (Fig. 180) is an unusual form, with only short hairs on the twigs, typical of the Highlands of

FIG 180. The dense woodland in Cwm Sere includes an unusual form of downy birch (Jonathan Mullard)

Scotland and resembling similar trees found in Scandinavia. Until the discovery here it was not known that this form occurred in South Wales.

WOODLAND INVERTEBRATES

The invertebrate life of the broadleaved woodlands in the Beacons has not been studied in any detail, but the dense woodland in Cwm Sere, dominated by oak, ash and alder, is known to be an extremely important area for invertebrates. It contains a rich and varied fauna, including both arthropods and molluscs associated with ancient woodland, including a number of rarities. Among the most interesting are the craneflies, 48 species of which were recorded in a single visit to the wood in 1981, and nine of these were rare. Probably the most notable cranefly found on this occasion was *Gonomyia limbata*, a very rare species of open or shaded seepages, which is known in Britain only from this woodland and a site in Yorkshire. In 2006 the wood was also the site of studies, by Adrian Plant of the National Museum of Wales and Ingnac Sivec, a Slovenian researcher, to investigate bioacoustic communication in stoneflies, *Perla* spp. The males vibrate their genitalia against stones or wood, which they seem to prefer as it is such a good resonator, to attract females. These stridulation songs are dramatic enough to be heard 3 m away in a quiet room but often it is difficult to hear it in the field, as it is usually inaudible to human ears. This time though the researchers were able to obtain good recordings in the field, and they were able to compare them with the songs of similar species in Europe.

There are few butterflies recorded from Cwm Sere, but in July 1978 the Biological Recording Group for Wales recorded a number of moths, including the very common heart and dart *Agrotis exclamationis*, dark arches *Apamea monoglypha* and white ermine *Spilosoma lubricipeda*, together with May high-flyer *Hydriomena impluviata*, clouded border *Lomaspilis marginata*, sandy carpet *Perizoma flavofasciata*, light emerald *Campaea margaritata* and the common pug *Eupithecia vulgata*. The beetle fauna in Cwm Sere is also rich and includes a number of uncommon species, including the long-horned beetle *Judolia cerambyciformis*, *Bembidion stomoides*, *Agonum assimile*, *Calathus piceus*, *Patrobus atrorufus*, orchid beetle *Dascillus cervinus* and frog beetle *Notiophilus rufipes*.

Broadleaved woodlands, including those at the margins of the otherwise species-poor conifer plantations, can support rich mollusc faunas. The shade, moisture and structure of the habitat, including the depth and type of leaf litter, are critical for some, quite literally, delicate molluscs. Wooded stream margins support the greater pellucid glass snail *Phenacolimax major*, a rare and elusive species of ancient woods, almost at the limit of its range in Britain. A 'semi-slug' that is unable to fit its soft body into its ear-like shell, these animals are surprisingly fast-moving when roused as they race to find shelter and avoid desiccation. Molluscs recorded from Cwm Sere include the equally thin-shelled (if uninspiringly named) brown snail *Zenobiella subrufescens*, which is a classic species of woods and wild places in western Britain and Ireland. While it is present in Cwm Sere and elsewhere, records suggest it is not as widespread in the Beacons as might be expected. The plated snail *Spermodea lamellata*, another western ancient woodland species, is very rare in southeast Wales but is known from a single site in the area, the Wildlife Trust's Pwll y Wrach reserve near Talgarth. Also very local are the three-toothed moss snail *Azeca goodalli* and the English chrysalis snail *Leiostyla anglica*, both recorded in a recent snail survey, the latter also present in Cwm Sere. The lemon slug *Malacolimax tenellus* is perhaps the best indicator of ancient woodland, even where the original trees have been replaced with conifers (Fig. 181). It has been recorded from Cwm Clydach National Nature Reserve and other woodlands in the east of the Beacons but may well be found in others if searched for when the macrofungi on which it feeds are fruiting.

Other rare and scarce invertebrates recorded from the beech woodland at Cwm Clydach include the craneflies *Gonomyia abbreviata* and *Limonia inusta* and the beetles *Epuraea longula*, *Hylecoetus dermestoides*, *Plegaderus dissectus*, *Rhizophagus nitidulus* and black-headed cardinal beetle *Pyrochroa coccinea*. Adult cardinal beetles take flying insects from flowers and leaves, while their larvae can be found beneath the bark of dead trees, where they feed on dead wood and fungi. The hornet *Vespa crabro* is regularly recorded in Llangynidr Gorge, probably nesting in

FIG 181. The lemon slug is one of the best indicators of ancient woodland, as it never seems to occur in other habitats. (James Turner/National Museum of Wales)

the dry, sheltered cliff woodland. This is our largest species of social wasp, with the queens averaging around 3 cm in length. Overwintering queens emerge in April and nests are started, usually in hollow trees or similar cavities, in May with the first workers appearing around June. New queens and males emerge from the nest in September or October, when they mate and disperse, the males to die and the queens to seek hibernation sites.

The red wood ant *Formica rufus* builds characteristic dome-shaped nests of twigs in deciduous woodlands. The ants can be up to 1 cm in length and are carnivorous, hunting out other insects. They are found only in a few undisturbed woodlands in the Brecon Beacons; they favour open clearings, so that the nest mound can catch the sun and keep the ants warm and active.

DORMICE

As well as being home to the plated snail, Pwll y Wrach also supports the most important colony of dormice *Muscardinus avellanarius* in the Brecon Beacons. The distribution of dormice almost exactly reflects the distribution of lesser horseshoe bats in the area, with two exceptions. In the Usk Valley there are lesser horseshoes, but no dormice, and in the Tawe Valley there are dormice, but no lesser horseshoes. The reason for this is not clear, but dormice are mainly ancient woodland specialists, preferring mature deciduous woodland with a wide variety of tree and shrub species, so areas of diverse broadleaved woodland such as Pwll y Wrach are ideal for them. In South Wales they are often found in other habitats, including mature hedgerows, reed beds, heathland and scrub, feeding on fruit, flowers, pollen, nuts and insects such as aphids. They need woodland, however, with a good diversity of trees and shrubs, to provide an all-year-round food supply. Early in the spring, hazel catkins and spring flowers provide a nutritious food and the dormouse's whiskers carry pollen from flower to flower, which helps pollination. Brambles are also a particularly important source of fruits in the autumn, while acorns and hazelnuts are vital in helping the animals increase their body weight before hibernation (Fig. 182). Gnawed hazelnuts, with a smooth inner edge to the neat round hole, are a clear sign that dormice are present in an area. Other mammals that eat hazelnuts either split the nuts, as do grey squirrels, or leave characteristic marks from their incisor teeth around the hole, like voles and wood mice *Apodemus sylvaticus*.

On the north side of the Black Mountains all of the woodlands contain dormice, but they do not occur in the hedgerows, even though these might be thought to be an equally suitable habitat. In contrast, on the western side of the

FIG 182. Hibernating dormice temporarily extracted from a nest box, as part of a survey in an area south of the Beacons. (Allan Nutt)

National Park, in Carmarthenshire, dormice are found almost exclusively in hedgerows. This has led researchers to speculate that there might be different subspecies of dormice, or that there could be distinct behavioural differences between populations.

Dormice are nocturnal, using their large eyes, long whiskers and excellent sense of smell to find their way about, and for this reason they are rarely seen. They spend the day asleep in spherical nests of shredded bark of honeysuckle, or clematis, constructed in trees, bushes or bramble patches up to 5 m from the ground. They also readily use nest boxes erected on trees for birds, or for small mammals. It is only when observers are checking nest boxes that they are likely to be found. Dormice are much more agile than other mice, spending a lot of time climbing around bushes and trees, rarely coming down to the ground, except to hibernate. They need to be able to move about within woodlands, through trees and bushes, or between woodlands using tall hedgerows. The design for the A479

FIG 183. An overhead crossing on the Talgarth and Bronllys Bypass at Pendre, specially designed for dormice but used mainly by grey squirrels. (Jonathan Mullard)

Talgarth Relief Road and Bronllys Bypass, which was opened in 2007, included an oversized culvert approximately 2 m in diameter which had an integrated 'high-level' dormouse ledge to link habitats on each side of the new road, and an innovative dormouse overhead crossing was installed at Pendre (Fig. 183). This was intended as a long-term mitigation measure to address the fragmentation of habitats caused by the construction of the road. The consultants on the project, in conjunction with the Countryside Council for Wales, were keen for the overhead crossing to be built, but dormice have been seen to run across the road, so they obviously don't feel the need to use it. Local people, however, say that the grey squirrels love it!

YELLOW-NECKED MICE

Another mouse, the yellow-necked mouse *Apodemus flavicollis*, is numerous in woodlands near Brecon and Hay on Wye. They are closely related to the wood mouse, with which they were long confused, only being recognised as a separate species in 1894. As with dormice, few people will have seen a yellow-necked mouse as they are nocturnal and largely confined to mature woodland. They are also superficially similar to the much more common wood mouse, so are easy to overlook. Yellow-necked mice are especially dependent on woodland with a good diversity of seed- and fruit-producing trees and shrubs, which makes them particularly vulnerable to woodland loss and fragmentation.

PINE MARTENS

Many of these small mammals are the prey of pine martens *Martes martes*, which are still present in the Beacons, with the broadleaved woodland in the vicinity of the Talgarth, Talybont and Usk as their stronghold. As well as small mammals, they will also eat birds and their eggs, invertebrates, fruits and nuts. Until about ten years ago there were numerous records of sightings, and it was thought that they had since become extinct in the area – but it is now clear that this is not the case, and the apparent disappearance is almost certainly a function of the lack of recording effort. Despite this, pine martens are probably not as common as they once were. The usual persecution in the Victorian period certainly affected their numbers. E. Cambridge Phillips reported in *The Zoologist* in 1887 that one was seen in a wood near Brecon in September 1886, and J. H. Salter, another local naturalist, also mentions other records in his diaries. For instance, on 9 September 1903 he writes, 'Mr Vaughan Powell, water bailiff at Senny Bridge, used to know the tracks of the marten cat in the snow in his youth.' Writing in 1926, T. R. Philips remarked that, 'the pine marten, *Mustela martes* is also, probably quite extinct in the neighbourhood' (Morgan 1992). Although pine martens are commonly referred to as nocturnal, they are frequently active during the day, especially in the summer months, and it is then that most of the sightings occur. In 2012 the Vincent Wildlife Trust started a two-year project to determine the status of the pine marten in Wales, and this will undoubtedly produce more records.

CONIFER PLANTATIONS

Substantial areas of the Brecon Beacons, particularly in the uplands, have been planted with conifers by the Forestry Commission, the largest plantation being Mynydd Du Forest, which covers 1,200 hectares. The primary purpose of these plantations is timber production and they are dominated by stands of single species (Fig. 184), with a variety of native trees and shrubs on the forest edge and alongside streams and gullies inside. Conifers planted in the Beacons include Corsican pine *Pinus nigra* ssp. *laricio*, Japanese larch *Larix kaempferi*, Sitka spruce *Picea sitchensis* and Norway spruce *P. abies*. Douglas fir *Pseudotsuga menziesii* and European larch *Larix decidua* are no longer considered suitable in these situations, but western red cedar *Thuya plicata* and western hemlock *Tsuga heterophylla* were grown experimentally in one or two areas. Most plantations are on ground that has been drained by a network of ditches and deep ploughed prior to tree planting, although more recent plantations may have been established using different

FIG 184. Sitka spruce plantation near the Storey Arms Centre, after a sudden fall of snow in May 2013. (Jonathan Mullard)

techniques. Planted mainly in the 1950s, most of the conifers in the Beacons have now reached maturity and quite extensive areas have been cropped in recent years.

Recently planted areas, where the trees are up to 12 years old, are the richest areas for wildlife, especially in first-rotation plantations where remnants of the previous habitat are present. During the middle period of a forest's life, up to 30 years old, the trees form a dense canopy which prevents light reaching the forest floor, resulting in an almost total absence of ground flora and understorey. In contrast, the high forest stage, from 30 to 70 years after planting, has a more open canopy, especially in deciduous larch plantations. This allows more light to reach the forest floor and some recovery of ground flora, especially near the forest edge. Conifers are frequently felled when the trees are around 40 years old, though continuous-cover forestry is increasingly being used.

The Forestry Commission is planning to gradually increase the amount of broadleaved woodland in the forests, keeping tree cover on the lower slopes and reshaping harsh coniferous edges on the upper slopes. This is to make the forests fit better in the wider landscape of open moorland and fields. The plan is to bring the moorland down valley slopes by removing conifers, whilst extending broadleaved woodland up the slopes from valley bottoms. In the last 20 years increasing attention has also been given to the wildlife value of conifer plantations, and many second-rotation forests have been managed in order to create a greater diversity of tree species and ages, with old stands of dead and dying trees being retained.

Conifers have been felled on National Trust land near the Storey Arms Centre due to an outbreak of ramorum dieback *Phytophthora ramorum*, a fungus-like pathogen of plants, in the Japanese larch there. Ramorum dieback is a virulent fungal disease that is notifiable, which means that any landowners who find it on their land are under instruction from the Forestry Commission to eradicate it. Symptoms include lesions that exude fluid from infected bark, visible as a black exudate that dries to a crust on the trunk. The inner bark under this bleeding area is usually discoloured and dying. When the lesions become extensive on the main trunk the tree dies. Signs of infection on Japanese larch include wilted, withered shoot tips with blackened needles. Originally, in Britain the majority of findings of *P. ramorum* have been in nurseries, where it affects container-grown ornamental plants such as *Rhododendron*, *Viburnum* and *Camellia*, but it has now been found at more than 700 sites in England and Wales, as well as a number of sites in Scotland, Northern Ireland and the Channel Islands.

FIG 185. Conifer forests provide good habitats for larger fungi, such as this fly agaric in Glasfynydd Forest, near the Usk Reservoir. (Harold Grenfell)

Conifer forests, even fairly recent ones, provide good habitats for larger fungi, such as fly agaric (Fig. 185). Larch bolete *Suillus grevillei* is found in larch plantations, but may become less common now that many of the larch are being felled because of ramorum dieback. The total number of species is lower than in native woodland, however, due to the fact that plantations are monocultures. Microfungi, including mycorrhizal species that are essential for the growth of most plants, are less common in conifer plantations, as they are often lost as a result of soil disturbance during the initial ploughing or the subsequent use of heavy machinery. The poor qualities of conifer bark, the lack of dead wood and old trees, excessive shade, and a lack of ecological continuity due to clear felling also make most conifer plantations poor habitats for lichens.

Large dense stands of conifers of uniform age do not provide a good habitat for invertebrates either, although those that do occur are often abundant. These are either recent arrivals to Britain, or common generalists that have spread from native plants. A number of new invertebrate species have been attracted to the canopy of conifer plantations, including several hoverflies such as *Eriozona erratica*, *E. syrphoides*, *Melangyna compositarum*, *Parasyrphus lineola* and *P. malinellus*. The caterpillars of red-necked footman moths *Atolmis rubricollis* feed on the few lichens that grow on conifers and there are sporadic records of this moth from various locations in the Beacons, but it is not clear whether they are from breeding colonies or migrants. They are on the wing in June and July and can sometimes be found flying in daytime.

Most invertebrates are found on the edges of conifer plantations. It was in such a location that a female comb-horn cranefly *Tanyptera atrata* was caught by Judy Webb during the Dipterists Forum summer field meeting held in Abergavenny in May 2011 (Fig. 186). These craneflies are impressive mimics, resembling large and dangerous social, or ichneumon, wasps. Their larvae are mainly associated with damp environments, living in and around moss, soil, fungal fruiting bodies and decaying wood. They appear to be largely detritus feeders, but also consume some living plants.

Another interesting fly recorded from Grwyne Fawr is the common awl robberfly *Neoitamus cyanurus*, which is only known from about 15 localities in Wales (Fig. 187). The name comes from the long ovipositor the female is equipped with, an awl being a long pointed spike, as in a bradawl – a tool for making holes in wood. The robberfly is generally a woodland species and is most usually found on foliage along woodland rides. It catches its prey, usually small moths, in flight (Stubbs & Drake 2001). The shelter provided by conifers also allows insects, particularly mosquitoes and midges, to fly in bad weather – and this can be a vital food source for several species of bats. Harvesting of the trees prior to maturity,

FIG 186. Female comb-horn cranefly caught as it was flying along the forest edge in the valley of the Grwyne Fawr, May 2011 (Judy Webb)

FIG 187. The common awl robberfly is found in ancient oak woodland as well as conifer plantations, and may be seen from May to October. The name comes from the female's long ovipositor. (Jeremy Early)

however, limits the availability of roosting holes, even at the high forest stage, and bat boxes have to be erected to compensate.

BIRDS IN CONIFER PLANTATIONS

While the insect life of conifer plantations is restricted they can, in contrast, provide excellent habitats for birds, especially in areas where there is little alternative cover available. The high forest stage, in particular, is the favoured habitat for a number of species, including song thrush *Turdus philomelos*, coal tit *Periparus ater*, willow warbler, goldcrest, siskin *Carduelis spinus* and common crossbill *Loxia curvirostra*. Most of these species also occur in a range of other habitats, but the crossbill is restricted to conifers, moving around between plantations depending on where cones have been produced in greatest abundance. A number of birds of prey also nest in plantations at this stage, and in areas that are being retained for the long term. These include buzzards, red kites, sparrowhawks and goshawks *Accipiter gentilis*.

Goshawks are very large birds of prey, but there is a marked difference in size between the sexes. Males are roughly the same size as a crow, while the much larger females are about the size of a buzzard. In many ways the goshawk is a large version of the much commoner sparrowhawk. They are grey above with whitish underparts, neatly barred with dark lines. Male goshawks usually have a striking head pattern with a dark crown, white eye stripe and dark 'ear' markings, which creates a masked appearance (Fig. 188).

The goshawk used to be widespread throughout Britain, but became extinct in the late nineteenth century due to deforestation and relentless persecution. They were reintroduced in the 1960s and the 1970s, not by conservation

FIG 188. Goshawk, several pairs of which nest in conifer plantations in the Beacons. They are still illegally persecuted and their nests frequently robbed. (Peter Beasley)

organisations, but by falconers who brought birds into the country from Finland and Scandinavia. Some of these imported birds escaped from captivity and others were deliberately released, possibly to allow them to breed in the wild and thereafter to harvest the young. These released and escaped birds established scattered populations throughout the country. There are only 200 pairs of goshawks in Wales, but a number of these nest in plantations in the Beacons.

Despite the high level of legal protection now given to the goshawk, its spread from these large forests into some of the surrounding privately owned woodlands has been restricted because of continuing harassment. In 2011, for example, during a routine visit to woodland near Chepstow a Forestry Commission Ranger discovered that a tree, home to a family of goshawks, had been felled. The tree had been cut down by hand and the chicks had disappeared, either stolen for falconry or killed. Nest destruction and egg theft unfortunately continue to be major factors affecting the recovery of the species, and the loss of just one or two clutches of eggs can have a considerable impact.

Goshawks return to the same nesting area each year, where they build a new nest, or alternatively refurbish and re-use an old nest. For such a large bird they can be surprisingly elusive, and can remain in an area for some time without being detected by the casual observer. In the spring though when they are establishing their nesting territory, and in the late summer when young fledged goshawks are calling for food, they can make a lot of noise and can be found comparatively easily. They feed on a wide variety of birds and small animals, but about two-thirds of their prey consists of crows, rooks *Corvus frugilegus* and woodpigeons *Columba palumbus*. Goshawks are also perhaps the only true natural predator of red kites.

Red kites, sometimes nesting in the same forests as goshawks, were also once regarded as vermin, and they were exterminated in England, Scotland and most of Wales by the end of the eighteenth century. Unlike the goshawk, however, they have noticeably increased in numbers. Around 20 years ago most red kite sightings were in the far west of the Beacons, but they are now commonly seen across the area. The kites continue to be targeted by egg thieves, however, and the illegal use of poisoned baits, not set specifically for red kite, is still a major threat.

Red kites are a wide-ranging species which occupy a wide variety of habitats. The only requirement is for a fairly large tree, with open access to it, in which to build a nest about 10–15 m above ground. Although it is a large bird, it is not strong or aggressive, only protecting the nest area, not the whole breeding territory. Most Welsh kites nest within 20 km of where they were reared. They are primarily scavengers, but they are also predators, especially when feeding young, taking a wide variety of live prey ranging from earthworms to birds and small mammals, such as rabbits, voles and mice. The bird uses a low, gliding flight to hunt live prey, searching for small movements on the ground. It then dives quickly and grasps the prey in its talons. One of the easiest places to see red kites feeding close up is at the feeding station in the village of Llanddeusant at the western edge of the Beacons. This is a commercial operation which puts out food for the kites every afternoon, and for a small fee spectacular views can be had.

There have been recent sightings of honey-buzzard *Pernis apivorus*, a large bird of prey similar to the buzzard. They are summer visitors to the area, spending the winter in Africa. Honey-buzzards are one of the most abundant raptors in Europe, with the population estimated to be around 160,000 pairs, the majority of birds being in Russia. In Britain, however, they were never recorded as common and probably became extinct around the turn of the twentieth century. They returned to breed occasionally, and until recently the number of pairs was believed to be very low. In the last few years they appear to be increasing, however, and the British population is now assessed to be at least 100 pairs. They were first recorded breeding in Wales around 1991, and the population here is now around 20 pairs.

Numbers are increasing, probably as a result of the upland conifer forests maturing, but the nest sites of birds breeding in Britain are being kept secret to protect them from egg collectors. They are secretive and elusive birds, spending a lot of time in the tree canopy. Honey-buzzards are unlike other large raptors in that they specialise in eating insects, with wasp larvae making up a large part of their diet. They have adaptations that protect them from stings and help them deal with their prey: their legs and feet are heavily scaled and the feathers around the bill are dense and scale-like. The bill is long and curved with an extended point suitable for holding insects, and their nostrils are reduced to long slits that are less likely to become blocked with soil as they dig for wasp nests.

Great grey shrike *Lanius excubitor* is a scarce winter visitor, usually associated with plantations on the upland edge. The best place to see one is around the Usk Reservoir, where they occur on an almost annual basis. Nightjars *Caprimulgus europaeus* also breed in young, or recently felled, plantations.

MAMMALS

A variety of mammals, including badgers (Fig. 189), roe deer and red deer, have also successfully adapted to living in conifer plantations. The distribution and abundance of badgers has historically been dependent on changing patterns of agriculture (Reason *et al.* 1993). Their diet consists mainly of earthworms, the importance of which cannot be underestimated – some animals have been known to eat over 200 earthworms in a single night.

Until the Badgers Act came into force in 1973, persecution was a contributory factor in determining population levels, and unfortunately snares and other forms of illegal persecution, which maim and kill badgers, continue to take their toll. In addition, bovine tuberculosis is a major, and controversial, issue for farmers in Wales. A cull of badgers in Wales aimed at cutting tuberculosis in cattle was, however, replaced in March 2012 by a vaccination programme.

BIG CATS

One of the most controversial members of the woodland mammal fauna in the Brecon Beacons and the surrounding area is the big cat. Over the years a number of reliable local naturalists have had clear sightings in and around woodland of what seem to be melanistic (i.e. black) pumas *Puma concolor* – including, on one occasion, one with cubs. Most of the records are from the north of the area, around Brecon and Sennybridge, although there are records of an animal being seen around Llangorse Lake between 2002 and 2004. More recently, in November 2010, a number of sheep kills, attributed to a big cat, were reported in Felindre, near Three Cocks, and in Crai, between Brecon and Sennybridge. There is anecdotal evidence amongst farmers and society at large that there are big cats wild within our countryside, and locals are aware of unusual sheep kills in the area but generally keep quiet and are unwilling to discuss the subject. Pumas are 'stalk and ambush' predators, pursing a wide variety of prey, including sheep. They prefer habitats such as woodland with dense undergrowth for stalking, but can also live in open areas.

The Welsh Government's Rural Affairs Department is responsible for investigating reports of sightings and attacks by big cats on livestock in Wales. All reported sightings are recorded on a database, held by the Wildlife Unit, which dates back to the early 1990s. Where evidence is available, staff from the Unit collect carcasses from alleged kills for post mortem, video footage or photographic evidence, casts of paw prints and any other signs indicating the possible presence of exotic species. In February 2011, for example, staff collected some casts of footprints taken in Crai, but they were poor-quality cement casts of footprints in snow so it was difficult to determine what had made them, although they were thought to be perhaps those of a large dog.

Wildlife advisers from the Department of Environment, Food and Rural Affairs and the Welsh Government have been investigating incidents allegedly involving big cats for over 15 years. In that time there have been several hundred sightings, but both organisations consider that not one piece of hard evidence has come to light to suggest that big cats are living in the Welsh countryside.

FIG 189. A very lifelike carving of badgers in Penmoelallt Community Woodland, a mixed coniferous and broadleaved woodland immediately north of Merthyr Tydfil. (Jonathan Mullard)

Other people, such as the naturalists who have spoken to the author, and seen them directly, have different views. Perhaps we just need to accept that these animals are now as much a part of our fauna as other naturalised species such as grey squirrels. As well as attacking sheep the cats are also thought to prey on deer, which are more numerous in the Beacons than might initially be thought.

DEER

The first record of deer in the Brecon Beacons comes from Gerald of Wales, who described Llanthony Priory in his *Journey Through Wales* in 1191 as follows:

> *As they sit in their cloisters in this monastery, breathing the fresh air, the monks gaze up at distant prospects which rise above their own lofty roof-tops, and there*

they see, as far as any eye can reach, mountain-peaks which rise to meet the sky and often enough herds of wild deer which are gazing on their summits.

These deer were probably red deer, the largest native land mammal in Wales – large adult stags weighing up to 200 kg. Although considered to be indigenous to Wales, most of the 200 or so red deer estimated to live in Wales are resident in the Beacons and originate from escapes from a deer farm in the 1980s. Infrared 'trail cameras' set up by the Forestry Commission have confirmed the presence of red deer in the area and provided valuable information on which woodlands they are using and at what time of year. The cameras can be left for up to six months before they need to be checked, and if the results indicate that deer are present this can be followed up with more detailed surveys into the impacts on trees and ground flora. One of the key areas for red deer appears to be Glasfynydd Forest, which surrounds the Usk Reservoir.

There are also occasional records of fallow *Dama dama* and roe deer, although the Beacons do not seem to be a key area for these species. Fallow deer were reintroduced to Britain during the eleventh or twelfth centuries and are medium-sized deer, with bucks weighing up to 95 kg. They are an attractive species and became popular in deer parks, from which escaped animals later established themselves in the wild. They are now amongst the most widespread of all the wild deer species in Wales, and large populations can often be seen at the western end of the Brecon Beacons near Llandeilo.

Milder winters and changes in land use have all contributed to an increase in the abundance of deer in Wales (Ward 2005). As well as increases for species already well established it is likely that other species will also be present in the future. Reeves's or Chinese muntjac *Muntiacus reevesi* are under-recorded, but certainly present in the Beacons. They were originally introduced to England through escapes from Woburn Park in Bedfordshire around 1925. Populations have expanded very rapidly, and they are now present in most English counties from South Yorkshire southwards, and have also expanded their range into Wales. They eat a wide range of foods, but seem to be primarily animals of dense woodland, although an analysis of the occurrence of sightings suggests they will also use a wide variety of other habitats.

As described previously, the landscape of Wales has been heavily influenced by people and, along with the loss of many of their natural predators, this provides a habitat in which deer can thrive. Although wild deer are not yet as numerous or widespread in Wales as in other parts of Britain, their impacts on agriculture, forestry and vulnerable habitats are becoming more obvious. The grazing of deer and indeed sheep can have a major effect on woodlands, including the rare and special trees described in the next chapter.

Chapter 10

Ancient and Special Trees

While the oak, ash, alder and beech woodlands described in the previous chapter are comparatively well known, the many ancient, or veteran, trees found in the Brecon Beacons are reminders of other, almost forgotten, landscapes, such as the black poplar *Populus nigra* woodlands which once covered the former floodplains of rivers such as the Usk. Similar woodlands can still be seen in the fragmentary floodplain forests on the River Drôme and River Loire in France. Old isolated oak and ash pollards are also evidence of previous management practices and remind us that trees were once a source of important products. Other ancient trees include the venerable specimens of yew *Taxus baccata* located in churchyards across the Beacons. As these are so firmly connected to the churches, and indeed characteristic of them in many cases, they are described in Chapter 11.

In contrast to these survivors of the past, the Beacons are also a source of new species, in the form of whitebeams *Sorbus* spp., the only endemic trees in Britain and Ireland. These species have arisen as a result of hybridisation between existing species of rowan, or whitebeam, and represent a new source of woodland diversity.

BLACK POPLARS

Although black poplar woodland is a landscape feature lost from the British countryside many centuries ago, isolated trees still exist along the river valleys. A tree of damp floodplains in eastern Wales and southern England, black polar is one of Britain's most endangered native tree species, and the best estimates indicate that there are only around 7,000 specimens remaining. Female trees are particularly rare, with no more than 400 recorded nationally. Seed germination is restricted to the unvegetated banks and bars of river systems, but our over-managed rivers have lacked suitable habitats for centuries.

Specialist floodplain trees that are currently rare and localised, such as black poplar, would have been much commoner in the extensive floodplain woodlands of the past. Much of this woodland was probably open in structure, similar to that of wood-pasture today, with the open areas consisting of grassland species tolerant of intermittent flooding. There would also have been extensive areas of scrub within which trees could regenerate, protected from grazing animals. All of these habitats would be in a dynamic mosaic, maintained by movement of the river channel and by grazing, with areas of swamp, fen, raised bog and wet woodland in former river channels and other areas with less permeable soils.

There is a significant population of black poplars in the Usk Valley, and it includes some of the best examples of standard trees in Britain. There is a particularly fine specimen, for example, used as an ornamental tree in the grounds of Nevill Hall hospital in Abergavenny. Mature standard specimens,

FIG 190. The largest black poplar in Britain, with a girth of 6.5 m and a height of 33.5 m, at the edge of the school playing fields at Christ College, Brecon. (Harold Grenfell)

such as this, often lean heavily and have lower branches that curve downwards, upper branches that curve upwards and deeply furrowed bark. The bright green leaves are deltoid to ovoid in shape, with hairy petioles and serrated margins, and the buds turn outwards. Prior to elongation the male catkins are red, while the females produce long pendulous seed capsules with copious amounts of white fluff when the seed is released. The largest black poplar in Britain is located on a field boundary at the edge of the school playing fields at Christ College in Brecon, which is one of the oldest schools in Wales, founded in 1541 by Henry VIII (Fig. 190). This black poplar again displays the archetypal profile of the tree, with arched boughs and leaning bole – a unique geometry that makes it clearly recognisable from other species of poplar. The school is immensely proud of its record-breaking tree, and cuttings have been taken, so that if anything happened to it replacements would be available.

Another large old black poplar is situated at the corner of the road just southwest of Llanwenarth Church, some 2 km west of Abergavenny (Fig. 191). These old trees are a haven for insects that rely on the very soft decaying wood of broadleaved trees, including species such as the lesser stag beetle *Dorcus parallelipipedus*, an adult male of which Graham Motley once watched entering the hole at the base. The males have distinctly knobbed antennae, and although their jaws are somewhat larger than those of the females, they are nowhere near as large as those of other male stag beetles *Lucanus cervus*. Lesser stag beetles have an even more secluded life cycle than stag beetles, since both larvae and adults spend their life mostly inside rotting wood. The adults may live for more than one year, perhaps up to three years, but not much is known about this species, as their small size and nocturnal habits mean that they have not attracted much attention from naturalists. It is quite likely that the females lay eggs for more than one season, as it is known that these beetles do not die at the end of the summer, as stag beetles do.

Other standard trees recorded nearby include one tree, unfortunately badly pollarded, on the side of the A40 near Pysgodlyn, one tree near the River Usk southeast of Mardy Farm, and three trees just west of Tyrewen. Few of these specimens are in good condition, owing to storm damage or unsympathetic management.

In the late 1990s DNA fingerprinting showed that many black poplars in Britain have been established by vegetative propagation, producing considerable clonal duplication, and this work has been augmented by a collaborative EU-funded project known as EUROPOP, which fingerprinted black poplars growing along river systems in nine countries. In highly dynamic river systems, such as those found in France, Spain, the Czech Republic and Ukraine, no duplication of clones

FIG 191. The old black poplar near Llanwenarth Church, an important habitat for lesser stag beetle and many other insects which rely on decaying wood. (Jonathan Mullard)

was detected, indicating that all the sampled trees were derived from seed rather than vegetative propagation. Similarly, less than 15 per cent clonal distribution was found in rivers in Italy, Austria and Germany, this low level of clonal duplication being considered to result naturally from the rooting of broken branches that had been carried downstream from the original trees. In contrast, there was much higher clonal duplication along the Rhine in the Netherlands (41 per cent), and the Usk had the highest recorded clonal duplication in Europe at 97 per cent. In the Usk Valley only two clones, consisting of 68 and 4 trees respectively, were found to be present, due to the fact that most of the trees had been deliberately planted. The current population therefore reflects former planting preferences rather than any natural distribution pattern, and it is not surprising that the genetic diversity is low. Male trees have also often been planted in preference to female trees, as the fluffy seeds were apparently unpopular with farmers, causing a nuisance at hay-making time.

The usual habitat of black poplars today is in hedgerows, since at the time of the enclosures in the eighteenth century the tree, together with alder and white willow *Salix alba*, would have been the obvious species to plant along the resulting ditches and hedgerows. Black poplars played an important role in the local economy, being pollarded to provide a crop of wood for bean sticks, scaffolding poles, thatching spars and fruit baskets. The owner of the 18 trees surviving in woodland near Abergavenny believes that they were planted to provide materials for the farm cart industry that was in existence in the Usk Valley some 200 years ago, the shock-absorbent qualities of the timber making it particularly suitable for this purpose (Cooper 2006). The fire-resistant qualities of the timber also made it the material of choice for barns and the manufacture of bellows and pumps for brickworks, limekilns and smithies.

All these black poplars are threatened by a pathogenic fungus, *Venturia populina*, which was first observed in the Manchester area in the summer of 2000. The symptoms are relatively easy to recognise: initially the usual dense canopy of the tree is much reduced, with many brown leaves visible throughout the tree, and then new leaves die rapidly. They first turn black and then develop a brown shrivelled appearance, staying on the tree longer than normal in the autumn, due to the inability to form an abscission layer at the base of the leaf stalk. The disease also leaves the tree vulnerable to attack by another fungus, *Dothichiza populea*, which, although not as serious, does cause further dieback, particularly in weakened specimens. Unfortunately there are recent reports of *Venturia populina* on trees in the Usk Valley, suggesting that the fungus has now spread throughout Britain. This could result in the loss of the whole population, severing our last link with the ancient floodplain forests.

VETERAN TREES

As well as the black poplars described above there are numerous other veteran trees in the Beacons which have been identified by the Ancient Tree Hunt, an initiative led by the Woodland Trust. The majority of the trees found to date are located, like the black poplars, in the Usk Valley above Abergavenny, but the details of these remain to be confirmed. Veteran trees are those which have passed through cycles of dieback and regeneration; as a result they typically support a range of characteristic features, including large amounts of dead wood, rot holes, sap runs, loose bark and bracket fungi. Different species of tree acquire these features at different ages; oaks, for example, usually take several hundred years to become veterans, whereas short-lived trees such as birch may develop the characteristics of veterans when they are less than 100 years old.

None of the historic parks mentioned in Chapter 3 was regarded as sufficiently interesting to include in the Parklands Survey carried out by the Countryside Council for Wales in the mid-1990s, so there very few wildlife records from these areas. Nor does the National Park Authority have any comprehensive details, although they have tried several times to encourage volunteers to undertake survey work. Parklands and wood-pastures with large mature or ancient trees within grazed grassland are some of the most valuable habitats in Europe, supporting a number of important species, the majority of which are associated with dead wood.

The most characteristic species associated with veteran trees are, not surprisingly, those which depend on dead wood, including many rare species of fungi and invertebrates, particularly beetles and flies. These saproxylic invertebrates, including hoverflies, beetles and false scorpions, can be divided into three types: those dependent on the habitats created by heartwood decay, those dependent on bark and sapwood decay, and those dependent on fungal fruiting bodies. The rare, bright red, Welsh oak longhorn beetle *Pyrrhidium sanguineum* is one species dependent on bark and sapwood decay that that has been recorded in the area. This small beetle, 6–15 mm long, is one of the commonest longhorn beetles in central Europe and, although it is listed as a Red Data Book species in Britain, it is being increasingly recorded across England and Wales. The larvae feed under the bark of dead branches and trunks but, unlike those of some other longhorn species, eggs are readily laid in newly cut timber. Although oak is the favoured host it will also use other deciduous trees.

Parkland is also an important habitat for lichens, partly because it has a number of features that are of particular significance, including the presence of mature trees to provide a continuity of substrate over hundreds of years. The trees are also well spaced so that the trunks receive high levels of light. Some parks may additionally be of ancient origin, or provide continuity with ancient woodland that formerly occupied the site. The hollow trunks and other crevices are used by roosting bats and nesting birds, such as kestrels, and provide an important resource for bats, which favour habitat mosaics with an abundance of insects.

Noctule bats are not as common in the Beacons as they once were. Their habitat still seems good enough, but something is clearly affecting populations and researchers are not sure what this might be. Noctule bats are primarily tree dwellers, living mainly in rot holes and woodpecker holes, so the Usk Valley and similar areas with a high proportion of ancient trees might be expected to be a stronghold for the species. Noctules are rarely found in buildings; most roosts in buildings are only 'gathering roosts', the colonies moving off at the end of May and early June. They fly in the open, often well above tree-top level, with repeated steep dives when chasing insects.

Despite the lack of a comprehensive survey it is likely that the parkland in the Beacons supports a wide range of scarce invertebrates associated with decaying wood. The priority is to conserve the mature and ancient trees and the associated dead-wood niches that support the rare saproxylic fauna, which includes some of Britain's most threatened invertebrates. Tidiness and over-zealous removal of dead wood and felling of trees on the grounds of a perceived threat to public safety are the greatest threats to the survival of such species. A major problem at many sites is that there is a gap in the age structure of trees, continuity being vital if the specialist invertebrate fauna is to survive.

ARMADA CHESTNUTS

One historic parkland that does have a significant number of veteran trees is that associated with Llanfihangel Court, in Llanfihangel Crucorney, which is among the oldest surviving mansions in Monmouthshire, dating from at least the sixteenth century. Here the remains of a formally designed park, originally a deer park, includes two avenues of trees centred on the mansion. The northern avenue consisted of pine, which was cut down in the 1940s, but the southern avenue of sweet, or Spanish, chestnut *Castanea sativa* survives to this day. The seeds for these trees, known as the Armada Chestnuts, are said to have been taken from the wreckage of ships from the Spanish Armada in 1588. The same tale is told about other similar plantings along the Welsh border, at Pedwardine, Monnington and Croft Castle.

Apparently, ornate urns containing chestnuts were salvaged from the remains of the Armada and the contents planted to celebrate the great victory. Whether this tale is true or not, at Croft Castle avenues of trees were established to commemorate the event – oaks to represent the English fleet and Spanish chestnuts to represent the Armada. Interestingly, the sixteenth-century Spanish poet Lope de Vega described the astonishing spectacle of the Armada as 'trees of the faith', and that it appeared as a 'jungle upon the sea'. The avenues at Croft and Llanfihangel were a reminder of ships of the line sailing in battle formation. Sweet chestnut is a long-lived tree, often surviving 500 years or more. With age the tree becomes grotesquely misshapen with a gigantic thick trunk, often partly hollow, and huge twisted branches which may touch the ground (Fig. 192).

FIG 192. One of the Armada chestnuts at Llanfihangel Court, veteran trees said to originate from chestnuts salvaged from the remains of the Spanish Armada. The complex structure of the trees provides valuable habitats for a variety of species. (Jonathan Mullard)

The complex structure of the trees includes cavities, splits, rot holes and bark flaps – all of which provide valuable habitats. The mature trees are extremely large, with many having huge hollow trunks.

This tradition of commemorating famous sea battles by planting trees was continued by the Woodland Trust in 2005, when they marked the bicentenary of the Battle of Trafalgar by highlighting the role played by native trees in providing the materials to build Nelson's fleet. They planted 33 new woods, to match the number of ships in the fleet, including one at Coed Tregib, near Llandeilo – at the opposite end of the Beacons to Llanfihangel.

POLLARDED TREES

Chestnuts are a familiar example of a non-native veteran tree, but there a number of other ancient native trees in the area. Two of the best of these, pollarded oaks more than 500 years old, are not within parkland but can be found in a field to the west of Llangorse Lake (Fig. 193). There is also a massive pollarded oak tree in

FIG 193. Two ancient pollarded pedunculate oaks, thought to be more than 500 years old, to the west of Llangorse Lake. (Gareth Ellis)

Cwm Oergwm, near Llanfrynach, which is a Brecknock Wildlife Trust reserve, and more undoubtedly remain to be discovered.

Many of the ancient oaks in Britain were pollarded in the past. Pollarding and shredding of trees were widespread and common practices in Britain until the eighteenth century. Trees were an important source of fodder, and their branches were regularly lopped so that sheep and cattle, and sometimes deer, could eat their twigs and leaves – the so-called 'pollard hay'. The tree was pruned in this way at intervals of 2–6 years so that the leafy material would be most abundant. Pollards being managed for timber were pruned at longer intervals of 8–15 years, a cycle that produces upright poles for use as fence rails and posts.

FIG 194. An ancient pollarded ash on the banks of the Nant Onneu southwest of Llangattock. (Jonathan Mullard)

By the mid-nineteenth century, however, the practice of pollarding was becoming increasingly rare, and it had virtually died out by the mid-twentieth century. In Europe, by contrast, pollarding remains common in several Mediterranean, Balkan and Scandinavian countries. The best time to cut pollards is in February and early March, because the new buds that form to replace the lost branches are then at less risk of frost damage.

One consequence of pollarding is that pollarded trees tend to live longer than unpollarded specimens, as they are maintained in a partially juvenile state and are less susceptible to wind damage. Pollarded trees develop a constantly rejuvenated, energy-creating young canopy, on top of an increasingly ancient trunk. This slows the tree's normal ageing processes. Old pollards are often hollow and can therefore be difficult to age accurately. They also tend to grow more slowly, with narrower growth rings in the years immediately after cutting.

There are also a number of pollarded ash trees in the Beacons, such as the one located to the southwest of Llangattock shown in Figure 194. Because the wood is both tough and flexible, ash has been used in the past to make spears, arrows and pike shafts. The tree's name, in fact, comes from the Anglo Saxon word *æsc*, which means lance or spear, while the scientific name *Fraxinus* means firelight and refers to the fact that the wood is well known for its ability to be burnt when it is still green, and *excelsior* means higher and alludes to the tree's ability to live at high altitudes. The larger timbers of ash were often used in wagon and furniture making and the smaller poles for hurdles, ladders, wheels, tool shafts and walking sticks. One early recommendation was that every Lord of the Manor should plant one acre of ash to every 20 acres of land because in future the wood would be worth more than the land itself.

HOLLINS AND HAGGS

Another formerly widespread source of pollard hay, this time evergreen, was holly. Despite its spiny leaves, holly is palatable to livestock and was once cultivated as a source of winter feed, being grown in parklands known as hollins. In the Middle Ages in particular, hollins were highly valued for their ability to supply supplementary fodder at the end of the farming year, the foliage being cut when needed. Apparently the shepherd, or cowherd, lopped a few upper branches from each tree, and this careful pollarding did not hurt it. Sheep are especially fond of the bark.

The practice occurred throughout the natural range of holly in England and Wales, but appears to have been most frequent in the Welsh Borders, Cumbria and the Pennines. For example, to the east of the Beacons, the Forest of Dean keepers are recorded, in the seventeenth century, cutting holly to feed deer in winter. The late-twelfth- or early-thirteenth-century tale *The Dream of Rhonabwy*, which survives in only one manuscript, the *Red Book of Hergest*, referred to in Chapter 4, includes a striking reference to the use of holly as fodder:

> *And as they came towards the house, they could see a black old hall with a straight gable end, and smoke a-plenty from it. And when they came inside, they could see a floor full of holes and uneven. Where there was a bump on it, it was with difficulty a man might stand thereon, so exceeding slippery was the floor with cows' urine and dung. Where there was a hole, a man might go over the ankle, what with the mixture of water and cow dung, and branches of holly a-plenty on the floor after the cattle had eaten off their tips.*

Relict hollins survive today at two sites in the Olchon Valley, on the Stiperstones in Shropshire, in the Peak District, in the New Forest and in Needwood Forest in Staffordshire. The scale of individual hollins could be enormous: when Needwood Forest, an area whose holly and oak foliage had long been used to feed deer, was disafforested and enclosed in 1802, 148,170 hollies were felled to make bobbins for the Lancashire cotton mills.

In the Olchon Valley the hollins occur towards the head of the valley on the west side just north of Upper Olchon Farm (Fig. 195). The largest hollin is situated on the slope to the east of the Olchon Brook, near the renowned Cae Thomas Well – the water emerging from which is said to have almost miraculous qualities in the treatment of affections of the skin. Despite its comparatively remote location the well attracts numerous visitors, and there is a permissive route to it from the nearby road which runs across the corner of the hollin field, but few people appear to notice the holly trees, despite the area being marked as woodland on the 1:25,000 Ordnance Survey map. The hollies surviving today are probably only a fraction of what was previously present, and some trees are dying, while others have fallen over. A rusty pair of garden loppers hung over a branch on one tree is testament to the fact that branches are still occasionally cut from these trees, not for feeding stock, but probably for sale as berried holly in the weeks leading up to Christmas. A second, smaller, site lies about 200 m to the southwest of the well and is easily viewed from the minor road, near the cattle grid. Both fields are grazed by sheep and there is a definite horizontal browse line visible on the trees, about 0.5 m above the ground, which indicates that the sheep are, at times, also eating the holly leaves on the lower branches.

FIG 195. The scattered remnants of a hollin in the upper Olchon Valley on the edge of the Black Mountains. (George Peterken)

There seem to be two distinct varieties of holly at the site, with some trees having smaller and less spiny leaves than others, and documentary evidence suggests that less spiny varieties of holly were indeed preferred. In 1697, for instance, the Yorkshire historian Abraham de la Pryme recorded that 'smooth-leaved holly' was used as fodder. In addition, the leaves growing near the top of the tree always have far fewer spines than those below, making them more suitable for fodder – as noted by Sir Herbert Maxwell in *Notes and Queries* in 1897:

> No matter what the age of the holly, so long as the twigs are within reach of being cropped by cattle, so long will the leaves on them remain armed with protective spines, but as soon as they attain a safe height their leaves become as smooth as a camellia.

By the eighteenth century, with the widespread introduction of turnips as a winter feed, the practice of feeding livestock with holly had largely died out, though as late as 1906 the *Chambers Encyclopaedia* noted that 'the leaves and small branches are sometimes used for feeding sheep in severe winters.' Evidence of this former practice still survives in farm, field and wood names, as well as in relict sites such as these in the Olchon Valley. Just as the word hollin is a collective term for a cluster of hollies, so a group of hollins was sometimes known as a hagg (or hag) of hollins. There is some confusion about terminology, however, because in the South Yorkshire dialect holly was known as hollin and what we would know as a hollin along the Welsh border was a hagg, so over the centuries the terms have become somewhat interchangeable. The Welsh *celyn* – as in Banc y Celyn on Mynydd Epynt, to the north of the Beacons – is derived from the same root word as hollin.

On some of the hillsides in the Black Mountains holly was once said to grow luxuriantly, almost to the exclusion of other trees and shrubs, and these pure holly stands were probably relict haggs. This phenomenon has been observed elsewhere, and A. G. Tansley in his book *The British Isles and their Vegetation* (1939) notes that 'Occasionally it [the holly tree] forms pure local woods whose origin and status are not known.' He was obviously not aware of the cultural background to these stands, which are now under threat. There is an urgent need to replant new trees, from locally collected seed, in these areas if they are to be conserved for future generations. The Christmas market for holly does not provide enough income to make them attractive on a commercial basis, but it would be a serious loss to the cultural and natural history of the area if the hollins of the Olchon Valley suffered the fate of those in Needwood Forest.

WHITEBEAMS

The Brecon Beacons are an important centre of diversity for whitebeams and are the sole location for six species: Ley's whitebeam *Sorbus leyana*, lesser whitebeam *S. minima*, Llanthony Valley whitebeam *S. stenophylla*, Welsh whitebeam *S. cambrensis*, thin-leaved whitebeam *S. leptophylla* and Motley's whitebeam *S. × motleyi*. All these trees are of great interest to naturalists, and recent research on their origins and ecology has been undertaken by a number of people, including Tim Rich, Head of Vascular Plants at the National Museum of Wales.

Found mostly on steep, sometimes almost vertical, slopes and usually on thin soils overlying limestone, whitebeams rarely exceed 6 m in height, and some are merely large shrubs. Despite being relatively small they are quite noticeable, with white-backed leaves, white blossom in spring and orange-brown to red berries in the autumn. Flowering and the setting of fruit vary from year to year, the open structure of the flowers allowing access to insects such as bees and flies which are attracted by the heavy, sweet, scent. The flowering time varies between species, with some flowering in April and others in June, while some trees have never been seen to flower. It may depend to some extent on weather conditions and environmental factors such as altitude and access to light. All whitebeams need high light levels, and they are therefore concentrated in these open, or cliff, habitats where they can obtain full sunlight.

One of the best-known rarities is Ley's whitebeam, with only 13 trees left (Fig. 196). Ley's whitebeam, or *cerdin darren fawr* in Welsh, was first described by Alfred James Wilmott, a professional taxonomist based at the British Museum (Natural History). He named it after Augustin Ley, who had first discovered it in 1896 at Darren Fawr, which is now a Brecknock Wildlife Trust Reserve. Ley noted around 15–20 mostly inaccessible shrubs and distributed specimens of it under the provisional name '*Pyrus scandica*?' Over 50 years later, J. E. Lousley in his New Naturalist volume *Wild Flowers of Chalk and Limestone* (1950), wrote that '*Sorbus leyanus* has its only known locality on a single short rock-face in the Merthyr Tydfil district. When I visited it in 1948 I found that a number of trees were dead. Others had their leaves so eaten by caterpillars that they were almost

FIG 196. The white blossom of Ley's whitebeam, one of the best-known endemic whitebeams found in the Beacons, on a tree at Penmoelallt. (Tim Rich)

FIG 197. Ley's whitebeam and interpretation panel at the National Botanic Garden of Wales, adjacent to a specimen of paperbark maple *Acer griseum* from China. (Jonathan Mullard)

unrecognisable.' The dead trees were probably a result of the severe winter of 1947/48, February 1948 being one of the coldest months on record. Jack Evans, a Merthyr forester and local naturalist, discovered the second site of Ley's whitebeam at Penmoelallt in 1958.

Many of the plants at Darren Fawr are bushes, approximately 2 m tall, which flower sporadically, while the trees at Penmoelallt are around 8–10 m tall and flower freely, though they produce fruit only occasionally. The numbers of trees at

Penmoelallt are increasing due to increased light on the woodland floor, caused by a number of fallen trees, which has encouraged the growth of saplings. This response to natural changes in the canopy suggests that coppicing the trees along the cliff edge at Darren Fawr could result in increases there too, provided grazing is excluded, as the combination of deer, sheep and rabbit grazing probably prevents the species colonising nearby grassland and scree. The cliffs at both sites are hazardous, but the easiest place to see Ley's whitebeam is at Penmoelallt, where a number of trees grown from seed and planted in the 1960s are easily accessible. Naturalists wishing to find Ley's whitebeam should not scramble on the cliffs, however, since the saplings, which are still relatively small, could easily be trampled in the process.

Because whitebeams do not root well from cuttings, material has been taken from most of the remaining specimens of Ley's whitebeam and grafted onto rowan stock, before being planted in the National Botanic Garden of Wales for safekeeping (Fig. 197). The Garden now has a large collection of whitebeams and is collaborating on a PhD project with the National Museum of Wales, the Whitley Wildlife Conservation Trust and Exeter University to investigate the origins and conservation of these rare trees.

Around 770 lesser (or least) whitebeams, *cerdin wen leiaf* in Welsh, have been recorded from the Beacons. The species was first found at Craig y Cilau on 12 June 1893 by Augustin Ley, who named it *Pyrus minima*, after observing it in flower and fruit. Ley reporting it as occurring 'in great abundance', clothing the limestone cliff to its head at an altitude of 600 m (Ley 1895a). This is still true today, and the National Nature Reserve at Craig y Cilau remains the best-known site (Fig. 198), with many specimens collected from the location in herbaria across Britain. In 1912 Charles Rothschild founded the Society for the Promotion of Nature Reserves, whose initial aim was to create a list of Britain's finest wildlife sites for potential purchase as nature reserves. Three years of information gathering followed, Rothschild and his colleagues looking for the 'breeding-places of scarce creatures', the 'localities of scarce plants' and areas of 'geological interest'. By 1915 they had compiled a list of 284 sites 'worthy of preservation', which included Craig y Cilau – the veteran British botanist Dr G. C. Druce having submitted a record in the hope of safeguarding *Pyrus minima*, as the species was then known. In 1947 though Craig y Cilau, which had been occupied as a military training ground during the Second World War, was in danger of being used permanently by the army for mortar practice, Lousley (1950) commenting that:

> The best place I know on the inland part of the limestone is a magnificent stretch of cliff high up above Crickhowell. Here there is a shrub allied to the Whitebeam and

known as Sorbus minima. *It grows freely on the precipitous rock and spreads freely from seed, and yet this cliff and another two miles to the west are the only places in the world where it is known to grow. There was recently a threat that the area would continue to be used as a military training ground where live shells would be employed. Energetic protests from botanists, supported by Members of Parliament, prevented this unique little shrub from any risk of being blown out of existence.*

By raising the issue in the House of Commons, and persuading the War Secretary Frederick Bellenger that the Army should pull out of the area, Tudor Watkins, Labour MP for Brecon and Radnorshire, was credited with preserving the species from extinction.

According to the *Red Data Book* (Wigginton 1999), the total world population of lesser whitebeam was fewer than 350 plants in two sites, but surveys by Tim Rich in 2002 have significantly revised this figure upwards. Many plants at Craig y Cilau and Darren Cilau have been destroyed by quarrying, the eastern specimens being the scattered fragments of what may have once been a more continuous population. Quarrying of the Llangattock ridge commenced sometime between 1797 and 1812 to provide stone for the construction of the Monmouthshire and Brecon Canal, with the workings eventually extending nearly 5 km along the scarp. The quarries were last worked in the 1940s. Although lesser whitebeam has recolonised some of the area, the density of plants is only around 40 per cent of that on unquarried rocks (Rich 2003). Before the quarrying started, the Craig y Cilau population could have consisted of over 1,000 plants. The differences between the historical and current population sizes reported probably reflect differences in survey quality but may include some real changes in populations. Smaller numbers grow further west at Cwm Cleisfer, and a single plant remains at Craig y Castell. It also used to be found at Blaen Onneu.

The current numbers of endemic whitebeams in the Beacons and their International Union for Conservation of Nature (IUCN) threat categories from the 2001 criteria now used for British plants are summarised in Table 5. Only in the case of Ley's whitebeam at Darren Fawr is there any evidence that the population has declined. In the other situations variations between survey methods are too large to separate real change from sampling effects. In order to address this issue Tim Rich has drawn up a standard monitoring protocol for Craig y Cilau (Rich 2003), with the intention that the same principles should be applied elsewhere for these and other rare *Sorbus* species.

The Llanthony Valley whitebeam was first found, as its name suggests, in the Llanthony Valley by Augustin Ley in 1874 and there are approximately 150 known trees. It is closely related to Welsh whitebeam, but recent biochemical studies

TABLE 5. Population sizes, number of sites and IUCN threat categories for whitebeams in the Brecon Beacons.

Species	No. of plants	No. of populations	IUCN category
Motley's whitebeam Sorbus × motleyi	4	1	Critically Endangered
Ley's whitebeam Sorbus leyana	13	2	Critically Endangered
Thin-leaved whitebeam Sorbus leptophylla	74	2	Endangered
Llanthony Valley whitebeam Sorbus stenophylla	120	5	Endangered
Welsh whitebeam Sorbus cambrensis	200	5	Endangered
Lesser whitebeam Sorbus minima	772	3	Vulnerable

Adapted from Rich et al. 2010, updated to 2012.

FIG 198. Tim Rich of the National Museum of Wales examining a fine specimen of lesser whitebeam at Craig y Cilau National Nature Reserve. (Jonathan Mullard)

have confirmed that the two species differ from each other and from the more widespread grey-leaved whitebeam *Sorbus porrigentiformis*, within which they were formally included. Llanthony Valley whitebeam occurs on Old Red Sandstone cliffs and grasslands on the northeast-facing slopes of Tarren yr Esgob, on east-facing cliffs, some quarried, at Darren Lwyd, and on west-facing crags at Cwmyoy, at altitudes of about 330–600 m. The upland location results in the tree flowering later than many other species of whitebeam. Some large old trees can reach a height of 14 m in more sheltered locations, but where conditions are more exposed they only reach 6–8 m. In some years the trees set abundant fruit, and on rocks ungrazed by sheep it has been noted that regeneration is occurring.

There are over 100 Welsh whitebeam trees known from the eastern Beacons, and it has been recorded scattered widely throughout Cwm Clydach, at Blackrock, at Craig y Cilau and at Coed Pantydarren. It occurs on limestone rocks and screes in old quarries and railway cuttings, and on field banks, associated with other species of whitebeam and hawthorn, ash and goat willow *Salix caprea*. Little is known about its reproductive biology, but it appears to set fruit irregularly. The leaves can vary in size quite markedly between trees.

Thin-leaved whitebeam, *cerddinen fannau* in Welsh, was first described by Warburg in 1952 (Warburg 1957) who reported it from two localities in the Brecon Beacons and probably also Montgomery, from where he had not seen fruiting material. The Montgomery material is now considered to be another species, Stirton's whitebeam *S. stirtoniana*. The specific epithet *leptophylla* means either 'thin-leaved' or 'narrow-leaved', and Warburg's description implies he meant the latter, but its leaves are not actually narrow, so botanists now call it thin-leaved! The type locality, the place where it was first recorded, is on the limestone at Craig y Cilau. The earliest collections that have been found were by William Charles Barton, an English botanist, in 1901 and by Ley in 1909. It has since been regularly recorded from this site, mostly from the well-known plants on the central cliffs. It usually occurs rooted directly into crevices, or occasionally on small ledges.

The classic growth form of thin-leaved whitebeam in the Brecon Beacons is as a shrub with its trunk pressed against a rock face, with a dense growth of small twigs at the base, often pendulous branches, and large, obovate, shallowly lobed leaves, with large fruits 11–16 mm long which are longer than wide (Fig. 199); such plants are well known at Craig y Cilau and also occur at Craig y Rhiwarth. On the exposed cliff tops and sides at both sites, the trees grow more erect and have smaller leaves of the same shape. The flowering and fruiting performance varies depending on location: plants in deep shade tend to be vegetative, while those growing along the cliff top are rather weather-beaten and rarely fruit, even if they flower, but those on the sheltered open cliff face flower and fruit regularly.

FIG 199. The classic form of thin-leaved whitebeam in the Beacons: a shrub with its trunk pressed against a rock face, with often pendulous branches, and large, obovate, shallowly lobed leaves. (Tim Rich)

HYBRIDISATION

Lousley noted in his New Naturalist (1950) that 'It is surprising how rich this Breconshire limestone is in rare *Sorbi*', new species of whitebeam developing as a result of hybridisation between their parent species. A recent example of this ongoing evolution is the discovery of Motley's whitebeam *Sorbus* × *motleyi*, which originated as a hybrid between Ley's whitebeam and rowan, at Penmoelallt near Merthyr Tydfil. The Great Storm of 1987 opened up the canopy and the extra light from the gap in the trees allowed seeds in the soil to germinate and grow. The plant was first found in 1999 by Graham Motley of the Countryside Council for Wales when he was monitoring the Ley's whitebeam, and it is named after him. Tim Rich was originally going to name it *motleyana*, with the name being a play on *S. leyana*, but the rules of botanical nomenclature meant it had to be called *motleyi* as Graham was involved in finding it, rather than it simply being named in his honour – so, as Tim puts it, 'my fun was spoiled.' A second, younger sapling was found nearby in 2004 and two more in 2011, so all four individuals of this hybrid known to date must have arisen independently. As so few specimens are known, care must be taken when visiting the site not to damage them accidentally.

Even though the flowers of these rare whitebeams attract insect pollinators, they generally reproduce asexually by apomixis, the seed developing directly from the female without any genetic input from the pollen. This asexual process is not perfect, however, and occasionally they can be fertilised by pollen from another species to generate new hybrids which may then, if biologically successful, go on to form new species. Ley's whitebeam itself was probably created shortly after the last glaciation, by hybridisation between rowan and either rock whitebeam *Sorbus rupicola* or grey-leaved whitebeam *S. porrigentiformis*, both of which grow with it today.

While these rare but relatively short-lived trees are really only known to naturalists, the seemingly eternal yew is regarded by some as the immortal tree of life and regarded with reverence throughout the land.

Chapter 11

Churches and Chapels

EVEN IN A RURAL AREA SUCH AS THE BRECON BEACONS, churchyards, cemeteries and burial grounds have become a refuge for wildlife and provide numerous opportunities for a variety of species. Churchyards, in particular, are often very old and, apart from burials, have not been disturbed for decades, or even centuries. Many are of medieval origin (Fig. 200), but a

FIG 200. The early medieval church at Llandetty on the southern bank of the Usk. The semicircular churchyard contains four yews, including three ancient ones situated between the lychgate and the east end of the church. (Jonathan Mullard)

number have nineteenth- or twentieth-century extensions. The soil is also mostly free from fertilisers and other agricultural chemicals, so churchyards are often the location for some of our most sensitive plants and fungi. As mentioned in Chapter 10, ancient trees such as yews also occur in churchyards and can be important features in the landscape, with significant cultural value, as well as being home to birds, bats and numerous species of insects. There is much less information on the wildlife of the chapel graveyards, which resulted from the great increase in Nonconformist denominations in Wales in the nineteenth century, although there is some evidence to suggest that they are of even greater interest than churchyards, since they were enclosed, like the churchyard extensions, before the use of agricultural chemicals. It would be a valuable project to survey these in more detail.

CHURCHYARD YEWS

Richard Mabey, in *Flora Britannica* (1996), notes that 'what sets yews most decisively apart from other trees in Britain is the remarkable and probably unique association they have with ancient churches ... Yews of great ages are rare outside churchyards and no other type of tree occurs so frequently inside the church grounds.' Mabey goes on to say that 'I do not know of any similarly exclusive relationship between places of worship and a single tree species existing anywhere else in the Western world.' The distribution of old yews in churchyards is reflected in the trees' distribution in the wild, and they are concentrated in Wales, southeast and central England and the Lake District. Many of these seem to be vastly older than the church – and since the planting of wild tree species was very rare before the Middle Ages, this suggests that the original sacred sites were located close to existing yew trees.

This association between churches and ancient yew trees is also clear in the Beacons. One of the earliest references dates from 27 October 1776, when Arthur Young, a tireless propagandist for agricultural improvement who spent most of his life travelling, using his journeys as the basis for a series of books, journeyed from Brecon to Crickhowell. Young was especially impressed by the churches on the route, including Llansantffraed, which he noted were 'surrounded by vast yew-trees'. The area has long been known for its ancient yews, and as far back as the eleventh century it was called Ystrad Yw, the vale of the yew trees. One of the best sites for yews in the Beacons though is the church of St Cynog's in Defynnog, near Sennybridge, which has four ancient female yews in the churchyard (Fig. 201). These are thought to be the oldest yew trees in Britain, being around 5,600 years

FIG 201. The ancient yews at St Cynog's church in Defynnog are thought to be the oldest yew trees in Britain, being around 5,600 years old. (Harold Grenfell)

old. Two trees on the north side of the churchyard, which grow close to each other, have been shown by the Ancient Yew Group to be genetically identical, the smaller tree being recorded, in 1998, as 'probably a layer' from the larger tree.

Another church noted for its yew trees is St Mary's church, Capel y Ffin, which has an interior of just 4 m × 8 m, making it one of the smallest churches in the country. It was described by the nineteenth-century diarist Francis Kilvert as 'the old chapel, short, stout and boxy, with its little bell turret, squatting like a stout grey owl among its seven great yews' (Fig. 202). The yews grow on the south side of the church, with an additional younger yew on the west side. In 1867 the Woolhope Naturalists Field Club noted that:

The yew trees at Capel y ffin are more remarkable for their mode of growth and apparent age than for their large size. They are, for the most part, tall upright trees with a central stem or stems. They are long past their prime, and present an appearance, at once rugged, grim and hoary. They are situated on the south side of the churchyard, and are planted in a semicircle. There are seven trees, two on the left, and five on the right of the entrance gate, and it almost seems as if one or two trees had been removed specially for the entrance.

FIG 202. St Mary's church, Capel y Ffin, described by the famous diarist Francis Kilvert, as 'the old chapel, short, stout and boxy, with its little bell turret, squatting like a stout grey owl among its seven great yews'. (Jonathan Mullard)

FIG 203. The burial ground of Capel y Ffin Baptist chapel, with its three yew trees, and the southern end of Darren Lwyd in the background. (Jonathan Mullard)

The trees were all measured by the Field Club, and when they were re-measured 145 years later in 2012, an average increase of only 36 cm in girth was recorded, showing these to be exceptionally slow-growing trees. It seems likely that they were all planted at the same time.

On the opposite side of the Afon Honddu is a small Baptist chapel built by two brothers, William and David Prosser, which bears a plaque commemorating their work in bringing 'The Ministry of the Gospel to their house in the year 1737'. Here again there are yews, this time three trees, planted closely together between the entrance gate and the chapel. They were probably planted when the chapel was built (Fig. 203).

As they become hollow and layer as they grow old, it might never be possible to determine accurate ages for our oldest yews, but one of the members of the Ancient Yew Group, Toby Hindson, has devised a set of protocols to help determine an individual yew's status as ancient, veteran, or notable. Under this system an ancient yew is a tree which is a minimum of 800 years old, with no upper limit, a veteran yew has a minimum age of 500 years, but may be up to 1200 years old, and a notable yew has a minimum age of 300 years, but may be up to 700 years old. Using this approach the Group has surveyed all the significant yew trees in the Beacons in some detail (Table 6). An earlier survey was carried out in 1970, the results being held at Brecknock Museum. It consists of a box filled with sheets of paper on which are rudimentary details of the girths of yews and sketches showing the position of the trees within the churchyard. The fact that every measurement is to the exact foot, six inches or three inches, however, indicates that they were trying to obtain a rough idea of girth rather than an exact measurement.

These old yews can be vulnerable to winter storms. On 2 January 2012 an ancient yew tree in the grounds of St Faith's Church, Llanfoist, which was believed to be up to 1,000 years old, was brought down by high winds (Skellon 2012). It is likely that the yew was weakened by fire damage that occurred before 1998. There was poor leaf growth on its damaged upper branches, but this was compensated by the development of new branches on the lower bole. Fortunately, one of these branches was below the point at which the tree snapped, so there is hope that a new tree will grow from the remains of the old one. Similarly, at Aberyscir, near Brecon, one of the two old yew trees collapsed under the weight of snow in the winter of 2007/08. A large stump showing new growth remains, however, and it is likely that the tree will recover. Some trees though have been lost completely. In 1884, for instance, the report of a visit by the Woolhope Society to Cwmyoy church noted that 'The very yew trees in the churchyard bore out the air of desolation that hangs on the place – two were dead and bare, and the others, ragged and worn, seemed scarcely able to sustain their existence.' Today, perhaps unsurprisingly, none of these trees remains.

TABLE 6. The most significant surviving churchyard yews in the Brecon Beacons.

Site	CLASSIFICATION		
	Ancient	Veteran	Notable
Defynnog	4		
Llanfeugan	1	6	4
Ystradfellte	1	3	2
Llanbedr Ystradyw	1	3	
Llanspyddid	1	1	1
Talgarth	1		2
Llanwenarth	1		
Llansantffraed	1		
Penpont	1		
Capel y Ffin		7	
Llanelly		4	8
Llanhamlach		3	
Cathedine		3	
Aberyscir		2	
Cantref		2	2
Llanfrynach		1	2
Llandetty		1	1
Llangenny		1	
Myddfai		1	
Llanfihangel Tal-y-llyn		1	
Partrishow		1	
Llangasty Talyllyn			2
Llanelieu			1
Llangattock			1
Llangorse			1

Adapted from material supplied by the Ancient Yew Group in 2012. The order is based on number of ancient, veteran or notable yews at the site. Sites in italics are those well worth a visit.

Yew trees are important havens for a wide variety of wildlife, and an ancient tree can support hundreds of different species, including mosses, lichens, birds and small mammals. The seeds develop within a bright red cup, the aril, that resembles a berry and are dispersed by birds, especially blackbird *Turdus merula* and song thrush, which are attracted to the fleshy arils. A few churches, such as those at Llangenny near Crickhowell and Llansantffraed have arched earthstars *Geastrum fornicatum* growing under their yew trees (Fig. 204). Earthstars are saprobic fungi, spending most of their life cycle as thin strands of mycelium

FIG 204. Arched earthstar under yew trees at Llansantffraed church, near Talybont-on-Usk. (Graham Motley)

and feeding off decomposing organic matter present in the soil. The fungal fruit bodies are generally found in summer and autumn. The arched earthstar is a large four-armed star, some 5–10 cm high when open, with the arms bent back and attached to tissue embedded in the soil. The central chamber, a rounded hollow ball containing the spores, is raised on a short stem. It does not appear to like totally bare soil, usually growing amongst open grass, herbs and light twig and leaf litter. Unfortunately the space beneath yew trees is often used to dump grass cuttings, probably because it is not considered of interest since the only plant able to grow in the deep shade is ivy, so it could be considered as a threatened habitat. Unmanaged churchyards, however, may become too shaded for the earthstar to survive.

OLD GRASSLANDS

Churchyards are often very old and have not been disturbed for decades, or even centuries, and as a result the soil is usually free from fertilisers and other chemicals, providing an excellent habitat for rare plants and fungi. Many, especially those enclosed in the nineteenth and early twentieth centuries, were derived from permanent pastures or hay meadows before modern agricultural practices depleted the number of species and altered the nature of most of our grasslands. Apart from where they have been disturbed by burials, they have been cut regularly ever since and have not been ploughed, treated with lime or chemicals, or grazed. For this reason, along with chapel burial grounds, they represent some of the best-preserved relics of semi-natural grassland in the Beacons. In contrast, medieval churchyards have been repeatedly excavated for burials and although they may be rich in species they are unlikely to represent remnants of medieval grassland (Chater 1996). What impact the change in management from grazing to cutting has had on the grassland is difficult to determine, but in many churchyards the vegetation is, perhaps surprisingly, more like continuously grazed grassland than the few remaining hay meadows, such as Boxbush Meadows.

One of the best churchyards in the Beacons is the one adjacent to the Libanus Congregational Church, where the area of grassland in the churchyard that has not yet been used for burials contains a good example of neutral grassland, with an upland element (Fig. 205). Species found here include wood anemone, devil's-bit scabious *Succisa pratensis*, black, or common knapweed, greater butterfly orchid *Platanthera clorantha*, greater twayblade *Listera ovata* and spotted orchids *Dactylorhiza* spp. Devil's-bit scabious is an interesting plant to find in churchyards, as it is so named because its roots are said to end abruptly where they have been bitten off by the devil!

Ten years or so ago the management of the grassland at Libanus was perfect for orchids, but recently it seems to have become more frequently mown and the plants do not appear to have been allowed to flower. The Brecknock Wildlife Trust

FIG 205. Libanus Congregational Church, near Brecon, which has one of the most wildlife-rich churchyards in the Beacons, with a good range of waxcap fungi. (Harold Grenfell)

FIG 206. Partrishow churchyard in early spring, with drifts of dog's mercury alongside common dog-violet, lady's smock and cultivated daffodils. The black marble tombstone is the only one without a covering of lichens. (Jonathan Mullard)

is now working with the local community to establish an appropriate management regime that keeps the area looking cared for, while allowing space for wildlife. Most of the better churchyards for fungi though seem to have fairly regularly mown grassland, and it is interesting to speculate how many good sites might have been lost through encouraging churches to allow their habitats to grow tall to encourage meadow flowers and other wildlife. A churchyard good for grassland fungi is not always good for wild flowers, so getting the balance right is extremely important. At Libanus there is a good range of waxcap fungi, with at least 12 species recorded from the site, including pink waxcap *Hygrocybe calyptriformis*. This has a pinkish-lilac conical cap with fine striations and a slightly greasy appearance. Pink waxcaps, which are seldom abundant, generally appear between August and October, and being a conspicuous species, it is thought that it may be better recorded than other waxcap fungi. Other churchyards with good grassland fungi include those at Bwlch and Cray, both of which, like Libanus, contain pink waxcaps.

Other species also occur frequently in churchyards. The churchyard at Partrishow, for example, has drifts of dog's mercury along with common dog-violet, lady's smock *Cardamine pratensis* and masses of cultivated daffodils *Narcissus pseudonarcissus* (Fig. 206). The native wild daffodil *Narcissus pseudonarcissus* ssp.

pseudonarcissus is, however, more or less absent from the Beacons. Dog's mercury and common dog-violet are so named because they were thought to be only good for dogs, since dog's mercury is highly poisonous and the violet lacks scent, as opposed to the 'sweet' violet *Viola odorata*. They are also indicative of former woodland habitats.

A notable feature of churchyards in several parts of Britain is the number of species in any one area that are confined to them. In Carmarthenshire, for example, dropwort *Filipendula vulgaris* has rarely been recorded from outside burial grounds and yet is well established in Myddfai churchyard, often found growing with Pyrenean lily *Lilium pyrenaicum*. The lily is certainly introduced, but, interestingly, dropwort is not recorded from any local grassland where it might be expected to occur if it were native, so there is a suggestion that this might be planted as well. Many other species have become naturalised from memorial posies and wreaths, including lily-of-the-valley, snowdrop *Galanthus nivalis*, primrose *Primula vulgaris*, garden forget-me-not *Myosotis* spp. and rosemary 'for remembrance' (Mabey 1996). The pink 'churchyard primrose' derives from the Victorian custom of planting primroses on the graves of small children. Occasionally ornamental plants, such as teasel *Dipsacus fullonum*, seed themselves near the church porch.

MOSSES AND LICHENS

The Old Red Sandstone tiles on buildings on the eastern edge of the Beacons are important for a suite of rare saxicolous (rock-dwelling) mosses. Church roofs represent particularly important habitats for these species, and some of these, including those at Llanwenarth, Llanfihangel Crucorney and Cwmyoy, are important for mosses able to tolerate the extreme conditions found on the south side. Rare grimmia species such as hoary grimmia *Grimmia laevigata* and flat-rock grimmia *Grimmia ovalis* may also be present, and occasionally fringed hoar-moss *Hedwigia ciliata* can be found. The latter species also occurs on the canopy above the entrance to the Rose and Crown, one of the pubs in Hay on Wye (Fig. 207).

Flat-rock grimmia has, in addition, been recorded by Sam Bosanquet on the roof at Llanthony Priory, and the nearby historic barn is also an important location, so there is a scatter of these mosses on rooftops along the Vale of Ewyas as far south as Llanfihangel Crucorney (Fig. 208). The Beacons are slightly too high, however, for these warmth-loving species to be found regularly, even in apparently the right habitat. Flat-rock grimmia does occur at higher altitudes, for example in Scotland, but is generally found on igneous rocks that probably

CHAPELS AND CHURCHES · 321

FIG 207. In Hay on Wye, the Rose and Crown pub has a noticeable population of fringed hoar-moss on the canopy above the entrance. (Jonathan Mullard)

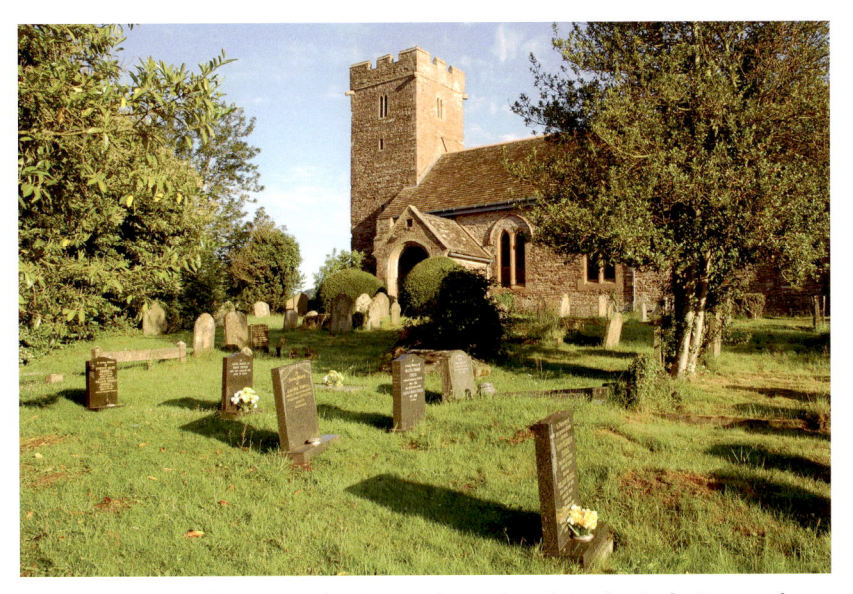

FIG 208. Llanfihangel Crucorney church, one of a number of churches in the Beacons that have stone tile roofs that are important for mosses. (Jonathan Mullard)

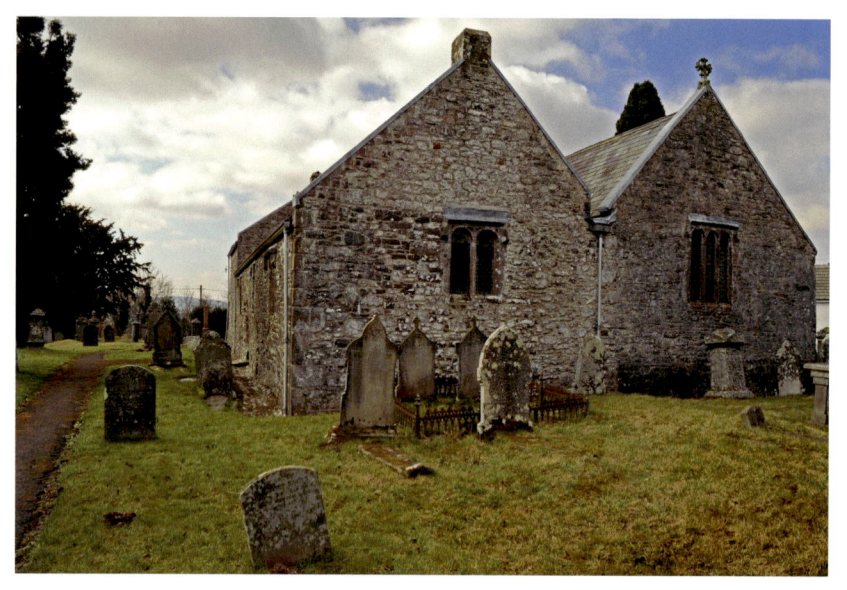

FIG 209. A total of 43 bryophyte species have been recorded from Llanddeusant church and churchyard. (Harold Grenfell)

absorb and then radiate heat differently, or better, than the sandstone. Another scarce member of the genus, north grimmia *Grimmia longirostris*, occurs on rocks amongst the landslips and below cliffs around Cwmyoy Darren.

Unfortunately many other churches in the area have had their roofs cleaned, while others have been slated or now have artificial tiles, and this has destroyed the habitat for many species. Most chapel roofs are constructed using slate, so they are poor locations for these species as well. Another similar and potentially interesting habitat, farm buildings with old tiles, appears to be too rich in nitrogen to be suitable for the grimmia species in particular, though some common species can be found here.

As well as the roofs of churches, churchyard walls and gravestones are also key habitats for mosses, the aspect and degree of shelter determining which species are present. Typically a whole suite of common mosses such as capillary thread-moss *Bryum capillare*, grey-cushioned grimmia *Grimmia pulvinata* and wall screw-moss *Tortula muralis* soften the stonework, while silky wall feather-moss *Homalothecium sericeum* spreads over gravestones. Churchyards are also the commonest habitat for tender feather-moss *Rhynchostegiella tenella*. Flat gravestones can quickly be covered with moss, which may have a protective effect on the inscriptions, so its removal is not advised. There are occasions, however, where moss can accelerate stone deterioration. It may be appropriate to remove moss from the top surface of standing sandstone gravestones to stop the rhizoids penetrating downwards. Llanddeusant church is probably typical of churches in the Beacons (Fig. 209), with 43 bryophyte species recorded from the site by Sam Bosanquet, including common calcicoles such as rock pocket-moss *Fissidens dubius*, spiral extinguisher-moss *Encalypta streptocarpa*, intermediate screw-moss *Syntrichia intermedia*, wall thread-moss *Bryum radiculosum* and tender feather-moss on the walls, and mosses of disturbed ground such as cylindric ditrichum *Trichodon cylindricus* and crimson tuber thread-moss *Bryum rubens* on graves. Mosses tend to like churchyard walls because they so often have old, crumbly lime-rich mortar.

The ancient stonework of churches and churchyards, when undisturbed and unpolluted by chemical sprays, also provides a sanctuary for lichens, which are able to colonise surfaces mostly unsuitable for flowering plants. Of the 2,000 British species, over a third have been found in churchyards, almost half of these being rare – and some, indeed, seldom if ever occur in other habitats. Gravestones also provide additional types of stone, and each type may support a particular range of lichens – acid stones, such as granite, slate and many sandstones, having a completely different lichen flora to basic stones such as limestone or marble (Fig. 210). Lichens are slow-growing, many only increasing in

FIG 210. Gravestones, such as these at Llandefalle, provide a variety of stone types which support a wide range of lichens. (Harold Grenfell)

size by around 1–2 mm a year. Some of the larger foliose lichens may eventually reach 150 mm in diameter, but this is an unusually high growth rate, and some individual crustose lichens have shown no discernible increase in size despite having been observed for over 10 years. Individual lichens may well be almost as old as the gravestones upon which they are found.

Surveys of churches in the Brecon Beacons by members of the British Lichen Society have recorded around 59–66 species of lichen, on average, on the churches themselves, churchyard walls and gravestones. In Defynnog churchyard there were 91 species found, and 82 were recorded at Llangasty. None of the species is particularly scarce, but some are of local interest, being rare or unknown outside churchyards in the Beacons. Three lichens, in particular, fall into this category: *Lecania turicensis* found at Defynnog, Llangasty Church and Talgarth; *Pertusaria lactescens* at Llangasty, Llangorse, Talgarth, Crickhowell, Llangattock; and *Ramalina canariensis* at Llangasty and Llanfilio, near Talgarth.

GHOST SLUG

The ghost slug *Selenochlamys ysbryda* was first discovered in late 2004, when Heike Reise and John Hutchinson, two mollusc experts based in Germany, found a single specimen in the churchyard of Brecon Cathedral, under wood and stones in an area of mown grass, with old gravestones overshadowed by trees. The significance of the find was not appreciated at first, as they believed the animal to be a juvenile albino *Testacella scutulum* that had lost its tiny vestigial shell. Like other species in its genus, this predatory slug spends most of its life underground, so it is rarely seen. It can reach 6.4 cm in length with its body extended, and it has no eyes. Like *T. scutulum*, the ghost slug is nocturnal and burrowing, feeding on earthworms at night using its blade-like teeth. It eats small worms whole, or attaches its teeth to one end of a larger one, which is then dragged around until it releases its hold.

The ghost slug (Fig. 211) is an alien species, apparently introduced to Britain in the roots of garden plants, and its nearest relatives live in the mountains of eastern Europe, Georgia and eastern Turkey. Originally reported as first being discovered in a Cardiff garden in 2007, the species was also photographed in Caerphilly in 2006. The slug was formally described and named in 2008 by Ben Rowson of the National Museum and Bill Symondson of Cardiff University. Because of the slug's white colour and nocturnal habits, and because it has been so rarely seen, it was given the species name *ysbryda*, the word *ysbryd* meaning ghost in Welsh. This in turn gave rise to the common name ghost

FIG 211. The ghost slug *Selenochlamys ysbryda*, a species new to science that was first discovered in the churchyard of Brecon Cathedral in 2004. (National Museum of Wales)

slug. It appears to be the first case of a species name having been taken from the Welsh language.

There have also been several sightings of this species in Talgarth over the last couple of years, on the grassy verge of an office car park in the centre of town. To date they have been seen crawling in the open there on at least seven occasions. Other ghost slugs have since been recorded from Hay on Wye, Gilwern near Abergavenny and Waterfall Cave in Blackrock Quarry off the Heads of the Valleys Road. There are no specimens or photos from the latter site though, so this record must be regarded as unconfirmed.

Inevitably, the intensively disturbed lowland areas of the Brecon Beacons harbour a number of introduced molluscs. These can be spread readily when they, or their eggs, are moved with plants or become attached to vehicles, livestock or rubbish. More common and less dramatic than the ghost slug, but still remaining enigmatic, is the Inishowen slug *Arion owenii*, a small brown and marmalade-coloured animal. This occurs in the Tawe Valley, including the broadleaved woods near Craig y Nos, and widely elsewhere in Wales, but its British distribution remains imperfectly known. It too may be spreading through human disturbance, as may the worm slug *Boettgerilla pallens*, a pale lavender-blue species named for its elongate appearance and subterranean habits. A native of the Caucasus, it expanded across Europe in the last century and may now be encountered under roadside stones in the Beacons.

BATS

Churches and churchyards play an important role in bat conservation, and in the Brecon Beacons several species are known to use the local churches, including common and soprano pipistrelle (*Pipistrellus pipistrellus* and *P. pygmaeus*), brown long-eared, lesser horseshoe, greater horseshoe and, in particular, Natterer's bat *Myotis nattereri*. Natterer's bat is the one species that seems to rely most heavily on churches. It is also one of the species which the Brecknock Bat Group has the most issues with, in relation to the attitude of the church authorities. Conflicts generally arise from the presence of bat droppings and urine staining inside the church, or when structural works such as re-roofing are required. Sadly some incumbents do not appreciate the value of their property for wildlife, and this is an area where voluntary conservation groups can play an important role.

Natterer's bat (Fig. 212) is a common and widespread bat, but one which has suffered particularly badly from the number of barn conversions in the area, so churches are increasingly important locations for their summer roost sites. Relatively few summer roost sites, apart from churches, are known, but those which have been found are in old stone buildings with large old timbered beams – crevices in those beams, or gaps in beam joints, being common locations. In winter Natterer's bats prefer to hibernate in the cool entrance areas of caves and mines, but they will hibernate in any underground shelter, and individual bats are occasionally found hibernating in churches, again in the crevices between beams. Natterer's start to arrive at their hibernation sites in December, with peak numbers in January or early February, most animals leaving by early March.

Inside a church, bats often roost in the corners of the naves and aisle, in the porch, or under roof tiles or lead-covered boarding. Contrary to popular belief, belfries are not a suitable location for bats. Individuals usually return annually and make use of beams, as described above, or occasionally locations behind pictures, where they feel safe. They are mainly active between spring and autumn, but some may also spend the winter hibernating in the unheated parts of a church. Bats seem to regard the interior of a church as a woodland canopy and may fly around inside before emerging to feed. They will also use porches

FIG 212. Natterer's bat, the one species that seems to rely most heavily on churches in the Beacons for its summer roosts, although it typically overwinters in limestone caves. (Melvin Grey)

as shelters between feeding sessions, even if they roost elsewhere, and the surrounding churchyard can be a good source of food for young bats learning to fly, or when the weather is unfavourable.

OTHER MAMMALS

Churches and churchyards can provide a good habitat for small mammals, and some of the larger and more unusual mammals will visit occasionally, the species present depending on the available food and shelter and the nature of the surrounding landscape. Usually the grassland is rich in worms and this attracts moles *Talpa europaea* and sometimes badgers, while mice, voles and shrews feed on vegetation and insects in the grassland. Hedgehogs *Erinaceus europaeus* and rabbits may live in hedges and banks on the boundaries, while foxes, weasels *Mustela nivalis*, stoats *M. erminea* and polecats *M. putorius* prey on all these species. Hedgehogs particularly need areas such as churchyards. The People's Trust for Endangered Species, which has been running counts of hedgehogs for over a decade, believes there are now fewer than a million hedgehogs left in the UK, against estimates of around two million in the mid-1990s and 36 million in the 1950s.

While the areas enclosed for churches, chapels and burial grounds have to some extent been protected from changes in the wider countryside, the farmland itself has evolved over the centuries, due to economic and social pressures. The wildlife and landscape that can now be found there is described in the following pages.

CHAPTER 12

Farmland

Most of the land area within the Brecon Beacons is owned and managed by individual landowners and farmers, and their activities are the dominant factor in the development and maintenance of the current landscape and the habitats within it. About 96 per cent of farmland in Wales is grazed by livestock, mainly cattle and sheep, with smaller numbers of horses and ponies. This figure includes the moorland and rough grazing land described in earlier chapters as well as lowland grassland, bogs and other grazed habitats. As farms continue to specialise, arable farming has virtually disappeared in the Beacons, although some cultivated land can still be found, particularly in the Usk and Wye valleys. As a result, many species of arable weed are now rare and the farmland birds that depend on mixed farming are in decline. Lowland fields are also intensively farmed to produce grass silage to feed cattle and sheep during winter months. These factors are liable to become more pronounced in the coming years, due to the rapidly increasing price of land. Farmland prices in Wales, due to strong demand, are among the highest in Britain; they have doubled in five years, with the average price of an acre (0.4 ha) of land now nearly £7,000. Despite these pressures, numerous traditional and non-intensive family farms still remain in the Beacons, and the historic farmsteads themselves are an important component of the landscape (Fig. 213).

SPECIES-RICH GRASSLAND

Before the 1940s, rich meadow grasslands would have covered much of the Welsh lowlands, especially on the fertile soils of river valleys and gently sloping ground.

FIG 213. A typical Beacons farmstead at Pantyffynnont, below Carreg Cennen. (Harold Grenfell)

Over the past 70 years the majority of lowland grasslands have been ploughed and sown with commercial grass varieties, which are heavily fertilised to enable more cattle or sheep to be kept. Making hay has also gone out of fashion. As mentioned earlier, many former hay meadows are now cut for silage (Fig. 214). Silage making involves cutting and baling fresh grass often twice a year, starting with a first cut as early as April or May, at a time when grassland birds would normally nest. Today lowland wildflower hay meadows and pastures mostly remain as small, isolated

FIG 214. Turning and baling grass silage on a farm in the shadow of Garn Goch hillfort. Silage is made by preserving the grass under naturally produced acidic conditions, which effectively pickles the crop. It is preferred by livestock to hay as it is more palatable. (Jonathan Mullard)

fragments surrounded by intensively farmed land, and are often associated with smallholdings that are not part of commercial farming enterprises. Even so, in many locations they are often subject to heavy grazing that prevents plants from flowering. At the most, species-rich grasslands in the lowlands and on the upland fringe make up less than 3.5 per cent of all the grazing land in Wales, and as a result they are now one of the country's most threatened habitats.

Most of the larger remaining species-rich grasslands found in Wales are 'mosaic' habitats of small unimproved pastures, hay meadows and rushy fields on the upland fringe – land that has traditionally been the most difficult to farm. They typically occur as rather small, isolated fields or groups of fields, often smaller than a hectare in size. Almost all are designated as Sites of Special Scientific Interest because of their botanical value.

MARSHY GRASSLAND

The lime-rich waters that run through Cwm Cadlan National Nature Reserve, a mosaic of wet grassland fields in a small valley to the northwest of Merthyr Tydfil, have created a fen-meadow. This is characterised by the prominence of purple moor-grass and meadow thistle *Cirsium dissectum*, along with tawny sedge *Carex hostiana* and flea sedge *C. pulicaris*. Associated species include sweet vernal-grass, quaking-grass *Briza media*, sharp-flowered rush, bog pimpernel, tormentil and devil's-bit scabious. The aptly named chalk comb-moss *Ctenidium molluscum* is also often a prominent component of the sward. Similarly scattered throughout the site are small stands of rhos pasture, the Welsh term for this particular type of grassland, which occurs on poorly drained soil and is dominated by purple moor-grass and rushes. In the northeast of the site some of the purple moor-grass vegetation is naturally less diverse, and occasional patches of wavy hair-grass, bilberry, heather and cross-leaved heath occur.

A large population of globeflower occurs in the fen-meadow and adjacent unimproved neutral grassland. Globeflower was previously a widespread species of upland meadows but has declined greatly due to agricultural intensification and improvement of land through drainage. Fertilisers also encourage the growth of more vigorous species with which globeflower cannot compete. In 2000 Graham Motley found the smut fungus *Urocystis trollii* on the globeflower here, and this seems to be the only Welsh record for the species.

A slightly larger area of marshy grassland at Cae Bryn Tywarch, in Cwm Nant Cil y Clawdd near Trecastle, supports a wide range of vegetation types once probably widespread in the upper Usk Valley, but which are now very scarce. As at Cwm Cadlan, the vegetation is dominated by purple moor-grass, plant communities ranging from wet heath with purple moor-grass, tormentil, cross-leaved heath, and sometimes lesser butterfly-orchid *Platanthera bifolia*, to a herb-rich community with wild angelica *Angelica sylvestris*, common marsh-bedstraw and sharp-flowered rush. Mires with purple moor-grass and meadow thistle are also frequent, with a particularly species-rich variant that includes an abundance of devil's-bit scabious, on which marsh fritillary butterflies *Eurodryas aurinia* feed (Fig. 215). Small pearl-bordered fritillaries *Boloria selene*, however, are much more abundant than marsh fritillaries in these marshy grasslands.

The marsh fritillary, like many other insects, often occurs in well-separated colonies that form part of a metapopulation, within which there is an interchange of individuals. These colonies, which are essentially temporary subpopulations, frequently die out and are recolonised. All the colonies are therefore interdependent and have to be protected, rather than just one or two sites. They are often small, however, and susceptible to extinction, so extensive mosaics of habitats are essential for the species' long-term survival. One of the largest metapopulations of marsh fritillary in South Wales can be found on the southern edge of the Brecon Beacons at Blaen Cynon, an extensive complex of damp pastures and heaths near Hirwaun.

FIG 215. Cae Bryn Tywarch, in Cwm Nant Cil y Clawdd near Trecastle, is one of the most important sites in the Brecon Beacons for marsh fritillary butterflies. (Graham Motley)

The females lay their eggs on the larger devil's-bit scabious plants, typically those growing where the height of the vegetation is between 8 and 20 cm. The fritillary is therefore very susceptible to grazing pressure, and most colonies occur where there is light grazing by cattle or horses. Very few occur in areas grazed by sheep, since sheep are highly selective feeders and graze the food plant preferentially, rendering it small and unsuitable for egg laying. In contrast, cattle and horses are less selective feeders but avoid devil's-bit scabious flower heads. Populations of the marsh fritillary fluctuate greatly in size from year to year, with larvae occasionally reaching enormous densities. The fluctuations appear to be dependent upon weather, food supply and the proportion of caterpillars killed by two parasitic braconid wasps, *Cotesia melitaearum* and *C. bignellii*, the latter apparently being more common in Wales than the former. In some years parasitic wasps can kill 75 per cent of the larval population. It is thought that the wasps control the size of marsh fritillary colonies, preventing them from outstripping the supply of food plants. They are thus an integral element in the butterfly's population dynamics and are themselves of significant conservation value. Weather conditions also affect the butterfly's breeding success, poor weather during the adult flight period reducing opportunities for mating, egg laying and dispersal.

HAY MEADOWS

Undoubtedly the best hay meadows in the Brecon Beacons are to be found on Berthlwyd Farm, a small, traditional upland farm, owned by the National Trust, near Ystradfellte (Fig. 216). The combination of so many habitats in one place is very unusual. As well as the high-quality hay meadows, acid grassland, limestone grassland, rhos pasture, wooded limestone pavement, native woodlands and heathland all combine to make a very rich and diverse landscape. Underneath Berthlwyd Farm lies the Little Neath River Cave described in Chapter 7, and the sympathic management of the land above the cave system undoubtedly has a beneficial effect on the wildlife of the cave.

Berthlwyd was brought to the attention of the National Trust by the Countryside Council for Wales, who were concerned about the long-term future of a farm that was extremely important for its nature conservation value. The farm had received little investment from the previous landlord and there was

FIG 216. The rich hay meadows at Berthlwyd, a small, traditional upland farm owned by the National Trust, are some of the most important in Wales. Plants found here include yellow rattle, eyebright, rough hawkbit, common knapweed, great burnet and a variety of orchids. (Joe Daggett)

significant pressure on the tenant to improve the farming system to be able to survive. This would have severely threatened the wildlife interest of the site. The farm fell within the National Trust's acquisition strategy for the area, which was to buy valley-head farms, so the holding was eventually purchased in 1992. Today the sixth generation of the same family to farm here are now tenants of the Trust, and the holding is a Site of Special Scientific Interest.

The ten hay meadows at Berthlwyd Farm contain a mixture of unimproved and semi-improved neutral grasslands, with several fields being of high quality, in terms of both species richness and abundance. Red clover *Trifolium pratense* is the most frequent species, along with yellow rattle *Rhinanthus minor* and another hemi-parasite, eyebright *Euphrasia* spp. The other most frequently recorded herbs are rough hawkbit *Leontodon hispidus*, common knapweed and great burnet, and these occur in the majority of fields. The typical hay-meadow legumes, bird's-foot-trefoil and meadow vetchling *Lathyrus pratensis* both occur at low frequencies, or are not recorded in many fields. Greater butterfly orchid *Platanthera chlorantha* (Fig. 217) and common spotted orchid *Dactylorhiza fuchsii* are found in some of the fields along with several different waxcap fungi species, such as golden waxcap *Hygrocybe chlorophana* and a small waxcap with an initially bell-shaped cap, scarlet in colour, known variously as scarlet hood, scarlet waxcap, or righteous red waxy cap *H. coccinea*.

The continuity of traditional hay-meadow management on this farm, over many generations, demonstrates the strong link between rich wildlife habitats and sustainable farming. Visits to the hay meadows are by appointment only, but the National Trust organises a number of guided walks on the farm during the summer. The meadows are quite high up, and in June, when hay meadows at lower altitudes are luxuriant and full of flowers, there is frequently not much growing in the fields. Early July is often a better time to visit if you want to see these splendid fields.

FIG 217. Greater butterfly orchid in the meadow at Berthlwyd Farm. (Joe Daggett)

In June 2005 the National Trust carried out a review of the farm, which concluded that the long-term aim of management should be to retain and enhance the complex and rich mosaic of habitats, including the flower-rich hay meadows. For the last ten years the farm has been managed by the tenants under a Tir Gofal agri-environment scheme, but under the current grassland management system, with no chemical inputs, a hay-cut after mid-July and subsequent grazing by sheep, the yield of the hay crop has fallen considerably in recent years, almost to the point where the tenant considers it to be unviable. There is also a concern that the drop in yield is being accompanied by a decline in species diversity that could result in the loss of the hay meadows.

One of the biggest problems has been a lack of manure to keep the fertility up in the meadows. The farm has largely been raising sheep, which are out-wintered or sent away for winter grazing, often to dairy farms which keep their cattle indoors over winter. This means that the sheep produce no manure over the winter to spread on the fields in spring to replace nutrients lost with annual removal of the hay crop. Some of the more flower-rich meadows on the farm have also become dominated by yellow rattle, a parasitic plant that feeds off the grass. This, combined with low nutrient levels and slightly acidic soil, has caused dramatic falls in the yields of hay. The problem has been addressed by applying lime to some of the more acidic fields, which has helped to make the fields less acidic and better suited to wild flowers. Early cutting and seed collecting in some fields to stop the yellow rattle from seeding has also been carried out. The rattle is an annual, so reducing the quantities of seed in any one year has a direct effect the following year. Cattle are also slowly being reintroduced to the farm, with three Welsh Blacks and one Hereford cow funded by the Trust, PONT (the Wales grazing animal project) and the tenant. The long-term aim is to re-establish a small herd of cattle, overwinter them in a shed and collect the manure. This can then be spread on the fields to increase the fertility.

Other hay meadows in the Beacons include Boxbush Meadows, two small meadows, located to the northwest of Capel y Ffin. Despite their small size these are an outstanding example of the once common herb-rich hay meadows of the eastern Welsh uplands. A number of unusual plant species have been recorded from the site, including greater butterfly orchid and wood crane's-bill *Geranium sylvaticum*, a plant more typically found in meadows in Scotland and northern England. Wood crane's-bill has undergone a substantial decline during the last 50 years, due to the increased use of chemical fertilisers and a change from hay making to silage production. At Boxbush it occurs towards the bottom of the wooded slope, close to the stream and on steeper banks at the margins of the hay meadows, sometimes under a thin canopy of bracken.

LOWLAND ACID GRASSLAND

One of the most extensive areas of agriculturally unimproved lowland grassland remaining in the Brecon Beacons can be found at Caeau Ty Mawr, four fields situated on level ground to the west of Llangorse Lake (Fig. 218). Over the majority of the area there is a grassy sward dominated by common bent, sweet vernal-grass, crested dog's-tail *Cynosurus cristatus*, red fescue and Yorkshire-fog *Holcus lanatus*, with common knapweed, common bird's-foot-trefoil, ribwort plantain *Plantago lanceolata*, tormentil, devil's-bit scabious and red clover. Other characteristic plants associated with this meadow include heath grass *Danthonia decumbens*, autumn hawkbit *Leontodon autumnalis* and betony *Stachys officinalis*. Glaucous sedge is locally abundant, and species such as meadow fescue *Festuca pratensis* and hairy lady's-mantle *Alchemilla filicaulis* occur occasionally in the sward.

The wetter parts of the fields are either dominated by species of rushes *Juncus* spp. or by purple moor-grass. The former community is characterised by abundant sharp-flowered rush with frequent meadowsweet, common marsh-bedstraw and greater bird's-foot-trefoil *Lotus uliginosus*, and also occasional marsh valerian. This latter community has affinities with the drier grassland, but also supports species such as tawny sedge and the regionally rare pepper-saxifrage *Silaum silaus*.

FIG 218. One of the best areas of unimproved lowland grassland occurs at Caeau Ty Mawr at the west end of Llangorse Lake. (Jonathan Mullard)

NEUTRAL GRASSLANDS

Neutral grasslands also occur in the Brecon Beacons, and one of the most interesting is Caeau Fferm, situated on the northeastern flank of the Grwyne Fawr valley around 3 km southwest of Llanthony. Surrounded on three sides by coniferous forest, it lies on a steep slope facing southwest at an altitude of 300–400 m. Until the nineteenth century the valley was intensively settled, with over 30 farmsteads surrounded by small stone-walled fields, but now almost no evidence of these remains. The dry pastures found here typically contain species such as common bent, sweet vernal-grass, crested dog's-tail, spring-sedge *Carex caryophyllea*, field wood-rush *Luzula campestris*, common bird's-foot-trefoil, red clover, meadow buttercup *Ranunculus acris* and cat's-ear *Hypochoeris radicata*. On the steeper slopes, where soils are more free-draining, heath-grass *Danthonia decumbens*, mouse-ear hawkweed *Pilosella officinarum*, fairy flax *Linum catharticum*, burnet-saxifrage *Pimpinella saxifraga*, tormentil and harebell are common. Scarce species recorded at Caeau Fferm include adder's-tongue fern *Ophioglossum*

FIG 219. Meadow saffron on Hen Allt Common, near Hay on Wye. The name is derived from the fact that the flowers, which have orange anthers, can be used to produce a form of saffron, a spice normally derived from a crocus. Despite appearances, however, meadow saffron is a lily rather than a crocus – having six, not three, stamens and broader leaves. (Jonathan Saville)

vulgatum, large thyme *Thymus pulegioides*, which here is close to the western limit of its geographical range, and meadow saffron *Colchicum autumnale*.

Meadow saffron, a plant of damp meadows and woods, is also known as autumn crocus or naked ladies, the latter name deriving from the fact that the flowers appear well after the leaves. The leaves appear in the spring and can be confused with ramsons – a potentially lethal mistake, since all parts of the plant carry a deadly poison called colchicine. For this reason, the grasslands where this plant once grew were typically managed for hay, as the leaves die down prior to harvest. In grazing meadows it was usually destroyed. Changes to agricultural practice have meant that meadow saffron is now comparatively rare, with only remnant populations in many locations. It does not spread easily, so protecting the grasslands where it still occurs and ensuring that these are well managed is a priority. Other key sites for the plant include Hen Allt Common near Hay on Wye (Fig. 219).

HEDGES

Hedges are an important part of the landscape in the Brecon Beacons and there are over 5,500 km of hedgerows in the area (Fig. 220). They are important not just

FIG 220. A frosty morning in Cwm Crai picks out the pattern of the hedgerows. Small fields such as this are typical of sheltered valleys in the Beacons. (Jonathan Mullard)

for farming but also for wildlife, landscape, culture and archaeology. Indeed, the town of Hay on Wye is said to derive its name from the Norman French word *haie*, which means a hedge or enclosure.

In the early 1800s the priest, poet and antiquary Walter Davies conducted a survey of the economic situation of South Wales at the request of the Board of Agriculture, and in 1815 he published the results of his work in two volumes as *A General View of the Agriculture and Domestic Economy of South Wales*. In these he noted that:

> In some parts, plashing of hedges is regularly attended to, Mr. Clark, in the Original Report of Brecknockshire, p. 13, 14, says – 'when the field is in wheat, the hedges are then pleached', that is, all the dead and superabundant wood is cut off from the hedge. The tall branches are half cut, but not wholly so, because it is intended, that when they are laid along the stakes, new sprouts may issue from them in this horizontal direction, the sap having still a passage from the parent root, by the half that was left uncut, to invigorate these young sprouts. Since the hedge undergoes this operation every six or eight years, the country has a neat husbandman-like appearance, and banishes from the spectator those unpleasant sensations of indolence and slovenliness, which the sight of overgrown hedges round small enclosures must ever inspire.

These hedges were composed of native plants, particularly blackthorn, hawthorn, sometimes with hazel, dogwood *Cornus sanguinea* and field maple. Davies also lists what he describes as 'Parasitical Plants, common in Hedge-Fences, but not able to support themselves as Fences without the assistance of others.' Most common in hedges in the Beacons was bramble, which he saw 'abundantly everywhere; creeping and striking root at every joint; troublesome in meadow lands, entangling and fleecing sheep in winter, &c. Some of the more careful farmers cut them close to the hedge once or twice a year, but more especially in autumn, before the mountain sheep have the run of the farm.' Also very common was dog rose *Rosa canina*, 'in Welsh, *march fieri*, or *mieriffreinig* ... A red and hairy excrescence growing on this briar was formerly accounted a specific in the chin-cough: but strange to be an effectual remedy, it was to be found without being sought for.'

The 'red and hairy excrescence' which Davies records as growing on dog rose is known as the rose bedeguar gall, Robin's pincushion gall, or moss gall (Fig. 221). While dog rose is the commonest host, sweet briar *Rosa rubiginosa* and field rose *R. arvensis* are often galled as well (Redfern 2011). The gall is caused by the gall wasp *Diplolepis rosae* (Fig. 222) and develops when the wasp lays its eggs in an unopened

ABOVE: **FIG 221.** Rose bedeguar gall, a chemically induced distortion caused by the gall wasp *Diplolepis rosae*. (Peter Birch)

FIG 222. The gall wasp *Diplolepis rosae*. Females are only four millimetres in length, while the male is even smaller. (Peter Birch)

FIG 223. Cowslips on a roadside verge in the Olchon Valley near Llanveynoe, in May 2012. Cowslips have declined dramatically over the last 60 years due to the increased use of herbicides and chemical fertilisers and the re-seeding of ancient grasslands. As a result roadside verges are now one of their main strongholds. (Jonathan Mullard)

leaf axillary or terminal bud. Being so noticeable, this gall has a considerable amount of folklore associated with it. The term bedeguar has French, and ultimately Persian, origins and means 'wind-brought', while Robin's pincushion refers to the woodland sprite of folklore, Robin Goodfellow.

Other hedgerow 'parasites' which Davies encountered on his travels included eglantine, or sweet briar, burnet rose and traveller's joy *Clematis vitalba*. The last of these, also known as the 'great wild climber', was thought, erroneously, to injure the hedges by killing the hawthorn. He recorded that the Breconshire farmers 'called this troublesome plant *coluddiony d—l*, i.e. the devil's guts'. All of these plants can be found in hedgerows in the area today. Davies also recorded that 'In hedges are found also all the varieties of timber trees; some permitted to attain their full growth; others indiscriminately plashed down into the fence: of these we may enumerate the following, in addition to the crab tree, alder, birch, &c. already inserted.' These timber trees included, amongst others, oak, ash, beech and sycamore, which was 'in much request for dairy vessels, turnery ware, &c.'

A number of butterflies breed in hedges, including the holly blue *Celastrina argiolus*, whose caterpillars are only found in hedges containing holly or ivy, whilst the brimstone *Gonepteryx rhamni* prefers buckthorn or alder buckthorn *Frangula alnus*. The pearl-bordered fritillary *Boloria euphrosyne* is one of a number of species that use hedgerows as a source of nectar, for basking, or as corridors. Hedges are also used by some species such as the peacock *Inachis io* as territorial sites, with males establishing perching sites and rising up to inspect other butterflies as they fly past.

Mature and diverse hedgerows also provide food and nesting habitat for harvest mice *Mus minutus*, with the main nest-supporting shrub species in field margins being bramble, hawthorn and blackthorn. There are only two or three records for harvest mice in the Beacons, but the species is almost certainly under-recorded.

In 2012 Keep Wales Tidy set up the Long Forest project, a new community hedgerow project funded by the Brecon Beacons Trust. The aim is for volunteers to help improve and protect the network of hedgerows in the area. Many hedges in the Beacons have never been surveyed and there is comparatively little information on their composition, age, or what other plants grow in the hedge banks. Cowslips are unfortunately no longer common in the Beacons, but several roadside verges have spectacular displays in the spring (Fig. 223).

DRYSTONE WALLS

Throughout upland Britain, where there are easily accessible rock outcrops and the climate is too extreme for hedgerows, there are drystone walls, and the Beacons are no exception. Such walls are an important feature of the mountain scenery, particularly where they separate the common grazing from the in-bye land. At one time the complete boundary between the fields and the open mountain would have been marked by walling (Fig. 224). Due to changes in farming practice, the lack of cheap labour and other economic pressures, drystone walls have not been repaired and maintained. Some walls have been stripped out and the material sold as building stone, but significant and dramatic walls still exist in the area. Walls of Llangynidr was started in 2000 as a village Millennium project to try and save the mountain walls in the parish. The project has two main aims, the first being to rebuild and replace fallen walls and the second to provide training in drystone walling for local people. It has been very successful to date, with a number of walls being rebuilt.

In these exposed situations drystone walls provide varied habitats and microclimates for plants and animals. There is an exposed, wet side and a dryer, warmer side, and while the top of the wall is often windswept the bottom is sheltered and dry. Even a well-maintained wall contains numerous holes

FIG 224. The mountain wall near Pal y Cwrt, separating the common grazing from the fields. (Jonathan Mullard)

providing habitats for a variety of arthropods including spiders, woodlice, millipedes, bees and wasps. Wood mice and bank voles *Myodes glareolus* also find the cavities in walls attractive. A semi-derelict wall is often better than a well-maintained one, since there are more sheltered spaces and more of it is covered in soil. However, such a condition is relatively short-lived, and once it is reduced to less than half its height the value of a wall for wildlife decreases considerably. Stone walls therefore need to be sympathetically maintained if they are to continue to be of interest for wildlife.

FARM BUILDINGS

There are still a number of traditional farm buildings surviving in the Brecon Beacons, though many barns have been converted to holiday accommodation. Two birds are intimately connected with this habitat, and indeed are named after it, the barn swallow and barn owl *Tyto alba*. Swallows feed on flying insects and have therefore been tolerated by people when building their nests.

Superstitions also abound regarding damage to the nest, and this may be another factor in ensuring their longevity; nests regularly survive, with suitable annual refurbishment, for 10–15 years. One of the easiest places to see nesting swallows is at Carreg Cennen farm, below the castle, where as part of the visitor facilities one of the original barns is filled with old farm machinery. Here during the summer numerous swallows fly in and out of the door and window openings just above the visitors' heads.

Barn owls, in contrast, are not numerous, though they may be sighted from time to time almost anywhere across the Beacons. Evidence suggests that the British barn owl population has declined by 70 per cent since the 1930s, due to the loss of habitats rich in prey species such as rough pasture, field margins, and woodland edges, the loss of barns and attics through demolition and conversion, and loss of veteran trees with suitable nesting holes. The loss of one roost site may precipitate the loss of a breeding pair entirely, since barn owls are so

FIG 225. Barn owl on a branch in Llangasty churchyard. This bird is probably a male, based on the clear white throat and white underwing colour (not visible in this photograph). It was using an owl box which had been erected on a nearby farm as a roost site. (Steve Wilce)

dependent on the security of their roosts from year to year. It is not clear what factors are limiting populations in the Beacons. The provision of owl boxes can, however, compensate to some extent for the loss of roosting spaces in barns. One evening in February 2013, Steve Wilce, who is an enthusiastic bird photographer, saw an adult bird in Llangasty churchyard. Barn owls will hunt over any open habitat that supports a population of small mammals, so churchyards, as described in the previous chapter, are ideal locations for them. Steve described taking the photograph (Fig. 225) as follows:

> *It was impossible to get near enough for a real close-up because he was quite spooky but I could see he was landing on a particular branch quite regularly. With this in mind I decided to set up my portable hide in some felled timber near to his favoured branch. This limited my view to that particular branch only but that's the way it is in these situations. I waited for 90 minutes before I saw him and he flew straight onto the branch passing within a metre of my hide. It's quite an experience to see a bird that big passing that close to you in absolute silence! As soon as he landed he looked straight at me and he must have realised that there was something different. I took the photo immediately, since I was afraid he would fly away, and he did so as soon as he heard the shutter, disappearing into the gloom. I haven't seen him perch on that branch since, so I'm glad I took the opportunity.*

ORCHARDS

A century ago almost every farm or smallholding in the Brecon Beacons had a small orchard of fruit trees to provide fresh fruit in the autumn and winter, but now only a few of these traditional orchards remain. Across Wales as a whole over the last 100 years around 80 per cent of orchards have been lost, some containing apple varieties dating back to Roman times. Fruit trees are known as 'early senescent hardwoods' – that is, they are short-lived in comparison to other hardwood species such as oak and ash and begin to produce features of veteran trees, such as hollow trunks, rot holes and split bark, relatively quickly. These all provide excellent habitats for wildlife.

Sites remaining today in the Brecon Beacons range from individual ancient fruit trees to neglected and abandoned farm orchards. Until recently their importance and the threats to remaining trees were often unrecognised, but a concerted effort by a number of organisations has redressed the situation, and interest in old varieties of apples and other orchard fruit is now increasing. The People's Trust for Endangered Species, for example, is currently running a project to map the traditional orchards of Wales, in order to create a baseline to guide future conservation work. This involves recording the condition, age, boundaries and management status of each orchard. To date they have located 307 orchards in the Beacons, most of which are in the area bounded by Talgarth, Gilwern and Llantilio Pertholey, with a focus in the Usk Valley. A total of 65 of these orchards probably have fewer than five trees remaining and so are considered relicts. About 20 per cent have been surveyed on the ground, with about a half being in good condition and the remainder in poor condition. One of the best is located near Groesffordd in the Usk Valley just to the east of Brecon (Fig. 226), but even this is affected by the use of chemicals. Over the border in the Olchon Valley and the Herefordshire Black Mountains the Trust has identified a cluster of sites south of Hay on Wye and another concentration around Longtown.

The cultivation of fruit trees in Wales has been practised for many centuries, and there is circumstantial evidence that apples were being cultivated as far back as the sixth century. From 1100 the Normans brought their own orchard culture to Britain. Norman French bishops and abbots controlled the monasteries and many had orchards and apple presses. By this time orchards were also beginning to play a vital part in the rural economy. Medieval orchards were associated

FIG 226. A relatively young orchard, planted within the last 30 years, near Groesffordd in the Usk Valley. Only a few old trees remained at this site before it was restored, well-managed traditional orchards now being rare within the farmed landscape. (Jonathan Mullard)

with manorial and monastic estates. A burst of fresh interest in fruit growing occurred in the sixteenth and seventeenth centuries, stimulated by court fashions and foreign influences. This brought new fruits and new varieties of old fruits (including apricots, cherries, nectarines, peaches and plums) into orchards, along with nut trees, and greatly enlarged their acreage in certain counties. Enthusiasm died away between 1750 and 1880, but then revived, giving fresh fruit, and especially jam, a larger place in people's diets. Many new varieties of apple were developed in the eighteenth and nineteenth centuries, when orchards expanded in size to meet demand, especially those orchards near large cities. Orchards prospered until the mid-twentieth century, but since then there has been a rapid decline in their area in England and Wales. In 1970 there were 65,200 hectares of orchards in the UK, but by 1997 the figure was 22,400 hectares, a decline of 66 per cent.

Rare varieties of Welsh fruits include varieties such as Pig yr Wydd, Saint Cecilia and Machen apples and Monmouthshire Burgundy pears. Pig yr Wydd translates as 'goose's bill', which is probably an allusion to the curved patterns on the sides of the fruit. This cooking apple seems to do well in farm orchards in the wetter western areas. This variety is often accompanied by Pig Aderyn, an early eating apple. Quite often in this variety the stalk projects horizontally from a fleshy bump on the base, so that the apples, when inverted, have a resemblance to a bird – hence the name, which means 'bird's bill'. Welsh apples are difficult to identify because, with the few exceptions mentioned above, no detailed descriptions of the varieties exist and there are no specimen trees in the national collections. As the Marcher Apple Network (2004) notes, 'There may be a few clues lurking somewhere in the literature, but quite often there is little beyond folk memories, which need to be corroborated by independent witnesses, to establish identity.' Landore, or Monmouth Green, is mentioned in Kilvert's diary and has been grown around the Black Mountains since Victorian times, but the variety could be far older. It is usually known as Landore in Herefordshire, but Monmouth Green in the Brecon area. Another local apple from the eastern end of the Beacons is Saint Cecilia, which was raised around 1900 at nurseries in Bassaleg, Monmouthshire, from a Cox's Orange Pippin seedling.

From the canopy of the fruit trees to the grassland beneath, traditional orchards are rich in native plants, including mistletoe (Fig. 227). As the only aerial tree parasite in Britain, and with customs and traditions stretching back into prehistory, the mistletoe has always attracted attention. Mistletoe is also well known for the insects associated with it. These obligate insects have been the focus of attention since concerns over the conservation of mistletoe were raised in the 1990s. At that time just four species were listed, all relatively unknown

FIG 227. Mistletoe on apple trees at Tretower Court. Most mistletoe in Britain grows on fruit trees, but it can also be found on other hosts, such as poplars, willows and hawthorns, in the wider countryside. (Jonathan Mullard)

(Briggs 2011), but since then two more have been discovered, and there may be more to find in future. Mistletoe in Europe hosts much larger numbers of insects. The current British list consists of one moth, the mistletoe marble moth *Celypha woodiana*, three sap-sucking bugs, *Cacopsylla visci*, *Pinalitus viscicola* and *Hypseloecus visci*, one predatory bug, *Anthocoris visci* (which feeds on the other bugs) and one beetle, the mistletoe weevil *Ixapion variegatum*. Little is known about the biology of these mistletoe specialist insects, and further research is needed.

Fungi are a common feature in old orchards, recycling nutrients, and the hollows they create are exploited by nesting birds and other creatures. Lichens, mosses and liverworts are also often abundant on the trunks and branches, providing food and shelter for invertebrates and nesting material for birds. One of the most distinctive mosses is a rare feather moss called supine plait moss *Hypnum resupinatum*. This is frequently found on the trunks of trees, where it is an indicator of relatively high pH and hence a diverse flora of mosses and lichens. The grassland in which the trees stand may also be an ancient and valuable habitat in itself, and there can be rare species here as well, such as waxcap fungi.

Traditional orchards are a particularly important habitat for invertebrates. Because of the wide tree spacing compared to that in woodlands, the dead and decaying wood is usually in open locations. This creates good habitats for insects and other invertebrate species which depend on decaying wood, and over 400 of these specialist species have been found in orchards. Springtime blossom, wild flowers on the ground and hedgerows surrounding orchards are also a good source of pollen and nectar for bumblebees, butterflies and other insects.

A great variety of birds take advantage of the feeding, nesting and roosting opportunities in the trees. Hollow branches, or trunks, are used as nesting sites by birds such as green woodpecker *Picus viridis*, great spotted woodpecker *Dendrocopos major* and the declining lesser spotted woodpecker. Blue tit *Cyanistes caeruleus* and chaffinch often nest in the branches, while in the winter months fieldfares and redwings feed on fallen fruit. Many of these species also feed on the wide range of insects present in the decaying wood.

The outlook for orchards, and indeed farming as whole, is bound up not only with the economic factors highlighted at the beginning of this chapter, but also with environmental issues. Climate change will undoubtedly have an effect on how land is farmed and the type of activities that take place in the Beacons. The final chapter therefore looks at these issues and examines what the future might hold for the wildlife of the Brecon Beacons.

Chapter 13

Landscape Futures

In the last 200 years the number of people on Earth has risen from one billion to the current population of seven billion. Although the United Nations predicts that growth will plateau at nine billion around mid-century, before slowly starting to fall, these rapidly increasing numbers are destroying ecosystems, polluting the air, land and sea, raising temperatures and melting icecaps. In doing so we are probably delaying the start of another glaciation, but with devastating consequences for wildlife across the globe. Many people find the issue of population growth difficult to address, yet it lies at the core of our current environmental problems. As a result we are living through a period of unprecedented global warming and this is having serious impacts on plants and animals. Trevor Beebee, joint author of *Amphibians and Reptiles* (New Naturalist 87), is one of many naturalists who have noted 'the uneasy relationship between human numbers and the sustainability of Britain's wildlife' (Beebee 2001).

Since the last glaciation, wildlife in Britain has been affected by fluctuating concentrations of atmospheric carbon dioxide, shifts in temperature and variation in precipitation, but it has been able to evolve and adapt. Such climate changes, however, occurred over an extended period of time, in a landscape that was not as fragmented as it is today, and with little or no pressure from people. In contrast, many species are now confined to relatively small areas within their previous ranges. Temperatures rising above those reached during the Pleistocene will therefore stress ecosystems and their wildlife far beyond the levels imposed by the global climatic changes that occurred in the recent evolutionary past. The warming climate is already forcing plants and animals to adapt, through moving habitat, changing life cycles, or adopting new behaviours. Species are likely to migrate northwards and upwards in response to the changing climate, but as described above the current situation is very different to anything ever experienced before. Wet and dull summers, such as that experienced in 2012, have been linked by recent research to ice melt in the Arctic shifting the position of the jet stream, which normally brings settled weather to the UK in the summer but has been moving for several years. According to the Met Office, the summers from 2007 to 2012 were duller and wetter than the long-term average.

ENVIRONMENTAL MONITORING

The upland areas of Wales, including the Brecon Beacons, are obviously not immune to these changes. Fifteen years of monitoring environmental change on Snowdon, for example, has revealed that shifts in temperature, atmospheric pollutants and land management are all having an impact on the mountain, far beyond what could be attributed to natural variation. Snowdon is one of a number of terrestrial Environmental Change Network (ECN) sites across the UK, and its records reveal that there is significantly less sulphur dioxide pollution (acid rain) contaminating natural habitats than there was at the start of the monitoring period, but that ongoing pollution from nitrogen oxides, mainly from vehicle exhausts, and ozone from industry, are still having a negative impact on vegetation. It is also apparent that the climate has already changed slightly on Snowdon: spring and summer temperatures having risen, while winters have become wetter and milder. Purple saxifrage is flowering significantly earlier and the numbers of ground beetles are decreasing, while spider numbers are stable and butterflies are increasing. On the positive side there is as yet no evidence of change in the vegetation communities. Conversely, some vegetation types, such as bracken-dominated grassland, are likely to benefit from warmer, drier summers. The already rapid spread of bracken may well increase, with invasion at higher elevations becoming possible if late frosts, which damage the emerging fronds, become less frequent and severe (Pakeman & Marrs 1996).

The ECN sites in Wales are all on National Nature Reserves, since there is already considerable information about their management, species and habitats. Two of these sites are at Cwm Cadlan (Fig. 228) and Ogof Ffynnon Ddu in the Brecon Beacons. The Electrical Supply Industry also has a similar site at Mynydd Llangatwg. Networks like these help to establish and maintain a coordinated system of long-term monitoring that increases our ability to detect, understand and predict the effects of climate change and air pollution on biodiversity. Importantly, each site monitors both the causes of environmental change, such as climate and pollution, and the effects upon ecosystems. The approach includes

FIG 228. One of the two Environmental Change Network monitoring sites in the Brecon Beacons, at Cwm Cadlan National Nature Reserve. (Jon Wohlgemuth/Countryside Council for Wales)

developing a long-term data set using an automatic weather station with a link to a website. There are also permanent quadrats for monitoring vegetation change at Ogof Ffynnon Ddu, Craig Cwm Du (part of Craig Cerrig Gleisiad National Nature Reserve) and at Craig y Cilau. Breeding bird surveys are also carried out twice a year around the weather stations, as is a butterfly survey, but the latter is proving difficult to implement reliably and regularly.

CLIMATE PREDICTIONS

It is thought that climate change may simply be too rapid for some species to migrate or adapt fast enough. Remnant arctic–alpine communities, such as those that occur in the Brecon Beacons, although of very limited occurrence in Wales, are of special concern since they are particularly vulnerable. It is argued that having survived since the last ice age in the few sites where they are able to compete with other vegetation, notably on cool, wet, north-facing cliffs and boulder screes, they have nowhere to go when the climate changes, since the mountains are not high enough to offer additional refuges. There is as yet though no evidence from studies in Wales or elsewhere to support this theory. Indeed, data from genetic studies of the Snowdon lily *Lloydia serotina*, which only occurs in North Wales, suggest that despite the total Welsh population numbering fewer than 100 bulbs, the Welsh plants, although isolated by considerable distances from the nearest populations in the Alps, are genetically more diverse than other populations of the same species (Jones *et al.* 2001). This suggests that the Snowdon lily may be able to respond to climate change more successfully than was previously supposed. Similar information is required for other key arctic–alpine species, as well as knowledge of their likely responses to climate change, based on experimental testing in carefully controlled experiments.

There is currently little understanding of which communities and species will be affected or how they will cope with the predicted changes. Summer droughts and higher temperatures might cause the drying out and subsequent oxidation and breakdown of peat. This could lead to wide-ranging ecological impacts, including dramatic changes in the vegetation cover of moorland areas and the loss of many plant and animal species (Fig. 229). Such changes would render national or international wildlife designations in the Beacons redundant. There

FIG 229. Upland habitats, like the Brecon Beacons, already under pressure from grazing livestock and atmospheric pollution, will be especially sensitive to climate change. (Jonathan Mullard)

is also little current understanding of the effects of interactions between climate change and other key factors affecting biodiversity. It is thought that changes in climate are already affecting the spread of epiphytic mosses and liverworts such as fingered cowlwort, which even 20 years ago had a very restricted distribution.

Land use, especially the intensity and pattern of sheep grazing, and changes to the acidity and fertility of soil and water due to the deposition of atmospheric nitrogen, are just two of the factors involved. Field experiments are currently being undertaken to investigate interactions in heather moorland and grassland ecosystems, but more research is needed. Some of the changes may be due to improving air quality, rather than climate change. A drop in sulphur dioxide levels, for example, may be the reason why formerly rare lichens, such as bearded lichen *Usnea articulata*, have spread into the Beacons. Bearded lichen was included in Section 42 of the Natural Environment and Rural Communities Act, as a species of 'principal importance for conservation of biological diversity in Wales', because of its rarity and the significant loss of historic sites. The increase in new sites for this species is therefore especially welcome.

Small advances such as this, however, are still outweighed by the massive changes which are certain to affect the Brecon Beacons over the decades to come. As well as climate change, there are also increasing pressures on habitats and wildlife arising from existing and proposed infrastructure projects such as gas pipelines, new roads and renewable energy developments.

GAS PIPELINES

In 2007, National Grid Gas commenced construction of the largest natural gas pipeline ever built in Britain, to connect liquid natural gas terminals at Milford Haven with the national gas network in Gloucestershire. Despite repeated objections from the National Park Authority it crossed the Brecon Beacons through Mynydd Myddfai and Mynydd Bach Trecastell commons (Fig. 230). Numerous other groups also protested against the development, but the pipeline went ahead. It cost around £700 million and was, according to the National Grid, expected to transport around 20 per cent of the gas needed to meet UK consumption in future. The diameter of the pipe itself is relatively small, but the 'working width' needed for the excavators and pipe-laying equipment varied between 48 m and 72 m and cut a path through both commons. National Grid was required, as a condition of consent, to continue restoration works for ten years following construction and to implement an enhancement package for the sensitive locations along the pipeline route, but fully restoring the commons will

FIG 230. Construction of the largest natural gas pipeline ever built in Britain crossing the ancient landscape of Mynydd Myddfai. (Jonathan Saville/Countryside Council for Wales)

be difficult. In many areas disturbance of the ground results in strips dominated by soft-rush that can be difficult to control. The location of water pipelines across several areas of common, such as Mynydd Llangynidr and Mynydd Llangatwg, for example, are clearly marked by the lines of rush that follow the route. The disturbance affects the hydrology and soil structure, with compaction leading to water retention, which creates an ideal habitat for such plants.

Indeed, the effectiveness of restoring habitats and landscapes is likely to vary depending on the nature of the site in question. Within the Beacons the National Grid were required to identify 11 'affected locations'; that is, sites that were particularly sensitive to the disturbance caused by pipeline construction and reinstatement. A variety of organisations, including the National Park Authority, have to agree that these sites have reached an acceptable level of restoration before National Grid's involvement is complete. This has not happened yet, though it is possible that a sufficient standard could be achieved for most of the sites in question. Mynydd Myddfai, the largest of the affected locations, will never be fully restored, and the Authority may have to accept this. In relation to the historic environment, sections have obviously been destroyed and all that remains is the archaeological record. It will also never be possible to return habitats and the landscape to their original condition, even though the area was already ecologically impoverished prior to the construction of the pipeline.

FIG 231. Silt runoff in the Nant Car, a tributary of the Usk, heading towards the main river in January 2008. (Graham Cowden)

Elsewhere along the route of the pipeline, farmers have concerns about the restoration of their pastures, and further remedial works will be required. Outside the area, Llandefalle Common is also considered to have been significantly damaged as a consequence of the restoration work. Throughout the construction period and 'reinstatement', the Authority was concerned that the environmental safeguards put in place by National Grid were insufficient to protect the environment. There was particular concern about the River Usk, because of the massive amounts of silt running into the watercourse. High levels of sediment as a result of construction work, even if relatively short-lived, can have damaging effects on a wide range of wildlife, affecting plants, invertebrates and fish. Long-term monitoring will be necessary to determine if this is the case in the Usk.

A smaller gas pipeline was constructed in 2002 from Gilwern to Hafodyrynys through the eastern side of the Beacons, crossing Mynydd Llangatwg and then south across Mynydd Coity to Pontypool. Various methods were tried, with varying degrees of success, to ensure the vegetation returned to its natural state. Not surprisingly, where turf was stripped and returned once the pipe was installed, the vegetation generally restored quite well and the heather has since returned to almost its original condition. Other areas have been less successfully restored, with soft-rush dominating some areas and other areas still relatively poorly vegetated ten years on. Hopefully, as methods of reinstatement improve, habitats may restore quicker. Often, however, these pipelines have a relatively short lifespan – and if they need to be replaced then the whole restoration process starts again.

HYDROELECTRIC SCHEMES

There has been a big increase in the number of small hydroelectric schemes constructed in the Beacons in the last few years, especially high-head schemes where water is diverted, via a pipe, away from a stream. Although there are obvious benefits from such a relatively clean energy source, if a scheme is inappropriately placed the result could be that fish, aquatic invertebrates, aquatic or semi-aquatic plants, bryophytes and lichens are affected by changing water levels. In gorges or areas with waterfalls that produce a lot of spray, for instance, there may be humidity-dependent species growing on rock outcrops or in the woodland, often some distance from the stream itself, that will be affected if average humidity levels drop. There is currently little information about the likely impacts on any of these species. It has been suggested that small changes in flow rates will have no impact because the species concerned will be able to adjust to the changes. There are, however, concerns that populations of rare species, which are thought to have poor rates of dispersal and establishment, may be affected, as commoner species adjust more readily and may end up dominating the changed habitat (Demars & Britton 2011).

NEW LANDSCAPES

While the wildlife-rich elements of the existing landscape must be protected, this must not prevent the consideration of ways in which they could be enhanced. As mentioned in the Foreword, the Brecon Beacons might well be one of the best places in Wales to create new landscapes. Indeed, the Beacons are one of a number of locations in Britain which were put forward by the Wilderness Foundation in 2005 as candidates for 'rewilding' (Vidal 2005). Most of the suggested localities were in upland areas with farms that the Foundation considered only marginally economic. One of the organisation's aims is returning land to be managed by natural processes, with multiple benefits to wildlife and people, and this is forming part of an increasing debate in Britain around how the uplands are best managed for the future.

Around 35 of the Sites of Special Scientific Interest in the Beacons are currently classified as 'ecologically unfavourable', including sites such as the Black Mountains, the Blorenge, the Brecon Beacons and Mynydd Du. As discussed in earlier chapters, the poor ecological status of these sites, and indeed of the wider upland and river landscape, results from a variety of factors including the acidification of upland waters, drainage and water abstraction, but particularly from the lack of appropriate grazing.

Today an estimated 8.62 million sheep are being kept in Wales, lower than the historic high of 11.77 million in 1999 but still a vast number. At that time subsidies were paid per breeding ewe, not per lamb produced, so to increase their profits farmers simply kept more sheep. Reform of the Common Agriculture Policy meant a new basis for payments to farmers, subsidy schemes being replaced in 2005 with the Single Payment Scheme. This 'decoupled' the link between payments and production, the intention being to allow farmers to produce what the market require and to farm environmentally.

While sheep numbers may have declined in recent years, grazing pressure has not been reduced to the same extent because heavier breeds are being favoured. Moreover, due to improved market prices the number of sheep in the Beacons has now returned to the level which existed before the outbreak of foot and mouth disease in 2001, limiting the recovery of the degraded moorland (Silcock *et al.* 2012). It is a rare sight to see traditional breeds of cattle grazing rough grassland in the uplands, the economics of beef production forcing most farmers to rear faster-growing continental breeds on intensively managed grasslands in the valleys. In the past, however, Welsh black cattle and sheep helped create the landscape and were central to the local economy (Figs 232, 233). These native breeds thrive on rough grazing, making them ideal for mountain areas, and at a low grazing density they actually improve conditions for wildlife.

FIG 232. A rare sight in the Beacons: cattle grazing the western slopes of Cefn Cul above the Afon Tawe. (Harold Grenfell)

Some people are concerned that remote tracts of countryside, which 'can be used only for grazing', will turn to scrub if there are less sheep in the hills. They fear that the Welsh countryside will be changed forever if the current methods of farming cease. Although this is presented as a negative outcome, the unforeseen side effects of the present regime of heavy grazing include a loss of wildlife, soil erosion and an increased risk of flooding in lowland areas, since the generally treeless landscape is unable to moderate the effects of heavy rain. In parallel, the drying out of peat soils causes oxidation which releases carbon dioxide into the atmosphere. Indeed, the uplands themselves could have a significant impact on climate change, because 500 million tonnes of carbon and up to 1.9 billion tonnes of carbon dioxide are estimated to be stored in Welsh soils. Peat, in particular, has the capacity to release far more carbon dioxide into the environment than previously realised, increasing the effects of climate change.

FIG 233. Welsh black mountain sheep, with a modern 'shepherd's hut' behind, at the Hay Festival in 2013. (Jonathan Mullard)

The Environment Agency's Foresight Programme has stated that Wales will be deficient in water supplies within 50 years as a consequence of climate change and rising demand. A comprehensive catchment management plan within the Brecon Beacons will be necessary to maintain supplies for a large proportion of Wales's population. Dŵr Cymru has already decommissioned two reservoirs within the National Park – the Neuadd Reservoir below Pen y Fan and the Grwyne Fawr Reservoir in the Black Mountains – because of water discolouration, dissolved organic carbon content and peat sediments. These water-quality problems can be attributed directly to the lack of catchment management, poor burning management and overgrazing, causing poor ecological condition of the surrounding land. In particular, problems arise from the extent of degraded blanket bog that surrounds the reservoirs.

Elsewhere in the Beacons, however, there are examples which show what could be done to reverse this situation. In 2008, for instance, Dŵr Cymru

FIG 234. Relict rowans growing alongside the waterfalls on the course of the Nant y Llyn above Cerrig Duon stone circle: a possible source of future woodlands. (Jonathan Mullard)

obtained permission from the National Park Authority to construct a new water treatment works in the upper Swansea Valley below Waun Fignen Felen. As a condition of the planning permission the water company funded research, which underlined the effectiveness of restoring bare peat to reduce dissolved organic carbon and discolouration in water. Works completed to date have produced a marked improvement in the quality and colour of water flowing through the Dan yr Ogof showcaves, which lie below the plateau.

With the reform of the Common Agriculture Policy, subsidies for upland farmers in Wales are likely to be focused on broader rural development themes, including the sustainable management of natural resources and action on climate change. In this context there is an opportunity to deliver not only food, but also a landscape much richer in wildlife. This could include promoting the growth of 'scrub' species, such as birch, rowan and willow, to create areas of woodland to connect upland habitats with lowland woodland. The trees would also improve the soil, reducing flooding, filtering water and providing habitats for a range of species. Relict specimens, often quite old but stunted trees, can be found in the Beacons along watercourses and on rocky ledges where the sheep cannot reach them (Fig. 234). A reduction in grazing pressure would allow seedlings from these trees to establish themselves, rapidly increasing the area of woodland. As described earlier in this book, there have been new areas of woodland planted in the Beacons, notably by the Woodland Trust, but these new plantings rarely establish as successfully, or as quickly, as those areas of woodland created by natural regeneration, and they are often much poorer in wildlife.

Conservation organisations face an interesting dilemma. While they value the history and traditions associated with the commons, and indeed value the cultural landscapes that have been produced as a result, the declining numbers of commoners and the poor quality of many of the upland habitats in the Beacons will require a new approach. This may not be popular, since it would involve substantial changes in the landscape and the way it is viewed by both residents and visitors.

A different approach to grazing, using cattle and sheep, as well as some habitat restoration, would re-establish large areas of woodland and heather moorland and protect soils. Local farmers and contractors could be paid to deliver these projects, providing new funding for those that live and work in the uplands. It all depends on a willingness to accept that the landscape will change. Decisions made now will affect what future generations see – but these mountains were more varied in the past and they could be so again. What price a new landscape for the Brecon Beacons, and how much richer would its wildlife be as a result?

Appendix 1

Designated Sites and Nature Reserves

SITES OF SPECIAL SCIENTIFIC INTEREST

The following table lists the main interests of each Site of Special Scientific Interest (SSSI) within the Brecon Beacons as at January 2013. Some of these sites also fall within areas designated as National Nature Reserves (NNR) or Special Areas of Conservation (SAC). SACs may include parts of more than one SSSI. Only a small part of sites indicated by * and without a grid reference fall within the area.

SSSI site name	Grid ref	Main interests
Abercriban Quarries	SO064123	Geological
Afon Llynfi *	Many	Biological – running water, otter, fish
Afon Wysg (Isafonydd)/River Usk (Tributaries) *	Many	Biological – running water, otter, fish
Alexanderstone Meadows *		Biological – marshy grassland, neutral grassland
Baltic and Tyle'r-bont Quarries	SO065115	Geological
Black Mountains	SO245300	Biological – upland habitats, woodland, flowering plants, bryophytes, birds
Blaen Nedd	SN914135	Geological and biological – caves, limestone pavement, calcareous grassland, neutral grassland, marshy grassland, wet heath, rock exposures, woodland

SSSI site name	Grid ref	Main interests
Blorenge	SO265105	Biological – upland heath, calcareous grassland
Boxbush Meadows	SO246318	Biological – neutral grassland, flowering plants
Brecon Beacons	SO010200	Geological and biological – upland habitats, flowering plants, bryophytes, lichens, cliffs
Bryn Bwch	SN920108	Biological – marshy grassland
Brynmawr Sections	SO197121	Geological
Buckland Coach House and Ice House	SO132215	Biological – bats
Cae Bryn Tywarch	SN853267	Biological – marshy grassland
Cae Cilmaenllwyd	SN670204	Biological – fen and marshy grassland
Cae Gwernllertai	SN943244	Biological – marshy grassland
Cae Maes y Ffynnon	SN747231	Biological – fen
Caeau Fferm	SO261258	Biological – neutral grassland
Caeau Cwmcoynant (Caeau Cwm Caenant)	SO232379	Biological – neutral grassland
Caeau Heol y Llidiart Coch	SN715213	Biological – marshy grassland
Caeau Nant y Llechau (Nant y Llechau Meadows)	SN902103	Biological – marshy grassland, neutral grassland
Caeau Tir Mawr	SN648206	Biological – marshy grassland
Caeau Ton y Fildre	SN865107	Biological – marshy grassland
Caeau Ty Mawr	SO121263	Biological – neutral grassland
Carreg Cennen	SN670191	Biological – woodland, flowering plants
Cathedine Common Wood	SO140247	Biological – woodland
Coed Blaen y Cwm (Blaen y Cwm Wood)	SO208370	Biological – woodland
Coed Mawr/Blaen Car	SN930285	Biological – neutral grassland, woodland
Coed Nant Menascin	SO059233	Biological – woodland
Coed y Cerrig	SO294212	Biological – woodland, plants
Coed Ynys Faen	SO240194	Biological – woodland
Coedydd Tregyb	SN641217	Biological – woodland
Coed y Person	SO279134	Biological – woodland

SSSI site name	Grid ref	Main interests
Craig y Rhiwarth	SN846158	Biological – woodland, flowering plants, calcareous grassland
Cwar Glas Quarry and Sawdde Gorge	SN726248	Geological
Cwar yr Ystrad a Cwar Blaen Dyffryn	SO085142	Geological
Cwm Cadlan	SN960096	Biological – fen, marshy grassland, neutral grassland, flowering plants
Cwm Clydach	SO218125	Geological and biological – woodland, flowering plants, fungi
Cwm Llanwenarth Meadows	SO254124	Biological – neutral grassland
Darren Fach	SO019105	Biological – woodland, flowering plants
Dyffrynoedd Nedd a Mellte, a Moel Penderyn	SN907100	Geological and biological – woodland, flowering plants, bryophytes, lichens
Foxwood	SO301217	Biological – bats
Gilwern Hill	SO249125	Geological and biological – woodland, calcareous grassland
Gweunydd Dyffryn Nedd	SN915115	Biological – marshy grassland
Gyfartha	SN992243	Biological – marshy grassland
Hen-allt Common	SO233399	Biological fen, neutral grassland, flowering plants
Heol Senni Quarry	SN914222	Geological
Illtyd Pools	SN965256	Geological and biological – fen, bog, water body, vascular plants, invertebrates
Llanfihangel Moraine	SO315203	Geological
Llanover Quarry	SO297079	Geological
Llyn Syfaddan (Llangorse Lake)	SO133265	Biological – fen, water body, flowering plants, invertebrates
Mandinam a Coed Deri *		Biological – woodland, grassland
Mynydd Du (Black Mountain)	SN706109	Geological and biological – upland habitats, flowering plants, bryophytes, calcareous grassland, water body, rock exposures, cliffs
Mynydd Llangatwg (Mynydd Llangattock)	SO187148	Geological and biological – caves, upland habitats, cliffs, woodland, calcareous grassland, raised bog, lichens, bryophytes, flowering plants, bats
Mynydd Llangynidr	SO140150	Geological

SSSI site name	Grid ref	Main interests
Nant Glais Caves (formerly Ogof y Ci)	SO040105	Geological
Nant Llech	SN842121	Geological and biological – woodland, bryophytes
Ogof Ffynnon Ddu	SN870165	Geological and biological – caves, invertebrates
Ogof Ffynnon Ddu Pant Mawr	SN880155	Geological and biological – caves, limestone pavement, calcareous grassland, dry heath, rock exposures, limestone pavement, flowering plants
Penllwyn yr Hendy	SN929227	Biological – marshy grassland, neutral grassland
Penmoelallt	SS017095	Biological – woodland, flowering plants
Pen y Graig Goch	SN742226	Biological – marshy grassland
Pen yr Hen Allt	SO229397	Biological – neutral grassland, flowering plants
Plas y Gors	SN921155	Biological – fen
Pwll y Wrach	SO165327	Biological – woodland
Rhos Cruglas	SN683240	Biological – marshy grassland, neutral grassland
Rhos Hen Glyn Isaf	SN787125	Biological – marshy grassland, flowering plants
River Usk (Upper Usk)/Afon Wysg (Wysg Uchaf)	SN834285	Biological – running water, fish, invertebrates, otter, fen, woodland, flowering plants
River Wye (Upper Wye)/Afon Gwy (Gwy Uchaf) *		Biological – running water, fish, otter
Siambre Ddu	SO250115	Geological and biological – bats
Strawberry Cottage Wood	SO314214	Biological – woodland
Sugar Loaf Woodlands	SO282175	Biological – woodland
Waun Ton y Spyddaden	SN864122	Biological – marshy grassland
Waun Ddu	SN822305	Biological – blanket bog
Woodland Park and Pontpren	SN946077	Biological – grassland habitats, invertebrates
Y Gors	SN876297	Biological – marshy grassland, fen
Ydw Valley and Fron Road Geological Exposures *		Geological

SPECIAL AREAS OF CONSERVATION AND NATIONAL NATURE RESERVES

This table lists Special Areas of Conservation (SACs) and National Nature Reserves (NNRs) and the Site of Special Scientific Interest (SSSI) with which they are associated.

SSSI site name	Associated SAC	Associated NNR
Cwm Cadlan	Cwm Cadlan	Cwm Cadlan
Cwm Clydach	Cwm Clydach Woodlands	Cwm Clydach
Dyffrynoedd Nedd a Mellte, a Moel Penderyn	Coedydd Nedd a Mellte	
Foxwood	Usk Bat Sites/Safleoedd Ystlumod Wysg	
Llyn Syfaddan (Llangorse Lake)	Llangorse Lake/Llyn Syfaddan	
Mynydd Llangatwg (Mynydd Llangattock)	Usk Bat Sites/Safleoedd Ystlumod Wysg	Craig y Cilau
Ogof Ffynnon Ddu		Ogof Ffynnon Ddu
Ogof Ffynnon Ddu Pant Mawr		Ogof Ffynnon Ddu
Penllwyn yr Hendy	River Usk/Afon Wysg	
River Usk (Upper Usk)/Afon Wysg (Wysg Uchaf)	River Usk/Afon Wysg	
River Wye (Upper Wye)/Afon Gwy (Gwy Uchaf)	River Wye/Afon Gwy	
Siambre Ddu	Usk Bat Sites/Safleoedd Ystlumod Wysg	
Sugar Loaf Woodlands	Sugar Loaf Woodlands	
Woodland Park and Pontpren	Blaen Cynon	Woodland Park

WILDLIFE TRUST RESERVES

Brecknock Wildlife Trust is responsible for 19 nature reserves, nine of which lie within the Brecon Beacons, while the Gwent Wildlife Trust manages one reserve in the area, Strawberry Cottage Wood. The majority of these sites are designated as Sites of Special Scientific Interest (SSSIs) and are also listed in the tables above.

Reserve	Grid ref	SSSI	Main interests
Cae Bryn Tywarch	SN853267	Yes	Meadow
Craig y Rhiwarth	SN846159	Yes	Limestone woodland, whitebeam
Cwm Claisfer	SO142166	No	Woodland
Cwm Oergwm	SO061235	Yes	Woodland
Darren Fawr	SO022102	Yes	Limestone scree, whitebeam
Daudraeth Illtyd	SN967256	Yes	Raised mire, pools
Pwll y Wrach	SO165326	Yes	Woodland, dormice
The Byddwn	SO087277	No	Former railway line
Trewalkin Meadow	SO155309	No	Meadow
Strawberry Cottage Wood	SO312215	Yes	Woodland

COED CADW RESERVES

Coed Cadw (Woodland Trust in Wales) own 10 reserves in the Brecon Beacons. Only one of these, Coed Tregib, is a Site of Special Scientific Interest (SSSI).

Reserve	Grid ref	SSSI	Designations
Abertreweren	SN920260	No	Ancient Semi-natural Woodland, Planted Ancient Woodland Site
Coed Cefn	SO226186	No	Ancient Semi-natural Woodland, Ancient Woodland Site, Scheduled Ancient Monument
Coed Glyn Gwennws	SN842137	No	Ancient Semi-natural Woodland
Coed Dyfodol Sarnau	SO022325	No	Ancient Semi-natural Woodland
Coed Letter	SN771305	No	Ancient Woodland Site, Planted Ancient Woodland Site
Coed Tregib	SN641217	Yes	Ancient Semi-natural Woodland
Great Triley Wood	SO311181	No	None
Park Wood	SO166346	No	Ancient Woodland Site, Planted Ancient Woodland Site
Punchbowl	SO281117	No	Ancient Semi-natural Woodland
Rook Wood	SO218407	No	Ancient Semi-natural Woodland, Ancient Woodland Site, Planted Ancient Woodland Site

GEOLOGICAL CONSERVATION REVIEW SITES

The Geological Conservation Review (GCR) identified sites of national and international importance which show the key elements of Britain's geology. There is now an inventory of over 3,000 Review Sites, selected for around 100 categories, known as the GCR 'blocks', encompassing the range of geological and geomorphological features.

GCR site name	GCR block
Abercriban Quarries	Non-marine Devonian
Afon Mellte and Afon Hepste	Fluvial geomorphology of Wales
Afon y Waen	Non-marine Devonian
Afon y Waen (fish)	Silurian-Devonian Chordata
Baltic Quarry	Dinantian of southern England and South Wales
Black Mountain	Fluvial geomorphology of Wales
Black Mountain (Mynydd Du)	Quaternary of Wales
Blaen Onneu Quarry	Dinantian of southern England and South Wales
Brynmawr Road Cutting	Westphalian
Clydach Halt Lime Works	Dinantian of southern England and South Wales
Craig Cerrig Gleisiad	Quaternary of Wales
Craig y Cwm	Non-marine Devonian
Craig y Ddinas	Variscan structures of South Wales and the Mendips
Craig y Fro Quarry	Palaeozoic palaeobotany
Craig y Fro Quarry	Non-marine Devonian
Cusop Dingle	Non-marine Devonian
Cwar Glas Quarry	Silurian-Devonian Chordata
Cwar yr Ystrad and Hendre	Dinantian of southern England and South Wales
Cwm Llwch	Quaternary of Wales
Dan yr Ogof	Caves
Duffryn Crawnon	Non-marine Devonian
Fron Road	Llandovery
Gilwern	Dinantian of southern England and South Wales
Heol Senni Quarry	Non-marine Devonian
Heol Senni Quarry	Silurian–Devonian Chordata
Hepste and Mellte Valleys	Karst
Little Neath River Caves	Caves

GCR site name	GCR block
Llammarch Dingle	Namurian of England and Wales
Llanelly Quarry	Dinantian of southern England and South Wales
Llanfihangel Moraine	Quaternary of Wales
Llanover Quarry	Palaeozoic palaeobotany
Llyn y Fan Fach	Mass movement
Mynydd Llangatwg Caves	Caves
Mynydd Llangynidr	Karst
Nant Glais Caves	Caves
Nant Llech	Westphalian
Nant Llech Plant Beds	Palaeozoic palaeobotany
Neath, Mellte and Sychryd	Namurian of England and Wales
Odynau Tyle'r Bont	Dinantian of southern England and South Wales
Ogof Draenen	Caves
Ogof Ffynnon Ddu Area	Caves
Pantymaes Quarry	Non-marine Devonian
Pontneddfechan	Westphalian
Porth yr Ogof	Caves
Sawdde Gorge	Ludlow
Sawdde Gorge	Wenlock
Sawdde Gorge	Non-marine Devonian
Siambre Ddu	Caves
Traeth Mawr	Quaternary of Wales

Appendix 2

Organisations and Contacts

There are numerous organisations concerned with British natural history and the countryside in general – far too many to list here. The following list therefore covers those especially relevant to the Brecon Beacons, or to topics covered in this book. Details of other organisations mentioned in the text can easily be found on the internet. All contact information was correct at the time of publication, but it should be noted that smaller organisations may change their contact address more frequently than larger bodies and may not be able to respond to enquiries as quickly.

AMPHIBIAN AND REPTILE CONSERVATION TRUST
The Trust is committed to conserving amphibians and reptiles and saving the disappearing habitats on which they depend. They have staff based in South Wales.
655A Christchurch Road, Boscombe, Bournemouth, Dorset BH1 4AP. www.arc-trust.org

ANCIENT YEW GROUP
The aims of the Group include raising public awareness of the national and worldwide importance of ancient yews. They have carried out extensive surveys, researching and collating all modern and historical references to trees across Britain.
c/o The Tree Register, 77a Hall End, Wootton, Bedford, MK43 9HP. www.ancient-yew.org

BRECKNOCK WILDLIFE TRUST
A charity working for the protection of the wildlife habitats and species in the old county of Brecknock.
Lion House, Bethel Square, Brecon, Powys, Wales, United Kingdom, LD3 7AY. www.brecknockwildlifetrust.org.uk

BRECON BEACONS NATIONAL PARK AUTHORITY
The duty of the Authority is to protect the natural beauty of the National Park, help visitors enjoy and understand it and foster the wellbeing of local people.
Plas y Ffynnon, Cambrian Way, Brecon, Powys, LD3 7HP. www.breconbeacons.org

BRITISH BRYOLOGICAL SOCIETY
The Society exists to promote the study of mosses and liverworts and has published the only modern field guide to mosses and liverworts of Britain and Ireland, enabling accurate identification in the field.
6 Church View, Wootton, Northampton NN4 7LJ. www.britishbryologicalsociety.org.uk

BRITISH LICHEN SOCIETY
The Society's aims are to promote and advance the teaching and study of lichens, to encourage and actively support the conservation of lichens, and to raise public awareness of the beauty of lichens and of their importance as indicators of the health of our environment.
c/o Deptartment of Botany, Natural History Museum, London SW7 5BD. www.thebls.org.uk

BUTTERFLY CONSERVATION
The charity is devoted to saving butterflies, moths and their habitats throughout the UK. The South Wales Branch runs guided walks, workshops, lectures and moth-trapping across the area.
South Wales Chairman, 6 Tai Canol, Llangorse, Brecon, Powys, LD3 7UR. www.southwales-butterflies.org.uk

CANAL AND RIVER TRUST
Formerly British Waterways, the charity is entrusted with the care of over 3,000 km of the inland waterways network in England and Wales.
South Wales and Severn Waterways, The Dock Office, Commercial Road, Gloucester GL1 2EB. www.canalrivertrust.org.uk

COED CADW (Woodland Trust in Wales)
The Trust wants to see a country rich in native woods and trees, enjoyed and valued by everyone.
3 Cooper's Yard, Curran Rd, Cardiff, CF10 5NB. www.woodlandtrust.org.uk

LLANGORSE RINGING GROUP
The Group was formed in 1978 and is affiliated to the British Trust for Ornithology. To date it has ringed some 58,000 birds of 102 species, all but a few hundred of these at the lake itself.
Group secretary: Jerry Lewis. jmsl2587@yahoo.co.uk

NATIONAL MUSEUM OF WALES
The Museum is an independent chartered body and a registered charity which receives its principal funding through grant-in-aid from the Welsh Government.
National Museum Cardiff, Cathays Park, Cardiff CF10 3NP. www.museumwales.ac.uk

NATIONAL TRUST
Founded in 1895 with the aim of saving the nation's heritage and open spaces, the Trust is currently running the Brecon Beacons Appeal to help meet the costs of managing the land it owns in the area.
Trinity Square, Llandudno, Conwy, LL30 2DE. www.nationaltrust.org.uk/brecon-beacons-central

NATURAL RESOURCES WALES
A Welsh Government sponsored body, responsible for the management of the natural resources of Wales. Formed from a merger of the Countryside Council for Wales, Environment Agency Wales, and Forestry Commission Wales.
Tŷ Cambria, 29 Newport Road, Cardiff, CF24 0TP. naturalresourceswales.gov.uk

PEOPLE'S TRUST FOR ENDANGERED SPECIES
The Trust was founded in 1977 with the aim of helping to ensure a future for many species of endangered creatures worldwide. One of its top priorities is the conservation of UK mammals and key cultural habitats, including orchards.
15 Cloisters House, 8 Battersea Park Road, London SW8 4BG. www.ptes.org

VINCENT WILDLIFE TRUST
A charity working to safeguard the future of mammals in Britain and Ireland, specialising in the conservation of rare or 'difficult to track' mammals, such as bats.
3 & 4 Bronsil Courtyard, Eastnor, Ledbury, Herefordshire HR8 1EP. www.vwt.org.uk

WYE AND USK FOUNDATION
The Foundation is a charity concerned with restoring the habitat, water quality and fisheries of the rivers Wye and Usk. Rivers trusts, like the Foundation, now represent catchments across a large part of England and Wales and their work is coordinated by the Rivers Trust. This is a completely separate organisation from the Canal and River Trust.
Coach House, Old Rectory, Llanstephan, Brecon, Powys LD3 0YR. www.wyeuskfoundation.org

References and Further Reading

The following list represents the main printed sources consulted during the preparation of this book. For reasons of space it does not include website references, specifically the various citations and management prescriptions for designated sites, but these are relatively easy to find. It also does not include unpublished material provided by staff of the various conservation agencies.

Adams, J. and Faure, H., eds. (1992) *Review and Atlas of Palaeovegetation: preliminary land ecosystem maps of the world since the Last Glacial Maximum*. Quaternary Environments Network. Oak Ridge National Laboratory, Tennessee. http://www.esd.ornl.gov/projects/qen/adams1.html.

Adams, J., Maslin, M. and Thomas, E. (1999) Sudden climate transitions during the Quaternary. *Progress in Physical Geography* **23** (1).

A'Hara, S., Samuel, S. and Cottrell, J. (2009) The role of DNA-fingerprinting in the conservation of the native black poplar. *British Wildlife* **21**, 110–15.

Alexander, K. N. A., and Harper, J. F. (2007) *Abida secale* (Drapanaud) in Wales. *Journal of Conchology* **39**, 481.

Aquatic Warbler Conservation Team (1999) World population, trends and threat status of the aquatic warbler *Acrocephalus paludicola*. *Vogelwelt* **120**, 65–85.

Babbs, H. (2013) The Woollen Line Gardening Blog. *The Guardian*, April 17.

Barclay, W. J, Taylor, K. and Thomas, L. P. (1988) *Geology of the South Wales Coalfield, Part V. The Country Around Merthyr Tydfil*, 3rd edition. Sheet memoir, England and Wales, British Geological Survey; sheet 231. HMSO, London.

Barker, G. (1985) *Prehistoric Farming in Europe*. Cambridge University Press, Cambridge.

Barrett, W. B. (1885) A contribution towards a Flora of Breconshire. *Journal of Botany* **1885**, 39–44, 83–9, 107–12, 145–9.

Beebee, T. (2001) British wildlife and human numbers: the ultimate conservation issue? *British Wildlife* **13** (1).

Bennion, H. and Appleby, P. (1999) An assessment of recent environmental change in Llangorse Lake using palaeolimnology. *Aquatic Conservation: Marine and Freshwater Ecosystems* **9**, 361–75.

Birks, H. J. B. (1989) Holocene isochrone maps and patterns of tree-spreading in the British Isles. *Journal of Biogeography* **16**, 503–40.

Bontadini, F., Schofield, H, and Naef-Daenzer, B. (2002) Radio-tracking reveals that lesser horseshoe bats (*Rhinolophus hipposideros*) forage in woodland. *Journal of Zoology* **258**, 281–90.

Borrow, G. H. (1906) *Wild Wales*. Everyman's Library. Dent, London.

Bosanquet, S. (2006) *Tortella bambergeri* (Schimp.) Broth. in the British Isles. *Journal of Bryology* **28**, 5–10.

Bosanquet, S. D. S. and Motley, G. S. (2008) The bryophytes of upland sandstone cliffs in the western and central Brecon Beacons National Park, Wales. CCW Staff Science Report 08/7/4. Countryside Council for Wales, Bangor.

Bradshaw, A. V. and Slater, F. M. (1999) Dead otters: post mortems and tissue analysis. R&D Technical Interim Report. Llysdinam Field Centre, Cardiff School of Biosciences, Cardiff.

Brecon Beacons National Park Authority (2001) Our Natural World: a Local Biodiversity Action Plan for the Brecon Beacons National Park. National Park Authority, Brecon.

Briggs, J. (1996) Canals: wildlife value and restoration issues. *British Wildlife* 7, 365–77.

Briggs, J. (2011) Mistletoe (*Viscum album*): a brief review of its local status with recent observations on its insect associations and conservation problems. *Proceedings of the Cotteswold Naturalists' Field Club*, **45** (2).

Bright, P. W., Morris, P. A. and Mitchell-Jones, A. (2006) *The Dormouse Conservation Handbook*, 2nd edn. English Nature (Natural England), Peterborough.

British Museum (undated) *A geographical Description of Brecknockshire, & of most of the Rarities, Wonders & Remarkable Places therein*. 20 pages in an old hand. Harleian MS 7017, 14.

Britton, J. (1810) The Beauties of England and Wales, Or, Delineations, Topographical, Historical, and Descriptive, Volume 11. Vernor and Hood, London.

Buller, F. (1979) *The Domesday Book of Mammoth Pike*. Hutchinson, London.

Cambridge Phillips, E. (1887) Marten Cat in Breconshire. *The Zoologist* Third Series, Vol XI, p.190. Simpkin, Marshall & Co., London.

Camden, W. (1607) *Britannia*. English translation by Philemon Holland. London.

Carr, S. J., Coleman, C. G., Humpage, A. J. and Shakesby, R. A., eds. (2007) *The Quaternary of the Brecon Beacons: Field Guide*. Quaternary Research Association, London.

Caseldine, A. (1990) *Environmental Archaeology in Wales*. St David's University College, Lampeter.

Chambers, F. M. (1982) Two radiocarbon-dated pollen diagrams from high altitude blanket peats in South Wales. *Journal of Ecology* **70**, 445–59.

Chambers, F. M. (1983) Three radiocarbon-dated pollen diagrams from upland peats north-west of Merthyr Tydfil, south Wales. *Journal of Ecology* **71**, 475–87.

Chater, A. O. (1986) The flora of Ceredigion churchyards (vc. 46). *Botanical Society of the British Isles Welsh Bulletin* **43**, 24–31.

Chatwin, B. (1982) *On the Black Hill*. Viking Press, New York.

Children, G. and Nash, G. (2001) *The Prehistoric Sites of Breconshire*. Logaston Press, Almeley.

Claridge, M. F. and Nixon, G. A. (1986) *Oncopsis flavicollis* (L.) associated with tree birches (*Betula*): a complex of biological species or a host plant utilization polymorphism? *Biological Journal of the Linnean Society* **27**, 381–97.

Cleal, C. J. and Thomas, B. A. (1995) *Palaeozoic Palaeobotany of Great Britain*. Geological Conservation Review Series 9. Chapman & Hall, London.

Collis, J. S. (1947) *Down to Earth*. Jonathan Cape, London.

Condry, W. (1981) *The Natural History of Wales*. New Naturalist 66. Collins, London.

Conolly, A. (1994) Castles and abbeys in Wales: refugia for 'medieval' medicinal plants. *Botanical Journal of Scotland* **46**, 628–36.

Conway, J. S. and Onslow, E. (1999) The impact of grazing management on limestone pavements in Wales. CCW Contract Science Report 346. Countryside Council for Wales, Bangor.

Cooke, J. A. L. (1967) New and rare British spiders. *Journal of Natural History* **1**, 135–48.

Cooper, F. (2006) The Black Poplar: Ecology, History and Conservation. Windgather Press, Bollington.

Cosgrove, P. J., Hastie, L. C. and Young, M. R. (2000) Freshwater pearl mussels in peril. *British Wildlife* **11**, 340–7.

Cottrell, J. (2004) Conservation of black poplar (*Populus nigra* L.). Forestry Commission Information Note 57.

Cowx, I. G. and Fraser, D. (2003) Monitoring the Atlantic Salmon. Conserving Natura 2000 Rivers: Monitoring Series 7. English Nature, Peterborough.

Cragga, B. A., Frya, J. C., Bacchusa Z. and Thurleya S. S. (1980) The aquatic vegetation of Llangorse Lake, Wales. Department of Applied Biology, University of Wales Institute of Science and Technology, Cardiff.

Cragg-Hine, D. and Hatton-Ellis, T. (1999) Lamprey habitat assessment using RHS in the River Usk. CCW Contract Science Report 365. Countryside Council for Wales, Bangor.

Crawford, L., Yeomans, W. E. and Adams, C. E. (2006) The impact of introduced signal crayfish *Pacifastacus leniusculus* on stream invertebrate communities. *Aquatic Conservation* **16**, 611–21.

Crofts, A. and Jefferson, R. G., eds. (1994) *The Lowland Grassland Management Handbook*. English Nature/The Wildlife Trusts, Peterborough.

Crowther, K. A. and Aitchison, I. W. (1996) Biological survey of common land no. 30: Brecknockshire. A survey of the biological characteristics and management of common land. CCW Contract Science Report 147. Countryside Council for Wales, Bangor.

Cundale, G. C. (1980) Llangorse Lake is dying: fact or fantasy? *Nature in Wales* **17**, 71–9.

Daggett, J. (2006) Cwm Sere stoneflies hit high notes on stridulation songs. Recorders Newsletter, Biodiversity Information Service for Powys and Brecon Beacons National Park **2**, 12.

Dance, S. P. (1972) Vertical range of molluscs on Ben Lawers, Scotland. *Journal of Conchology* **27**, 509–15.

Davies, M. (1967) *Brecon Beacons*. National Park Guide 5. HMSO, London.

Davies, W. (1814) A General View of the Agricultural Economy of South Wales (2 volumes). London.

Deacon, J. (1997) Identification of limestone pavements in Wales and their flora. CCW Contract Science Report 159. Countryside Council for Wales, Bangor.

Decu, V. G. and Iliffe, T. M. (1983) A review of the terrestrial cavernicolous fauna of Romania. *Bulletin of the National Speleological Society* **45**, 86–97.

Defoe, D. (1724–27) A Tour Thro' the Whole Island of Great Britain, Divided into Circuits or Journies. Edited by G. D. H. Cole; Dent, London, 1927.

Demars, B. O. L. and Britton, A. (2011) Assessing the impacts of small scale hydroelectric schemes on rare bryophytes and lichens. *Scottish Natural Heritage Commissioned Report* **421**.

De Vere, N. (2009) New trees are taking root in Britain. *Ardd: National Botanic Garden of Wales Magazine*, summer issue.

Dipper, F. (2001) *Extraordinary Fish*. Dorling Kindersley, London.

Doward, J. (2013) Fears over future of lamb farming as prices fall and imports soar. *The Observer*, 3 February.

Drake, C. M., Hewitt, S. M. and Godfrey, A. (2010) Flies of exposed riverine sediments. *British Wildlife* **21**, 320–5.

Dry Stone Walling Association of Great Britain (2007) Dry stone walls and wildlife. DSWA, Milnthorpe.

Dudman, A. A. and Richards, A. J. (1997) *Dandelions of Great Britain and Ireland*. BSBI Handbooks for Field Identification 9. Botanical Society of the British Isles, London.

Dyson, C. (2009) Floodplain habitats in Wales and their potential for delivering multiple benefits: a pilot study in the Usk catchment using GIS. Countryside Council for Wales South & East Region.

Eddington, J. (1977) Biospeleology of Dan-Yr-Ogof. *Transactions of the British Cave Research Association* **4**, 331–41.

Edington, J. M. (1967) Report on Cwm Sere and Cwm Llwch. Unpublished report, Zoology Department, University College, Cardiff.

Edwards, D. (1970) Further observations on the Lower Devonian Plant, *Gosslingia breconensis* Heard. *Philosophical Transactions of the Royal Society of London B* **258**, 225–43.

Edwards, S. R. (2012) *English Names for British Bryophytes*, 4th edn. British Bryological Society, Wootton.

Ellis, G. (2009) Mapping and cataloguing the limestone pavements of the Brecon Beacons National Park. Brecon Beacons National Park Authority.

Ellis, R. G. (1991) Welsh plant records 1988. *BSBI Welsh Bulletin* **51**.

Evans, R. (2002) Blast from the past. *Smithsonian Magazine*, July issue.

Evans, S. and Holden, E. (2003) Collation of data and information on mycologically important semi-natural grasslands in Wales. Report to Countryside Council for Wales, Bangor.

Ford, T. D., ed. (1989) *Limestones and Caves of Wales*. Cambridge University Press, Cambridge.

Foulds, A. (2006) Berthlwyd Farm Hay Meadows Project hay meadow survey 2006. Unpublished report to the National Trust.

Foulds, A. (2007) Berthlwyd Farm Hay Meadows Project hay meadow survey 2007. Unpublished report to the National Trust.

Fowles, A. (1994) A provisional checklist of the invertebrates recorded from Wales. 1. False scorpions, harvestmen and spiders. Countryside Council for Wales.

Fox, A. D. and Cham, S. A. (1994) Status, habitat use and conservation of the scarce blue-tailed damselfly *Ischnura pumilio*. *Biological Conservation* **68**, 115–22.

Fuller, R. J., Atkinson, P. W., Garnet, M. C. *et al.* (2006) Breeding bird communities in the upland margins (ffridd) of Wales in the mid-1980s. *Bird Study* **53**, 177–86.

Geodata Institute (2005) Fluvial audit of the upper Usk tributaries. Unpublished report to Countryside Council for Wales, Bangor.

George, T. N. (1926) The Carboniferous limestone (Avonian) succession of a portion of the North Crop of the South Wales coalfield. *Quarterly Journal of the Geological Society* **83**, 38–95.

Gibbs, D. J. (2008) Monitoring invertebrate features on SSSI – *Donacia bicolora* at Llangorse Lake, Breconshire. CCW Contract Science Report 813. Countryside Council for Wales, Bangor.

Gilbert, O. (2001) Wildlife report: lichens. *British Wildlife* **12**, (4).

Goodier, R. (1967) Welsh mountain spiders. *Nature in Wales* **10** (3), 106–14.

Goodier, R. (1967) Welsh mountain beetles. *Nature in Wales* **11** (2), 57–67.

Green, M. (2007) Welsh Ring Ouzel Survey 2006. *Welsh Birds* **5** (1), 37–41.

Griffith, G. W., Bratton, J. L. and Easton, G. L. (2004) Charismatic megafungi: the conservation of waxcap grasslands. *British Wildlife* **15** (3), 31–43.

Griffith, G. W., Easton, G. L. and Jones, A. W. (undated) *Ecology and Diversity of Waxcap (Hygrocybe* spp.) *Fungi*. Institute of Biological Sciences, University of Wales Aberystwyth.

Griffiths, B. M. (1939) Early references to waterblooms in British lakes. *Proceedings of the Linnean Society (London)* **151**, 14–19.

Griffiths, J. (1967) Summer flocks of mute swans in Breconshire. *Nature in Wales* **10** (3).

Griffiths, S. W., Collen, P. and Armstrong, J. D. (2004) Competition for shelter among overwintering signal crayfish and juvenile Atlantic salmon. *Journal of Fish Biology* **63**, 436–47.

Grogan, A. L., Philcox, C. K., Macdonald, D. W. (2001) Nature conservation advice in relation to otters. In Highways Agency, *Design Manual for Roads and Bridges. Volume 10, Section 4*. Department of Transport, London.

Guan, R. Z. and Wiles, P. R. (1997) Ecological impact of introduced crayfish on benthic fishes in a British lowland river. *Conservation Biology* **11**, 641–7.

Guile, D. P. M. (1965) The vegetation of the Brecon Beacons National Park. Unpublished PhD thesis, University of Cardiff.

Gunn, J., Hardwick, P. and Wood, P. J. (2000) The invertebrate community of the Peak–Speedwell cave system, Derbyshire, England: pressures and considerations for conservation management. *Aquatic Conservation: Marine & Freshwater Ecosystems* **10**, 353–69.

Gunther, R. W. T. (ed.) (1945) *Life and Letters of Edward Lhuyd 1660–1709*. Printed for the subscribers, Oxford.

Hansard, G. A. (1834). *Trout and Salmon Fishing in Wales*. London.

Harding, P. T. (2007) Baseline survey of the woodlouse *Armadillidium pictum* on Tarren yr Esgob, Black Mountains (East) SSSI. Countryside Council for Wales Contract No: FC 73-01-576.

Harding, P. T. and Sutton, S. L. (1985) *Woodlice in Britain and Ireland: Distribution and Habitat*. Institute of Terrestrial Ecology, Huntingdon.

Hardwick, P. and Gunn, J. (1996) The conservation of Britain's limestone cave resource. *Environmental Geology* **28**, 121–7.

Hartnup, R. (2011) *Gold under Bracken: the Land of Wales*. Y Lolfa, Talybont.

Harvey, J. P. and Cowx, I. G. (2003) Monitoring the River, Brook and Sea Lamprey, *Lampetra* fluviatilis, L. planeri and Petromyzon marinus. Conserving Natura 2000 Rivers: Monitoring Series 5, English Nature, Peterborough.

Harvey, L. A. and St Ledger Gordon, D. (1953) *Dartmoor*. New Naturalist 27. Collins, London.

Hazleton, M. (1972) Biological records 1970 and 1971. *Transactions of the Cave Research Group of Great Britain* **14**, 205–31.

Heads, P. A. and Lawton, J. H. (2008) Bracken, ants and extrafloral nectaries, III. How insect herbivores avoid ant predation. *Ecological Entomology* **10**, 29–42.

Heard, A. (1927) On Old Red Sandstone plants showing structure from Brecon (South Wales). *Quarterly Journal of the Geological Society of London* **83**, 195–207.

Henderson, D. M. (1992) A new spiral variant of *Juncus effusus* L. (Juncaceae). *Watsonia* **19**, 133–4.

Henderson, H. M. (1994) The Physicians of Myddfai: the Welsh herbal tradition. *Botanical Journal of Scotland* **46**, 623–7.

Highways Agency (1998) Design Manual for Roads and Bridges. Volume 10, Environmental Design: Section 1, Part 5. Department of Transport, London.

Hill, M. O., Preston, C. D. and Smith, A. J. E. (1994) *Atlas of the Bryophytes of Britain and Ireland*. Volume 3, Mosses. Harley Books, Colchester.

Holmes, N. T. H. (2004) A review of water quality monitoring on the Usk catchment using macrophytes. Environment Agency Wales, South East Area.

Homans, G. C. (1991) *English Villagers of the Thirteenth Century*. Harvard University Press, Cambridge, MA.

Hoskins, W. G. and Stamp, L. D. (1963) *The Common Lands of England and Wales*. New Naturalist 45. Collins, London.

Hughes, G., ed. (1985) Looking around Llanelli. Llanelli Borough Council.

Hughes, T. J. (2006) *Wales's Best One Hundred Churches*. Poetry Wales Press, Bridgend.

Hull International Fisheries Institute (2006) Monitoring of lamprey in the rivers Wye and Usk SACs 2005–2006. Unpublished report to Countryside Council for Wales.

Hyde, H. A. (1961) *Welsh Timber Trees*. National Museum of Wales, Cardiff.

Ingram, G. C. S. and Salmon, H. M. (1957) *The Birds of Brecknock*. Brecknock Society, Brecon.

Jackson, P. and Alexander, K. (1995) A biological survey of Berthlwyd Farm. National Trust, Cirencester.

James, B. D. (1992) *Myddfai, Its Land and Peoples*. Privately published.

Jefferson, G. T., Chapman, P., Carter, J. and Proudlove, G. (2004) The invertebrate fauna of the Ogof Ffynnon Ddu cave system, Powys, South Wales. *Cave and Karst Science* **31** (2), 63–76.

Jenkins, D. C. (ed.) (1986) Selections from the Diary of Thomas Jenkins of Llandeilo 1826–1870. Dragon Books, Bala.

Joint Nature Conservation Committee (2007) Second Report by the UK under Article 17 on the implementation of the Habitats Directive from January 2001 to December 2006. JNCC, Peterborough.

Jones, B. (2007) A framework to set conservation objectives and achieve favourable condition in Welsh upland SSSIs. Countryside Council for Wales.

Jones, B., Gliddon, C. and Good, J. E. G. (2001) The conservation of variation in geographically peripheral populations: *Lloydia serotina* (Liliaceae) in Britain. *Biological Conservation* **101**, 147–56.

Jones, D. (2003) *Welsh Wildlife*. Y Lolfa, Talybont.

Jones, E. V. (1973) Perlau Taf. In *The Carmarthenshire Historian*, **10**. Carmarthenshire Community Council, Carmarthen.

Kennedy, C. E. J. and Southwood, T. R. E. (1984) The number of species of insects associated with British trees: a re-analysis. *Journal of Animal Ecology* **53**, 455–78.

Kerney, M. (1999) Atlas of the Land and Freshwater Molluscs of Britain and Ireland. Harley Books, Colchester.

Killeen, I. J. (2007) A survey of Welsh rivers supporting populations of the freshwater pearl mussel *Margaritifera margaritifera* (L., 1758). Report to Countryside Council for Wales.

Killeen, I. J. and Oliver, P. G. (1998) The status and distribution of the freshwater pearl mussel (*Margaritifera margaritifera* [L., 1758]) in Wales: report on the 1997 survey. CCW Contract Science Report 185. Countryside Council for Wales, Bangor.

Kilvert, R. F. (1960) *Kilvert's Diary: Selections from the Diary of the Rev. F. Kilvert ...* Chosen, edited and introduced by William Plomer. Jonathan Cape, London.

King, J. and Varney, H. (1994) *Brecon Beacons National Park Common Land Project*. Brecon Beacons National Park Authority.

Knight, J. K. (2010) *Caerleon Roman Fortress*. Cadw, Cardiff.

Knight, L. (undated) *Cave Life in Britain*. Freshwater Biological Association, Far Sawrey.

Ladich, F. (1989) Sound production by the river bullhead, *Cottus gobio* L. (Cottidae, Teleostei). *Journal of Fish Biology* 35, 531–8.

Langan, S., Cooksley, S., Young, M. *et al.* (2007) The management and conservation of the freshwater pearl mussel in Scottish catchments designated as Special Areas of Conservation or Sites of Special Scientific Interest. Scottish Natural Heritage Commissioned Report 249.

Larson, D. W., Matthes, U. and Kelly, P. E. (2005) *Cliff Ecology: Pattern and Process in Cliff Ecosystems*. Cambridge University Press, Cambridge.

Lawley, M. (undated) A social history and biographical history of British and Irish field-bryologists. British Bryological Society.

Leake, J. R., Mckendrick, S. L., Bidartondo, M. and Read, D. J. (2004) Symbiotic germination and development of the myco-heterotroph *Monotropa hypopitys* in nature and its requirement for locally distributed *Tricholoma* spp. *New Phytologist* **163**, 405–23.

Lenton, T. M., Crouch, M., Johnson, M., Pires, N. and Dolan, L. (2012) First plants cooled the Ordovician. *Nature Geoscience* **5**, 86–9.

Leroy, S. A. G. and Simms, M. J. (2006) Iron Age to Medieval entomogamous vegetation and *Rhinolophus hipposideros* roost in south-eastern Wales (UK). *Palaeogeography, Palaeoclimatology, Palaeoecology* **237**, 4–18.

Lewis, S. (1833) *A Topographical Dictionary of Wales*. S. Lewis, London.

Ley, A. (1874–86) Plants of Breconshire. *Botanical Record Club Report* 1874, 80–6; 1881–82, 243–6; 1883, 53–63; 1884–86, 144.

Ley, A. (1895a) A new form of *Pyrus*. *Journal of Botany* **33**, 84.

Ley, A. (1895b) Recent additions to the flora of Breconshire. *Journal of Botany* **33**, 135–7.

Light, J. J. and Belcher, J. H. (1968) A snow microflora in the Cairngorm Mountains, Scotland. *British Phycological Bulletin* **3**, 471–3.

Liles, G. and Colley, R. (2000) Otter *Lutra lutra* road deaths in Wales: identification of accident blackspots and establishment of mitigation measures. Environment Agency Wales, Aberystwyth.

Linnard, W. (1982) *Welsh Woods and Forests*. National Museum of Wales, Cardiff.

Linnard, W. (1984) Bogwood. *Nature in Wales* N.S. **3** (1&2), 74–8.

Lousley, J. E. (1950) *Wild Flowers of Chalk and Limestone*. New Naturalist 16. Collins, London.

Lovegrove, R. (2007) *Silent Fields: The Long Decline of a Nation's Wildlife*. Oxford University Press, Oxford.

Lovegrove, R., Williams, G. and Williams, I. (1994) *Birds in Wales*. Poyser, London.

Luiselli, L., Capula, M., Rugiero, L. and Anibaldi, C. (1994) Habitat choice by melanistic and cryptically coloured morphs of the adder, *Vípera berus*. *Bolletino di Zoologia* **61**, 213–16.

Mabey, R. (1996) *Flora Britannica*. Sinclair-Stevenson, London.

McGrail, S. (1978) *Logboats of England and Wales*. National Maritime Museum, London.

Majerus, M. (2002) *Moths*. New Naturalist 90. HarperCollins, London.

Malkin, B. H. (1804) The Scenery, Antiquities, and Biography of South Wales. Longman, London.

Mapstone, L. (2009) Landscapes for lessers: phase 2 project report. CCW Science Report 896. Countryside Council for Wales, Bangor.

Marcher Apple Network (2004) Apples of the Welsh Marches: Old Varieties Grown in the Traditional Orchards of the West Midlands and Wales. MAN.

Marren, P. (2012) Atlas of British and Irish Hawkweeds (book review). *British Wildlife* **23** (3).

Marrs, R. H. and Watt, A. S. (2006) Biological flora of the British Isles 245: *Pteridium aquilinum* (L.) Kuhn. *Journal of Ecology* **94**, 1272–321.

Mason, E. J. (1975) Portrait of the Brecon Beacons and Surrounding Area. Robert Hale, London.

Mason-Williams, A. and Benson-Evans, K. (1958) A Preliminary Investigation into the Bacterial and Botanical Flora of Caves in South Wales. Cave Research Group, Berkhamsted.

Massey, M. E. (1976) *The Birds of Breconshire*. Brecknock Naturalists Trust, Brecon.

Maxwell, H. (1897) *Holly Meadows. Notes and Queries* 8th Series, Vol XI, May 22nd, p.411.

May, L., Dudley, B., Spears, B. M. and Hatton-Ellis, T. W. (2008) Nutrient modelling and a nutrient budget for Llangorse Lake. CCW Contract Science Report 831. Countryside Council for Wales, Bangor.

May, L., Spears, B. M., Dudley, B. J. and Hatton-Ellis, T. W. (2010) The importance of nitrogen limitation in the restoration of Llangorse Lake, Wales, UK. *Journal of Environmental Monitoring* **12**, 338–46.

Meade, R. and Wheeler, B. D. (1990) Illtyd Pools, Brecon: description and conservation. *New Phytologist* **115** (1), 187–99.

Meyer, J. L., and Wallace, J. B. (2001) Lost linkages and lotic ecology: rediscovering small streams. In M. C. Press, N. J. Huntly and S. Levin, eds., *Ecology: Achievement and Challenge*. Blackwell Science, Oxford, pp. 295–317.

Milne-Redhead, E. (1990) The B.S.B.I. Black Poplar survey, 1973–88. *Watsonia* **18**, 1–5.

Monbiot, G. (2012) The great riches of our seas have been depleted and forgotten. *The Guardian*, 7 September.

Monteith, D. T., ed. (1996) Integrated classification and assessment of lakes phase III: final Report. CCW Science Report 167. Countryside Council for Wales, Bangor.

Morgan, I. (1992) Interim notes on the status of the pine marten in South and Mid Wales. *Llanelli Naturalists Newsletter* Winter 1992/93.

Morris, M. G. (1965) Records of weevils (Col., Curculionidae) from Wales and Monmouthshire, including *Otiorhynchus nodosus* (Müll) from the Brecon Beacons. *Entomologists' Gazette* **16**, 125–8.

Motley, G. and Bosanquet, S. D. S. (2003) Summary of recent bryological recording at waterbodies in South Wales, with particular reference to populations of the priority BAP species *Riccia huebeneriana* (Violet crystalwort) and other scarce or local species. Unpublished CCW report. Countryside Council for Wales, Bangor.

Motley, G. S. and Graham, J. J. (2001) The Bryophyte flora of the area around Bannau Sir Gaer and Llyn Y Fan. *Llanelli Naturalists Newsletter*, April 2001 (5).

Mullard, J. (2006) *Gower*. New Naturalist 99. HarperCollins, London.

Mullard, J. (2010) New Naturalist: Brecon Beacons. *Natur Cymru* **35**, 22–7.

Murchison, R. I. (1839) *The Silurian System*. John Murray, London.

National Caving Association (1995) *Cave Conservation Policy*. The Association, London.

Nelson, E. C. (1993) Corkscrew rush (*Juncus effusus* L. forma *spiralis* (J. McNab) Hegi) (Juncaceae) in Ireland and Britain. *Watsonia* **19**, 275–8.

Norton, M. G., Savage, D. and Standing, P. A. (1967) The Little Neath River Cave, South Wales. *Proceedings of the University of Bristol Spelaeological Society* **11** (2), 186–200.

Orange, A. (1996) A survey of lichens in Welsh parklands. CCW Contract Science Report 138. Countryside Council for Wales, Bangor.

Orange, A. (2002) Literature review of upland saxicolous lichen and bryophyte communities Scottish Natural Heritage Commissioned Report F01AC201/1.

Orange, A. (2008) Saxicolous lichen and bryophyte communities in Upland Britain. JNCC Report 404.

Ormerod, S. J. and Tyler, S. J. (1991) Exploitation of prey by a river bird, the dipper, *Cinclus cinclus* (L.), along acidic and circumneutral streams in upland Wales. *Freshwater Biology* **25**,105–16.

Owen, H. W. and Morgan, R. (2007) *Dictionary of the Place-names of Wales*. Gomer Press, Ceredigion.

Owen, T. M. (1969) Historical aspects of peat

cutting in Wales. In Jenkins, G., ed., *Studies in Folk Life*. RKP, London, pp. 123–55.

Page, C. N. (1988) *Ferns*. New Naturalist 74. Collins, London.

Pakeman, R. J. and Marrs, R. H. (1992) The conservation value of bracken *Pteridium aquilinum* dominated communities in the UK, and an assessment of the ecological impact of bracken expansion or its removal. *Biological Conservation* **62**, 101–14.

Pakeman, R. J. and Marrs, R. H. (1996) Modelling the effects of climate change on the growth of bracken (*Pteridium aquilinum*) in Britain. *Journal of Applied Ecology* **33**, 561–75.

Parker, A. G., Goudie, A. S., Anderson, D. E. and Bonsall, C. (2002) A review of the mid-Holocene elm decline in the British Isles. *Progress in Physical Geography* **26**, 1–45.

Parry, D. and Westwood S. (1996) Berthlwyd Hayfields (part SSSI): site description. CCW unpublished document. Countryside Council for Wales, Bangor.

Peers, M. F. (1985) *Birds of Radnorshire and mid-Powys*. M. Peers, Llangammarch Wells.

Peers, M. F. and Shrubb, M. (1990) *Birds of Breconshire*. Brecknock Wildlife Trust, Brecon.

Peterken, G. F. (1993) *Woodland Conservation and Management*. Chapman & Hall, London.

Peterken, G. F. (2009) Woodland origins of meadows. *British Wildlife* **20**, 161–70.

Philcox, C. K., Grogan, A. L. and Macdonald, D. W. (1999) Patterns of otter *Lutra lutra* road mortality in Britain. *Journal of Applied Ecology* **36**, 748–61.

Philip, A. (1986) Heads, bracken, ants and extrafloral nectaries. IV. Do wood ants (*Formica lugubris*) protect the plant against insect herbivores? *Journal of Animal Ecology* **55**, 795–809.

Phillips, E. C. (1899) *The Birds of Breconshire*. Edwin Davis, Brecon.

Phillips, R. W. (1892) Notes on the Flora of Breconshire. *Journal of Botany* **1892**, 854–5.

Plantlife (2005) *Looking after Rare Mosses and Liverworts Beside Lakes and Reservoirs*. Back from the Brink Management Series. Plantlife, Salisbury.

Pratt-Heaton, C. (1999) Visitors and visitor pressure in the Brecon Beacons National Park. Occasional Paper from the Brecon Beacons National Park Authority.

Preston, C. D. (1994) *Juncus effusus* var. *spiralis* in the Inner Hebrides. *Watsonia* **20**, 153–4.

Procter, E. (2011) Llanthony Priory in the Vale of Ewyas: the landscape impact of a medieval priory in the Welsh Marches. *Archaeology in Wales* **51**.

Pye, H. (2010) Waterfall Country: management plan 2010–2019. Brecon Beacons National Park Authority, Brecon.

Quick, H. E. (1938) The Medicinal Leech, *Hirudo medicinalis* Linn. in Breconshire, with notes on other species of Hirudinea found in South Wales. *Proceedings of the Swansea Scientific and Field Naturalists Society* **2**, 12–14.

Rackham, O. (2006) *Woodlands*. New Naturalist 100. HarperCollins, London.

Radley, J. (1961) Holly as a winter feed. *Agricultural History Review* **9**, 89–92.

Railton, C. L. (1953) *The Ogof Ffynnon Ddu Cave System*. Publication 6, Cave Research Group.

Ratcliffe, D. A. (1977) *A Nature Conservation Review: Volume 2, Site Accounts: the Selection of Biological Sites of National Importance to Nature Conservation in Britain*. Cambridge University Press, Cambridge.

Raven, J. and Walters, M. (1956) *Mountain Flowers*. New Naturalist 33. Collins, London.

Read, H. J., ed. (2000) *Veteran Trees: a Guide to Good Management*. Veteran Trees Initiative. English Nature, Peterborough.

Reason, P., Harris, S., Cresswell, P. (1993) Estimating the impact of past persecution and habitat changes on the numbers of badgers *Meles meles* in Britain. *Mammal Review* **23**, 1–15.

Redfern, M. (2011) *Plant Galls*. New Naturalist 117. HarperCollins, London.

Redknap, M. and Lane, A. (1994) The Early Medieval crannog at Llangors, Powys: an interim statement on the 1989–1993 seasons. *International Journal of Nautical Archaeology* **23**, 189–205.

Redwood, P. (1996/7) Crickhowell Manor in 1587. *Brycheiniog* **29**, 15–38.

Reise, H. and Hutchinson, J. M. C. (2009) An earlier record of the slug *Selenochlamys*

ysbryda, from Brecon, UK. *Journal of Conchology* **40**, 103.
Rhodes, J. (2002) A Calendar of the Registers of the Priory of Llanthony by Gloucester 1457–1466, 1501–1525. Bristol and Gloucester Archaeological Society, Gloucester.
Rhys, J. (1901) *Celtic Folklore, Welsh And Manx*. Clarendon Press, Oxford.
Rich, T. C. G. (1999) Distribution and conservation of *Hieracium tavense*, Black Mountain hawkweed. National Museums and Galleries of Wales, Cardiff.
Rich, T. C. G. (2001) Distribution and conservation of *Hieracium asteridiophyllum*, Llangattock hawkweed. National Museums and Galleries of Wales, Cardiff.
Rich, T. C. G. (2001) Distribution and conservation of *Hieracium cillense*, Craig y Cilau hawkweed. National Museums and Galleries of Wales, Cardiff.
Rich, T. C. G. (2002) Conservation of Britain's biodiversity: *Hieracium asteridiophyllum* and *H. cillense* (Asteraceae). *Watsonia* **24**, 101–6.
Rich, T. C. G. (2003) Establishment of a monitoring regime for *Sorbus* species at Craig y Cilau NNR. Unpublished contract report to CCW. Countryside Council for Wales, Bangor.
Rich, T. C. G. (2005) Conservation of Britain's biodiversity: *Hieracium neocoracinum* (Asteraceae), Craig Cerrig-gleisiad hawkweed. *Watsonia* **25**, 283–7.
Rich, T. C. G. and Proctor, M. C. F. (2009) Some new British and Irish *Sorbus* L. taxa (Rosaceae). *Watsonia* **27**, 207–16.
Rich, T. C. G. and Rumsey, F. (2004) *Hymenophyllum tunbrigense* Hymenophyllaceae. *Curtis's Botanical Magazine* **21**, 70–6.
Rich, T. C. G. and Smith, P. A. (2007) Conservation of Britain's Biodiversity: Hieracium cacuminum, Summit Hawkweed (Asteraceae). *Watsonia* **26**, 463–8.
Rich, T. C. G, Motley, G. S. and Kay, Q. O. N. (2005) Population sizes of three rare Welsh endemic *Sorbus* species (Rosaceae). *Watsonia* **25**, 381–8.
Rich, T. C. G., Houston, L., Robertson, A. and Proctor, M. C. F. (2010) *Whitebeams, Rowans and Service Trees of Britain and Ireland*. Botanical Society of the British Isles, London.
Richards, P. W. and Evans, G. B. (1972) Biological flora of the British Isles: *Hymenophyllum*. *Journal of Ecology* **60**, 245–68.
Roach, F. A. (1985) Cultivated Fruits of Britain: Their Origin and History. Blackwell, Oxford.
Roberts, B. F. (2010) Edward Lhwyd in Carmarthenshire. *Carmarthen Antiquary* **46**, 24–43.
Roberts, G. C. S. (1994) The Welsh hill farm: a cultural landscape in decline. *Landscape Research* **19**, 149–50.
Roberts, S. J., Lewis, J. M. S. and Williams, I. T. (1999) Breeding European honey-buzzards in Britain. *British Birds* **92**, 326–45.
Robertson, J., Everett, S. and Berkshire, I. (2008) Manifesto for the wild meadows of Wales. Flora Locale and the Grasslands Trust.
Rogers, A. E. F. and Gault, L. N. (1968) The distribution of sand martins on the River Usk. *Nature in Wales* **11** (1), 15–19.
Rose, F. and Harding, P. T. (1978) Pasture and woodlands in lowland Britain and their importance for the conservation of the epiphytes and invertebrates associated with old trees. Nature Conservancy Council and The Institute of Terrestrial Ecology.
Rotherham, I. D., ed. (2008) *Orchards and Groves: their History, Ecology, Culture and Archaeology*. Landscape Archaeology and Ecology **7**. Wildtrack Publishing, Sheffield.
Rotheroe, M. (2001) A preliminary survey of waxcap grassland indicator species in South Wales. In D. Moore, M. M. Nauta, S. E. Evans and M. Rotheroe, eds., *Fungal Conservation: Issues and Solutions*. Cambridge University Press, Cambridge, pp. 120–35.
Rowson, B. (2010) The rare lapidary snail *Helicigona lapicida* at Dryslwyn Castle, Carmarthenshire. Report to Cadw, October 2010.
Rudeforth, C. C. (1984) *Soils and their Use in Wales*. Soil Survey of England and Wales Bulletin 11. National Soil Resources Institute, Harpenden.

Sadler, J. P., Bell, D. and Hammond, P. M. (2005) Assessment of the distribution of *Bembidion testaceum* and reasons for its decline. Environment Agency Science Report: SC030199/SR.

Saunders, D. (2001) Brecon Beacons National Park. *British Wildlife* **13**, 109–17.

Schlee, D. (2013) CALCH: getting on the trail of Welsh industrial heritage. *The Archaeologist* **87**.

Sharrock, J. T. R. and Sharrock, E. M. (1976) *Rare Birds in Britain and Ireland.* Poyser, Berkhamsted.

Sier, A. R. J. and Scott, W. A., eds. (2008) *Climate Change Impacts: Evidence from ECN Sites.* Centre for Ecology & Hydrology, Lancaster.

Silcock, P., Brunyee, J. and Pring, J. (2012) Changing livestock numbers in the UK Less Favoured Areas: an analysis of likely biodiversity implications. Cumulus Consultants Report prepared for the Royal Society for the Protection of Birds.

Simmons, I. G. (2003) The Moorlands of England and Wales: an Environmental History, 8000 BC – AD 2000. Edinburgh University Press, Edinburgh.

Simms, M. (1988) *Caves and Karst of the Brecon Beacons National Park: a Field Guide.* Cave Studies Series 7. British Cave Research Association.

Simpson, V. R. (1998) A post mortem study of otters (*Lutra lutra*) found dead in south west England. R&D Technical Report W148. Environment Agency, Bristol.

Sinnadurai, P. (2009) The Brecon Beacons National Park: a good place for Glastir Sustainable Land Management Scheme. Brecon Beacons National Park Authority.

Sinnadurai, P. (2011) Beetle bling: warriors of chaos. *Natur Cymru* **39**.

Skellon, K. (2012) '1,000 year-old' Llanfoist tree felled by gales. *South Wales Argus* Friday 6 January.

Skinner, A., Young, M. and Hastie, L. (2003) *Ecology of the Freshwater Pearl Mussel.* Conserving Natura 2000 Rivers: Ecology Series 2. English Nature, Peterborough.

Slater, F. M. (1981) Peat cutting in Mid-Wales: a brief introduction. *Nature in Wales* **17**, 149–52.

Smith, A. G. and Cloutman, E. W. (1988) Reconstruction of Holocene vegetation history in three dimensions at Waun-Fignen-Felen, an upland site in South Wales. *Philosophical Transactions of the Royal Society of London B* **322**, 159–219.

Smith, S. J. (2001) A study of whinchats *Saxicola rubetra* on the moorland edge. *Welsh Birds* **3**, 183–90.

Smith, S. J. and Lawrence, M. (2002) Ringing recoveries at sparrowhawk sites: the impact on whinchats. British Trust for Ornithology, Thetford.

Smulders, M. J. M., Cottrell, J. E., Lefèvre, F. *et al.* (2008) Structure of the genetic diversity in Black Poplar (*Populus nigra* L.) populations across European river systems: consequences for conservation and restoration. *Forest Ecology and Management* **255**, 1388–99.

Southwood, T. R. E. (1961) The numbers of species of insect associated with various trees *Journal of Animal Ecology* **30**, 1–8.

Spray, M. (1981) Holly as fodder in England. *Agricultural History Review* **29**, 97–110.

Stamp, L. D. (1969) *Nature Conservation in Britain.* New Naturalist 49. Collins, London.

Standing, P. and Lloyd, O. C. (1970) Porth yr Ogof, Breconshire. *Proceedings of the University of Bristol Spelaeological Society* **12** (2), 213–29.

Stephens, N. (1990) *Natural Landscapes of Britain from the Air.* Cambridge Air Surveys, Cambridge.

Stringer, R. N. and Davies R. H. (1984) Llygad Llwchwr: an area to keep an eye on (Bryophyte Survey). *Llanelli Naturalists Newsletter*, June.

Stubbs, A. E. and Drake, M. (2001) *British Soldierflies and Their Allies: a Field Guide to the Larger British Brachycera.* British Entomological & Natural History Society, London.

Szweykowski, J., Buczkowska, K., Odrzykoski, I. J. (2005) *Conocephalum salebrosum* (Marchantiopsida, Conocephalaceae): a new Holarctic liverwort species. *Plant Systematics and Evolution* **253**, 133–58.

Tansley, A. G. (1939) *The British Isles and their Vegetation.* Cambridge University Press, Cambridge.

Thorpe, L. (1978) *Gerald of Wales: The Journey Through Wales/The Description of Wales.*

Translated by L. Thorpe. Penguin Classics. Penguin, Harmondsworth, 1978.
Tomlinson, M. L. and Perrow, M. R. (2003) Ecology of the Bullhead. Conserving Natura 2000 Rivers: Ecology Series 4. English Nature, Peterborough.
Toulmin Smith, L. (ed.) (1906) The Itinerary in Wales of John Leland in or about the Years 1536–1539. Vol. 3 of The Itinerary of John Leland in or about the years 1535–1543. George Bell & Sons, London.
Vidal, J. (2005) Wild herds may stampede across Britain under plan for huge reserves. *The Guardian*, 27 October.
Walker, M. J. C. (1982) The late-glacial and Early Flandrian deposits at Traeth Mawr, Brecon Beacons, South Wales. *New Phytologist* **90**, 177–94.
Wallace, A. R. (1847) Capture of *Trichius fasciatus* near Neath. *Zoologist* **5**, 1676.
Wallace, A. R. (1905) *My Life: a Record of Events and Opinions*. Chapman and Hall, London.
Walter, D. (1815) A General View of the Agriculture and Domestic Economy of South Wales. Board of Agriculture.
Ward, A. I. (2005) Expanding ranges of wild and feral deer in Great Britain. *Mammal Review* **35**, 165–73.
Ward, S. D. and Evans, D. F. (1975) The Limestone Pavements of Wales: a Botanical and Conservation Assessment Based on Botanical Criteria. Institute of Terrestrial Ecology, Bangor.
Warburg, E. F. (1957) Some new names in the British flora. *Watsonia* **4**, 41–8.
Waring, P. (1996) The status and ecology of the Silurian moth in Wales. CCW Contract Science Report 140. Countryside Council for Wales, Bangor.
Warren, R. D. and Witter, M. S. (2002) Monitoring trends in bat populations through roost surveys: methods and data from *Rhinolophus hipposideros*. *Biological Conservation* **105**, 255–61.
Watson, J., Hamilton-Smith, E., Gillieson, D. and Kiernan, K. (1997) *Guidelines for Cave and Karst Protection*. IUCN, Cambridge.
Webb, S. and Glading, P. (1998) The ecology and conservation of limestone pavement in Britain. *British Wildlife* **10**, 103–13.

Westcombe, T. (1844) List of plants observed in Brecknockshire and Radnorshire. *Phytologist* **1**, 781.
Wheeler, A. (1977) The history and distribution of the freshwater fishes of the British Isles. *Journal of Biogeography* **4**, 1–24.
Wigginton, M. J., ed. (1999) *Red Data Books of Britain and Ireland 1: Vascular Plants*, 3rd edn. Joint Nature Conservation Committee, Peterborough.
Williams, R. (1989) *People of the Black Mountains*. Chatto & Windus, London.
Willing, M. (2012) The status and distribution of Geyer's whorl snail *Vertigo geyeri* at Craig y Cilau National Nature Reserve in 2011, with a wider search of other sites in south-east Wales supporting base-rich seepages. Unpublished report to CCW. Countryside Council for Wales, Bangor.
Wolton, R. (2008) Where dormice nest in hedgerows. *The Dormouse Monitor*, Spring 2008. People's Trust for Endangered Species, London.
Woodroffe, G. (2001) *The Otter*. Mammal Society, London.
Woods, R. G. (2003) *The Lichen Flora of Brecknock*. R. G. Woods, Builth Wells.
Woods, R. G. (2009) A strategy and action plan for the conservation of lower plants and fungi in Wales 2009–2015. Plantlife International, Salisbury.
Woolmore, R. (2011) *Brecon Beacons National Park. Designation History Series*. Countryside Council for Wales and Natural England.
Wright, P. S. (1980) Soils in Dyfed IV (Llandeilo). Rothamsted Experimental Station.
Young, M. R., Cosgrove, P. J. and Hastie L. C. (2000) The extent of, and causes for, the decline of a highly threatened naiad: *Margaritifera margaritifera*. In G. Bauer and K. Wächtler, eds., *Ecology and Evolutionary Biology of the Freshwater Mussels Unionoidea*. Springer-Verlag, Berlin.
Zuiganov, V., Zotin, A., Nezlin, L. and Tretiakov, V. (1994) *The Freshwater Pearl Mussels and their Relationships with Salmonid Fish*. VNIRO, Moscow.

Indexes

SPECIES INDEX

Page numbers in **bold** include illustrations.

Abida secale (large chrysalis snail) 119
Abramis brama (bream) 240
Accipiter gentilis (goshawk) **283–4**
  nisus (sparrowhawk) 149, 150, 283
Acer campestre (field maple) 261, 340
  pseudoplatanus (sycamore) 162, 341
Achillea millefolium (yarrow) 81 335
Acicula fusca (point snail) 218
Acrocephalus paludicola (aquatic warbler) **236–7**
  schoenobaenus (sedge warbler) 236, 237
  scirpaceus (reed warbler) 237
Actitis hypoleucos (common sandpiper) 142
adder (*vipera berus*) **151–2**
aeshna, common (*Aeshna juncea*) 246, 248
agaric, fly (*Amanita muscaria*) 272, **280**, 281
Agonum assimile (long-horned beetle) 273
Agrostis canina (velvet bent) 102
  capillaris (common bent) 99, 104, 271, 337, 338
  stolonifera (creeping bent) 164
Agrotis exclamationis (heart and dart moth) 273
Alauda arvensis (skylark) 142, 146, 147
Alcedo atthis (kingfisher) 178, **180**, 181, 260
Alces alces (elk) 61
Alchemilla filicaulis (hairy lady's-mantle) 337
  glabra (smooth lady's-mantle) 106
alder (*Alnus glutinosa*) 60, 61, 162, 267–8
Alexanders (*Smyrnium olusatrum*) 81
algae 161, 230–1
  Chlamydomonas nivalis **121–2**

Chroococcus giganteus 209
Synechoccus aeruginosum 209
  elongates 211
blue-green (*Nostoc muscorum*) 209, **231**
filamentous red (*Lemanea fluviatilis*) 161
red (*Hildenbrandia rivularis*) 161
Allium schoenoprasum (wild chives) 126–7
  ursinum (ransoms) 133
Alnus glutinosa (alder) 60, 61, 162, 267–8
Alopecurus aequalis (orange foxtail) 245
  geniculatus (marsh foxtail) 164, 245
Alosa alosa (allis shad) 157, 173, 175
  fallax (twaite shad) 157, **173–4**
Amanita muscaria (fly agaric) 272, **280**, 281
Amblystegium fluviatile (brook-side feather-moss) 161
Anagallis tenella (bog pimpernel) 250, 332
Anas acuta (pintail) 247
  crecca (teal) 258
  penelope (wigeon) 164, 247
  platyrhynchos (mallard) 260
Anastrophyllum hellerianum (Heller's notchwort) 193
Ancylus fluviatilis (freshwater limpet) 227
Andreaea alpina (alpine rock-moss) 109
  rothii falcata (dusky rock-moss) 109
  rupestris (black rock-moss) 109
Andromeda polifolia (bog rosemary) 102
anemone, wood (*Anemone nemorosa*) 131, 263, 318
Anemone nemorosa (wood anemone) 131, 263, 318

Aneugmenus (sawfly) 146
angelica, wild (*Angelica sylvestris*) 332
Anguilla anguilla (eel) 157, 177, 223, 225, 240
Anoectangium aestivum (summer-moss) 109
ant, red wood (*Formica rufus*) 275
  yellow meadow (*Lasius flavus*) 132
Antennaria dioica (mountain everlasting) 130
Anthocoris visci (bug) 349
Anthoxanthum odoratum (sweet vernal-grass) 102, 332, 338
Anthriscus sylvestris (cow-parsley) 132
Anthus petrosus (rock pipit) 142
  pratensis (meadow pipit) 142, 146, 147
  trivialis (tree pipit) 146, 147, 148
Antichaeta analis 250
ants 145–6
  red wood (*Formica rufus*) 275
  yellow meadow (*Lasius flavus*) 132
Apamea monoglypha (dark arches moth) 273
Aphanorhegma patens (spreading earth-moss) 254
Aphileta misera 244
Aphodius lapponum (northern dung beetle) 111
Apium inundatum (lesser marshwort) 163, 245
Apodemus flavicollis (yellow-necked mouse) 277
  sylvaticus (wood mouse) 275, 344
apple 346–8
Apus apus (swift) 142, 215
Aquilegia vulgaris (columbine) 268
Arabidopsis thaliana (thale cress) 81
Archaegonaspis ludensis 23
archangel, yellow (*Lamium galeobdolon*) 133, 263
Archidium alternifolium (clay earth-moss) 256
Arctium minimum (lesser burdock) 133
Arctosa cinerea (wolf spider) **168–9**
Ardea cinerea (grey heron) 177, 178, 245, 260
Argynnis aglaja (dark green fritillary) 133, 144, **145**
Arion ater (large black slug) 113, 117
  intermedius (hedgehog slug) 117–18
  owenii (Inishowen slug) 325–6
  subfuscus (orange-staining dusky slug) 117–18
Armadillidium pictum (woodlouse) **113–14**
Arrhenatherum elatius (false oat grass) 133
Artemisia absinthium (wormwood) 59
  frigida (sagewort) 58
  tridentata (sagebrush) 58
  vulgaris (mugwort) 58, 164
Arum maculatum (lords-and-ladies) 133, 209

Arvicola amphibious (water vole) **59**, 177, 242–3
ash (*Fraxinus*) 43, 93, 162, 261, 265–6, **298**, 299, 341, 346
asphodel, bog (*Narthecium ossifragum*) 102
Aspicilia calcarea (white crustose lichen) 126
Asplenium adiantum-nigrum (black spleenwort) 131
  ruta-muraria (wall-rue) 133, 209
  trichomanes (maidenhair spleenwort) 133, 209
  viride (green spleenwort) 131, 133, 193, 264
Athyrium felix-femina (lady-fern) 133, 161, 264, 267
Atolmis rubricollis (red-necked footman moth) 281
Atropa belladonna (deadly nightshade) 81
auroch (*Bos primigenius*) 61
Austropotamobius pallipes (white-clawed crayfish) **175–7**
avens, mountain (*Dryas octopetala*) 59
  water (*Geum rivale*) 106
  wood (*Geum urbanum*) 132, 271
awlwort (*Subularia aquatic*) 225, 234
Aythya farina (pochard) 239
  fuligula (tufted duck) 239, 258
Azeca goodalli (three-toothed moss snail) 274

badger (*Meles meles*) 181, 220, 285–6, 328
Baetis scambus (small dark olive mayfly) 172
  niger (southern iron blue mayfly) 172, **173**
  rhodani (March brown mayfly) 172
  vernus (medium olive mayfly) 172
Baldellia ranunculoides (lesser water plantain) 248
Ballota nigra (black horehound) 81
Barbilophozia attenuata (trunk pawwort) 136
bat, brown long-eared (*Plecotus auritus*) 186, 326
  common pipistrelle (*Pipistrellus pipistrellus*) 186, 260, 326
  Daubenton's (*Myotis daubentoni*) 184, 260
  greater horseshoe (*Rhinolophus ferrumequinum*) 187, 326
  lesser horseshoe (*Rhinolophus hipposideros*) **185–7**, 219–20, 326
  Natterer's (*Myotis nattereri*) **326–7**
  noctule (*Nyctalus noctula*) 260, 295
  soprano pipistrelle (*Pipistrellus pygmaeus*) 326
Bazzania trilobata (greater whipwort) 136
bear, brown (*Ursus arctos*) 61, 71

beaver (*Castor fiber*) 61
bedstraw, heath (*Galium saxatile*) 98, 248
  limestone (*Galium sterneri*) 133
  northern (*Galium boreale*) 106
beech (*Fagus sylvatica*) 62, 261, 269–71
beetle:
  Agonum assimile 273
  Bembidion testaceum 166
    stomoides 273
  Calathus piceus 273
  Clivina fossor 112
  Ctenicera cuprea 112
  Dyschirius globosus 112
  Elmis aenea 113
  Epuraea longula 274
  Hypnoides riparius 111–12
  Hylecoetus dermestoides 274
  Leistus rufomarginatus 112
  Lionychus quadrillum 167
  Nebria gyllenhali 113
    salina 112
  Olisthopus rotundatus 112
  Patrobus atrorufus 273
  Plegaderus dissectus 274
  Pterostichus madidus 112
    diligens 250
  Rhizophagus nitidulus 274
  Scolytus scolytus 61–2
  bee (*Trichius fasciatus*) **194–5**
  black-headed cardinal (*Pyrochroa coccinea*) 274
  dung, northern (*Aphodius lapponum*) 111
  fen soldier (*Cantharis thoracica*) 250
  frog (*Notiophilus rufipes*) 273
  great diving (*Dysticus marginalis*) 246
  heather (*Lochmaea suturalis*) 98
  leaf (*Plateumaris affinis*) 250
  lesser stag (*Dorcus parallelipipedus*) 291
  long-horned (*Judolia cerambyciformis*) 273
  minotaur (*Typhaeus typhaeus*) **111**
  New Forest mud (*Helophorus laticollis*) 218
  orchid (*Dascillus cervinus*) 273
  river shingle 166–8
  stag (*Lucanus cervus*) 291
  two-tone reed (*Donacia bicolora*) **235**
  Welsh oak longhorn (*Pyrrhidium sanguineum*) 294
bell flower, ivy-leafed (*Wahlenbergia hederacea*) 144

Bembidion stomoides (beetle) 273
  testaceum (beetle) 166
bent, common (*Agrostis capillaris*) 99, 104, 271, 337, 338
  creeping (*Agrostis stolonifera*) 164
  velvet (*Agrostis canina*) 102
betony (*Stachys officinalis*) 337
Betula (birch) 59, 65, 69, 262, 272–3, 341
  pendula (silver birch) 272
  pubescens (downy birch) 261, 263, 272–3
Bibio pomonae (heather-fly) 115
bilberry (*Vaccinium myrtillus*) 97, 98, 105, 248, 271, 332
birch (*Betula*) 59, 65, 69, 262, 272–3, 341
  silver (*Betula pendula*) 272
  downy (*Betula pubescens*) 261, 263, 272–3
bird's-foot-trefoil, common (*Lotus corniculatus*) 129, 335, 337, 338
  greater (*Lotus uliginosus*) 337
bird's-nest, yellow (*Monotropa hypopitys*) **170**, 271
bistort, amphibious (*Persicaria amphibia*) 163, 254
bittern (*Botaurus stellaris*) 239
bittersweet (*Solanum dulcamara*) 164
blackbird (*Turdus merula*) 146, 147, 316
blackthorn (*Prunus spinosa*) 132, 143, 340, 342
bladder-fern, brittle (*Cystopteris fragilis*) 133
bladder-moss, dwarf (*Physcomitrium sphaericum*) 256
blanketweed (*Cladophora*) 177
Blechnum spicant (hard-fern) 264
Blepharostoma trichophyllum (hairy threadwort) 109
blue, holly (*Celastrina argiolus*) 341
bluebell (*Hyacinthoides non-scripta*) 13, 263
boar, wild (*Sus scrofa*) 61
Boettgerilla pallens (worm slug) 326
bog-moss (*Sphagnum*) 98, 244
  acute-leaved (*Sphagnum capillifolium*) 248
  cow-horn (*Sphagnum auriculatum*) 102
  feathery (*Sphagnum cuspidatum*) 102
  five-ranked (*Sphagnum quinquefarium*) 271
  Magellanic (*Sphagnum magellanicum*) 250
  papillose (*Sphagnum papillosum*) 248
  Russow's (*Sphagnum russowii*) 109
bogbean (*Menyanthes trifoliate*) 234, 248
bolete, larch (*Suillus grevillei*) 281
Boloria euphrosyne (pearl-bordered fritillary) 342
  selene (small pearl-bordered fritillary) 332

Boreus hyemalis (snow flea) **122**
Borrelia burgdorferi (bacterium) 145
Botaurus stellaris (bittern) 239
bow-moss, beaked (*Dicranodontium denudatum*) 266
Brachypodium sylvaticum (false brome) 132, 264, 271
bracken (*Pteridium aquilinum*) 50, 133, 143, 145, 271
braconid wasps 333
bramble (*Rubus iscanus*) 162, 271, 342
　stone (*Rubus saxatilis*) 132, 143
Branta canadensis (Canada goose) 232, 237
bream (*Abramis brama*) 240
briar, sweet (*Rosa rubiginosa*) 34–5
brimstone (*Gonepteryx rhamni*) 342
Briza media (quaking grass) 332
brome, false (*Brachypodium sylvaticum*) 132, 264, 271
brook-moss, claw (*Hygrohypnum ochraceum*) 161
brooklime (*Veronica beccabunga*) 162
broom (*Cytisus scoparius*) 143
Bryum capillare (capillary thread-moss) 322
　gemmiferum (small-bud bryum) 256
　radiculosum (wall thread-moss) 323
　rubens (crimson tuber thread-moss) 323
Bucephala clangula (goldeneye) 239, 258
buckler-fern, hay-scented (*Dryopteris aemula*) 192, 264
　rigid (*Dryopteris submontana*) 139
buckthorn (*Rhamnus cathartica*) 266, 342
　alder (*Frangula alnus*) 343
Bufo bufo (common toad) 247
bugs, sap-sucking:
　Cacopsylla visci 349
　Hypseloecus visci 349
　Pinalitus viscicola 349
bulin, lesser (*Ena obscura*) 218
bullhead (*Cottus gobio*) 157, 178, **219**
bunting, reed (*Emberiza schoeniclus*) 237
burdock, lesser (*Arctium minimum*) 133
Buteo buteo (buzzard) 89, 146, 147, 283
burnet, great (*Sanguisorba officinalis*) 130, 335
　salad (*Sanguisorba minor*) 129
bur-reed (*Sparganium angustifolium*) 225
　branched (*Sparganium erectum*) 162
Butomus umbellatus (flowering rush) 234
buttercup, creeping (*Ranunculus repens*) 267
　meadow (*Ranunculus acris*) 338

butterwort (*Pinguicula vulgaris*) 248
buzzard (*Buteo buteo*) 89, 146, 147, 283

caddis fly 172, 225, 227
　Polycentropus flavomaculatus 227
　Sericostoma personatum 227
Callitriche (water-starworts) 232
Calluna vulgaris (heather) **104**, 105, 332
Caloplaca citrina (common yellow lichen) 126
Calopteryx splendens (banded demoiselle) 188, **189**
Calathus piceus (long-horned beetle) 27
Caltha palustris (marsh marigold) 161
chamomile (*Chamaemelum nobile*) 81
Campaea margaritata (light emerald moth) 273
Campanula rotundifolia (harebell) 133, 338
Campylophyllum calcareum (chalk feather-moss) 271
Campylopus flexuosus (rusty swan-neck moss) 136
canary-grass (*Phalaris arundinacea*) 162
Canis lupus (wolf) 61
Cantharellus ferruginascens 271
Capreolus capreolus (roe deer) 61, 285, 288
Cardamine pratensis (lady's smock) 319
Carduelis cannabina (linnet) 146, 147
　spinus (siskin) 282
Carex acutiformis (lesser pond-sedge) 162
　echinata (star sedge) 102
　flacca (glaucous sedge) 133, 337
　lasiocarpa (slender sedge) 244
　montana (soft-leaved sedge) 131
　nigra (common sedge) 98
　panacea (carnation sedge) 102
　paniculata (greater tussock-sedge) 248, 249
　pulicaris (flea sedge) 332
　remota (remote sedge) 161
　rostrata (bottle sedge) 248
　viridula (yellow sedge) 102
carpet moth, grey mountain (*Entephria caesiata*) 114
　gallium (*Epirrhoe galiata*) 114
　sandy (*Perizoma flavofasciata*) 273
Carychium minimum (herald snail) 218
Castanea sativa (Spanish/sweet chestnut) **295–7**
Castor fiber (beaver) 61
cat's-ear (*Hypochoeris radicata*) 338
cedar, western red (*Thuya plicata*) 278
celandine, lesser (*Ranunculus ficaria*) 263

Celastrina argiolus (holly blue) 341
Celypha woodiana (mistletoe marble moth) 349
Centaurea nigra (black/common knapweed) 162, 318, 335
Centranthus ruber (red valerian) 81, 133
Certhia familiaris (treecreeper) 74
Cervus elaphus (red deer) 61, 65, 285, 287–8
Ceterach officinarum (rustyback) 133, 209
Cetrariella commixta (lichen) 136
Cettia cetti (Cetti's warbler) 237
chaffinch (*Fringilla coelebs*) 146, 147, 272, 350
Chalara fraxinea 266
Chamaemelum nobile (chamomile) 81
Chamerion angustifolium (rosebay willowherb) 62
Chara (stonewort) 232, 233–4
Charadrius morinellus (dotterel) 142
  dubius (little ringed plover) 180
cherry, bird (*Prunus avium*) 267
chestnut, sweet/Spanish (*Castanea sativa*) **295–7**
chickweed (*Stellaria media*) 99
Chiloscyphus polyanthus (St Winifrid's moss) 161
chives, wild (*Allium schoenoprasum*) 126–7
Chlamydomonas nivalis (alga) **121–2**
Chloroperla torrentium (large yellow sally stonefly) 172
Chroicocephalus ridibundus (black-headed gull) 246–7
Chroococcus giganteus 209
Chrysosplenium oppositifolium (opposite-leaved golden saxifrage) 102, 209, 267
Chrysothrix chlorine (bright yellow mustard/gold dust lichen) 194
chub (*Leuciscus cephalus*) 175
cicely, sweet (*Myrrhis odorata*) 268
Cinclidotus fontinaloides (smaller lattice-moss) 161
Cinclus cinclus (dipper) **178–9**, 215
Circaea alpina (alpine enchanter's-nightshade) 124
  lutetiana (enchanter's-nightshade) 132, 271
Cirsium arvense (creeping thistle) 99, 164
  dissectum (meadow thistle) 332
  heterophyllum (melancholy thistle) 195
  palustre (marsh thistle) 133
  vulgare (spear thistle) 133
Cladium mariscus (fen-sedge) 244
Cladonia (lichen) 137
  impexa 244
Cladophora (blanketweed) 177

clary, wild (*Salvia verbenaca*) 81
Clausilia bidentata (door snail) 113, 218
Clavaria rosea (rose spindles) **130**
Clavariadelphus pistillaris (giant club) 271
Clavulinopsis fusiformis (golden spindles) 129
cleavers (*Galium aparine*) 133
Clematis vitalba (traveller's joy) 342
click beetles:
  Ctenicera cuprea 112
  black (*Hypnoidus riparius*) 111, 112
Climacium dendroides (tree-moss) 256
Cliorismia rustica (southern silver stiletto-fly) 168
Clivina fossor (beetle) 112
Cloeon dipterum (mayfly) 228
clover, red (*Trifolium pratense*) 335, 337, 338
  zigzag (*Trifolium medium*) 132
club, giant (*Clavariadelphus pistillaris*) 271
clubmoss, stag's horn (*Lycopodium clavatum*) **27**
club-rush (*Schoenoplectus*) 234
  wood (*Scirpus sylvaticus*) 163
cock's-foot (*Dactylis glomerata*) 133
Coenagrion mercuriale (southern damselfly) 248
  puella (azure damselfly) 236, 248
  pulchellum (blue damselfly) 236
Colchicum autumnale (meadow saffron) **338**, 339
collar-moss, cruet (*Splachnum ampullaceum*) 138
  round-fruited (*Splachnum sphaericum*) 138
Columba palumbus (woodpigeon) 284
columbine (*Aquilegia vulgaris*) 268
Colura calyptrifolia (fingered cowlwort) 193
comb-moss, chalk (*Ctenidium molluscum*) 332
comfrey (*Symphytum*) 162
Conium maculatum (hemlock) 81, 164
Conocephalum conicum (great-scented liverwort) 161, 209
  salebrosum 161
Convallaria majalis (lily-of-the-valley) 131, 133, 266, 320
Cooksonia hemisphaerica 30
coot (*Fulica atra*) 239, 245, 260
Cordulegaster boltonii (golden-ringed dragonfly) 248
Cornicularia normoerica 136
Cornus sanguinea (dogwood) 340
Corvus (crows) 177
  corax (raven) **140–1**, 146, 147
  corone (carrion crow) 88, 146, 147, 284
  frugilegus (rook) 284
  monedula (jackdaw) 215

Corylus avellana (hazel) 60, 65, 69, 263, 267, 340
Cotesia bignellii (parasitic wasp) 333
  melitaearum (parasitic wasp) 333
cottongrass, common (*Eriophorum angustifolium*) 102, 103, 248
  hare's-tail (*Eriophorum vaginatum*) 100, 102, 248
Cottus gobio (bullhead) 157, 178, **219**
couch, bearded (*Elymus caninus*) 132
cow parsley (*Anthriscus sylvestris*) 132
cow parsnip (*Heracleum sphondylium*) 133
cowberry (*Vaccinium vitis-idaea*) 105, 106
cowlwort, fingered (*Colura calyptrifolia*) 193
cowslip (*Primula veris*) 106, 133, **341**
cow-wheat (*Melampyrum pratense*) 132
craneflies 250
  Gonomyia abbreviata 274
    limbata 273
  Limonia inusta 274
  Limnophila abdominalis 250
  Rhabdomastix laeta 168
  Rhizophagus nitidulus 274
  Tipula marginata 250
  comb-horn (*Tanyptera atrata*) 281, **282**
crane's-bill, shining (*Geranium lucidum*) 81
  wood (*Geranium sylvaticum*) 336
Crataegus monogyna (hawthorn) 107, 132, 143, 340, 342
Craterellus cornucopioides (horn of plenty) 271
crayfish, signal (*Pacifastacus leniusculus*) 176, 178
  white-clawed (*Austropotamobius pallipes*) **175–7**
crazed cap (*Dermoloma cuneifolium*) 129
Crenobia alpina (grey flatworm) 218
cress, thale (*Arabidopsis thaliana*) 81
  yellow (*Rorippa*) 162
crestwort, fragrant (*Lophocolea fragrans*) 271
crisp-moss, Bamberger's (*Tortella bambergeri*) 136, **137**
  frizzled (*Tortella tortuosa*) 109
crossbill, common (*Loxia curvirostra*) 283
crows (*Corvus*) 177
  carrion (*Corvus corone*) 88, 146, 147, 284
crowberry (*Empetrum nigrum*) 105, 248
crowfoot, round-leaved (*Ranunculus omiophyllus*) 102
cruet-moss, slender (*Tetraplodon mnioides*) **138**
Cryptogramma crispa (parsley fern) 138

crystalwort, cavernous (*Riccia cavernosa*) 254
  common (*Riccia sorocarpa*) 254
  glaucous (*Riccia glauca*) 254
  purple (*Riccia beyrichiana*) 254
  violet (*Riccia huebeneriana*) **252–5**
Ctenicera cuprea (click beetle) 112
Ctenidium molluscum (chalk comb-moss) 332
Ctenopharyngodon idella (Chinese grass-carp) 240
cuckoo (*Cuculus canorus*) 146, 147
Culex pipiens (common mosquito) 211
curlew (*Numenius arquata*) 142, 164
Cuthbert's beads (sea lilies) 33, 34
Cyanistes caeruleus (blue tit) 146, 147, 350
Cygnus olor (mute swan) 181, **237–9**, 245
Cymbalaria muralis (ivy-leaved toadflax) 81
Cynosurus cristatus (dog's-tail) 337, 338
Cystoderma amianthinum (earthy powdercap) 271
Cystopteris fragilis (brittle bladder-fern) 133
Cytisus scoparius (broom) 143

dace (*Leuciscus leuciscus*) 175
Dactylis glomerata (cock's-foot) 133
Dactylorhiza spp. (spotted orchid) 318
daffodil (*Narcissus pseudonarcissus*) 319–20
Dama dama (fallow deer) 288
damselfly, azure (*Coenagrion puella*) 236, 248
  blue (*Coenagrion pulchellum*) 236
  blue-tailed (*Ischnura elegans*) 248
  common blue (*Enallagma cyathigerum*) 236, 246, 248
  emerald (*Lestes sponsa*) 248
  large red (*Pyrrhosoma nymphula*) 246, 248
  scarce blue-tailed (*Ischnura pumilio*) 248
  southern (*Coenagrion mercuriale*) 248
dandelion (*Taraxacum*) 133
  Brecon (*Taraxacum breconense*) 27, 162
  Degelius's (*Taraxacum degelii*) 162
Danthonia decumbens (heath grass) 337, 338
darter, black (*Sympetrum danae*) 245, 248
Dascillus cervinus (orchid beetle) 273
Dawsonites arcuatus 30
dead-nettle, white (*Lamium album*) 81
deer, fallow (*Dama dama*) 288
  red (*Cervus elaphus*) 61, 65, 285, 287–8
  roe (*Capreolus capreolus*) 61, 285, 288
deergrass (*Scirpus cespitosus*) 105
Delichon urbicum (house martin) 142

demoiselle, banded (*Calopteryx splendens*) 188, **189**
  beautiful (*Calopteryx virgo*) 248
Dendrocoelum lacteum (flatworm) 218
Dendrocopos major (great spotted woodpecker) 350
  minor (lesser spotted woodpecker) 74, 350
Dermoloma cuneifolium (crazed cap) 129
Deroceras reticulatum (grey field slug) 113
Deschampsia cespitosa (tufted hair-grass) 267, 271
  flexuosa (wavy hair-grass) 98, 102, 103, 332
Dichodontium denudatum (yellowish fork-moss) 194
Dicranodontium denudatum (beaked bow-moss) 266
Dicranum fuscescens (dusky fork-moss) 136
  majus (greater fork-moss) 271
  scoparium (broom fork-moss) 109
Dicrostonyx torquatus (arctic lemming) 59
Diplolepis rosae (gall wasp) **340–1**
Diplophyllum albicans (white earwort) 109
dipper (*Cinclus cinclus*) **178–9**, 215
Dipsacus fullonum (teasel) 320
Discus rotundatus (rounded snail) 113, 218
distichium (*Distichium capillaceum*) 109
ditrichum, Alpine (*Ditrichum zonatum*) 109
  cylindric (*Trichodon cylindricus*) 323
Dixa (meniscus midge) 218
dog-violet (*Viola riviniana*) 133, 144, 209, 319, 320
  early (*Viola reichenbachiana*) 271
dog's mercury (*Mercurialis perennis*) 133, 209, 263, 319, 320
dog's-tail (*Cynosurus cristatus*) 337, 338
dogwood (*Cornus sanguinea*) 340
Donacia bicolora (two-tone reed beetle) **235**
Dorcus parallelipipedus (lesser stag beetle) 291
dormouse (*Muscardinus avellanarius*) **275–7**
dotterel (*Charadrius morinellus*) 142
dragonfly, golden-ringed (*Cordulegaster boltonii*) 248
Drepanophycus spinaeformis 30
dropwort (*Filipendula vulgaris*) 320
Drosera intermedia (oblong-leafed sundew) 249
  rotundifolia (round-leaved sundew) 102, 248, 250
Dryas octopetala (mountain avens) 59
Dryopteris aemula (hay-scented buckler-fern) 192, 264
  felix-mas (male-fern) 133

Dryopteris submontana (rigid buckler-fern) 139
duck, tufted (*Aythya fuligula*) 239, 258
duckweed, great (*Lemna polyrhiza*) 233
  greater (*Spirodela polyrhiza*) 233
dung beetle, northern (*Aphodius lapponum*) 111
dungfly (*Leria serrata*) 211
dunnock (*Prunella modularis*) 146, 147
Dyschirius globosus 112
Dysticus marginalis (great diving beetle) 246
Dytroptis pteridis (planthopper) 145

earth-moss, clay (*Archidium alternifolium*) 256
  delicate (*Pseudephemerum nitidum*) 254
  serrated (*Pseudephemerum nitidum*) 254
  sessile (*Ephemerum sessile*) 257
  spreading (*Aphanorhegma patens*) 254
earthstar, arched (*Geastrum fornicatum*) **316–17**
earwort, narrow-lobed (*Scapania gymnostomophila*) 109
  water (*Scapania undulate*) 161
  western (*Scapania gracilis*) 136
  white (*Diplophyllum albicans*) 109
Ecdyonurus dispar (autumn dun mayfly) 172
  torrentis (large blue dun mayfly) 172
eel, European (*Anguilla anguilla*) 157, 177, 223, 225, 240
elder (*Sambucus nigra*) 143
elecampane (*Inula helenium*) 81
Eleocharis palustris (common spike-rush) 162
  quinqueflora (few-flowered spike-rush) 250
elk (*Alces alces*) 61
elm (*Ulmus* spp.) 61–2
  wych (*Ulmus glabra*) 267
Elmis aenea (beetle) 113
Elymus caninus (bearded couch) 132
Emberiza citronella (yellowhammer) 146, 147, 148
  schoeniclus (reed bunting) 237
emperor moth (*Saturnia pavonia*) **114**
Empetrum nigrum (crowberry) 105, 248
Ena obscura (lesser bulin) 218
Enallagma cyathigerum (common blue) 236, 246, 248
Encalypta ciliata (extinguisher-moss) 136
  streptocarpa (spiral extinguisher-moss) 323
enchanter's-nightshade (*Circaea lutetiana*) 132, 271
  alpine (*Circaea alpina*) 124
Entephria caesiata (grey mountain carpet moth) 114

Enterographa hutchinsii (lichen) 194
Entoloma porphyrophaeum (lilac pinkgill) 129
Ephemerum sessile (sessile earth-moss) 257
Epidalea calamita (natterjack toad) 247
Epilobium hirsutum (great willowherb) 162
 montanum (broad-leaved willowherb) 133
Epipactis helleborine (broad-leaved helleborine) 132
Epipterygium tozeri (Tozer's thread-moss) 256
Epirrhoe galiata (gallium carpet moth) 114
Epuraea longula (beetle) 274
Equisetum (horsetail) 255
 hyemale (rough horsetail) 268
 telmateia (giant horsetail) 268
Erica cinerea (bell heather) 105
 tetralix (cross-leaved heath) 105, 248, 332
Erinaceus europaeus (hedgehog) 328
Eriophorum angustifolium (common cottongrass) 102, 103, 248
 vaginatum (hare's-tail cottongrass) 100, 102, 248
Eriopygodes imbecilla (Silurian moth) **115–17**
Eriozona erratica (hoverfly) 281
 syrphoides (hoverfly) 281
Erithacus rubecula (robin) 146, 147
Erophila verna (common whitlowgrass) 81
Erysimum cheri (Aegean wallflower) 81
Esox lucius (pike) 61, 177, **240–2**, 260
Eupatorium cannabinum (hemp-agrimony) 132
Euphorbia amygdaloides (wood spurge) 266
Euphrasia (eyebright) 335
Eupithecia vulgate (common pug moth) 273
Eurhynchium schleicheri (twist-tip feather-moss) 271
Eurodryas aurinia (marsh fritillary) **332–3**
extinguisher-moss (*Encalypta ciliata*) 136
 spiral (*Encalypta streptocarpa*) 323
eyebright (*Euphrasia*) 335

Fagus sylvatica (beech) 62, 261, 269–71
Falco columbarius (merlin) **141**
 peregrinus (peregrine) 140
 subbuteo (hobby) 237
Fallopia japonica (Japanese knotweed) 164–5
feather-moss, blunt (*Homalia tricholmanoides*) 162
 brook-side (*Amblystegium fluviatile*) 161
 chalk (*Campylophyllum calcareum*) 271
 fox-tail (*Thamnobryum alopecurum*) 161

long-beaked water (*Rhynchostegium riparioides*) 161
 neat (*Pseudoscleropodium purum*) 264
 silky wall (*Homalothecium sericeum*) 322
 tender (*Rhynchostegiella tenella*) 322, 323
 tufted (*Scleropodium cespitans*) 162
 twist-tip (*Eurhynchium schleicheri*) 271
 wall (*Rhynchostegium murale*) 209
Fontinalis (willow moss) 177
Felis sylvestris (wildcat) 61
fennel (*Foeniculum vulgare*) 81
fen-sedge (*Cladium mariscus*) 244
fern, adder's-tongue (*Ophioglossum vulgatum*) 338
 beech (*Phegopteris connectilis*) 106, 193
 hart's-tongue (*Phyllitis scolopendrium*) 131, 133, 209, 263
 lemon-scented (*Oreopteris limbosperma*)
 limestone (*Gymnocarpium robertianum*) 125, 133, **139**
 oak (*Gymnocarpium dryopteris*) 106
 parsley (*Cryptogramma crispa*) 138
 royal (*Osmunda regalis*) 192, 249
fescue, meadow (*Festuca pratensis*) 337
 red (*Festuca rubra*) 133
 sheep's (*Festuca ovina*) 98, 99, 103
 wood (*Festuca altissima*) 264, 266
feverfew (*Tanacetum parthenium*) 81
fieldfare (*Turdus pilaris*) 142, 350
Filipendula ulmaria (meadowsweet) 106, 132, 161, 267, 337
 vulgaris (dropwort) 320
filmy-fern, Tunbridge (*Hymenophyllum tunbrigense*) **192–3**
 Wilson's (*Hymenophyllum wilsonii*) 106, 192
fingerwort, rock (*Lepidozia cupressina*) 136
fir, Douglas (*Pseudotsuga menziesii*) 278
Fissidens celticus (Welsh pocket-moss) 194
 curnovii (Curnow's pocket-moss) 194
 dubius (rock pocket-moss) 323
 rivularis (river pocket-moss) 161
 rufulus (beck pocket-moss) 161
flapwort, autumn (*Jamesoniella autumnalis*) 193
 matchstick (*Odontoschisma denudatum*) 193
flatworms:
 Crenobia alpina 218
 Dendrocoelum lacteum 218
 Phagocata vitta 218
flax, fairy (*Linum catharticum*) 338

SPECIES INDEX · 393

Flodea canadensis (Canadian waterweed) 163
fly, snail-killing:
  Antichaeta analis 250
  Psacadina verbekei 250
Foeniculum vulgare (fennel) 81
Folsomia palearctica (springtail) 218
Fontinalis (willow moss) 177
  antipyretica (greater water-moss) 156, 226–7, 256
forget-me-not (*Myosotis*) 320
  water (*Myosotis scorpioides*) 162, 248
fork-moss, broom (*Dicranum scoparium*) 109
  dusky (*Dicranum fuscescens*) 136
  greater (*Dicranum majus*) 271
  yellowish (*Dichodontium denudatum*) 194
Formica rufus (red wood ant) 275
  lemani (ant) 146
Fossombronia foveolata (pitted frillwort) 255
  incurva (weedy frillwort) 255
  pusilla (common frillwort) 255
  wondraczekii (acid frillwort) 255
fox (*Vulpes vulpes*) 220, 328
foxtail, marsh (*Alopecurus geniculatus*) 164, 245
  orange (*Alopecurus aequalis*) 245
Frangula alnus (alder buckthorn) 342
frillwort, acid (*Fossombronia wondraczekii*) 254
  common (*Fossombronia pusilla*) 254
  pitted (*Fossombronia foveolata*) 254
  weedy (*Fossombronia incurve*) 254
fringe-moss, green mountain (*Racomitrium fasciculare*) 109
  narrow-leaved (*Racomitrium aquaticum*) 109
  woolly (*Racomitrium lanuginosum*) 136
  yellow (*Racomitrium aciculare*) 161
Fringilla coelebs (chaffinch) 146, 147, 272, 350
fritillary, dark green (*Argynnis aglaja*) 133, 144, **145**
  marsh (*Eurodryas aurinia*) **332–3**
  pearl-bordered (*Boloria euphrosyne*) 342
  small pearl-bordered (*Boloria selene*) 332
frog, common (*Rana temporaria*) 152, 228, 247
Fulica atra (coot) 239, 245, 260
Fusarium (fungus) 211
Fuscidea cyathoides (lichen) 137
  kochiana (lichen) 137
  lygea (lichen) 137

Galanthus nivalis (snowdrop) 320
Galba truncatula (dwarf pond snail) 113

Galium aparine (cleavers) 133
  palustre (common marsh bedstraw) 102, 337
  saxatile (heath bedstraw) 98, 248
  sterneri (limestone bedstraw) 133
gall, rose bedeguar **340–1**
gall wasp (*Diplolepis rosae*) **340–1**
Gallinago gallinago (snipe) 247
Gallinula chloropus (moorhen) 260
Gallium boreale (northern bedstraw) 106
Gammarus (amphipod crustacean) 215
  pulex 215, 228
Garrulus glandarius (jay) 146, 147
Geastrum fornicatum (arched earthstar) 316–**17**
Genista pilosa (hairy greenweed) 131
Geranium lucidum (shining crane's-bill) 81
  robertianum (herb-Robert) 131, 133, 209
  sylvaticum (wood crane's-bill) 336
Geum rivale (water avens) 106
  urbanum (wood avens) 132, 271
globeflower (*Trollius europaeus*) 133, 332
Glyceria fluitans (floating sweet-grass) 161, 164, 245
gnat, common cave (*Speleolepta leptogaster*) 211
goldcrest (*Regulus regulus*) 74
goldeneye (*Bucephala clangula*) 239, 258
Gonepteryx rhamni (brimstone) 342
Gonomyia abbreviata (cranefly) 274
  limbata (cranefly) 273
goosander (*Mergus merganser*) 258
goose, Canada (*Branta canadensis*) 232, 237
gorse, common (*Ulex europaeus*) 143
  western (*Ulex gallii*) **104**, 105, 143
goshawk (*Accipiter gentilis*) **283–4**
Gosslingia breconensis 27, **28–9**
grass-carp, Chinese (*Ctenopharyngodon idella*) 240
grebe, little (*Tachybaptus ruficollis*) 245, 246
greenweed, hairy (*Genista pilosa*) 131
Grimmia laevigata (hoary grimmia) 320
  longirostris (north grimmia) 322
  ovalis (flat-rock grimmia) 320
  pulvinata (grey-cushioned grimmia) 322
  torquata (twisted grimmia) 109
Grimmia, flat-rock (*Grimmia ovalis*) 320
  grey-cushioned (*Grimmia pulvinata*) 322
  hoary (*Grimmia laevigata*) 320
  north (*Grimmia longirostris*) 322
  thickpoint (*Schistidium crassipilum*) 136
  twisted (*Grimmia torquata*) 109

grouse, black (*Tetrao tetrix*) 97
red (*Lagopus lagopus*) 141–2
gull, black-headed (*Chroicocephalus ridibundus*) 246–7
Gymnocarpium dryopteris (oak fern) 106
robertianum (limestone fern) 125, 133, **139**
Gymnostomum aeruginosum (verdigris tufa-moss) 109, 209

Haemopis sanguisuga (horse leech) 228, 234, **251**
hagfish 23
haircap, alpine (*Polytrichum alpinum*) 109
common (*Polytrichum commune*) 102, 248
hair-grass, tufted (*Deschampsia cespitosa*) 267, 271
wavy (*Deschampsia flexuosa*) 98, 102, 103, 332
hard-fern (*Blechnum spicant*) 264
hare, mountain (*Lepus timidus*) 59
harebell (*Campanula rotundifolia*) 133, 338
hawkbit, autumn (*Leontodon autumnalis*) 337
rough (*Leontodon hispidus*) 335
hawkweed (*Hieracium*) 17, 106–7, 123–4
Craig Cerrig Gleisiad (*Hieracium neocoracinum*) 107
Craig y Cilau (*Hieracium cillense*) 123, **124**
Llangattock (*Hieracium asteridiophyllum*) 123–4
long-bracted (*Hieracium cinderella*) 162
mouse-ear (*Pilosella officinarum*) 338
Stenström's (*Hieracium stenstroemii*) 162
summit (*Hieracium cacuminum*) 106
Riddelsdell's (*Hieracium riddelsdellii*) 17
hawthorn (*Crataegus monogyna*) 107, 132, 143, 340, 342
hazel (*Corylus avellana*) 60, 65, 69, 263, 267, 340
heath, cross-leaved (*Erica tetralix*) 105, 248, 332
heath grass (*Danthonia decumbens*) 337, 338
heather (*Calluna vulgaris*) **104**, 105, 332
bell (*Erica cinerea*) 105
heather beetle (*Lochmaea suturalis*) 98
heather fly (*Bibio pomonae*) 115
Hedera helix (ivy) 132, 209
hedgehog (*Erinaceus europaeus*) 328
Hedwigia ciliata (fringed hoar-moss) 320
Helianthemum nummularium (common rock-rose) 129
Helicogona lapicida (lapidary snail) 119
helleborine, broad-leaved (*Epipactis helleborine*) 132

Helophorus laticollis (New Forest mud beetle) 218
hemlock (*Conium maculatum*) 81, 164
western (*Tsuga heterophylla*) 278
hemp-agrimony (*Eupatorium cannabinum*) 132
Heptagenia sulphurea (yellow may dun mayfly) 172
Heracleum mantegazzianum (giant hogweed) 164, **165**
Heracleum sphondylium (cow parsnip) 133
herb-Paris (*Paris quadrifolia*) 268
herb-Robert (*Geranium robertianum*) 131, 133, 209
heron, grey (*Ardea cinerea*) 177, 178, 245, 260
Heterocladium heteropterum (wry-leaved tamarisk-moss) 109
Hieracium (hawkweed) 17, 106–7, 123–4
asteridiophyllum (Llangattock hawkweed) 123–4
cacuminum (summit hawkweed) 106
cillense (Craig y Cilau hawkweed) 123, **124**
cinderella (long-bracted hawkweed) 162
neocoracinum (Craig Cerrig Gleisiad hawkweed) 107
riddelsdellii (Riddelsdell's hawkweed) 17
stenstroemii (Stenström's hawkweed) 162
Hildenbrandia rivularis (red alga) 161
Himalayan balsam (*Impatiens glandulifera*) **164–6**
Hippuris vulgaris (mare's-tail) 232–3
Hirudo medicinalis (medical leech) 234–5
Hirundo rustica (barn swallow) 142, 215, 237, 344–5
hoar-moss, fringed (*Hedwigia ciliata*) 320
hobby (*Falco subbuteo*) 237
hoglouse, freshwater (*Proasellus cavaticus*) **216**
hogweed, giant (*Heracleum mantegazzianum*) 164, **165**
Holcus lanatus (Yorkshire-fog) 337
holly (*Ilex aquifolium*) 93, 143, 261, 263, **299–302**
hollywort, Hutchins' (*Jubula hutchinsiae*) 193
Homalia trichomanoides (blunt feather-moss) 162
Homalothecium sericeum (silky wall feather-moss) 322
honey-buzzard (*Pernis apivorus*) 285
honeysuckle (*Lonicera periclymenum*) 132
hook-moss, sickle-leaved (*Sanionia uncinata*) 109

horehound, black (*Ballota nigra*) 81
　white (*Marrubium vulgare*) 81
horn of plenty (*Craterellus cornucopioides*) 271
hornet (*Vespa carbo*) 274
Hornungia petraea (hutchinsia) 124
horsetail (*Equisetum*) 255
　giant (*Equisetum telmateia*) 268
　rough (*Equisetum hyemale*) 268
Hostiniella beardii 30
hoverflies 281
　Eriozona erratica 281
　　syrphoides 281
　Melangyna compositarum 281
　Parasyrphus malinellus 281
　　lineola 281
hutchinsia (*Hornungia petraea*) 124
Hyacinthoides non-scripta (bluebell) 13, 263
Hydriomena impluviata (May high-flyer moth) 273
Hydrocotyle vulgaris (marsh pennywort) 102
Hygrocybe calyptriformis (pink waxcap) 319
　chlorophana (golden waxcap) 335
　coccinea (scarlet waxcap) 335
　colemanniana (toasted waxcap) 129–30
　glutinipes (glutinous waxcap) 129–30
　panacea (crimson waxcap) 129–30
　persistens (persistent waxcap) **129–30**
Hygrohypnum ochraceum (claw brook-moss) 161
Hylecoetus dermestoides (beetle) 274
Hylocomium brevirostre (short-beaked wood-moss) 266
Hymenophyllum tunbrigense (Tunbridge filmy-fern) **192–3**
　wilsonii (Wilson's filmy fern) 106, 192
Hymenoscyphus pseudoalbidus 266
Hypericum elodes (St John's-wort) 248
Hypnoidus riparius (black click beetle) 111, 112
Hypnum cupressiforme (cypress-leaved plait-moss) 271
　jutlandicum (heath plait-moss) 109
　resupinatum (supine plait-moss) 349
Hypochoeris radicata (cat's-ear) 338

Ilex aquifolium (holly) 93, 143, 261, 263, **299–302**
Impatiens glandulifera (Himalayan balsam) **164–6**
Inachis io (peacock) 342
Inula helenium (elecampane) 81
Ischnura elegans (blue-tailed damselfly) 248
　pumilio (scarce blue-tailed damselfly) 248

Isoetes lacustris (quillwort) 224, 226, 228
Isothecium holtii (Holt's mouse-tail moss) 194
ivy (*Hedera helix*) 132, 209
Ixapion variegatum (waxed mistletoe) 349
Ixodes ricinus (sheep tick) 145–6

jack snipe (*Lymnocryptes minimus*) 164
jackdaw (*Corvus monedula*) 215
Jamesoniella autumnalis (autumn flapwort) 193
jay (*Garrulus glandarius*) 146, 147
Jubula hutchinsiae (Hutchins' hollywort) 193
Judolia cerambyciformis (long-horned beetle) 273
Juncus (rush) 102, 161, 337
　acutiflorus (sharp-flowered rush) 102, 332, 337
　bulbosus (bulbous rush) 102, 225, 228
　conglomeratus (compact rush) 248
　effusus (soft-rush) 99, 228, 248, 357
　effusus spiralis (corkscrew/spiral) **99**, **101**
　squarrosus (heath rush) 98
juniper (*Juniperus communis*) 59, 97

kingfisher (*Alcedo atthis*) 178, **180**, 181, 260
kite, red (*Milvus milvus*) 89, **90**, 142, 283, 284–5
knapweed, black/common (*Centaurea nigra*) 162, 318, 335
　Japanese (*Fallopia japonica*) 164–5
Krithodeophyton croftii (fossil) 29–30

Lacerta vivipara (common lizard) 151
lady's-mantle, hairy (*Alchemilla filicaulis*) 337
　smooth (*Alchemilla glabra*) 106
lady's smock (*Cardamine pratensis*) 319
lady-fern (*Athyrium felix-femina*) 133, 161, 264, 267
Lagopus lagopus (red grouse) 141–2
Lamium album (white dead-nettle) 81
　galeobdolon (Yellow archangel) 133, 263
lamprey, brook (*Lampetra planeri*) 157
　river (*Lampetra fluviatilis*) 157, 173, 175
　sea (*Petromyzon marinus*) 157
Lanius excubitor (great grey shrike) 285
lapwing (*Vanellus vanellus*) 142, 164
larch, European (*Larix decidua*) 278
　Japanese (*Larix kaempferi*) 278, 280
Lasius flavus (yellow meadow ant) 132
Lathraea squamaria (toothwort) 271
Lathyrus pratensis (meadow vetch) 335
lattice-moss, smaller (*Cinclidotus fontinaloides*) 161

leafhopper (*Oncopsis flavicollis*) 272
leaf-miners 146
Lecania turicensis (lichen) 324
leech, horse (*Haemopis sanguisuga*) 228, 234, **251**
  medical (*Hirudo medicinalis*) 234–5
Lehmannia marginata (tree slug) **118**
Leiostyla anglica (English chrysalis snail) 274
Leistus rufomarginatus (beetle) 112
Lemanea fluviatilis (filamentous red algae) 161
lemming, arctic (*Dicrostonyx torquatus*) 59
  Norway (*Lemmus lemmus*) 59
Lemmus lemmus (Norway lemming) 59
Lemna polyrhiza (great duckweed) 233
Leontodon autumnalis (autumn hawkbit) 337
  hispidus (rough hawkbit) 335
Lepidozia cupressina (rock fingerwort) 136
Lepthyphantes pallidus (spider) 215
Leptobryum pyriforme (golden thread-moss) 256
Lepus timidus (mountain hare) 59
Leria serrata (dungfly) 211
leskea, Spruce's (*Platydictya jungermannioides*) 271
Lessertia denticulata (spider) 215
Lestes sponsa (emerald damselfly) 248
Leuciscus cephalus (chub) 175
  leuciscus (dace) 175
Leucobryum juniperoideum (smaller white-moss) 136
Leucodon sciuroides (squirrel-tail moss) **66**
lichen:
  Cetrariella commixta 136
  Cladonia 137
    impexa 244
  Fuscidea cyathoides 137
    kochiana 137
    lygea 137
  Lecania turicensis 324
  Micarea alabastrites 194
    hedlundii 194
    pycnidiophora 194
    stipitata 194
  Opegrapha dolomitica 105
  Peltigera polydactyla 105
  Pertusaria lactescens 324
  Phyllopsora rosei 194
  Polyblastia allobata 194
  Pseudephebe pubescens 136
  Ramalina canariensis 324
  Rhizocarpon geographicum 137

Umbilicaria cylindrica 136
  proboscidea 136
  torrefacta 136
Verrucaria 161
  viridula 105
bearded (*Usnea articulata*) 355
bright yellow mustard powder/gold dust
  (*Chrysothrix chlorine*) 194
common yellow (*Caloplaca citrina*) 126
white crustose (*Aspicilia calcarea*) 126
lily, Pyrenean (*Lilium pyrenaicum*) 320
  Snowdon (*Lloydia serotina*) 354
lily-of-the-valley (*Convallaria majalis*) 131, 133, 266, 320
Limax cinereoniger (ash-black slug) 118
lime (*Tilia*) 61
  small-leaved (*Tilia cordata*) 271
Limnophila abdominalis (cranefly) 250
Limonia inusta (cranefly) 274
limpet, freshwater (*Ancylus fluviatilis*) 227
linnet (*Carduelis cannabina*) 146, 147
Linum catharticum (fairy flax) 338
Lionychus quadrillum (river shingle beetle) 167
Lissotriton helveticus (palmate newt) 228, 247
  vulgaris (smooth/common newt) 228, 247
Listera ovate (greater twayblade) 318
Lithostrotion (fossil coral) **32**
Littorella uniflora (shoreweed) **224**, 226, 228
liverwort, crescent-cupped (*Lunularia cruciata*) 162
  great scented (*Conocephalum conicum*) 161, 209
  mushroom-headed (*Preissia quadrata*) 109
  star-headed (*Marchantia polymorpha*) 161
lizard, common (*Lacerta vivipara*) 151
Lloydia serotina (Snowdon lily) 354
Lochmaea suturalis (heather beetle) 98
Lolium perenne (perennial ryegrass) 99
Lomaspilis marginata (clouded border moth) 273
Lonicera periclymenum (honeysuckle) 132
Lophocolea fragrans (fragrant crestwort) 271
Lophozia ventricosa (tumid notchwort) 109
lords-and-ladies (*Arum maculatum*) 133, 209
Lotus corniculatus (common bird's-foot-trefoil) 129, 335, 337, 338
  uliginosus (greater bird's-foot-trefoil) 337
lousewort (*Pedicularis sylvatica*) 248
Loxia curvirostra (common crossbill) 283
Lucanus cervus (stag beetle) 291

Lunularia cruciata (crescent-cupped liverwort) 162
Lutra lutra (otter) 61, 177, 182–4, 220, 260
Luzula campestris (field wood-rush) 338
　multiflora (heath wood-rush) 98
　sylvatica (great wood-rush) 106
Lychnis floscuculi (ragged robin) 102
Lycopodium clavatum (stag's horn clubmoss) **27**
Lyginopteris hoeninghausii (fossil) 46
Lymnocryptes minimus (jack snipe) 164
lynx (*Lynx lynx*) 61
Lysimachia nemorum (yellow pimpernel) 263, 267
Lythrum salicaria (purple loosestrife) 234

mosquito, common (*Culex pipiens*) 211
Macromonas (bacterium) 211
magpie (*Pica pica*) 147
Malacolimax tenellus (lemon slug) **274**
male-fern (*Dryopteris felix-mas*) 133
mallard (*Anas platyrhynchos*) 260
mallow (*Malva sylvestris*) 81
mammoth, woolly (*Mammuthus primigenius*) 59
Mammuthus primigenius (woolly mammoth) 59
maple, field (*Acer campestre*) 261, 340
Marchantia polymorpha (star-headed liverwort) 161
Marchesinia mackaii (MacKay's pouncewort) 271
mare's-tail (*Hippuris vulgaris*) 232–3
Margaritifera margaritifera (freshwater pearl mussel) **169–71**
marigold, marsh (*Caltha palustris*) 161
Marrubium vulgare (white horehound) 81
marsh-bedstraw, common (*Galium palustre*) 102, 337
marshwort, lesser (*Apium inundatum*) 163, 245
Marsupella emarginata (notched rustwort) 109
marten, pine (*Martes martes*) 278
Martes martes (pine marten) 278
martin, house (*Delichon urbicum*) 142
　sand (*Riparia riparia*) 180–1, 237
mat-grass (*Nardus stricta*) 93, 98
mayfly (*Cloeon dipterum*) 228
　Ecdyonurus 156, 172, 225
　Heptagagenia 156, 172, 225
　autumn dun (*Ecdyonurus dispar*) 172
　blue-winged olive (*Serratella ignita*) 172
　large brook dun (*Ecdyonurus torrentis*) 172
　large olive (*Baetis rhodani*) 172
　March brown (*Rithrogena germanica*) 172
　medium olive (*Baetis vernus*) 172
　olive upright (*Rithrogena semicolorata*) 172
　small dark olive (*Baetis scambus*) 172
　southern iron blue (*Baetis niger*) 172, **173**
　yellow may dun (*Heptagenia sulphurea*) 172
meadow-grass, annual (*Poa annua*) 99
　smooth (*Poa pratensis*) 99
meadow rue (*Thalictrum flavum*) 59
　lesser (*Thalictrum minus*) 106, 131
　rough (*Poa trivialis*) 267
meadowsweet (*Filipendula ulmaria*) 106, 132, 161, 267, 337
Meioneta gulosa 112
Melampyrum pratense (cow-wheat) 132
Melangyna compositarum (hoverfly) 281
Meles meles (badger) 181, 220, 285–6, 328
Melica nutans (mountain melick) 124, 131
Mentha pulegium (pennyroyal) 245
　aquatica (water mint) 162, 234, 267
Menyanthes trifoliate (bogbean) 234, 248
Meotica anglica 167
Mercurialis perennis (dog's mercury) 133, 209, 263, 319, 320
Mergellus albellus (smew) 239
Mergus merganser (goosander) 258
merlin (*Falco columbarius*) **141**
Meta menardi (orb-web spider) **211–13**
Metellina merianae (cave spider) 214
Micarea alabastrites (lichen) 194
　hedlundii (lichen) 194
　pycnidiophora (lichen) 194
　stipitata (lichen) 194
Microtus gregalis (narrow-headed vole) 59
midge, meniscus (*Dixa*) 218
milkwort, heath (*Polygala serpyllifolia*) 248
Milvus milvus (red kite) 89, **90**, 142, 283, 284–5
mink, American (*Neovison vison*) 243
minnow (*Phoxinus phoxinus*) 157
mint, water (*Mentha aquatica*) 162, 234, 267
mistletoe (*Viscum album*) 271, **348–9**
Mnium hornum (swan's-neck thyme-moss) 109, 271
mole (*Talpa europaea*) 328
Molinia caerulea (purple moor-grass) 93, 102, 105, 332, 337
Monotropa hypopitys (yellow bird's-nest) **170**, 271
moor-grass, purple (*Molinia caerulea*) 93, 102, 105, 332, 337
moorhen (*Gallinula chloropus*) 260

moss:
  acuteleaf small limestone (*Seligeria acutifolia*) 125
  brown's four-tooth (*Tetradontium brownianum*) 194
  Haller's apple (*Bartramia Hallerana*) 194
  Holt's mouse-tail (*Isothecium holtii*) 194
  red leskea (*Orthothecium rufescens*) **110**
  rose (*Rhodobryum roseum*) 132
  small limestone (*Seligeria pusilla*) 125
  summer (*Anoectangium aestivum*) 109
  squirrel-tail (*Leucodon sciuroides*) **66**
  St Winifrid's (*Chiloscyphus polyanthus*) 161
  tree (*Climacium dendroides*) 256
  willow (*Fontinalis*) 177
Motacilla alba yarrellii (pied wagtail) 146, 147, 237
  cinerea (grey wagtail) 180
  flava (yellow wagtail) 150, 237
moth, brown silver-lined (*Petrophora chlorosata*) 145
  clouded border (*Lomaspilis marginata*) 273
  common pug (*Eupithecia vulgate*) 273
  dark arches (*Apamea monoglypha*) 273
  gold spot (*Plusia festuca*) 112
  heart and dart (*Agrotis exclamationis*) 273
  herald (*Scoliopteryx libatrix*) **211–12**, 213
  light emerald (*Campaea margaritata*) 273
  map-winged swift (*Pharmacis fusconebulosa*) 145
  May high-flyer (*Hydriomena impluviata*) 273
  mistletoe marble (*Celypha woodiana*) 349
  red-necked footman (*Atolmis rubricollis*) 281
  scarce silver y (*Syngrapha interrogationis*) 114, 117
  Silurian (*Eriopygodes imbecilla*) **115–17**
  tissue (*Triphosa dubitata*) 211–12
  white ermine (*Spilosoma lubricipeda*) 273
mountain everlasting (*Antennaria dioica*) 130
mountain melick (*Melica nutans*) 124, 131
mouse, harvest (*Mus minutes*) 342
  wood (*Apodemus sylvaticus*) 275, 344
  yellow-necked (*Apodemus flavicollis*) 277
mudwort, water (*Limosella aquatica*) 244
mugwort (*Artemisia vulgaris*) 58, 164
muntjac, Chinese/Reeves's (*Muntiacus reevesi*) 288
Mus minutes (harvest mouse) 342
Muscardinus avellanarius (dormouse) **275–7**

mussels, freshwater pearl (*Margaritifera margaritifera*) **169–71**
Mustela erminea (stoat) 328
  nivalis (weasel) 328
Mycelis muralis (wall lettuce) 133
Myodes glareolus (bank vole) 344
Myosotis (forget-me-not) 320
  scorpioides (water forget-me-not) 162, 248
Myotis daubentoni (Daubenton's bat) 184, 260
  nattereri (Natterer's bat) **326–7**
Myriophyllum (water-milfoil) 156
  alternifolium (alternate water-milfoil) 161, 225
Myrmica (ants) 146
Myrrhis odorata (sweet cicely) 268

Narcissus pseudonarcissus (daffodil) 319–20
Nardus stricta (mat-grass) 93, 98
Narthecium ossifragum (bog asphodel) 102
Nasonovia saxifragae (aphid) 112
Nasturtium officinale (water-cress) 177, 248
Natrix natrix (grass snake) 152
Nebria gyllenhali (beetle) 113
  salina 112
Neoitamus cyanurus (common awl robberfly) 281, **282**
Neottia nidus-avis (bird's-nest orchid) 270
Neovison vison (American mink) 243
Nesticus cellulanus (comb-footed cellar spider) 214
nettle, stinging (*Urtica dioica*) 99, 133, 164, 209
Neuralethopteris schlehanii (fossil) 46
Neuropteris jongmansii (fossil) 46
  rectinervis (fossil) 46
newt, great crested (*Tritus cristatus*) 74, 228, 247
  palmate (*Lissotriton helveticus*) 228, 247
  smooth/common (*Lissotriton vulgaris*) 228, 247
nightshade, deadly (*Atropa belladonna*) 81
Niphargus fontanus (well shrimp) **216–17**
Nitella flexilis (stonewort) 225
nodding-moss, crookneck (*Pohlia camptotrachela*) 256
Nostoc muscorum (blue-green alga) 209, **231**
notchwort, Heller's (*Anastrophyllum hellerianum*) 193
  larger cut (*Tritomaria exsectiformis*) 266
  tumid (*Lophozia ventricosa*) 109
Notiophilus rufipes (frog beetle) 273
Numenius arquata (curlew) 142, 164
Nuphar × *spenneriana* (yellow water-lily) 233

SPECIES INDEX · 399

Nyctalus noctula (noctule bat) 260, 295

oak (Quercus) 60, 65, 341, 346
   pedunculate (Quercus robur) 62–3, 162, 263, **297–9**
   sessile (Quercus petraea) 144, 263, 265, 270
oat-grass, false (Arrhenatherum elatius) 133
Ochotona pusilla (steppe pika) 59
Odontoschisma denudatum (matchstick flapwort) 193
oedipodium, Griffith's (Oedipodium griffithianum) 109
Oedipodium griffithianum (Griffith's oedipodium) 109
Oenanthe fistulosa (tubular water-dropwort) 234
   crocata (hemlock water-dropwort) 162
Oenanthe oenanthe (wheatear) 139, 140, 146, 147
Olisthopus rotundatus 112
Oncorhynchus mykiss (rainbow trout) 221
Oniscus asellus (common shiny woodlouse) 218
Oncopsis flavicollis (leafhopper) 272
Opegrapha dolomitica (lichen) 105
Ophioglossum vulgatum (adder's-tongue fern) 338
orchid, bird's-nest (Neottia nidus-avis) 270
   early purple (Orchis mascula) 106
   greater butterfly (Platanthera chlorantha) 318, **335**, 336, 338
   lesser butterfly (Platanthera bifolia) 332
   spotted (Dactylorhiza) 318
Oreopteris limbosperma (lemon-scented fern) 138
Orthetrum coerulescens (keeled skimmer) 248
Orthilia secunda (serrated wintergreen) 106
Orthothecium rufescens (red leskea) **110**
Oryctolagus cuniculus (rabbit) 129
Osmunda regalis (royal fern) 192, 249
osprey (Pandion haliaetus) 258
Otiorhynchus nodosus (weevil) 111
otter (Lutra lutra) 61, 177, 182–4, 220, 260
ouzel, ring (Turdus torquatus) **97–8**, 139, 140, 146, 147
owl, barn (Tyto alba) 344, **345–6**
Oxalis acetosella (wood sorrel) 133, 209
oxychilus cellarius (cellar snail) 218

Pacifastacus leniusculus (signal crayfish) 176, 178
Pandion haliaetus (osprey) 258
Parasyrphus malinellus (hoverfly) 281
   lineola (hoverfly) 281
Parietaria judaica (pellitory-of-the-wall) 81

Paris quadrifolia (herb-Paris) 268
Parmelia saxatilis (lichen) 137
Parus major (great tit) 146, 147
Patrobus atrorufus (beetle) 273
pawwort, trunk (Barbilophozia attenuata) 136
peacock (Inachis io) 342
Pedicularis sylvatica (lousewort) 248
pellia (Pellia epiphylla) 161
   endive (Pellia endiviifolia) 162, 209
pellitory-of-the-wall (Parietaria judaica) 81
Peltigera polydactyla (lichen) 105
pennyroyal (Mentha pulegium) 245
pennywort, marsh (Hydrocotyle vulgaris) 102
perch (Perca fluviatilis) 177, 240, 260
peregrine (Falco peregrinus) 140
Periparus ater (coal tit) 282
periwinkle (Vinca minor) 81
Perizoma flavofasciata (sandy carpet moth) 273
Perla (stonefly) 273
Pernis apivorus (honey-buzzard) 285
Persicaria amphibia (amphibious bistort) 163, 254
   hydropiper (water-pepper) 163
   maculosa (redshank) 163
Pertusaria lactescens (lichen) 324
Petromyzon marinus (sea lamprey) 157
Petrophora chlorosata (brown silver-lined moth) 145
Phagocata vitta (flatworm) 218
Phalaris arundinacea (canary-grass) 162
Pharmacis fusconebulosa (map-winged swift moth) 145
Phegopteris connectilis (beech fern) 106, 193
Phenacolimax major (greater pellucid glass snail) 273–4
Phoenicurus phoenicurus (redstart) 146, 147
Phoxinus phoxinus (minnow) 157
Phragmites australis (common reed) 234, 249
Phyllitis scolopendrium (hart's-tongue fern) 131, 133, 209, 263
Phyllopsora rosei (lichen) 194
Phylloscopus trochilus (willow warbler) 146, 147, 272, 282
Physcomitrium sphaericum (dwarf bladder-moss) 256
Phytophthora ramorum (ramorum) 280
Pica pica (magpie) 147
Picea abies (Norway spruce) 278
   sitchensis (Sitka spruce) 278
Picus viridis (green woodpecker) 350

pike (*Esox lucius*) 61, 177, **240–2**, 260
pillwort (*Pilularia globulifera*) **244–5**
Pilosella officinarum (mouse-ear hawkweed) 338
Pilularia globulifera (pillwort) **244–5**
pimpernel, bog (*Anagallis tenella*) 250, 332
  yellow (*Lysimachia nemorum*) 263, 267
Pimpinella saxifrage (burnet saxifrage) 338
pine, Corsican (*Pinus nigra*) 278
  Scots (*Pinus sylvestris*) 60, 262
Pinguicula vulgaris (butterwort) 248
pinkgill, lilac (*Entoloma porphyrophaeum*) 129
pintail (*Anas acuta*) 247
Pinus nigra (Corsican pine) 278
  sylvestris (Scots pine) 60, 262
Pipistrellus pipistrellus (common pipistrelle) 186, 260, 326
  pygmaeus (soprano pipistrelle) 326
pipit, meadow (*Anthus pratensis*) 142, 146, 147
  rock (*Anthus petrosus*) 142
  tree (*Anthus trivialis*) 146, 147, 148
Plagiomnium undulatum (thyme-moss) 209
Plagiothecium denticulatum (donnian silk-moss) 109
plait-moss, cypress-leaved (*Hypnum cupressiforme*) 271
  heath (*Hypnum jutlandicum*) 109
  supine (*Hypnum resupinatum*) 349
plantain, ribwort (*Plantago lanceolata*) 337
planthopper (*Dytroptis pteridis*) 145
Platanthera bifolia (lesser butterfly orchid) 332
  chlorantha (greater butterfly orchid) 318, **335**, 336, 338
Plateumaris affinis (leaf beetle) 250
Platydictya jungermannioides (Spruce's leskea) 271
Plegaderus dissectus (beetle) 274
plover, golden (*Pluvialis apricaria*) 141
  little ringed (*Charadrius dubius*) 180
Plusia festuca (gold spot moth) 112
Pluvialis apricaria (golden plover) 141
Poa annua (annual meadow-grass) 99
  pratensis (smooth meadow-grass) 99
  trivialis (rough meadow-grass) 267
pochard (*Aythya farina*) 239
pocket-moss, beck (*Fissidens rufulus*) 161
  Curnow's (*Fissidens curnovii*) 194
  river (*Fissidens rivularis*) 161
  rock (*Fissidens dubius*) 323
  Welsh (*Fissidens celticus*) 194

Pohlia camptotrachela (crookneck nodding-moss) 256
  nutans (nodding thread-moss) 109
polecat (*Mustela putorius*) 328
Polyblastia allobata (lichen) 194
Polycelis nigra (flatworm) 228
Polycentropus flavomaculatus (caddis fly) 227
Polygala serpyllifolia (heath milkwort) 248
Polygonatum odoratum (Solomon's seal) 124
polypody (*Polypodium vulgare*) 133
  southern (*Polypodium cambricum*) 81
Polystichum aculeatum (hard shield-fern) 133
Polytrichum 98
  alpinum (alpine haircap) 109
  commune (common haircap) 102, 248
pond-sedge, lesser (*Carex acutiformis*) 162
pondweed (*Potamogeton crispus*) 232
  bog (*Potamogeton polygonifolius*) 102, 228, 248
  broadleaved (*Potamogeton natans*) 163
  fennel (*Potamogeton pectinatus*) 230
  horned (*Zannichellia palustris*) 230
  lesser (*Potamogeton pusillus*) 232
  long-stalked (*Potamogeton praelongus*) 233
  perfoliate (*Potamogeton perfoliatus*) 232
  shining (*Potamogeton lucens*) 232
  various-leaved (*Potamogeton gramineus*) 233
poplar (*Populus*) 245
  black (*Populus nigra*) **289–93**
poppy, Welsh 268
Populus (poplar) 245
  nigra (black poplar) **289–93**
Porrhomma rosenhaueri (spider) 214
Potamogeton crispus (pondweed) 232
  gramineus (various-leaved pondweed) 233
  lucens (shining pondweed) 232
  natans (broad-leaved pondweed) 163
  pectinatus (fennel pondweed) 230
  perfoliatus (perfoliate pondweed) 232
  polygonifolius (bog pondweed) 102, 228, 248
  pusillus (lesser pondweed) 232
  praelongus (long-stalked pondweed) 233
Potentilla anserina (silverweed) 163
  erecta (tormentil) 98, 248, 332, 337, 338
pouchwort, straggling (*Saccogyna viticulosa*) 194
pouncewort, MacKay's (*Marchesinia mackaii*) 271
powdercap, earthy (*Cystoderma amianthinum*) 271
  strangler (*Squamanita paradoxa*) 271

Preissia quadrata (mushroom-headed liverwort) 109
primrose (*Primula vulgaris*) 320
Primula veris (cowslip) 106, 133, **341**
 vulgaris (primrose) 320
Proasellus cavaticus (freshwater hoglouse) **216**
Prunella modularis (dunnock) 146, 147
 vulgaris (selfheal) 133
Prunus avium (bird cherry) 267
 spinosa (blackthorn) 132, 143, 340, 342
Psacadina verbekei (fly) 250
Pseudephemerum nitidum (serrated earth-moss) 254
 nitidum (delicate earth-moss) 254
Pseudephebe pubescens (lichen) 136
Pseudoscleropodium purum (neat feather-moss) 264
Pseudotaxiphyllum elegans (elegant silk-moss) 109
Pseudotsuga menziesii (Douglas fir) 278
Pteridium aquilinum (bracken) 50, 133, 143, 145, 271
Pterostichus madidus (ground beetle) 112
 diligens (ground beetle) 250
Puma concolor (puma) 286–7
puma (*Puma concolor*) 286–7
purple-loosestrife (*Lythrum salicaria*) 234
Pyramidula pusilla (rock snail) 119
Pyrochroa coccinea (black-headed cardinal beetle) 274
Pyrrhidium sanguineum (Welsh oak longhorn beetle) 294
Pyrrhosoma nymphula (large red damselfly) 246, 248

quaking grass (*Briza media*) 332
Quercus (oak) 60, 65, 341, 346
 petraea (sessile oak) 144, 263, 265, 270
 robur (pedunculate oak) 62–3, 162, 263, **297–9**
quillwort (*Isoetes lacustris*) 224, 226, 228

rabbit (*Oryctolagus cuniculus*) 129
Racomitrium aciculare (yellow fringe-moss) 161
 aquaticum (narrow-leaved fringe-moss) 109
 fasciculare (green mountain fringe-moss) 109
 lanuginosum (woolly fringe-moss) 136
ragged robin (*Lychnis flos-cuculi*) 102
Ramalina canariensis (lichen) 324
 ramorum (*Phytophthora ramorum*) 280
Rana temporaria (common frog) 152, 228, 247

Rangifer tarandus (reindeer) 59
ransoms (*Allium ursinum*) 133
Ranunculus acris (meadow buttercup) 338
 aquatilis (common water-crowfoot) 156, 248
 circinatus (fan-leaved water-crowfoot) 233
 ficaria (lesser celandine) 263
 flammula (lesser spearwort) 161, 245, 248
 fluitans (river water-crowfoot) **156**, 177, 225
 lingua (greater spearwort) 163
 omiophyllus (round-leaved crowfoot) 102
 repens (creeping buttercup) 267
rat, brown (*Rattus norvegicus*) 177
rattle, yellow (*Rhinanthus minor*) 335, 336
raven (*Corvus corax*) **140**–1, 146, 147
redshank (*Persicaria maculosa*) 163
redstart (*Phoenicurus phoenicurus*) 146, 147
redwing (*Turdus iliacus*) 142, 350
reed, common (*Phragmites australis*) 234, 249
reedmace, lesser (*Typha angustifolia*) 234
Regulus regulus (goldcrest) 74
reindeer (*Rangifer tarandus*) 59
Rhabdomastix laeta (cranefly) 168
Rhamnus cathartica (buckthorn) 266, 342
Rhinanthus minor (yellow rattle) 335, 336
Rhinolophus ferrumequinum (greater horseshoe bat) 187, 326
 hipposideros (lesser horseshoe bat) **185–7**, 219–20, 326
Rithrogena germanica (March brown) 172
 semicolorata (olive upright mayfly) 172
Rhizocarpon geographicum (lichen) 137
Rhizophagus nitidulus (cranefly) 274
Rhodobryum roseum (rose-moss) 132
Rhynchostegiella tenella (tender feather-moss) 322, 323
 murale (wall feather-moss) 209
Rhynchostegium riparioides (long-beaked water feather-moss) 161
Rhytidiadelphus squarrosus (springy turf-moss) 130, 264
 subpinnatus (scarce turf-moss) 194
Riccia beyrichiana (purple crystalwort) 254
 cavernosa (cavernous crystalwort) 254
 glauca (glaucous crystalwort) 254
 hueberiana (violet crystalwort) **252–5**
 sorocarpa (common crystalwort) 254
Riparia riparia (sand martin) 180–1, 237
Rivularia haematites (bacterium) 251
roach (*Rutilius rutilius*) 175

robberfly, common awl (*Neoitamus cyanurus*) 281, **282**
robin (*Erithacus rubecula*) 146, 147
rock-bristle, bentfoot (*Seligeria campylopoda*) 125
   Donn's (*Seligeria donniana*) 125
   Irish (*Seligeria oelandica*) 125
   triangular/trifid (*Seligeria patula*) 125
rock-cress, hairy (*Seligeria*) 125
rock-moss, alpine (*Andreaea alpina*) 109
   black (*Andreaea rupestris*) 109
   dusky (*Andreaea rothii falcata*) 109
rock-rose, common (*Helianthemum nummularium*) 129
rook (*Corvus frugilegus*) 284
Rorippa (yellow cress) 162
Rosa arvensis (field rose) 340
   canina (dog/wild rose) 143, 340
   pimpinellifolia (burnet rose) 132, 341
   rubiginosa (sweet briar) 34–5
   villosa (apple rose) 132
rose, apple (*Rosa villosa*) 132
   burnet (*Rosa pimpinellifolia*) 132, 341
   dog/wild (*Rosa canina*) 143, 340
   field (*Rosa arvensis*) 340
   guelder (*Viburnum opulus*) 132
rosemary (*Rosmarinus officinalis*) 320
   bog (*Andromeda polifolia*) 102
rose-moss (*Rhodobryum roseum*) 132
Rosmarinus officinalis (rosemary) 320
rowan (*Sorbus aucuparia*) 107, 143, 262, 263
Rubus breconensis (bramble) 27
   iscanus (bramble) 162, 271, 342
   saxatilis (stone bramble) 132, 143
rush (*Juncus*) 102, 161, 337
   bulbous (*Juncus bulbosus*) 102, 225, 228
   compact (*Juncus conglomeratus*) 248
   corkscrew/spiral (*Juncus effuses*) 99–100, **101**
   flowering (*Butomus umbellatus*) 234
   heath (*Juncus squarrosus*) 98
   sharp-flowered (*Juncus acutiflorus*) 102, 332, 337
   soft (*Juncus effusus*) 99, 228, 248, 357
Russula minutula 271
rustwort, notched (*Marsupella emarginata*) 109
rustyback (*Ceterach officinarum*) 133, 209
Rutilius rutilius (roach) 175
ryegrass, perennial (*Lolium perenne*) 99

Saccogyna viticulosa (straggling pouchwort) 194
saffron, meadow (*Colchicum autumnale*) **338–9**
sage, wood (*Teucrium scorodinia*) 132
sagebrush (*Artemisia tridentata*) 58
sagewort (*Artemisia frigida*) 58
Salix (willow) 59, 143, 162, 249
   alba (white willow) 293
   cinerea (grey willow) 267
   oleifolia (rusty willow) 161
   fragilis (crack willow) 163
   herbacea (dwarf willow) 105
   triandra (almond willow) 163–4
Salmo salar (Atlantic salmon) 157, 170–2
   trutta (brown trout) 157, 172, 177, 219, 225
salmon, Atlantic (*Salmo salar*) 157, 170–2
salmon salad (*Tremiscus helvelloides*) 271
Salvia verbenaca (wild clary) 81
Sambucus nigra (elder) 143
sandpiper, common (*Actitis hypoleucos*) 142
   green (*Tringa ochropus*) 164
Sanguisorba minor (salad burnet) 129
   officinalis (great burnet) 130, 335
sanicle (*Sanicula europea*) 133
Sanionia uncinata (sickle-leaved hook-moss) 109
Saturnia pavonia (emperor moth) **114**
sawfly (*Aneugmenus*) 145, 146
Saxicola rubetra (whinchat) 97, 146, 147, **148**–50
   rubicola (stonechat) 148
Saxifraga hypnoides (mossy saxifrage) 112, 130, **131**, 133
   oppositifolium (purple saxifrage) **96**, 105, 352
   tridactylites (rue-leaved saxifrage) 81
saxifrage, burnet (*Pimpinella saxifraga*) 338
   mossy (*Saxifraga hypnoides*) 112, 130, **131**, 133
   opposite-leaved golden (*Chrysosplenium oppositifolium*) 102, 209, 267
   purple (*Saxifraga oppositifolium*) **96**, 105, 352
   rue-leaved (*Saxifraga tridactylites*) 81
Scabiosa columbaria (small scabious) 131, 132, 133
scabious, devil's-bit (*Succisa pratensis*) 318, 332, 333, 337
   small (*Scabiosa columbaria*) 131, 132, 133
Scapania gracilis (western earwort) 136
   gymnostomophila (narrow-lobed earwort) 109
   undulate (water earwort) 161
Schistidium crassipilum (thickpoint grimmia) 136
Schoenoplectus (club-rush) 234

Sciadophyton steinmanni (fossil) 30
Scirpus cespitosus (deergrass) 105
  sylvaticus (wood club-rush) 163
Sciurus vulgaris (red squirrel) 176
  carolinensis (grey squirrel) 176
Scleropodium cespitans (tufted feather-moss) 162
Scoliopteryx libatrix (herald moth) 211–12, 213
Scolopax rusticola (woodcock) 247
Scolytus scolytus (beetle) 61–2
screw-moss, intermediate (*Syntrichia intermedia*) 323
  wall (*Tortula muralis*) 322
Scutellaria minor (lesser skullcap) 250
sedge flies 172
sedge, bottle (*Carex rostrata*) 248
  carnation (*Carex panacea*) 102
  common (*Carex nigra*) 98
  flea (*Carex pulicaris*) 332
  glaucous (*Carex flacca*) 133, 337
  green-ribbed (*Carex binervis*) 98
  remote (*Carex remota*) 161
  slender (*Carex lasiocarpa*) 244
  soft-leaved (*Carex montana*) 131
  star (*Carex echinata*) 102
  tawny (*Carex hostiana*) 332, 337
  yellow (*Carex viridula*) 102
Sedum forsteranum (rock stonecrop) 105
Selenochlamys ysbryda (ghost slug) 324–5
selfheal (*Prunella vulgaris*) 133
Seligeria (rock-bristle) 125
  acutifolia (small acuteleaf limestone moss) 125
  campylopoda (bentfoot rock-bristle) 125
  donniana (Donn's rock-bristle) 125
  oelandica (Irish rock-bristle) 125
  patula (triangular/trifid rock-bristle) 125
  pusilla (small limestone moss) 125
Sennicaulis hippocrepiformis (fossil) 30
Sericostoma personatum (caddis fly) 227
Serratella ignite (blue-winged olive mayfly) 172
service tree, wild (*Sorbus torminalis*) 271
shad, allis (*Alosa alosa*) 157, 173, 175
  twaite (*Alosa fallax*) 157, **173–4**
shield-fern, hard (*Polystichum aculeatum*) 133
shoreweed (*Littorella uniflora*) 224, 226, 228
shrike, great grey (*Lanius excubitor*) 285
shrimp, well (*Niphargus fontanus*) **216–17**
silk-moss, donnian (*Plagiothecium denticulatum*) 109
  elegant (*Pseudotaxiphyllum elegans*) 109

Silurian moth (*Eriopygodes imbecilla*) **115–17**
silverweed (*Potentilla anserina*) 163
siskin (*Carduelis spinus*) 282
skimmer, keeled (*Orthetrum coerulescens*) 248
skullcap, lesser (*Scutellaria minor*) 250
skylark (*Alauda arvensis*) 142, 146, 147
slug, ash-black (*Limax cinereoniger*) 118
  ghost (*Selenochlamys ysbryda*) **324–5**
  grey field (*Deroceras reticulatum*) 113
  hedgehog (*Arion intermedius*) 117–18
  Inishowen (*Arion owenii*) 325–6
  large black (*Arion ater*) 113, 117
  lemon (*Malacolimax tenellus*) **274**
  orange-staining dusky (*Arion subfuscus*) 117–18
  tree (*Lehmannia marginata*) **118**
  worm (*Boettgerilla pallens*) 326
smew (*Mergellus albellus*) 239
smut fungus (*Urocystis trollii*) 332
snail, cellar (*Oxychilus cellarius*) 218
  crystal (*Vitrea contracta*) 218
  dwarf pond (*Galba truncatula*) 113
  English chrysalis (*Leiostyla anglica*) 274
  furrowed/strawberry (*Trochulus striolata*) 218
  Geyer's whorl (*Vertigo geyeri*) 250
  greater pellucid glass (*Phenacolimax major*) 273–4
  hairy (*Trochulus hispida*) 218
  herald (*Carychium minimum*) 218
  hollowed glass (*Zonitoides excavatus*) 117
  lapidary (*Helicogona lapicida*) 119
  large chrysalis (*Abida secale*) 119
  plated (*Spermodea lamellata*) 274
  point (*Acicula fusca*) 218
  rock (*Pyramidula pusilla*) 119
  rounded (*Discus rotundatus*) 113, 218
  thin-shelled brown (*Zenobiella subrufescens*) 274
  three-toothed moss (*Azeca goodalli*) 274
  two-toothed door (*Clausilia bidentata*) 113, 218
snake, grass (*Natrix natrix*) 152
snipe (*Gallinago gallinago*) 247
snow flea (*Boreus hyemalis*) **122**
snow lichen, Vesuvius (*Stereocaulon vesuvianum*) 137
snowdrop (*Galanthus nivalis*) 320
Solanum dulcamara (bittersweet) 164
Solomon's seal (*Polygonatum odoratum*) 124

Sorbus (whitebeam) 123, 289, 302–10
  aucuparia (rowan) 107, 143, 262, 263
  cambrensis (Welsh whitebeam) 302
  leptophylla (thin-leaved whitebeam) 302, 308, **309**
  leyana (Ley's whitebeam) 302, **303–5**, 310
  minima (lesser whitebeam) 302, 305, **307**
  × *motleyi* (Motley's whitebeam) 302, 307, 310
  porrigentiformis (grey-leaved whitebeam) 308, 310
  rupicola (rock whitebeam) 310
  stenophylla (Llanthony Valley whitebeam) 302, 306–7
  torminalis (wild service tree) 271
Sparganium angustifolium (bur-reed) 225
  erectum (branched bur-reed) 162
sparrowhawk (*Accipiter nisus*) 149, 150, 283
spearwort, greater (*Ranunculus lingua*) 163
  lesser (*Ranunculus flammula*) 161, 245, 248
speedwell, spiked (*Veronica spicata spicata*) 126–9
Speleolepta leptogaster (common cave gnat) 211
Spermodea lamellata (plated snail) 274
Sphagnum (bog-moss) 98, 244
  auriculatum (cow-horn bog-moss) 102
  capillifolium (acute-leaved bog-moss) 248
  cuspidatum (feathery bog-moss) 102
  fallax (recurved sphagnum) 102
  magellanicum (Magellanic bog-moss) 250
  papillosum (papillose bog-moss) 248
  quinquefarium (five-ranked bog-moss) 271
sphagnum, recurved (*Sphagnum fallax*) 102
Sphenolobopsis pearsonii (horsehair threadwort) 193
spider:
  Aphileta misera 244
  Lepthyphantes pallidus 215
  Lessertia dentichelis 215
  Metellina merianae 214
  Porrhomma rosenhaueri **214**
  Tegenaria 214
  Wackenaera kochi 244
    unicornis 244
  comb-footed cellar spider (*Nesticus cellulanus*) 214
  orb-web cave (*Meta menardi*) **211–13**
  wolf spider (*Arctosa cinerea*) **168–9**
spike-rush, common (*Eleocharis palustris*) 162
  few-flowered (*Eleocharis quinqueflora*) 250

Spilosoma lubricipeda (white ermine moth) 273
spindles, golden (*Clavulinopsis fusiformis*) 129
  rose (*Clavaria rosea*) **130**
Spiriverpa lunulata (northern silver stiletto-fly) 168
Spirodela polyrhiza (greater duckweed) 233
Splachnum ampullaceum (cruet collar-moss) 138
  sphaericum (round-fruited collar-moss) 138
spleenwort, black (*Asplenium adiantum-nigrum*) 131
  green (*Asplenium viride*) 131, 133, 193, 264
  maidenhair (*Asplenium trichomanes*) 133, 209
Sporogonites exuberans (fossil) 30
springtails 113, 121, 122, 217–18
spruce, Norway (*Picea abies*) 278
  Sitka (*Picea sitchensis*) 278
spurge, wood (*Euphorbia amygdaloides*) 266
Squamanita paradoxa (strangler powdercap) 271
squirrel, grey (*Sciurus carolinensis*) 176
  red (*Sciurus vulgaris*) 176
St John's-wort (*Hypericum elodes*) 248
Stachys officinalis (betony) 337
starling (*Sturnus vulgaris*) 239
Staurothele succedens 105
Stellaria alsine (bog stitchwort) 102
  media (chickweed) 99
steppe pika (*Ochotona pusilla*) 59
Stereocaulon vesuvianum (Vesuvius snow lichen) 137
stiletto-fly, southern silver (*Cliorismia rustica*) 168
  northern silver (*Spiriverpa lunulata*) 168
stitchwort, bog (*Stellaria alsine*) 102
stoat (*Mustela erminea*) 328
stonechat (*Saxicola rubicola*) 148
stonecrop, rock (*Sedum forsteranum*) 105
stonefly (*Perla*) 273
  large yellow sally (*Chloroperla torrentium*) 172
stonewort (*Chara*) 232, 233–4
stonewort (*Nitella flexilis*) 225
Streptomyces (bacterium) 211
Sturnus vulgaris (starling) 239
Subularia aquatic (awlwort) 225, 234
Succisa pratensis (devil's-bit scabious) 318, 332, 333, 337
Suillus grevillei (larch bolete) 281
summer-moss (*Anoectangium aestivum*) 109
sundew, oblong-leafed (*Drosera intermedia*) 249
  round-leaved (*Drosera rotundifolia*) 102, 248, 250

Sus scrofa (wild boar) 61
swallow, barn (*Hirundo rustica*) 142, 215, 237, 344–5
swan, mute (*Cygnus olor*) 181, **237–9**, 245
swan-neck moss, rusty (*Campylopus flexuosus*) 136
sweet-grass, floating (*Glyceria fluitans*) 161, 164, 245
swift (*Apus apus*) 142, 215
sycamore (*Acer pseudoplatanus*) 162, 341
Sylvia borin (garden warbler) 146, 147
 sarda (Marmora's warbler) 150–1
 undata (Dartford warbler) **150–1**
Sympetrum danae (black darter dragonfly) 245, 248
Symphytum (comfrey) 162
Syntrichia intermedia (intermediate screw-moss) 323
Synechoccus aeruginosum (alga) 209
 elongatus (alga) 211
Syngrapha interrogationis (scarce silver y moth) 114, 117

Tachybaptus ruficollis (little grebe) 245, 246
Talpa europaea (mole) 328
tamarisk-moss, wry-leaved (*Heterocladium heteropterum*) 109
Tanacetum parthenium (feverfew) 81
Tanyptera atrata (comb-horn cranefly) 281, **282**
Taraxacum (dandelion) 133
 breconense (Brecon dandelion) 27, 162
 degelii (Degelius's dandelion) 162
 vachellii 162
Tarella trowenii 27, 29
Taxus baccata (yew) 289, **312–17**
teal (*Anas crecca*) 258
teasel (*Dipsacus fullonum*) 320
Tegenaria (spider) 214
Tetradontium brownianum (brown's four-tooth moss) 194
Tetrao tetrix (black grouse) 97
Tetraplodon mnioides (slender cruet-moss) **138**
Teucrium scorodinia (wood sage) 132
Thalictrum flavum (meadow rue) 59
 minus (lesser meadow-rue) 106, 131
thistle, creeping (*Cirsium arvense*) 99, 164
 marsh (*Cirsium palustre*) 133
 meadow (*Cirsium dissectum*) 332
 melancholy (*Cirsium heterophyllum*) 195
 spear (*Cirsium vulgare*) 133

Thamnobryum alopecurum (fox-tail feather-moss) 161
thread-moss, capillary (*Bryum capillare*) 322
 crimson tuber (*Bryum rubens*) 323
 golden (*Leptobryum pyriforme*) 256
 nodding (*Pohlia nutans*) 109
 Tozer's (*Epipterygium tozeri*) 256
 wall (*Bryum radiculosum*) 323
threadwort, hairy (*Blepharostoma trichophyllum*) 109
 horsehair (*Sphenolobopsis pearsonii*) 193
thrush, mistle (*Turdus viscivorus*) 146, 147
 song (*Turdus philomelos*) 282
Thuya plicata (western red cedar) 278
thyme, large (*Thymus pulegioides*) 339
 wild (*Thymus polytrichus*) 129
thyme-moss (*Plagiomnium undulatum*) 209
 swan's-neck (*Mnium hornum*) 109, 271
Thymus polytrichus (wild thyme) 129
 pulegioides (large thyme) 339
tick, sheep (*Ixodes ricinus*) 145–6
Tilia (lime) 61
 cordata (small-leafed lime) 271
Tipula marginata (cranefly) 250
tit, blue (*Cyanistes caeruleus*) 146, 147, 350
 coal (*Periparus ater*) 282
 great (*Parus major*) 146, 147
toad, common (*Bufo bufo*) 247
 natterjack (*Epidalea calamita*) 247
toadflax, ivy-leaved (*Cymbalaria muralis*) 81
Tomocerus minor 217
toothwort (*Lathraea squamaria*) 271
tormentil (*Potentilla erecta*) 98, 248, 332, 337, 338
Tortella bambergeri (Bamberger's crisp-moss) 136, **137**
 tortuosa (frizzled crisp-moss) 109
Tortula muralis (wall screw-moss) 322
traveller's joy (*Clematis vitalba*) 342
treecreeper (*Certhia familiaris*) 74
tree-moss (*Climacium dendroides*) 256
Tremiscus helvelloides (salmon salad) 271
Trichodon cylindricus (cylindric ditrichum) 323
Trichius fasciatus (bee beetle) **194–5**
Tricholoma (fungus) 271
Trifolium medium (zigzag clover) 132
 pratense (red clover) 335, 337, 338
trimerophyte (fossil) 30
Tringa ochropus (green sandpiper) 164
Triphosa dubitata (tissue moth) 211–12

Tritus cristatus (great crested newt) 74, 228, 247
Trochulus hispida (hairy snail) 218
  striolata (furrowed/strawberry snail) 218
Troglodytes troglodytes (wren) 146, 147, 215
Trollius europaeus (globeflower) 133, 332
trout, brown (*Salmo trutta*) 157, 172, 177, 219, 225
  rainbow (*Oncorhynchus mykiss*) 221
Tsuga heterophylla (western hemlock) 278
tufa-moss, verdigris (*Gymnostomum aeruginosum*) 109, 209
Turdus iliacus (redwing) 142, 350
  merula (blackbird) 146, 147, 316
  philomelos (song thrush) 282
  pilaris (fieldfare) 142, 350
  torquatus (ring ouzel) 97, **98**, 139, 140, 146, 147
  viscivorus (mistle thrush) 146, 147
turf-moss, scarce (*Rhytidiadelphus subpinnatus*) 194
  springy (*Rhytidiadelphus squarrosus*) 130, 264
tussock-sedge, greater (*Carex paniculata*) 248, 249
twayblade, greater (*Listera ovata*) 318
Typha angustifolia (lesser reedmace) 234
Typhaeus typhaeus (minotaur beetle) **111**
Tyto alba (barn owl) 344, **345–6**

Ulex europaeus (common gorse) 143
  gallii (western gorse) **104**, 105, 143
Ulmus glabra (wych elm) 267
Umbilicaria cylindrica (lichen) 136
  proboscidea (lichen) 136
  torrefacta (lichen) 136
upwinged flies 172
Urocystis trollii (smut fungus) 332
Ursus arctos (brown bear) 61, 71
Urtica dioica (stinging nettle) 99, 133, 164, 209
Usnea articulata (bearded lichen) 355

Vaccinium myrtillus (bilberry) 97, 98, 105, 248, 271, 332
  vitis-idaea (cowberry) 105, 106
valerian, marsh (*Valeriana dioica*) 267, 337
  red (*Centranthus ruber*) 81, 133
Valeriana dioica (marsh valerian) 267, 337
Vanellus vanellus (lapwing) 142, 164
Venturia populina (fossil) 29
Verbena officinalis (vervain) 81
vernal-grass, sweet (*Anthoxanthum odoratum*) 102, 332, 338

Veronica beccabunga (brooklime) 162
  catenata (pink water-speedwell) 163
  spicata hybrida (spiked speedwell) 126–9
Verrucaria (lichen) 161
  viridula 105
Vertigo geyeri (Geyer's whorl snail) 250
vervain (*Verbena officinalis*) 81
Vespa carbo (hornet) 274
vetch, upright (*Vicia orobus*) 144
vetchling, meadow (*Lathyrus pratensis*) 335
Viburnum opulus (guelder rose) 132
Vicia orobus (upright vetch) 144
Vinca minor (periwinkle) 81
Viola palustris (marsh violet) 102
  reichenbachiana (early dog-violet) 271
  riviniana (dog-violet) 133, 144, 209, 319, 320
violet, marsh (*Viola palustris*) 102
Viscum album (mistletoe) 271, **348–9**
Vitrea contracta (crystal snail) 218
vole, bank (*Myodes glareolus*) 344
  narrow-headed (*Microtus gregalis*) 59
  water (*Arvicola amphibious*) **59**, 177, 242–3
Vulpes vulpes (fox) 220, 328

Wackenaera kochi (spider) 244
  unicornis (spider) 244
wagtail, grey (*Motacilla cinerea*) 180
  pied (*Motacilla alba yarrellii*) 146, 147, 237
  yellow (*Motacilla flava*) 150, 237
Wahlenbergia hederacea (ivy-leafed bell flower) 144
wall lettuce (*Mycelis muralis*) 133
wallflower, Aegean (*Erysimum cheri*) 81
wall-rue (*Asplenium ruta-muraria*) 133, 209
warbler, aquatic (*Acrocephalus paludicola*) **236–7**
  Cetti's (*Cettia cetti*) 237
  Dartford (*Sylvia undata*) **150–1**
  garden (*Sylvia borin*) 146, 147
  Marmora's (*Sylvia sarda*) 150–1
  reed (*Acrocephalus scirpaceus*) 237
  sedge (*Acrocephalus schoenobaenus*) 236, 237
  willow (*Phylloscopus trochilus*) 146, 147, 272, 282
water-cress (*Nasturtium officinale*) 177, 248
water-crowfoot, common (*Ranunculus aquatilis*) 156, 248
  fan-leaved (*Ranunculus circinatus*) 233
  river (*Ranunculus fluitans*) **156**, 177, 225

water-dropwort, hemlock (*Oenanthe crocata*) 162
  tubular (*Oenanthe fistulosa*) 234
water-lily, yellow (*Nuphar* × *spenneriana*) 233
water-milfoil (*Myriophyllum*) 156
  alternate (*Myriophyllum alternifolium*) 161, 225
water-moss, greater (*Fontinalis antipyretica*) 156, 226–7, 256
water-pepper (*Persicaria hydropiper*) 163
water-plantain, lesser (*Baldellia ranunculoides*) 248
water-speedwell, pink (*Veronica catenata*) 163
water-starwort (*Callitriche*) 232
waterweed, Canadian (*Elodea canadensis*) 163
waxcap 349
  crimson (*Hygrocybe panacea*) 129–30
  glutinous (*Hygrocybe glutinipes*) 129–30
  golden (*Hygrocybe chlorophana*) 335
  persistent (*Hygrocybe persistens*) **129–130**
  pink (*Hygrocybe calyptriformis*) 319
  scarlet (*Hygrocybe coccinea*) 335
  toasted (*Hygrocybe colemanniana*) 129–30
weasel (*Mustela nivalis*) 328
weevil:
  Otiorhynchus nodosus 111
  mistletoe (*Ixapion variegatum*) 349
wheatear (*Oenanthe oenanthe*) 139, 140, 146, 147
whinchat (*Saxicola rubetra*) 97, 146, 147, **148–50**
whipwort, greater (*Bazzania trilobata*) 136, 193
whitebeam (*Sorbus*) 123, 289, 302–10
  lesser (*Sorbus minima*) 302, 305, **307**
  grey-leaved (*Sorbus porrigentiformis*) 308, 310
  Ley's (*Sorbus leyana*) 302, **303–5**, 310
  Llanthony Valley (*Sorbus stenophylla*) 302, 306–7
  Motley's (*Sorbus* × *motleyi*) 302, 307, 310
  rock (*Sorbus rupicola*) 310
  thin-leaved (*Sorbus leptophylla*) 302, 308, **309**
  Welsh (*Sorbus cambrensis*) 302
white-moss, smaller (*Leucobryum juniperoideum*) 136
whitlowgrass, common (*Erophila verna*) 81
wigeon (*Anas penelope*) 164, 247

wildcat (*Felis sylvestris*) 61
willow (*Salix*) 59, 143, 162, 249
  almond (*Salix triandra*) 163–4
  crack (*Salix fragilis*) 163
  dwarf (*Salix herbacea*) 105
  grey (*Salix cinerea*) 267
  rusty (*Salix cinerea oleifolia*) 161
  white (*Salix alba*) 293
willowherb, broad-leaved (*Epilobium montanum*) 133
  great (*Epilobium hirsutum*) 162
  rosebay (*Chamerion angustifolium*) 62
wintergreen, serrated (*Orthilia secunda*) 106
wolf (*Canis lupus*) 61
woodcock (*Scolopax rusticola*) 247
woodlouse 113, 133, 218, 344
  Armadillidium pictum **113–14**
  common shiny (*Oniscus asellus*) 218
  rosy/pink (*Androniscus dentiger*) 218
wood-moss, short-beaked (*Hylocomium brevirostre*) 266
woodpecker, great spotted (*Dendrocopos major*) 350
  green (*Picus viridis*) 350
  lesser spotted (*Dendrocopos minor*) 74, 350
woodpigeon (*Columba palumbus*) 284
wood-rush, field (*Luzula campestris*) 338
  great (*Luzula sylvatica*) 106
  heath (*Luzula multiflora*) 98
wood-sorrel (*Oxalis acetosella*) 133, 209
wormwood (*Artemisia absinthium*) 59
wren (*Troglodytes troglodytes*) 146, 147, 215

yarrow (*Achillea millefolium*) 81, 335
yellowhammer (*Emberiza citronella*) 146, 147, 148
yew (*Taxus baccata*) 289, **312–17**
Yorkshire-fog (*Holcus lanatus*) 337

Zannichellia palustris (horned pondweed) 230
Zenobiella subrufescens (thin-shelled brown snail) 274
Zonitoides excavates (hollowed glass snail) 117

GENERAL INDEX

Page numbers in **bold** include illustrations.

Abercraf 245
Abercynrig 82
Abergavenny 30, 48, 56, 263, 281, 290, 293, 294, 325
　Priory Deer Park **82**, 83
Aberyscir 315, 316
Abingdon Chronicle 76
Afanc 240–1
agriculture, earliest 61
alder woodland 267–8
algae problems 230–2
Allt yr Esgair 141, 229
Anglezarke series soils 56
Arthurian legends 2, 41, 94
ash woodland 43

Bachawy Gorge 113
badger cull 286
Bannau Sir Gaer 7, 99, 105, 108, **120**
Barrett, W. Bowles 17
bats 184–7, 209–11, 219–20, 326–7
Beacon Hills 3
bears 71–2
Berthlwyd Farm 334–6
big cats sightings 286–7
birch woodland 272–3
birds 88–90, 97, 140–2, 146–51, 178–81, 236–9, 282–5, 345–6
　wintering and passage 258
Bishopston Mudstone 44
Black Death 79
Black Hill *see* Mynydd Du
Black Mountains 4–6, 8, 55, 62, 66–8, 93, 114, 116, 119, 160, 178, 263, 265, 275, 302, 358
Black Rock Quarry 325
Blaen Cynon 332
Blaen Nedd 37
Blaen Onneu 306
Blaen y Glyn 50
Blaenau (Pen y Beacon) Stone Circle 67–8
Blaenavon Industrial Landscape World Heritage Site 7–9, **87**, 88, 141
Blaencamlais Pool 247
Blaenllynfi Castle 77

Blaentillary Quarry 117
Blorenge, the 19, 27, 33, 104, 125, **136**, 139, 141, 148, 149, 150, 151, 261–2, 358
Blue-Grey Hills 26
bog wood 86
bogs 57–8, 86, 100–2, 154, 234, 246–7, 248–50, 360
Boreal, the 60–2
Borrow, George 10–11
Borth Bog 86
Bosanquet, Sam 110, 122, 137, 320, 323
Boxbush Meadows 318, 336
Brechfa Pool 244–5
Brecknock 10, 79
Brecknock County Naturalist's Trust/Wildlife Trust 43, 182–4, 198, 228, 236, 303, 318
Brecknock and Abergavenny Canal 259
Brecknock Bat Group 326
Brecknock Mere 239
Brecon 178, 182, 247, 259, 260, 277, 286
　Castle 74
　Cathedral 23, 324
　Christ College **290**, 291
Brecon Beacons Commoners' Association 92
Brecon Beacons National Park 2, 4, 6–9, 90, 111, 189
Brecon Canal 160, 172
British Bryological Society 11, 109
British Lichen Society 324
Bronllys Castle 77
Bronze Age 44, 65–9
Brownstones 25–6, 50, 52
Brychan 76
Brycheiniog 72–7
Brynamman 38, 223
Bryniau Gleision 26
Buckland House 82, 186–7
Buckland, William 21
Bugle Bridge 84
butterflies 133, **144–5**, 273, **332–3**, 342–3, 353
Bwa Maen 41–2
Bwlch 141, 230

Cadair Fawr 132
Cae Thomas Well 300
Caeau Fferm 338–9
Caeau Ty Mawr **337**

GENERAL INDEX · 409

Cae Bryn Tywarch 332
Caerwent 81
cairns, round 69–70
calcareous flushes 250–1
Camden, William, *Britannia* 12, 16
canals 160, 172, 185, 213, 259–60
Cantref reservoir 176, 252, 254, 258
Capel Horeb quarry 30–1
Capel y Ffin 336
Capel y Ffin, St Mary's Church 313, **314**, 315, 316
    Baptist Chapel **314**, 315
carboniferous rocks 19, 31ff
Cardiff University 21, 27, 207, 324
Carmarthen 81, 97
Carn y Goetre **134**
Carnau Gwynion **40**
Carreg Cennen 34, 119, 125–9
    Castle **126**, 198, 345
Carreg Cennen Disturbance 43, 126
Carreg Fryn Fras 2
Carreg Waun Llech Stone Circle 66
Cathedine 316
cattle farming 84, 359
caves 157, 197–219
    exploration 203–7
    flora and fauna 208–20
    formation 199–202
Cefn Carn Fadog 56
Cefn Coed y Cymmer 265
Cefn Cul **359**
Cefn Esgair-carnau 68, **99**
Celtic Church 73–4
Cennen, Afon 125
Cerrig Duon Stone Circle 66, **67**
charcoal production 264, 268, 270
Chatwin, Bruce, *On the Black Hill* 4
churchyards 311–28
cliff ledges 104–8
climate change 351–5
clog making 268
Clydach, Afon 87–8
coal extraction 8, 87–8
coal measures 21, 45–6
Coed Aberedw 113
Coed Fenni-fach 70, **78**, 79
Coed Nant Menascin 144, 263, **264**, 267
Coed Pantydarren 308
Coed Tregib 297
Coed y Cerrig National Nature Reserve 268

Coed y Rhaeadr 21
Coed Ynys Faen 267
Common Agricultural Policy 359, 362
common land, rights 91–4
conifer plantations 278–88
coppicing 62
Corn Du **1**, **3**, 48, 142, 227, 228
corries 123
Countryside Council for Wales 31, 43, 130, 294, 310, 334
Cox, Prof A. H. 27, 28
Craig Cerrig Gleisiad 105, 106, **107**, 118, 138
Craig Cerrig Gleisiad Natural Nature Reserve 49, 105, **107–8**, 110, 118, 138, 353
Craig Cwareli 105
Craig Cwm Clyd 97
Craig Cwm Cynwyn 105
Craig Cwm Llwch 105
Craig Cwm Sere 105, **106**
Craig Fran Gorge 2
Craig y Castell 306
Craig y Cilau National Nature Reserve 119, **123**–5, 197, 204, 250, 305, 306, **307**, 353
Craig y Dinas *see* Dinas Rock
Craig y Fro Quarry 27–30, 50, 106, **196**
Craig y Nos 17, 43, 48, 56, 82, 265, 325
    Castle 82, 155
    Country Park 43, 190
Craig y Rhiwarth 43, 265, **266**, 308
Crannog 74–6
Cribarth Disturbance 43
Crickhowell 6, 50, 63, 77, 135, 161, 172, 173, **174**, 181, 182, 305, 312, 316, 324
    Manor 83
Croft 296
Cwar Glas Quarry 23, **24**
Cwar y Gigfran 50
Cwm Cadlan National Nature Reserve 250–1, 331, 352, **353**
Cwm Camlais 248
Cwm Cleisfer 306
Cwm Clydach 130, **269–70**, 274, 308
Cwm Crai 56, **339**
Cwm Crew 49
Cwm Llwch 48, **49**
Cwm Nant Cil y Clawdd 332
Cwm Sere **272**, 273–4
Cwm Taf Fechan 125
Cwmyoy 50–2, 134, 308, 315, 320

Cwmyoy Darren 322

Dan yr Ogof caves 12, 157, 190, 198, 200, **201–2**, 203, 208, 218, 362
dark sky reserve, international 13
Darren 50
Darren, Black 52, **53**
Darren, Red 52
Darren Cilau 119, 308
Darren Fawr 124, **135**, **139**, 303–4, 305, 306, 308
Darren Lwyd 308
Davies, David 99
Davies, Walter 340, 342
Defoe, Daniel 4, 9–10
deforestation 65
Defynnog, St Cynog's Church 312, **313**, 316, 324
Devil's Table 52
Devonian rocks 23–6
Dinantian period 36
Dinas Rock 2, 41, **42**
Dryslwyn Castle 119
drystone walls 343–4

Eardiston Series soils 54
Eglwys Faen **204**, 205
Elm Disease 61–2
Enclosure 78, 84, 293
eutrophication problems 230–2
Ewyas, Vale of 187
Exeter University 31, 305

Fan Brycheiniog **7**, 99, **120**, 157
Fan Llia 50
Fan y Big 2
Farewell Rock 45–6
farm buildings, as habitats 344–6
Feddyg, Rhiwallon 95
Felindre 286
fern collecting 89
feudal system 78–9
Fforest Fawr 68, 86, 263
  Geopark 20, 21, **43**
Fforest Series soils 55
Ffrwdgrech 82
Ffridd, the 143–52
field systems, medieval 78
fish 157, 170–5, 218–19, 239–42, 344
Foel Fawr 125
Foel Fraith 56

folds and fractures, geological 41–3
Forestry Commission 41, 278–9, 280, 284, 288
Forgotten Landscapes Project 9, 141, 289
fossils 23, 26–31, 33–4, 45–6, 57
Friends of Friendless Churches 12
fruit growing 346–8
  rare varieties 348
fungi 129–30, 281, 349

Gafenni, Afon 48
Garn Goch hillfort **70**, **331**
Garnddyrys Forge 245–6
Garreg Lwyd 56
gas pipelines 355–7
George, T. N. 37
Gerald of Wales 9, 75, 232, 239, 287
Giedd, Afon 157
Gilwern Hill 125, 139, 325, 357
glaciation 21, 46–50, 57–8
Glangrwyne 88
Glangrwyney Court 82
Glanusk Park 82
Glasbury 180
Glasfynydd Forest 288
Glyndwr Revolt 79
Gliffaes 82
Glyn Tarell 50
Golden Valley 7, 240
Gorse Llwyn 248–9
Gospel Pass 5
Gossling, F. N. 27–8
grasslands 317–20, 329–39
Great Llwygy farm 265
Grey Grits 26
Greywacke sandstone 22
Groesffordd 347
Gruffudd ap Rhys 239
Grwyne Fawr 178 338
Grwyne Fechan 178
Gwernvale 62, 63–5, **64**

Haffes, Afon **155**
Hafodyrynys 357
Hatterall Ridge 5, 52, 116–17
Hay Common pools 254
hay meadows 334–6
Hay on Wye 66, 93, 139, 277, 320, **321**, 325, 339, 340, 347
  Castle **77**, 82

Heard, Albert 28–9, 30
heath 104–5
hedges 339–43
helictite 205
Hen Allt Common 339
Henllys Vale 37, **38**
Henrhyd Falls 45, 190, **191**
Hepste, Afon 153, 178, 189, 190, 164
herbalism 93–4
Herbert's Quarry 38, **39**
hillforts 70
hollins 299–302
Holocene Period 62
Honddu river and valley 48, 56, 84, 88, 187, **188**
hydroelectric schemes 358

Illtyd Pools 243–4, 254
Industrial Revolution 7–9, 87–8
invasive plants 164–6
Iron Age 69–70
Isca, Roman fort 71

Jenkins, Thomas 203

karst, glaciated 34

'Lady of the Lake' 93, 222, 223
Leland, John 4, 5, 240
Lenton, Timothy 31
Lesser Garth Cave 214
Lewis, Samuel, *A Topographical Dictionary of Wales* 4–5
Ley, Augustin 4, 17, 107, 303, 305, 306, 308
Lhuyd, Edward 15–16, 33–4, 96, 105, 199, 219, 234
Libanus Church **318**, 319
lime industry 37–8, 270
limestone 19, 32–43
limestone grassland 129–30
limestone pavements 34–7, 131–3
Lindisfarne 33
Little Neath River Cave 207–8, 219, 334
liverworts 50, 93, **94**, 105, 108–10, 161–2, 252–5, 266, 271, 349
Llanddeusant church **322**, 323
Llanbedr 316
Llandefalle **323**, 357
Llandegfedd reservoir, Newport 257
Llandeilo 54, 288, 297

Llandetty **311**, 316
Llandovery 79
Llandyfan 25, 88
Llaneliau 316
Llanelly 223, 256, 316
Llanfair Kilgeddin, St Mary's Church 12, **13**
Llanfeugan 316
Llanfihangel 47–8, 82, 295, **296**, 297, 320, **321**
Llanfihangel Tal-y-llyn 316
Llanfilio 324
Llanfoist Church 213, 315
Llanfrynach 71, 245, 263, 316
Llangasty 236, 316, 324, 346
Llangattock 82, 83, **298**, 299, 316, 324
Llangattock escarpment 206
Llangenny 83, 267, 316
Llangetty 48
Llangoed Common 244
Llangorse churchyard 316, 324
Llangorse Lake 9, 49, 56, 57, 60, 61, **75**, **76**, 181, 221, 228–32, 239–43, 254, 258, 337
Llangynidr 160, 182, 269, 270, 274–5, 343
Llanover Quarry 30
Llansantffraed **14**, **15**, 169, 312
Llanspyddid 316
Llanthony Priory 7, 68, 84, **85**, 116, 239, 257, 287–8, 306–8, 320, 338
Llanwenarth Church 291, **292**, 316, 320
Lloyd, John 89
Llwchwr river (Afon) 157, 203
Llwyn-on reservoir 176
Llwynywermod 82
Llygad Llwchwr 157, **158**
Llyn Brianne 97, 258
Llyn Cwm Llwch **227**–8
Llyn Traeth Bach 246–7
Llyn y Fan Fach 93, 97, 105, 122, 221, **222**–5
Llyn y Fan Fawr 118, 221, **226**–7
Llyn y Garn Fawr 247
Llynfi river and valley 79, 228, 230, 240
Llys Brychan, Roman villa 71
Loch Lomond Stadial 47, 48
log boats 76–7
Logan, Sir William Edmond 45
Longtown 347
Loughor river 88
Lower Llicdi reservoir 256
Lower Neuadd reservoir 252, 255, **256**
Lugwardine series soils 56

Lwyd, Afon 7
Lyme Disease 145–6

Maen Du Holy Well 74
Maen Grwydr **46**, 47
Maen Llia **66**
Maen Madoc stone **73**
Maen Mawr 66, **67**
medicinal plants 79–81, 94–5
Medieval Period 78–9
Mellte, Afon 41, 153, **154**, 178, 179, 189, 198, 264
Mendip cave fauna 217
Merthyr Tydfil 18, 28, 125, 303, 310, 331
mesolithic hunter-gatherers 61
migration 88
Milford Series soils 54
Millstone Grit 19, 20, 123
Minera caves 207
molluscs 113, 117–19, 218, 250, 273–4, 324–6
moonmilk 211
monastic buildings 73–4
  see also Llanthony Priory
Monmouthshire and Brecon Canal **160, 213**, 221, **259–6**, 306
Monnow river 12, 48, 188
moraines 47–50
mosses and lichens 51, 93, **94**, 105, 108–10, 126, 135, 136–8, 161–2, 194, 255–8, 266, 271, 320–4, 349, 358
moths 112, 114–15, 145, 211–12, 273, 281, 349
Motley, Graham 110, 122, 254, 310, 332
Mudstones 23, 44, 108
Murchison, Sir Roderick Impey 21–2, 30–1
Myddfai 94–5, 316, 320
Myddfai, Physicians of 2, 94–5, 97, 222
Mynydd Bach Trecastell 355
Mynydd Coity 357
Mynydd Du (Black Hill) 2, 4, 10, 38, 47, 49, 56, 57, 69, 122, 129, 135, 137, 142, 159, 198, 203, 226, 263, 278, 358
Mynydd Gader 5
Mynydd Garn Clochdy 148
Mynydd Illtyd 86, **92**, 93, 243–4, 248
Mynydd Llangattwg 40, 102, 119, **144**, 197, 204, 208, 245, 247, 356, 357
Mynydd Llangorse 229
Mynydd Llangynidr 40, 56, 245, 247, 356
Mynydd Mallaen 97
Mynydd Myddfai 25, 94, **95**, 97, 355, **356**

Mynydd Troed **64**, 65
Mynydd y Garn Fawr 148

Namurian Rocks 44–5
Nant Carr 357
Nant Cwm Llwch 227
Nant Glais Caves 208, 210, 214, 218
Nant Lech valley 46, 190
Nant Tarw 67
Nant y Llyn **361**
National Botanic Garden of Wales 124, **304**, 305
National Museum of Wales 75, 99, 113, 169, 171, 218, 273, 302, 305
National Soil Map 54
National Trust 9, 91, 111, 112, 164, 280, 334–6
native beech woodland 269–71
Neath 16
  vale of 43, 190
Neath Disturbance 43, 48
Nedd Fechan 153, 178, 189, 264
Nedd, Afon 12, 48, 189, 190, 264
Neolithic period 61, 62–5, 77
Newport 159, 257, 259
Nevill Hall/Llanfoist moraine 48
Norman Invasion 77

Offa's Dyke National Trail 5, 116
Ogof Agen Allwedd 204, 219, 220
Ogof Craig ar Ffynnon 205
Ogof Draenen 197, 205, 219, 220
Ogof Ffynnon Ddu 32, **35**, 49, 119, 130, **131**, 133, 197, 203, 207, 208, 209, 216, 219, 352
Ogof y Ci 214
Ogof y Darren Cilau 197, 204, 205, **206**
Olchon valley 5, 7, **8**, 300, **342**, 347
Old Red Sandstone 2, 19, 23–5, 34, 41, 45, 48, 50, 54, 68, 105, 123, 136, **137**, 228, 254
orchards 346–50
Ordovician period 22, 31
otter conservation 182–4
Otter Hole Cave 208, 209
oxbows 162–4

Pal y Cwrt **128**, 129, 344
palaeoecological studies 57–8
Pant Brwyn Trorum 99, **100**
Pant Mawr 37, 247
Pant y blodau 97

Pant y Meddygon 94, **95**, 97
Pantyffynnont **330**
parks and gardens, historic 82–3, 294–5
Partrishow 316, **319**
passage birds 258
pearl mussel fishing **169–7**
peat 55–6, 86–7
peat erosion 100, 102–5
Pen Ffordd Goch Pond (Keeper's Pool) 245–6
Pen Point 316
Pen Trumau 102–**103**
Pen y Crug 70
Pen y Fan 1, 2–4, 16, 18, 23, 25, 26, 96, 106, **107**, 108, 112, 119, 142, **165**, 227, 261, 272
Pen y Gadair Fawr 5
Pencelli 77, **163**
Penderyn 26, 41, 252
Pendre **277**
Penlan ponds **247**
Penmoelallt 304–5, 310
Penmyarth 82
Penpont 82
Pentwyn reservoir 252
Penwyrlod 62, **63**
Phillips, Edward Cambridge 6, 88
Phillips, Reginald W. 17
Picws Du **7**
Plas Llangattock 82
Plateau Beds 25, 26
Pliny the Elder 33
podzolic soils 54
pollarding 297–9
pollen analysis 57–8, 60–1
pollution 100, 134, 2, 170, 172, 176, 181, 230, 351–3
  light 13–14, 172
Pont Melin Fach 159
Pontneddfechan 2, 41, 264
Pontnewydd 259, 260
Pontsticill reservoir 252, 257
pools 243–7
population growth 351
Porth yr Ogof 16, 34, **198**–9, 209, 211, 215, 218
Post Office Surveyors Department 27
prehistoric remains 62–70
pro-talus ramparts 49
Punchbowl, the 261, **262**, 269
Pwll Du 9, 159
Pwll Gwy Rhoc 247

Pwll Pant Mawr 247
Pwll y Felin **159**
Pwll y Wrach 274, 275
Pwllcoediog 165
Pyrddin, Afon 178, 189, 264
Pysgodlyn 291

rainfall 11–12, 36, 54–55, 154, 172, 179, 232, 252
recreational use 18, 90, 112, 141, 190, 197, 207, 229, 257, 259–60
Red Marl 25
reptiles 151–2
reservoirs 221, 252–60
Rhiangoll river and valley 56
Rhiw Cwrw 240
Rhiw Pyscod 240
Rich, Tim 302, 306, 310
rivers, characteristics 152–9
Roberts, Dr Nicholas 97
Roman period 71–2

Saith Maen 67
Sandstones 2, 19, 23–6, 44
Sarn Helen 73
Sawdde Gorge 23
Sawdde, Afon **11**, 223
scree 134–9
Sedgewick, Adam 21
Senni river and valley 25, **26**, 30
Sennybridge 286, 312
Sgwd yr Eira 153, 190, **192**
sheep farming 84–6, 93, 359–60
siltstones 23
Silures tribe 22, 71
Silurian period 22–3
Sinc Ger y Ffordd 157, **158**
sinkholes 40–1, 157–9, 196, 245
Skirrid (Ysgyryd Fawr) 9, 50, 52, **53**, **134**
Skirrid Mountain Inn 52, **53**
Slwch Tump 70
Smith, Steve 148–9, 150
snow, and wildlife 119–23
snow, watermelon 121–2
soils 54–6
Sorgwm valley **64**, 65
spiders 112, 211, 213–15, 244
stalactites and stalagmites 200–2
standing stones and stone circles 65–8
Strawberry Cottage Wood 265

Sugar Loaf **8**, 9, 48, **82**, 83, 264–5
Sumner, Heyward 12
Swansea valley 43, 47, 362
Sychlwch, Afon **156**
Sychryd, Afon 41, **42**, **120**, 121, 189
Symonds, W. S. 48

Taf Fawr river and valley 2, 26, 41, 265
Taf Fechan 41, 265
Tair Carn Isaf 69
Tair Carn Uchaf 44, **69**
Tales from the Wildwood (TV programme) 265
Talgarth 77, 263, 274, 277, 278, 316, 324, 325
Talybont **55**, 181, 278
Talybont reservoir 26, 252, **253**, 257, 258
Tarren yr Esgob 113, 139, 263, 308
Tawe river and valley 12, 17, 48, 56, 66, 110, 153, 155, 157, 226, 263, 265, 275, 325
tilestones 25
tombs, megalithic 62–5
Towy anticline 22
Towy river and valley 77, 125, 140
Traeth Bach, Illtyd 243–4
Traeth Mawr 57–8, 248, **249**
transhumance 84–5
Treberfydd 82
Trecastle 160, 247, 332
Trecastle Mountain 71
tree line 261–3
Trefecca Fawr 82
Tretower 79, **80**, 81, 82
 Castle 77
Trewyn 82
Twrch Sandstone 44, 49
Twrch, Afon 2, 37, 44
Twyn y Beddau 245
Twyn y Gaer 70
Ty Mawr Pool 245, **246**
Tyrewen 291
Tywi river 12, 173

Usk reservoir 252, 254, 255, 285, 288
Usk river and valley 12, 48, 56, 70, 71, 72, 79, 82, 88, 159–87, 248, 254, 259, 260, 263, 275, 278, 290, 291, 292, 293, 332, 347, 357
 oxbows 162–4
 shingle banks 166–9
 vegetation 161–2

Vans, the 4
Vaughan, Henry 14–15
Victorians and wildlife 88–9
Vincent Wildlife Trust 187, 278
volcanic events 86

Waen Ddu 250
Wallace, Alfred Russel 16–17, 19, 66, 194–5
Wars of the Roses 126
water supplies, future 360–2
water voles, conservation 242–3
waterfalls 189–96
Waun Fignen Felen 57, **58**, 61, 102, 362
Waun Lysiog 55
Waun Wen 55
weather 11–12
 see also climate change; rainfall
Welsh black cattle **359**
Welsh mountain ponies **92**, 93
Welsh mountain sheep 93, 359
Wenallt Series soils 55
Westwood reservoir 257
Wilcocks Series soils 56
Wilderness Foundation 358
Williams, Raymond, *People of the Mountains* 5–6
winter sports 119
Woodland Trust 262, 294, 297, 362
Woolf, Pip, 'Woollen Line' project **103**
Wye river and valley 12, 82, 173, 180, 263
Wynne, Robert 16

Y Gaer 70, 71, **72**,
Y Gaer Fawr **70**
Y Pigwn 71
Ystrad Yw 312
Ynys Bwlc **75–6**
Younger Dryas period 59
Ysgyryd Fawr (The Skirrid) 9, 50, 52, **53**, 134
Ystradfellte 37, **40**, 44–5, 50, 73, 132–3, 153, 245, 316
Ystradffin 97
Ystradgynlais 157

The New Naturalist Library

1. *Butterflies* — E. B. Ford
2. *British Game* — B. Vesey-Fitzgerald
3. *London's Natural History* — R. S. R. Fitter
4. *Britain's Structure and Scenery* — L. Dudley Stamp
5. *Wild Flowers* — J. Gilmour & M. Walters
6. *The Highlands & Islands* — F. Fraser Darling & J. M. Boyd
7. *Mushrooms & Toadstools* — J. Ramsbottom
8. *Insect Natural History* — A. D. Imms
9. *A Country Parish* — A. W. Boyd
10. *British Plant Life* — W. B. Turrill
11. *Mountains & Moorlands* — W. H. Pearsall
12. *The Sea Shore* — C. M. Yonge
13. *Snowdonia* — F. J. North, B. Campbell & R. Scott
14. *The Art of Botanical Illustration* — W. Blunt
15. *Life in Lakes & Rivers* — T. T. Macan & E. B. Worthington
16. *Wild Flowers of Chalk & Limestone* — J. E. Lousley
17. *Birds & Men* — E. M. Nicholson
18. *A Natural History of Man in Britain* — H. J. Fleure & M. Davies
19. *Wild Orchids of Britain* — V. S. Summerhayes
20. *The British Amphibians & Reptiles* — M. Smith
21. *British Mammals* — L. Harrison Matthews
22. *Climate and the British Scene* — G. Manley
23. *An Angler's Entomology* — J. R. Harris
24. *Flowers of the Coast* — I. Hepburn
25. *The Sea Coast* — J. A. Steers
26. *The Weald* — S. W. Wooldridge & F. Goldring
27. *Dartmoor* — L. A. Harvey & D. St Leger Gordon
28. *Sea Birds* — J. Fisher & R. M. Lockley
29. *The World of the Honeybee* — C. G. Butler
30. *Moths* — E. B. Ford
31. *Man and the Land* — L. Dudley Stamp
32. *Trees, Woods and Man* — H. L. Edlin
33. *Mountain Flowers* — J. Raven & M. Walters
34. *The Open Sea: I. The World of Plankton* — A. Hardy
35. *The World of the Soil* — E. J. Russell
36. *Insect Migration* — C. B. Williams
37. *The Open Sea: II. Fish & Fisheries* — A. Hardy
38. *The World of Spiders* — W. S. Bristowe
39. *The Folklore of Birds* — E. A. Armstrong
40. *Bumblebees* — J. B. Free & C. G. Butler
41. *Dragonflies* — P. S. Corbet, C. Longfield & N. W. Moore
42. *Fossils* — H. H. Swinnerton
43. *Weeds & Aliens* — E. Salisbury
44. *The Peak District* — K. C. Edwards
45. *The Common Lands of England & Wales* — L. Dudley Stamp & W. G. Hoskins
46. *The Broads* — E. A. Ellis
47. *The Snowdonia National Park* — W. M. Condry
48. *Grass and Grasslands* — I. Moore
49. *Nature Conservation in Britain* — L. Dudley Stamp
50. *Pesticides and Pollution* — K. Mellanby
51. *Man & Birds* — R. K. Murton
52. *Woodland Birds* — E. Simms
53. *The Lake District* — W. H. Pearsall & W. Pennington
54. *The Pollination of Flowers* — M. Proctor & P. Yeo
55. *Finches* — I. Newton
56. *Pedigree: Words from Nature* — S. Potter & L. Sargent
57. *British Seals* — H. R. Hewer
58. *Hedges* — E. Pollard, M. D. Hooper & N. W. Moore
59. *Ants* — M. V. Brian
60. *British Birds of Prey* — L. Brown
61. *Inheritance and Natural History* — R. J. Berry
62. *British Tits* — C. Perrins
63. *British Thrushes* — E. Simms
64. *The Natural History of Shetland* — R. J. Berry & J. L. Johnston

65. *Waders* — W. G. Hale
66. *The Natural History of Wales* — W. M. Condry
67. *Farming and Wildlife* — K. Mellanby
68. *Mammals in the British Isles* —
    L. Harrison Matthews
69. *Reptiles and Amphibians in Britain* — D. Frazer
70. *The Natural History of Orkney* — R. J. Berry
71. *British Warblers* — E. Simms
72. *Heathlands* — N. R. Webb
73. *The New Forest* — C. R. Tubbs
74. *Ferns* — C. N. Page
75. *Freshwater Fish* — P. S. Maitland &
    R. N. Campbell
76. *The Hebrides* — J. M. Boyd & I. L. Boyd
77. *The Soil* — B. Davis, N. Walker, D. Ball &
    A. Fitter
78. *British Larks, Pipits & Wagtails* — E. Simms
79. *Caves & Cave Life* — P. Chapman
80. *Wild & Garden Plants* — M. Walters
81. *Ladybirds* — M. E. N. Majerus
82. *The New Naturalists* — P. Marren
83. *The Natural History of Pollination* —
    M. Proctor, P. Yeo & A. Lack
84. *Ireland: A Natural History* — D. Cabot
85. *Plant Disease* — D. Ingram & N. Robertson
86. *Lichens* — Oliver Gilbert
87. *Amphibians and Reptiles* — T. Beebee &
    R. Griffiths
88. *Loch Lomondside* — J. Mitchell
89. *The Broads* — B. Moss
90. *Moths* — M. Majerus
91. *Nature Conservation* — P. Marren
92. *Lakeland* — D. Ratcliffe
93. *British Bats* — John Altringham
94. *Seashore* — Peter Hayward
95. *Northumberland* — Angus Lunn
96. *Fungi* — Brian Spooner & Peter Roberts
97. *Mosses & Liverworts* — Nick Hodgetts &
    Ron Porley
98. *Bumblebees* — Ted Benton
99. *Gower* — Jonathan Mullard
100. *Woodlands* — Oliver Rackham
101. *Galloway and the Borders* — Derek Ratcliffe
102. *Garden Natural History* — Stefan Buczacki
103. *The Isles of Scilly* — Rosemary Parslow
104. *A History of Ornithology* — Peter Bircham
105. *Wye Valley* — George Peterken
106. *Dragonflies* — Philip Corbet & Stephen
     Brooks
107. *Grouse* — Adam Watson & Robert Moss
108. *Southern England* — Peter Friend
109. *Islands* — R. J. Berry
110. *Wildfowl* — David Cabot
111. *Dartmoor* — Ian Mercer
112. *Books and Naturalists* — David E. Allen
113. *Bird Migration* — Ian Newton
114. *Badger* — Timothy J. Roper
115. *Climate and Weather* — John Kington
116. *Plant Pests* — David V. Alford
117. *Plant Galls* — Margaret Redfern
118. *Marches* — Andrew Allott
119. *Scotland* — Peter Friend
120. *Grasshoppers & Crickets* — Ted Benton
121. *Partridges* — G. R. (Dick) Potts
122. *Vegetation of Britain & Ireland* —
     Michael Proctor
123. *Terns* — David Cabot & Ian Nisbet
124. *Bird Populations* — Ian Newton
125. *Owls* — Mike Toms